The Business of Beauty

The Business of Beauty

Gender and the Body in Modern London

Jessica P. Clark

BLOOMSBURY VISUAL ARTS
LONDON • NEW YORK • OXFORD • NEW DELHI • SYDNEY

BLOOMSBURY VISUAL ARTS
Bloomsbury Publishing Plc
50 Bedford Square, London, WC1B 3DP, UK
1385 Broadway, New York, NY 10018, USA

BLOOMSBURY, BLOOMSBURY VISUAL ARTS and the Diana logo are trademarks of
Bloomsbury Publishing Plc

First published in Great Britain 2020

Cover design by Adriana Brioso
Cover image: Two Ladies and Little Girl Before Hairdresser's Shop, by Hablot Knight
Browne, England, 1835–1882. Gift of Mrs. James Ward Thorne. The Art Institute of Chicago.

A catalogue record for this book is available from the British Library.

A catalog record for this book is available from the Library of Congress.

ISBN: HB: 978-1-3500-9851-0
PB: 978-1-3500-9850-3
ePDF: 978-1-3500-9853-4
eBook: 978-1-3500-9852-7

Typeset by Newgen KnowledgeWorks Pvt. Ltd., Chennai, India
Printed and bound in India

To find out more about our authors and books visit www.bloomsbury.com
and sign up for our newsletters.

For Linda Clark

Contents

Plates

Illustrations

Figures

Map

Acknowledgments

Colleagues, friends, and family have made the writing of this book a truly collaborative experience; to them I'm deeply indebted. At Johns Hopkins, Judy Walkowitz was an outstanding mentor. She demonstrated the dynamic possibilities of life as a feminist scholar by connecting, building, and inspiring. I strive to do the same and am fortunate to have such a wonderful model. Toby Ditz, Mary Fissell, and Mary Ryan fostered a rich and rigorous intellectual environment that pushed me to delve deeper and expand my ambitions. This was bolstered by the camaraderie and enduring friendship of Claire Cage, Natalie Elder, Laurel Flinn, Katie Jorgensen Gray, Jason Hoppe, Ren Pepitone, Olivia Weisser, and members of the Johns Hopkins Gender History "Geminar." New friends and colleagues have been equally generous, first at McGill and now at Brock, with special thanks to Sarah Brand, Helen Dewar, Elizabeth Elbourne, Renée Lafferty-Salhany, Brian Lewis, Jai Virdi, and Elizabeth Vlossak. I'm lucky to know and work with so many outstanding people.

This book would not exist without the generous support of the Social Sciences and Humanities Research Council of Canada, the American Historical Association, the Bodleian Libraries, the Royal Bank of Canada, Johns Hopkins, Brock University, and Brock's Humanities Research Institute. A number of people helped me locate the diverse sources that shaped this project. Alexandra Franklin, Michelle Chew, and Colin Harris at the Bodleian Libraries, Oxford, Carol Holliger at the Archives of Ohio United Methodism, Julie-Anne Lambert at the John Johnson Collection, Victoria West at the Worshipful Company of Barbers, and Emma White at Croydon Museum and Archives Service offered assistance and expertise at key junctures. Edward Bodenham of Floris, Simon, Amanda, Kate, and Eleanor Brooke of Grossmith, and individuals at John Gosnell & Co. Ltd. shared private company records and family stories. I'm grateful for their time and help.

I also extend my thanks to Palgrave Macmillan for permission to reproduce parts of "Grooming Men: The Material World of the Nineteenth-Century Barbershop" from *Gender and Material Culture in Britain since 1600*, edited by Hannah Greig, Jane Hamlett, and Leonie Hannan (New York: Palgrave Macmillan, 2015). Portions of Chapter 5 first appeared as "*Pomeroy v. Pomeroy*: Beauty, Modernity, and the Female Entrepreneur in *Fin-De-Siècle* London," *The Women's History Review* 22, no. 6 (2013): 877–903, https://doi.org/10.1080/09612025.2013.780844, with thanks to Taylor & Francis for allowing its reproduction. I am also grateful to John Wiley and Sons for permission to reproduce elements of "Buying Beauty: Female Beauty Consumption in the Modern British World," *History Compass* 14, no. 5 (May 2016): 206–17. The map in Chapter 1, created by Rebecca Nickerson, includes material from Open Roads, London: Ordnance Survey Data, which contains OS data © Crown copyright and database right (2010); and Joseph Meyer's "London, 1845, nach den besten Materialien entworfen," from the David Rumsey Historical Map Collection.

I've been fortunate to learn from mentors, editors, anonymous readers, students, and friends who have each informed this project in different ways. My deepest thanks to Stephen Brooke, Alison Matthews David, Paul Deslandes, Lara Kriegel, Dellores Laing and Jonathan Faiers, Erika Rappaport, Kevin Siena, Tori Smith, and Alun Withey. Anthony Salvador and Judy Walkowitz read some of the final versions of the manuscript, offering fresh insights at an important stage. Frances Arnold and Yvonne Thouroude thoughtfully guided me through the publishing process. Lisa DeBoer, Brandon Harrison, Gabrielle Marshall, Rebecca Nickerson, and Danielle Sinopoli did important work that made this a better book. Amanda Herbert and Katie Hindmarch-Watson provided round-the-clock support—and line edits—when I needed it most. Nigel Lezama, an exceptional friend and collaborator, was a source of so much joy and motivation.

Friends and family have enhanced this experience, offering encouragement, laughter, and new memories on both sides of the Atlantic. In the UK, Barbara Collier, Peter Jenkins, the late Queenie Collier, Marcia Cooper, and Naor Aloni always made me feel at home, whether in Worthing or in London. Kristy Boone, Evan McKie, Michelle Seniuk, Kenny and Candace Sheppard, and Christy Whetter were enthusiastic cheerleaders, confidantes, and companions. In one of my last conversations with my father, the late Randy Clark, I excitedly mapped out a dissertation project that would, more than ten years later, become this book. I've thought of him every day of its writing. My mother, Linda Clark, taught me to think critically, work hard, and love even harder. I continue to learn from her, and it's to her that I dedicate this book. Pamela Collier, my brothers, and their beautiful families ground me with their love. Emma, Liam, Owen, Declan, Isla, and baby Clark remind me to keep it fun. Finally, I'm grateful to Dan Pacella for his deep, unwavering belief in me. He also makes me laugh every single day. For that, and so much more, I thank him.

Introduction

In 1860, an article entitled "Real Mysteries of Paris and London" appeared in Charles Dickens's popular periodical *All the Year Round*. From the outset, the author emphatically declared that he had no interest in "mysteries of crime." Instead, he embarked on a satirical investigation into the mysterious sustainability of various urban trades, detailing silversmiths on Oxford Street, West End fur traders, and jewelers of Paris's Rue de Rivoli. Included in this list was the "inexplicable" profusion of London's beauty businesses and their financial success. "How are they kept up?" he wondered. This indeed was a "mystery of unfathomable nature." On Bond Street alone there were seven large perfumery shops and six "haircutting temples." According to the author, their prosperity challenged the conventional wisdom that "so few people we know" bought perfumers' wares. Would not, he wondered, a "single shop on the scale of a Bond-street Emporium … have proved enough, not only for all England, but for all the world?" *All the Year Round*'s columnist could offer no explanation for their profitability. The prospect of a substantial British market for perfumery and hairdressing was simply unthinkable.[1]

Perhaps the "Real Mystery" of the 1860 account was not the shops' profitability, but the transactions that transpired beyond their doors, as provided by those who controlled these lucrative emporiums. *All the Year Round*'s focus on perfumers' wares did not only fail to mention the broad range of goods and services on offer in such establishments (Figure 0.1). Also missing from its exposé were the tradespeople who made possible the Victorian proliferation of artificial beauty: those practitioners, male and female, who provided perfumery but also helped what journalist Eliza Linton called the "Girl of the Period" to "dy[e] her hair and pain[t] her face."[2] The mystification of both goods and traders reflected their ambiguous role in London's modern retailing scene. The purchase of beautifying goods—perfumes, false hair, rouge, and creams—was not always a respectable pursuit for British consumers, and especially women. Throughout

Figure 0.1 "Perfumer" by Benjamin Waterhouse Hawkins (*c.*1845). SSPL/Getty Images.

the nineteenth century, many observers remained deeply suspect of the use of beautifying goods, as the article from *All the Year Round* suggests.[3] Beauty goods were not only dangerous, argued critics, but also deceptive since commercial beautification tainted any outward manifestations of inner morality.[4] Popular criticism turned on the supposed "inauthenticity" of the enhanced body, not to mention the perceived duplicity of beauty consumers.[5]

This does not mean, however, that products were not seen as necessary and valued, even as they may have been sources of shame. Widespread reservations about beauty consumption subsequently demanded discretion in the sale of beauty goods and services, shaping the lives and pursuits of women and men who discreetly helped consumers to enhance their appearance. London's beauty providers responded in a number of ways to this demand for discretion; some aligned themselves with professional allies in more reputable fields, while others embraced the "mystery" of their craft to entice and protect clientele. In this way, public criticism of self-fashioning and beautification organized both the buying and selling of beauty goods, as many Britons kept their beautifying practices under wraps.

All the Year Round's characterizations of British beauty businesses—as both ubiquitous and discreet—frame the two major aims of this study. The first is to show that, despite Victorians' alleged rejection of artificial beauty aids, both women and men developed tacit strategies to alter their appearance. Consumers with means used beautifying wares on a regular basis. They developed a repertoire of strategies to conceal this type of consumption, producing a form of discretion capitalism that was anchored in visual enhancement.[6] In this way, beauty practices mirrored a similar paradox as that introduced by Michel Foucault in relation to Victorian sexuality: the proliferation of practices in the face of official denunciation and prohibition.[7] While there have been many critical and correct reassessments of Foucault's work, particularly those that challenge his marginalization of gender, race, and colonialism, his theories of proliferation and denunciation are relevant here; Victorian consumers condemned artifice yet actively participated in processes of beautification, both under cover and in plain sight.[8] Yet, this study differs from Foucault's selective approach in its second aim, which is to chart the social and material effects of these prohibitions, in this case on the lives and careers of modern London's beauty practitioners. The proliferation of beauty practices, as covert yet visible, had material consequences for the selling of beauty goods and services. Commercial beauty traders developed specific strategies to make beauty purchases possible. This book interrogates these commercial developments, bringing modern beauty retailers and their practices to the fore. London's beauty consumers and traders negotiated fraught conditions regulating nineteenth- and early-twentieth-century retail, including competing ideas about "authenticity" and "artificiality" that affected commercial relationships with neighbors, fellow traders, and customers. In London's rapidly expanding urban scene, traders were expected to promote reliability when dealing with customers to quell concerns over commercial fraud and trickery. This was particularly pressing for those in the beauty trades given widespread concerns over goods' promotion of duplicity, especially among female customers. To navigate these pressures, London's beauty brokers adopted a complex range of business identities and strategies, mobilizing a different type of artifice to generate the appearance of commercial transparency. These tactics had mixed success; some traders garnered national respect while others stood trial—literally and figuratively—before the British public.

Who were these London traders seeking patronage from fashionable consumers? Despite resounding criticism of beauty products and services from the nineteenth century, there emerged a modest but growing trade in commercial beauty. Between 1850 and 1914, the scale of this business transformed. From humble small-scale firms that were often concentrated in distinct spaces in London, fluid categories of traders expanded their beauty businesses, with some even growing into international operations serving a global market of consumers. This group consisted of traders who remedied and enhanced women's and men's bodies, placing them at the center of Victorian and Edwardian body politics: hairdressers, barbers, perfumers, wigmakers, complexion specialists, hair-restorers, chiropodists, electrolysis operators, manicurists, and beauty "culturists." Their business initiatives were deliberately subdued compared to the beauty industries of other nations, but they nonetheless set the stage for a subsequent market explosion in the twentieth century. Through their products and promotions—and endorsement of a cultivated, bourgeois body—these early traders established the foundations for the eventual surge of interest in the "cult of the body" that came to underpin twentieth-century consumer capitalism.[9]

Victorian beauty traders in particular laid the groundwork for modern attention to the consumer body, aided in part by nineteenth-century advances in manufacturing and distribution.[10] But it was also due to shifting attitudes toward bodily manipulation, engendered, in part, by the expanding accessibility of beautifying goods and services. Through these items, British consumers engaged in processes of self-fashioning, by which I mean the cultivation of particular modes of appearance—but also identities or personas—to meet dominant expectations of one's gender, class, or race. These performances of the self occurred through "artful processes," which could include patronage of arts and culture, the adoption of certain fashions, or, in this instance, the pursuit of goods and services that transformed the body.[11] London's beauty brokers attempted to influence these processes of self-fashioning through a range of publicity stunts and marketing schemes. In doing so, they met the demand of Victorian consumers who, despite their claims to the contrary, sought out bodily goods and services to produce an idealized version of a refined Anglo beauty. Most markedly, this enhanced bourgeois beauty was "fair"—or white—in complexion. The ordered body could also take feminine or masculine forms, was free of blemishes, wrinkles, or marks of disease and debility, abundant in hair (but only in the right places), trim in figure, rosy in countenance, sweet smelling, smoothed, and buffed.[12] The enactment of this nineteenth-century aesthetic did not necessarily demand overt color cosmetics or dyed hair, tell-tale signs of the supposed transgression of a deliberately transformed self. But it did require discreet consumer engagement in bodily goods and services, a pursuit so private that it could transpire beyond the scrutiny of critics, peers, and, until recently, many historians. Practices in commercial beautification would only intensify through the early twentieth century, propelled in part by earlier generations of female and male traders who rendered the modern body "beautiful."[13]

Modern Beauty

The potency of modern London's beauty scene has remained hidden, in part, due to the different consumer cultures that developed around beauty industries in the United States and France, Britain's earliest international competitors. In the case of the United States, historian Kathy Peiss argues that a national beauty industry engendered not only early female enterprise but also personal freedom and expression among an American consuming public. In a pioneering study, she finds that reticence and concerns over respectability were ultimately trumped by consumer desires to become beautiful, propelling the emergence of the US beauty market as a global trendsetter. Many key players in its early beauty industry were women, including African-American businesswomen who took up commercial beautification as economic and civic pursuits, forging new possibilities in enterprise and self-fashioning.[14] Historian Morag Martin notes similar advances in France, albeit at an earlier moment. In the eighteenth and early nineteenth centuries, the French perfumery industry experienced a period of transition when appearances transformed from those of aesthetic excess— elaborate wigs and thick paint—to the natural countenance of the Romantic school. Eighteenth-century French beauty entrepreneurs countered moralistic critics by appealing to notions of health and science in promoting the benefits of their rouges and powders. As in the British context, early-modern French perfumers promoted a "natural" aesthetic that facilitated the uninterrupted flow of consumption.[15] An unadulterated look remained the ideal through most of the nineteenth century.[16] French women nonetheless developed a reputation, among British critics, for adopting brighter colors and obvious styling, trends that allegedly contrasted British values around bodily discipline, concealment, and the illusion of "naturalness."[17]

Beauty industries flourished not only in western markets but also around the world, and historians have shown how beauty consumption proved central to the fashioning of localized identities across global geographies.[18] To date, such national studies do not extend to early British markets in commercial beauty despite Britain's role as a colonizing force and its subsequent implication in transnational flows of ideas about appearance, the body, and race.[19] This is changing, however, with a growing number of explorations of British bodily practices and consumption in the nineteenth and early twentieth centuries. Scholars have used beauty and grooming practices to elucidate historical experiences as diverse as the reading of print periodicals and military duty in the Boer War.[20] Others look to the intersections of health and beauty to chart early-nineteenth-century fashionable trends like a "tubercular chic" or enduring discourses of "naturalness" that informed beauty advertising into the late nineteenth century.[21] Recent developments in the history of male beauty further corroborate the centrality of bodily grooming to a range of consumers, highlighting the influential ways that bodily health and fitness intersected with notions of citizenship, gender, and race.[22]

Despite these important revelations, some historians of Britain—like their historical contemporaries—continue to perceive the nineteenth and early twentieth centuries as devoid of beauty praxis, let alone a commercial beauty culture. In fact, the buying and selling of beauty goods not only occurred but was integral to processes of modern self-making, particularly in London's urbanized setting. Historians have foregrounded London as a key site in the development of British modernity as the rapid expansion of an increasingly mobile population created what James Vernon terms "a new society of strangers."[23] The anonymous modern metropolis "was governed by the principles of visual exchange," argues Lynda Nead, "by the display of goods and advertisements, by the fashioning of self and society."[24] Propelling this modern visual economy, in part, was the proliferation of new technologies in print, photography, and bodily display. Indeed, modernity turned on visual forms, which encouraged the "sizing up" of strangers on metropolitan streets increasingly populated by anonymous crowds.[25] As Sadiah Qureshi shows, women and men moving through heterogeneous urban space relied on observation to decipher differences of class, gender, race, and ethnicity, understanding the power of appearance to determine the character of London's inhabitants.[26] These visual codes were mutable and untrustworthy, however, and were cultivated, manipulated, or transformed through new developments particular to the modern city.[27] This included the rise of London's nineteenth-century fashion industry, as publicity and promotion, ready-made clothing, and new spaces of commerce intensified the reliance on clothing to forge modern gendered identities.[28] But there also existed opportunities for transforming the body itself, a phenomenon that is central to the history of nineteenth-century urban modernity.[29]

Figure 0.2 A Woman Having Her Hair Cut in Her Hairdresser's Studio (*c.*1865). London Stereoscopic Company/Stringer/Getty Images.

This book argues that the deliberate fashioning of bodies—complexions, hair, hands, and figures—was an essential tool for London consumers who depended on beautifying goods to align with visual codes of display regulating the modern city (Figure 0.2). This occurred across a number of major urban centers, but what made the modern British context unique was the culture of concealment that defined their beauty practices and purchases. Unlike urban improvement schemes or commercial spectacles, the fashioning of modern bourgeois bodies was not initially celebrated as a triumph of modernity. Instead, overt beautification symbolized the dangers of modern urban life in which "imposters were everywhere and could not be reliably identified by location or dress."[30] Despite some shifting values, the body remained contested terrain into the early twentieth century, bounded by dominant social and gender norms regulating ideas about artifice, health, and inner beauty.[31] Consumers subsequently turned to discreet goods and services to fashion unremarkable bodies that aligned with circulating expectations of legibility, order, and "naturalness" (Figure 0.3). To do so, consumers went to great lengths to conceal their beautifying practices, engaging in tacit processes of self-making that owed their modernity, in part, to the parameters of secrecy confining them.[32]

The importance of beauty to modern self-fashioning developed in relation to urban conditions, but it was also linked to Britain's role as a colonizing force,

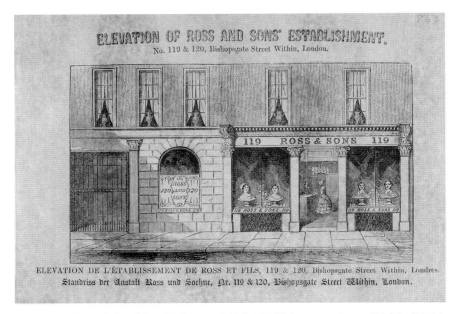

Figure 0.3 Ross & Sons' Establishment, 119 & 120 Bishopsgate Street Within (1851). Courtesy of the John Johnson Collection, Bodleian Libraries, University of Oxford, Beauty Parlour 1 (36).

something that was especially evident in representations of race. In her pivotal work, Stephanie M. H. Camp argued that "ideas about beauty and ugliness were and remain entangled with the invention and ongoing reinvention of race itself."[33] Nineteenth-century discourses on personal beauty were frequently imbued with messages about race and specifically fairness, purity, and "Englishness." Traders' insistence on whiteness as "natural" subsequently implicated them in the promotion of racialized aesthetics throughout the nineteenth century. Some London-based beauty entrepreneurs circulated discourses about appearance and ethnic ascendency, actively promoting the desirability of unblemished complexions like an "English rose." As we will see, some of these traders were not themselves British and operated within modern London's cosmopolitan commercial milieu. Despite these traders' foreign origins, patriotic messages heralding the unsurpassed beauty of white British women became a means to encourage consumption of beauty goods in domestic and colonial markets, while circulating dangerous messages about the ascendency of whiteness in the context of nineteenth-century colonialism.[34]

In addition to fashioning consumers in an idealized image of white bourgeois beauty, London's beauty providers participated in their own processes of modern self-making. Tradespeople themselves crafted commercial personas, and attention to these strategies offers important new insights into the navigation of urban geographies, the development of consumer trust, and the ways that gender operated on the ground in modern commercial settings. London's central role comes to the fore, repositioning a familiar cast of early-twentieth-century innovators—who often take the credit as pioneers of the "modern" beauty business—as inheritors rather than inventors of Britain's commercial beauty industry. Leading entrepreneurs like Helena Rubinstein followed on the heels of existing traders and specifically a number of small-scale beauty "culturists" operating in *fin de siècle* London. Rubinstein and others were also indebted to an earlier generation of mid-century beauty traders whose work was an integral part of modern London's fashionable scene.

By beautifying and "whitening" the body via scent, cosmetics, and false hair, nineteenth- and early-twentieth-century traders were an essential element of modern life. They enabled consumers' attempts to meet dominant western beauty standards. They simultaneously bolstered London's standing as a western fashion capital where consumers' quests for beauty could be realized. Yet, traders and consumers could only meet these desires by maintaining discretion. In doing so, they conformed to widespread cultural conditions regulating and periodically concealing British people's participation in modern beauty culture and the true extent of Britain's ethnic and cultural heterogeneity.[35]

London Beauty

British beauty brokers circulated discreet messages about an idealized white Anglo beauty from their headquarters in London, the imperial capital and alleged "heart" of the empire. The modern city was not only a geopolitical capital; as an exclusive hub for luxury consumption, it was also the epicenter of Britain's early fashion industries. Alongside Paris, and eventually New York and Berlin, London produced the latest in luxury trends, goods, and services in this period, functioning as a central node in a constellation of western fashion capitals.[36] International elites flocked to London for the annual social season, fraternizing with politicians, diplomats, and members of the aristocracy.[37] To support their presence at court, Parliament, and lavish private functions, visitors and residents alike procured bespoke alternatives to continental fashions, as crafted by reputable—and local—luxury traders. In this way, argues historian Christopher Breward, London traders served a distinct purpose by providing wares based on heritage and prestige, fulfilling "craving[s] for a subtle code of social distinction that protected [elite] interests and discouraged crude imitation."[38] It was out of this metropolitan network of celebrated luxury tailors, dressmakers, and fancy goods providers that London's beauty brokers carved a discreet niche, offering elite clientele the latest in scent, hairstyles, and bodily transformations to complement their sartorial selections.

In this way, Victorian and Edwardian beauty providers were an integral part of a modern milieu, contributing to what Breward characterizes as the "ubiquitous presence of fashion in the day-to-day rhythms of city life."[39] Across London, fashionable consumption and its production mapped onto the capital's unique social geographies, something that modern shoppers would have experienced firsthand as they moved through the capital's distinct commercial and residential enclaves. Most notably, London hosted a concentration of wealth in the west that diminished as travelers moved eastward or ventured south of the Thames, a characteristic that informed the location and distribution of fashionable businesses.[40] Through the nineteenth century, as Erika Rappaport has shown, the West End stood as the hub of London's luxury retailing, and its fashionable enterprises established the early contours of the city's modern commercial map.[41] Shops on St. James's Street catered to aristocratic masculine tastes, providing gentlemen shoppers with the headwear, shirts, and accoutrements demanded when patronizing the adjacent "Clubland," London's preeminent site of male leisure and sociability.[42] To the north of St. James's in the parish of St. George Hanover Square lay Mayfair, a residential district that housed the city's elites but also some of the most exclusive commercial avenues in Europe. There, streets like Savile Row hosted skillful tailors who produced the finest in men's fashions and formalwear, alongside more discreet court dressmakers and milliners who set the trends in Britain's fashionable feminine toilettes.[43] Tucked among the West End's stately town houses, residential squares, and broadly paved thoroughfares, providers maintained their clients' aristocratic status by adorning their bodies in fashions that communicated cultural cachet and superior economic standing.

Among this urban latticework of fashionable retailers, London's leading beauty entrepreneurs discreetly staked their claim in the West End's carriage trades. Along Mayfair's most affluent vistas—including the archetypal Bond Street—beauty tradespeople consistently did good business throughout the nineteenth century (Figure 0.4). In fact, two of Old Bond Street's longest tenants worked in the beauty trades; James Atkinson and William Francis Truefitt were designated perfumers and hairdressers to the Royal Family from 1799 and 1805, respectively, and continued in these roles through the nineteenth century.[44] They

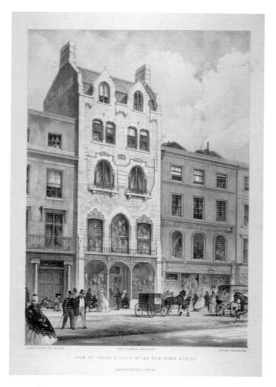

Figure 0.4 "New Bond Street" by Robert Dudley (*c*.1860). Guildhall Library & Art Gallery/Heritage Images/Getty Images.

were not the only beauty traders on Bond Street. By 1856, a street directory registered some nineteen vendors providing some type of beauty goods or services. This included chemists, hairdressers, wig makers, and perfumers, such as long-standing industry leaders Francis Henry Breidenbach, Gattie & Pierce, and Septimus Piesse.[45] In this moment, some years before the more visible presence of female custom in the West End, men were the primary patrons of these elite beauty businesses. Before the late 1860s, high-end perfumery shops and hairdressing saloons primarily functioned as masculine sites of discreet grooming and gathering, offering opportunities for men to commune while refining their appearance to meet classed standards of respectability.[46]

Despite functioning as a symbolic site of privileged exclusivity, the West End and its residents were not a world unto themselves, and through the nineteenth century there was considerable intermingling of luxury with less affluent areas bordering Mayfair.[47] A shopper rambling eastward toward the trafficked streets of Piccadilly to the south, Oxford to the north, and Regent to the east could find reputable options for fashionable pursuits at relatively reasonable costs, including hairdressing operations that catered to those seeking out the latest follicular trends[48] (Figure 0.5). The parishes east of Regent Street, St. James Westminster and St. Anne's Soho, also harbored a number of small-scale perfumery and hairdressing businesses like that of Solomon Lloyd and family. These more humble neighborhoods included communities of immigrant newcomers to London, some of which mobilized their continental beauty expertise to serve British clientele. A number of French-born hairdressers, perfumers, and assistants resided among Soho's considerable Francophone community, in an area sometimes referred to as "La Petite France."

Contrasting the dense byways of Soho were expansive commercial conduits like the Strand, which bounded the lowest edges of London's theater district, Covent Garden. Scattered among the Strand's showy retail and theatrical offerings were the dignified premises of perfumers and hairdressers like Eugène Rimmel and Alfred Low, who met shoppers' beautifying needs via scent, cosmetiques, soap, lotions, and pomades.[49] Additional establishments welcomed the urban traveller as they trekked further east toward the bustling City, London's financial and publishing hub[50] (Figure 0.6). From the mid-nineteenth century, the City

Figure 0.5 "Regent Street Looking towards the Quadrant" by Thomas Shotter Boys (1842). Courtesy of the Art Institute of Chicago.

Figure 0.6 "St. Paul's Cathedral and Ludgate Hill" by John O'Connor (1900). Fine Art Photographic Library/Corbis via Getty Images.

gained a reputation as a public domain of masculine work and life when an influx of male white-collar workers swelled its numbers each weekday morning. This daily concentration of middle-class clerks, brokers, and newspaper men gave rise to a unique brand of grooming businesses specifically catering to their professional needs: barbershops like that of Tom Skelton and his wife Margaret at 17 Fleet Street, which offered City workers a speedy lunchtime shave or trim.[51]

Venturing further east or south introduced travelers to plebeian pockets in the East End and South London, whose heterogeneous populations included laborers, middling merchants, craftspeople, the working or indigent poor—and the humble hairdressers and barbers who served them. In the Victorian period, popular understandings of London's social geographies included an imaginative rupture dividing an allegedly civilized West End from its squalid neighbor to the East.[52] However, these sensational narratives obscured the presence of respectable East End traders, such as hairdresser Edwin Creer who was a vocal advocate for improving the lives and working conditions of London's barber assistants. As we will see, ordinary businesspeople like Creer were integral to the development of London's early beauty industries, despite operating outside the spatial and imaginative boundaries that privileged West End developments. Manufacturing districts in more humble locales also served as essential sites of production and wholesale operations when leading perfumers and hairdressers expanded their businesses—and stock—in the second half of the nineteenth century. By organizing their manufacturing operations across London's industrializing boroughs, trade leaders took advantage of existing urban infrastructures to grow their firms. Perfume wholesalers and distillers, as well as hair merchants and soap makers, cropped up in the center of London and to the east: Clerkenwell, Farringdon, particularly around Hatton Garden, Shoreditch, in and around Commercial Street. Successful perfumers augmented their West End retail outfits by taking up industrial real estate in London's docklands, where industry leaders relied on bonded warehouses to receive raw materials and ship finished products to global markets.[53] It was in these more humble neighborhoods that much of the backstage labor also occurred, as male and female laborers—dubbed "chemical manufacturers"—produced, packed, and shipped growing quantities of commercial beauty goods. From these warehouses in London's laboring quarters, traders transported beautifying goods to flagship West End shops, provincial agents, and perfumery and hairdressing branches established across British colonies.

The rise of London's nineteenth-century beauty industry reflected a competitive urban commercial scene, cultivated by a small but interconnected group of luxury fashion traders operating across the imperial capital. The broad urban distribution of Victorian and Edwardian beauty businesses speaks to their centrality in the luxury scene, with clothing, accessories, and beauty goods bolstering the city's reputation as a fashionable western entrepôt. Nineteenth-century perfumers, hairdressers, and complexion experts offered goods and services that allowed consumers to embody new forms of modern bourgeois respectability, by rendering their bodies "beautiful." To do so, traders took up residence across London's diverse commercial landscapes—from the metropolis' fashionable enclaves to its modest alleys to manufacturing suburbs to the global market—generating popular interest, patronage, and imaginative possibilities in the buying of beauty.

Selling British Beauty

That a British beauty industry developed at all is striking given widespread public criticism of self-fashioning—and especially *female* self-fashioning—that

Figure 0.7 "Progress of the Toilet—The Wig" by James Gillray (n.d.). Courtesy of the Victoria & Albert Museum, London.

guided nineteenth-century luxury consumption (Figure 0.7). These critiques had very real effects on the development of a national industry in the ways that it demanded a concealing of consumers' desires, practices, and pursuits. It could even be argued that, despite London's standing as a preeminent western fashion capital, the story of Britain's beauty industry is not one of resounding success when compared to those of its competitors across the English Channel and the Atlantic. Paralleling general characteristics of the second industrial revolution, nineteenth-century British beauty providers did not match the scale of French and American operations.[54] Economic trends and trade policy also affected the international ranking of beauty industries in this period. Perhaps no force was stronger than domestic consumer attitudes to beautification, as the cultural values regulating beauty and grooming practices in Britain—those of negation, reservation, and concealment—laid the ideological groundwork for a national beauty culture that seemingly prioritized personal privacy over conspicuous consumption. Rather than succumb to critiques, however, traders mobilized these values to inform the design and sale of specifically British beautifying goods and services. In this way, traders simultaneously adhered to and advanced a discreet national aesthetic grounded in "natural" beauty, which bolstered London's global reputation for "social prestige and affluence."[55]

By the twentieth century, this understated approach to beauty nonetheless translated into challenges for the British industry more generally. When tastes for overt beautification ramped up in this period, Britain's beauty providers found themselves competing with the brassy advertising campaigns and exciting new color cosmetics offered by their American competitors and the elegant art deco luxuries afforded by France's leading perfumers.[56] In the opening decades of the twentieth century, a growing contingent of European and American émigrés arrived in London to entice elite British consumers with the bolder bodily treatments flourishing in alternate national beauty markets. Yet future magnates like Helena Rubinstein were not the first to stoke the beauty demands and imaginative possibilities of the British consuming public. As we will see, entrepreneurial insiders and "outsiders" flourished in Britain's nineteenth-century beauty trades, repackaging beautifying goods as cosmopolitan luxuries available to even the most demure of British nationals. They did steady business with British clients, whose seeming resistance to commercial beautification masked the realities of their bodily and consumer practices. London traders cultivated this consistent, albeit concealed demand by tailoring their professionalizing efforts, marketing schemes, and product development to meet popular and consumer desires for discretion.

In addition to widespread cultural critiques over overt beautification, a trader's class, gender, and location in London space could also affect the visibility—and viability—of their beauty enterprise. From the late 1860s, general anxieties over beauty goods coalesced around purported "backroom beauty dealings" and shady traders, labels that took on increasingly gendered associations. Following the public trials of Sarah "Madame Rachel" Leverson in 1868, the onus increasingly fell on small-scale entrepreneurs to defend the respectability of their work, shop space, and wares. Modest firms subsequently lagged behind the efforts of a small but powerful cohort of professionalized trade leaders, who mobilized what Alison C. Kay dubs "masculine-controlled organizational bodies" to establish industry dominance: the British Hairdressers' Benevolent and Provident Institution (1831), La Société du Progrès de la Coiffure (1863), the Hairdressers' Guild (1881).[57] Paralleling these professional affiliations were expanded scales of production to meet new demand for greater quantities of goods. The ensuing ascendency of trade professionals through the 1870s and

1880s arguably came at the cost of their competition: smaller, less capitalized British perfumers and hairdressers who failed to expand their businesses at similar rates. But professionalized firms also suffered from no longer being able to meet personalized needs of high-end female customers. Thus, while trade imbalances based on gender and scale of operations continued into the late nineteenth century, a new category of female beauty entrepreneur—the beauty culturist—eventually excelled by promoting feminine intimacy to a generation of women who sought explicitly female expertise.

For much of the nineteenth century, however, misgivings over beauty providers prevailed, deriving in no small part from more general discomfort with the instabilities of the Victorian market; it is subsequently worth pausing to review the commercial context in which our protagonists labored. Tammy Whitlock has charted pervasive cultural interest among Victorian observers in the apparent perils of Britain's modern retailing scene.[58] Commentators alleged widespread deceit in the course of daily commercial dealings, including those involving sensitive issues of health and the body.[59] Bolstering public misgivings were a number of dramatic cases of commercial food and drug adulteration that unnerved the Victorian consuming public, cases that periodically involved beautifying goods.[60] Court cases, editorials, literature, and satire from the period betray the extent of merchant and consumer discomfort.[61] In many cases, these anxious rhetorics developed to the detriment of the common shopkeeper, who emerged as a prime suspect in the defrauding of the uninformed and increasingly vulnerable urban shopper.[62] Across the Anglo world, nineteenth-century shoppers and retailers struggled with the perceived incompatibility of monetary gain and personal virtue.[63]

This included beauty traders, who navigated modernizing initiatives that transformed both the material conditions of retailing—most notably via new spectacles like the department store—and conceptions of commercial relationships between vendors and patrons.[64] Some historians have argued that the development of standardized practices like cash sales and fixed prices precipitated a move away from traditional sociable shopping exchanges to impersonal transactions that defined modern commerce. However, others have made compelling cases for a continuity in vendor–patron relations through the late nineteenth century rather than a comprehensive (and alienating) modern overhaul.[65] But if intensely local commercial relationships based on character and familiarity endured, nineteenth-century commentators still fixated on the *perceived* anonymity of modern urban commercial interactions, perceptions that had significant consequences for the trade in beauty, perfumery, and grooming.[66]

Commerce — Spermaceti, Ambergris.

Figure 0.8 "Commerce—Spermaceti, Ambergris" by Benjamin Waterhouse Hawkins (*c*.1845). SSPL/Getty Images.

Critics especially warned against the dangers of shopping for increasingly ambulatory female consumers. Susceptible to the lure of commercial pomp and puffery, women ostensibly succumbed to unbridled feminine fantasies propelled by luxury offerings[67] (Figure 0.8). Not coincidentally, many traders offering these goods had access not only to women's pocketbooks but also to their bodies: milliners, dressmakers, perfumers.

It is here that the protagonists of *The Business of Beauty* come to the fore, serving as a lightning rod for circulating anxieties that coalesced in reaction to London's burgeoning beauty trades. To be sure, it was beauty consumers who propelled demand, flouting popular convention in the hopes of altering their looks and, sometimes, their lots in life. But consumers were not the only subjects involved in processes of self-fashioning; all the while, beauty traders fashioned business personas, employing marketing and promotional strategies particular to the modern retail scene. Beauty consumers and merchants were subsequently bound by relationships of trust and discretion, relationships that, in many ways, defied the allegedly impersonal nature of modern urban life.

Yet both beauty consumers and merchants became suspect when they embarked on their commercial exchange: consumers for their desire to conceal their natural or "true" selves and merchants for profiting from these activities.[68] Given its transgressive possibilities, the modern beauty business subsequently produced a number of explosive cases of commercial fraud in various forms. This included conflicts over patents and copyright, adulterated goods, deceptive marketing, and trademark infringement.[69] This study addresses examples from each of these categories, showing how both purchasers and retailers of beauty goods were implicated in contested commercial transactions ranging from the seemingly honest to the far more dubious. Encounters between and among consumers and traders also generated intermittent but powerful ruptures in local courtrooms, shops, and even on the streets of London. Such conflicts throw into relief the careful navigation—by both shoppers and merchants— of the shifting terrains of British beauty ideals and "modern" commercial relationships, revealing how beauty consumption was periodically at the center of these negotiations.

Locating Beauty Brokers

To chart the history of beauty consumption and production in nineteenth- and early-twentieth-century London, this study offers a social, cultural, and urban history of a small group populating a specific metropolitan trade, some of whom faced intense public scrutiny over the propriety of their dealings. The high stakes governing beauty consumption periodically heightened critiques of small-scale operations. At risk was not only the respectability of small-scale beauty providers but also the standing of their customers. At times, the alleged protection of beauty consumers—and especially women—could marginalize small-scale businesses, including those run by women, given traders' "threats" to consumer bodies and health. Navigating this fraught commercial and cultural landscape subsequently proved more difficult for some beauty traders than others, as gender, class, and location in London defined merchants' ability to develop trustworthy commercial reputations and align with circulating expectations of respectability. Much of vendors' success, then, was not only a matter of business prowess but also driven by sociocultural and individual qualities: class, ethnicity, and gender, but also personality, kinship networks, and luck.[70] Incorporating these contingent factors into a historical study of a specific industry foregrounds the importance of circumstance to business success, not to mention the daily realities of small-scale entrepreneurship.

Focusing on the sociocultural and personal contingencies that shaped individual beauty enterprise demands an exploration of both marginal and major players in London's early beauty industry. The nineteenth-century beauty business was built, in part, out of complex relationships between and among male and female traders of varying success who battled for dominance over small niche markets. This competitive atmosphere was often fostered by traders' location in urban space, as ordinary and oftentimes unsuccessful traders lived and worked alongside merchants who would go on to dominate the industry. In other words, both women and men, successful and unsuccessful, were part of a dynamic interplay that propelled the industry by fostering a competitive atmosphere in a densely local market.[71] But beauty providers were not passive players; they developed a variety of strategies for enhancing the respectability of beauty goods, which, in turn, fueled their economic success. Small-scale, female, and foreign traders forged significant connections to the market, regardless of the scale, duration, or viability of their operations. Thus, ordinary traders were central to the development of the early British beauty business despite being on the spatial and imaginative boundaries of the trade. In this light, *The Business of Beauty* devotes equal attention to famous beauty culturists and previously unacknowledged commercial players striving for economic stability in the beauty business, arguing for the significance of even the most fleeting enterprise. It focuses on what was arguably the most important element of Britain's nineteenth-century luxury market to highlight both economic and interpersonal realities of everyday entrepreneurial life.[72]

This study also aligns with histories of women in business and studies of subjectivity and enterprising families by devoting careful attention to space; this provides an entry point for linking daily life and economic relationships in London's early beauty industry.[73] A focus on London as a western fashion capital highlights the intimate overlap—the messiness—of social networks, gendered experience, and commercial activities in the modern metropolis.[74] Historical actors moved through the built environment, engaging in economic exchange but also what has been termed "emotional practices" in response to social and environmental situations.[75] The application of these concepts to nineteenth-century urban commerce suggests that dense concentrations of businesses—and bodies—created intimate economic but also personal webs linking local players.

Charting the commercial and interpersonal "highways and byways" of the metropolis thus allows us to expand our cast of characters beyond traditional economic actors, giving equal weight to both major and minor figures—women and men—doing business in a particular locale. This repopulation of the commercial landscapes of the city ultimately complicates a standard entrepreneurial story, moving away from the lauding of individual achievements of industry leaders toward an appreciation of secondary players and the nuanced interplay between location, proximity, and enterprise. It simultaneously draws attention to the ways that beauty consumers and providers created distinct markets, navigating the spatial politics and interpersonal interactions demanded by the muted culture of British beauty consumption.

If cultural prescriptions regulating British beauty demanded the concealment of beautifying practices and purchases, they could also work to obscure their presence in the historical record. No single archive offers a uniform picture of commercial beauty in the nineteenth and early twentieth centuries. Rather, consumers and traders provide glimpses of their activities and interactions across a range of sources: periodical press articles, beauty manuals, trade journals, business directories. This study uncovers some of these concealed practices by piecing together these archival elements, exposing an active urban trade more productive than previously acknowledged.

The type and availability of sources nonetheless has consequences for selecting the case studies in this book; as much as possible, I devote attention to both extraordinary and ordinary traders. Some individuals, like Eugène Rimmel or Aimée Lloyd, were exceptional because they experienced incredible financial success or an acrimonious divorce. The resulting court proceedings, firm records, limited liability registration, and newspaper coverage of notable events enabled me to construct the major case studies appearing in this book. A handful of more detailed sources, such as the letters of Jeannette Scalé preserved in a Methodist archive in Ohio, chart daily business activities, expressed in deeply intimate terms that vivify the personal consequences of entrepreneurial ambition. These exceptional holdings provide us with evocative glimpses of the emotional toll of the beauty business, which so often accompanied the highs and lows of individual enterprise.

But what of other, ordinary traders haunting the margins of the historical record? How do we account for struggling and failing beauty businesses, operating out of backroom parlors and workrooms, never to feature in an advertisement or trade journal? Historians of women and enterprise have developed a number of productive strategies to illuminate such players, from mining fire insurance records to mapping trade directories and census records.[76] Such sources are of particular importance in the case of London's beauty businesses, where many traders figure in official records as a single line in a single volume of a city directory or as a brief reference to failure in the *London Gazette*. In those cases, I rely on census records, probates, and directory listings to determine the social and urban contexts in which these traders lived and worked, reconstructing the interpersonal contours of their lives.[77] When mapped onto modern London, with its highways and byways demarcated by class and rank, a focus on neighborhoods' social makeup—occupations of neighbors, size of family units, numbers of dependents—brings to life the environments in which these people conducted their business. By situating these traders within a populous commercial setting, we can begin to construct localized relationships built on proximity as well as economic strategies.

The women and men showcased in this book are not representative of all traders' experiences, but they are most certainly important examples of ordinary women's and men's labor in the early beauty trades.[78] When situated within overlapping social, professional, and geographic circles, we can begin to reconstruct the interweaving of traders' lives and work. This historical reality is mirrored in the structure of this book, in which characters move in and out of intersecting case studies, some appearing across multiple chapters and life stories. As the book's freestanding but interconnected case studies progress, we can begin to see the localized relationships connecting players as part of a complex modern network of those trading in beauty but also concealment.

* * *

The Business of Beauty opens with a tight focus on localized space before moving outward in scope, to consider the capital, the continent, and colonial markets, before concluding in the same intimate spaces that open the book. Our journey begins and ends in Mayfair, where elite retailers bumped up against less affluent proprietors in the neighboring "backmews" east of Regent Street and along the borders of Soho. Chapter 1 reveals the importance of "backmewsy" small-scale beauty providers, including some women, to London's early beauty industry. By tracking hair restorer Agnes Headman and hairdresser Aimée Lloyd, we learn how competitors on New and Old Bond Streets, not to mention double-crossing assistants and abusive spouses, shaped their success in the mid-nineteenth century. Chapter 2 explores how the respectability of London's beauty businesses met significant challenges by the late 1860s following the rise of one particularly notorious female trader, Sarah "Madame Rachel" Leverson. Leverson's 1868 fraud trials inspired national outrage over duplicitous "tricks" of backroom beauty providers. Sensational media coverage of Leverson's practices heightened public criticism of artificial beauty, affecting both consumers and producers. As we will see, perfumers across London worked to affirm their respectability in the wake of the "Madame Rachel" scandal, moves that reorganized the trade along professional versus "disreputable" lines.

Chapter 3 expands our focus eastward from the "court" end of town to explore the City, the East End, and the South, showing how London's hairdressers and barbers worked alongside perfumers to enhance consumers' appearances. Barbers' and hairdressers' traditional, masculine work was challenged, however, with the introduction of a "new" innovation of the late 1860s: female hairdressers to serve elite women customers. The response of London's leading hairdressers and perfumers to feminized labor illuminates the ways that new professional organizations and their members came to dominate the British beauty industry, maintaining clear gender divisions in the trade through the 1870s and 1880s. In Chapter 4, we follow one such professional trade leader, émigré perfumer Eugène Rimmel, as he relocated from Soho's Francophone networks to the Strand in a move that enhanced his cosmopolitan authority for British consumers. Moving beyond the boundaries of the nation, we see how leading perfumers like Rimmel established a masculine perfumery class, adopting roles as imperial traders and exporting not only goods but also competing discourses about race and beauty across the British world.

Chapters 5 and 6 return from colonial markets to our point of departure—Mayfair—where a new contingent of female entrepreneurs emerged at the *fin de siècle* to counter increasingly depersonalized beauty firms: the beauty culturist. This included a number of foreign nationals like American Jeannette Scalé Pomeroy who introduced British ladies to a new generation of beauty services, including electrolysis, electric massage, and facials. Chapter 6 follows this cohort of female beauty culturists into the twentieth century, charting the early British experiences of a future star: twentieth-century beauty magnate Helena Rubinstein. In doing so, the study concludes by situating Rubinstein as a successor to rather than originator of luxury beauty retailing, reconnecting her to a longer history of modern London's lesser-known but equally significant beauty brokers.[79]

1

"Backmewsy" Beauty: Agnes Headman and Aimée Lloyd

In February 1858, Mrs. Agnes Headman of 24 Savile Row died, leaving behind her a profitable London-based business as a "Hair Restorer and Advisor to Ladies on the State of their Hair." Headman (c.1808–1858) had developed a following of West End customers who patronized her hair dyeing services, but also purchased manufactures like "Rejuvenescent Hair Cream" and "Botanic Hair Wash and Curling Fluid," which she produced in her backroom laboratory. Through services and goods, Headman promised to enhance female clients' natural beauty, all the while maintaining discretion about their patronage of her West End location.[1]

Just around the corner on Glasshouse Street, another female trader worked to produce one of London's best-selling and enigmatic grooming products marketed to men, a waterless shaving cream known as "Euxesis." In contrast to Agnes Headman's independent venture, Aimée Lloyd (b. 1828) labored as part of a family unit and contributed to the Lloyds's household economy. When her husband proved abusive and indolent, she found herself "wholly destitute" in both the economic and personal sense. She subsequently turned to profits from "Euxesis" for her survival. Her efforts did not go unnoticed; before long, celebrated London wholesaler Robert Hovenden (1830–1908) attempted to procure the secret formula for "Euxesis." When Lloyd refused, she and Hovenden embarked on a protracted legal battle over the shaving cream, which she eventually won with the support of character witnesses from the local business community. Euxesis continued to be produced into the twentieth century, although Lloyd herself disappears from the historical record.[2]

Despite their differences, Agnes Headman and Aimée Lloyd's experiences suggest those of a handful of beauty businesswomen who lived and worked in London's West End in the mid-nineteenth century. Their stories highlight shared elements that periodically featured in small-scale beauty enterprises, both male- and female-owned. They speak to the presence of small-scale ventures in modest "backmewsy" spaces, contiguous to more successful luxury beauty "emporiums" located on London's leading commercial corridors like Bond Street. They also demonstrate the ways that traders' linkages to family networks could both engender and work against their commercial enterprise. Alternatively, traders could depend upon particular commercial actors, specifically agents and wholesalers, to help substantiate their local reputation. Indeed, Headman, Lloyd, and other small-scale entrepreneurs operated in broader occupational networks of retail and manufacturing perfumers, hairdressers, and "beauty advisors." These communities could function as a site of belonging, but also as a mechanism of exclusion for traders who transgressed conventional social mores, as we will explore further in Chapter 2. Finally, the cases of Headman and Lloyd provide examples of mid-century beauty marketing campaigns in popular print periodicals, revealing the ways that elaborate, increasingly expensive forms of self-promotion came to be dominated by more successful, oftentimes male counterparts.

As part of London's small contingent of mid-nineteenth-century beauty businesses, women's enterprises contributed to the foundations of Britain's modern commercial beauty industry, alongside those of increasingly elaborate, typically male-owned firms. Clustered in London's West End, men's and women's shops were scattered along Mayfair and St. James's stately commercial thoroughfares and the more contested terrain of its plebeian neighbors to the east, St. James Westminster and St. Anne's Soho. Hierarchies of space operated in these contiguous spaces and shaped the material conditions of the West End perfumery and hairdressing market. In the West End, male and female vendors capitalized on a burgeoning Victorian beauty culture to consolidate a new luxury trade for elite and middle-class consumers.

Charting the stories of Agnes Headman and Aimée Lloyd—and their personal and economic connections to family-in-law, business rivals, and occupational communities—is an exercise in complicating standard stories about entrepreneurial success. By moving away from the lauding of singular achievements of industry leaders, we craft alternative entrepreneurial narratives that repopulate the commercial landscapes of West End enterprise. Traders operating at the center and on the margins of London's beauty business were part of a dense spatial concentration of mid- and small-sized firms, in a dynamic business environment engendered by their close proximity.[3] Headman and Lloyd were just two of a number of traders populating the West End beauty trades, and yet their stories offer general insights into economic challenges and resourcefulness, interleaved with moments of love and violence. They also allow us to observe the complex nature of London's mid-century urban geography and its inhabitants, how gender operated "on the ground," and the interconnections between urban networks and business practices, all as they unfolded in a discreet commercial milieu. Ultimately, male and female beauty traders' spatial concentration in the West End and along the borders of St. James Westminster and St. Anne's Soho contributed to a commercial atmosphere that was not only dynamic and creative but also competitive.[4] Regardless of merchants' class or gender, their intense concentration in this geographic and economic atmosphere engendered what economist Alfred Marshall characterized as "a continuous interplay between competition and cooperation," in this case in the beauty market.[5] This included the "backmewsy" operations of more humble beauty providers; an exploration of them moves them from the peripheries of scholarly considerations of Victorian enterprise to center stage as representative entrepreneurs in a metropolitan commercial environment out of which successful individual ventures emerged.[6] In other words, small-scale entrepreneurs—including some women—were important players in Victorian London's beauty business. Their presence contributed to later successes of London's professionalizing perfumers and hairdressers on national and global stages.

Building a British Beauty Business

Agnes Headman and Aimée Lloyd were part of a compact network of mid-century traders who discreetly enhanced Londoners' appearance. Until the late nineteenth century, however, there was no formal, capitalist "beauty industry" in London and especially not one catering exclusively to female clientele.[7] Through the eighteenth century, London's commercial scene featured a notable perfumery trade based on skill and craftsmanship that serviced men and women of the city's prosperous classes.[8] Along with hairdressers and wig makers, these traders proffered the requisite items for elite eighteenth-century consumers to meet late-century trends: perfume, paint, powder, and towering perukes (Plate 1). Elite patronage reflected not only expanding urban markets in commodities but also new cultural and aesthetic associations relating to whiteness and British identity. Kim Hall argues that the early years of European colonization generated—and depended on—a new set of cultural connotations around a racialized hierarchy of lightness over darkness. The subsequent idealization of fairness imbued male and female beauty with symbolic functions related to moral purity as well as social and ethnic hegemony.[9] These powerful new connotations expanded public interest in beautification beyond the elite and urban consuming classes. For example, early modern medical and domestic recipe books reveal that middling men and women practiced what Edith Snook terms "beautifying physic." Early modern women engaged in home production, eschewing the overt "paints" targeted by anti-cosmetic satires in favor of cleansing washes, unguents, and complexion creams that "were manifestly a component of medical practice."[10]

By the nineteenth century, London traders continued to offer consumers, primarily elite men, grooming tools and services necessary for communicating the civilized status of a fashionable public figure.[11] Meanwhile, new conceptions of bourgeois femininity consolidated linkages between physical beauty and women's moral purity.[12] Emerging evangelical domestic ideology prescribed an idealized femininity, in which a woman's physical appearance conveyed "the seasons of a woman's life" or her connections to the natural world.[13] This transformed the nature and appearance of women's self-fashioning, when, by the mid-century, a domesticated white femininity defined by authenticity and artlessness emerged as the desirable form for a bourgeois wife. Pamphlets and didactic health literature deplored female cosmetic use as a sign of women's duplicitous and immoral inner character.[14] Middle-class women's magazines, new cultural forms flourishing in the 1850s and 1860s, also reinforced the rejection of artifice in lieu of honesty about one's physical beauty.[15] Middle-class authors and critics derided beauty consumption as a habit of the debauched aristocratic classes, whose artifice mirrored their doubtful moral character.[16]

At the same time, the promotion of natural beauty foregrounded the importance of an attractive physical appearance as a marker of mental and bodily health. Public censure subsequently could not dissuade Victorian men and women from engaging in discreet practices of bodily self-fashioning in order to attain an effect of what critic Amy Montz terms "artificial naturalness."[17] While home production persisted through the mid-nineteenth century, advice on self-modification in the name of beauty began to address the need to purchase various products rather than concoct them at home, a shift engendered by a growing commercial market for consumable beauty goods.[18] Responding to the rising demand for grooming products, advice authors alternated between critiquing artificial adornment and endorsing the latest retailer.[19] Toilet books condemned unnatural artifice while simultaneously detailing complex recipes and beauty techniques in "the embellishment of nature by means of art."[20] One *Handbook of the Toilette* instructed female readers how to dye the eyelashes using "a strong aqueous solution of carbonate of soda, applied by means of a fine camel-hair pencil," while 1858's *Arts of Beauty* suggested using a piece of leather and "pitch-plaster" to tear off superfluous hair.[21]

While prescriptive authors identified Britain's middle-class wives and mothers as the primary keepers of the cult of domesticity, they also targeted members of the upper ranks, the principal consumers of beauty goods and services.[22] Testing the boundaries of respectability, elite clientele and London beauty providers seem to have discounted or ignored criticism appearing in the didactic and periodical press.[23] It certainly did not prevent a cohort of perfumers, hairdressers, and wigmakers, operating through the first half of the nineteenth century, from advertising their goods via elaborate promotional campaigns. Perfumers like Alexander Ross of Bishopsgate Street published comprehensive tracts, pamphlets, and illustrated advertisements, inviting consumers to patronize his equally spectacular perfumery showroom in the City[24] (Plate 2). Meanwhile, West End traders including Francis Breidenbach and James Atkinson hawked their unique versions of items like bear's grease, a fatty pomade used to shine, style, and encourage hair growth[25] (Figure 1.1). Yet, London's privileged clientele seemingly understood that they could avoid criticism only if they did not appear to be "made up" or artificially enhanced. In

Figure 1.1 Pharmacy: Bear's Grease for Hair (n.d.). Courtesy of the Wellcome Library, London.

this way, tensions between transparency and invisibility pervaded nineteenth-century beauty culture and manifested themselves conceptually and practically.

Scholars have argued that these tensions intensified in 1859 with the development of aniline dyes that produced new varieties of brightly colored textiles (Plate 3). Britain's middle- and upper-class women excitedly transformed vibrant mauve, magenta, and "near-neon green" fabrics into the latest French fashions. Historian Tammy Whitlock argues that these showier forms of dress in turn engendered a renewed interest in not just hair, perfumery, and complexion care, but also cosmetics use.[26] While a natural aesthetic remained the fashion through the 1860s, new technologies in "making up" and a growing sensitivity to beautifying goods suddenly increased the visibility of artificial embellishment.[27] The "woman of artifice" dramatically figured in literary productions of the period, sensationalized in serial novels like Mary Elizabeth Braddon's *Lady Audley's Secret* (1862) and Wilkie Collins's *Armadale* (1866).[28] Contrary to these sensational accounts of female self-fashioning, many middle- and upper-class women stayed true to discreet measures to enact a "natural," unadulterated aesthetic in an effort to avoid criticism. They adopted beauty products that eliminated gray hairs, whitened discolored teeth, and produced a fair, blemish-free complexion, idealized as an "English rose."[29]

The slowly shifting terrain in standards of bodily manipulation was propelled by an expanding array of commercial providers, who encouraged upper- and middle-class consumers to purchase rather than produce beautifying products.[30] A consumer's class status and geographic location in London space determined the appropriate venue for such beauty consumption. London's West End was unquestionably the heart of commercial beauty culture, with its complementary associations of luxury services and elite patronage.[31] There, according to *Fun*, ladies wishing "to commit a social felony by stealing a march upon time" needed only "appl[y] to a perfumer," an imprecise category that could describe manufacturing or retail perfumers, hairdressers and wigmakers, or enigmatic "consultants" like Agnes Headman.[32] In West End perfumery shops, retailers like Atkinson, Eugène Rimmel, and Septimus Piesse manufactured and sold a new scent every year, alongside an expanding array of face powders, eye pencils, rouge for the face, and cosmetiques for the hair[33] (Figure 1.2). Other high-end commercial retailers stocked similar goods while offering services in haircutting, singeing, and dyeing.[34] Skin and nail care also fell under the purview of perfumers and hairdressers, and it would not be until the *fin de siècle* that trade directories included the categories of manicurist (1891), complexion specialist (1897), and electrolysis operator (1903).[35] Only

Figure 1.2 J.&E. Atkinson's (1832, n.d.). Courtesy of the John Johnson Collection, Bodleian Libraries, University of Oxford, Beauty Parlour 2 (64).

periodically did vendors characterize themselves as "Hair Dye Makers" and "Hair Restorers," which seemed to imply service providers' ability to color and condition but not cut hair.

While female consumers were the most frequent targets of anti-artifice critiques, there also existed a healthy market for male self-fashioning and beauty through the nineteenth century. Perfumers' goods were typically unisex in design, and it was not until the end of the century that traders actively marketed their goods to specific genders.[36] *Eau de Cologne*, lavender water, and toilet soaps prominently featured in gender-neutral advertisements, courting both male and female custom. Remarkable records from Floris, the contemporary perfumery house established on Jermyn Street in 1730, attest to the mixed gender composition of consumption. A sample of one hundred purchases from January 1871 reveals some sixty-two purchases by men investing in a broad range of goods: cologne, toothbrushes, cold cream, soap, and sponges.[37] While such records are exceptional, the books offer a tantalizing glimpse into the diverse categories of goods represented in women's and men's patronage of London beauty businesses.

More often, historians of self-fashioning and material culture are faced with the difficult task of charting women's and men's daily grooming practices, practices often effaced by the subjects themselves. Popular censure restricted people's candor about beauty practices. Perusal of personal letters and diaries does little to uncover individual practices of beautification.[38] Fortunately, a handful of noteworthy business sources like the Floris accounts help to illuminate the number and class of consumers patronizing mid-century beauty businesses. Cashbooks from Breidenbach's Bond Street perfumery business also identify private patrons, in addition to commercial purchases by provincial and local chemists, wholesalers, and hairdressers.[39] Transactions from 1869 betrayed a diverse range of customers, including a number of visible members of London society: Baron Calthorpe, a never-married former MP; the Countess of Caledon, a Lady of the Bedchamber to Queen Victoria; and Amelia Curzon, wife of a popular local barrister and mistress at Scarsdale House, Kensington.[40]

But Breidenbach's elite location did not prevent men and women of the respectable middle classes from also soliciting the shop. Traveling from outside of London or ordering goods by post, upper-middle-class customers represented provincial political influence—like Mrs. Henrietta Tindal, the wife of the Clerk of the Peace for Buckinghamshire or William Bowdidge, an alderman in Brighton—and High Street trade, including Brighton-based "Professor of Notation" Frederick Cavile and never-married Devon stationer Ann Crowther.[41] In addition to business records, Old Bailey trial proceedings suggest that beauty consumption extended to a more lowly class of customer who also desired to beautify their bodies. In 1858, Georgiana Percy, a 22-year-old waistcoat maker in Euston Square, spent 3d. on a bar of soap at Madame Mara's on Regent Street.[42] In 1864, 19-year-old Charlotte Watts of Bermondsey purchased a packet of violet powder at James Bates's hairdressing and perfumery business on Glasshouse Street.[43]

While illuminating, such sources do not reveal the full extent to which different strata of British society consumed beautifying goods. Not until the final years of the nineteenth century and the rise of the "New Woman" did there emerge a growing acceptance of the visibly "made up," as "the use of pigments" became "general."[44] By this period, technological developments made for new advances in beauty treatments, including techniques in facial massage, electrolysis, and even chemical peels. At the turn of the twentieth century, these procedures, which expanded upon traditional beauty products, were readily available to those women and men who, according to the *Daily Mirror* in 1906, would "suffer anything and pay anything for a good complexion."[45]

"Hangers-On to a Fashionable Situation"

Some years before this, in the mid-nineteenth century, tensions around the visibility of people's beauty practices extended beyond clientele to implicate the purveyors of beauty products. Yet, in spite of cultural censure, a trade directory of 1857 records an active group of some 1,254 Londoners representing the fluid categories used to classify beauty providers: haircutters, barbers, wigmakers, hair workers (producing chignons, frizettes, and partings), retail perfumers, wholesale perfumers, hair dye makers, and chiropodists.[46] Surnames and census records suggest that many of these tradespeople were non-British nationals, who dominated perfumery and hairdressing throughout the latter half of the nineteenth century. Less often, these figures appeared in middle-class trades selling general beauty supplies, such as chemists and druggists.[47]

References in trade directories and census returns only begin to suggest the practice of these traders at the mid-century, but historians of women and business have demonstrated that we can glean some important information from these data sets.[48] However limited, the sources suggest the presence of a handful of female tradespeople working in close proximity to male traders who periodically left more historical records than their female counterparts, including trade listings and professional memberships, advertisements in the popular press, or, after 1855, registration of their businesses as limited liability companies. References in newspaper advertisements, trade directories, census records, and fire insurance policies suggest the presence of at least 255 female traders operating beauty businesses in London between 1840 and 1870.[49] A few more detailed cases of female enterprise surface when women became entangled in formal interventions and legal proceedings. Records from Britain's Court of Chancery, in its dealings with equity law, describe practices of a few exemplary female beauty providers and help to identify notable trends in their business practices.[50]

Trade directories suggest that, despite their low numbers, a geographic concentration of female retail perfumers emerged in the West End's burgeoning beauty business. Business historian Alison C. Kay estimates that women made up approximately 10 percent of all London traders in the mid-nineteenth century. The beauty business registers only slightly higher than Kay's estimates. Between 1852 and 1870 women made up approximately 15 percent of London's small contingent of "Retail Perfumers," reaching 21 percent in 1863.[51] Significantly, the majority of female retail perfumers listed in London's *Post Office Directory* through the mid-nineteenth century were based in St. George Hanover Square or St. James Westminster.[52] To be sure, these demographics, based on trade listings, fail to account for all female beauty merchants. As scholars have noted, trade directories can be "notoriously incomplete," ignoring down-market or itinerant vendors serving informal sectors of the urban economy.[53] It is nonetheless significant that some women elected to advertise their businesses in trade directories aimed at London's expanding population of consumers, publicizing their discreet goods and services.

While female beauty providers contributed to trade networks of West End perfumers and hairdressers, circulating ideas about feminine bourgeois respectability could affect their public visibility as trade leaders, given the nature of their work. Historians Kay and Jennifer Aston have shown that economic and legal factors like lack of credit and legal inequalities—that is, factors traditionally depicted as curbing female business participation—did not limit women to the extent that scholars have previously imagined.[54] Aston's ongoing research compellingly demonstrates that, despite enduring narratives about women's relegation to the private sphere from the mid-nineteenth century, female entrepreneurs were visible players helming viable, long-term business ventures in dynamic urban locales like Birmingham and Leeds.[55] Yet, despite the sustained and public presence of businesswomen across trades and urban centers, Victorian cultural mores around commercial beautification, beauty consumption, and bodily services could seemingly affect the visibility and public profile of enterprising women in the mid-century beauty business. Popular conceptions of bourgeois femininity also seems to have resulted in what Katrina Honeyman describes as women's "sectoral concentration."[56] Throughout the 1850s and 1860s, some trades related to beauty providers, including the aforementioned chemists and druggists, featured few women.[57] Nor did women manage distilleries, which were central to the perfumery trades in their provision of requisite oils and essences. In perfumery, demands for ample start-up capital could potentially limit the scale of business for both women and men. Wholesale or retail perfumery required abundant stock, not to mention manufacturing oils and chemicals.[58] The sundry nature of perfumers' wares amplified these costs. Items liquidated at an 1854 auction betray the variety of goods required, including "fancy soaps, distilled perfumes, essential oils, pomades, marrows, and oils, a large stock of hair, clothes, nail, tooth, and other brushes." This did not begin to account for shop fixtures and furniture[59] (see Appendix II).

As Kay and Aston have argued, a woman's physical and material circumstances in commercial space shaped her enterprise, and this was no different for West

End beauty traders.[60] Their typical location adjacent to London's leading avenues of consumption suggests that women's mid-century beauty businesses were somewhat less visible than increasingly professionalized counterparts.[61] Their situation could owe, in part, to the disparate rental rates demanded on neighboring West End streets. At mid-century, Kay notes that a shop on elite St. James's Street rented for nearly £400 a year, while adjacent New Bond Street offered shop space for £375. Rates on "the Strand, Coventry Street, Piccadilly, Regent, and Oxford Street" were comparably high.[62] But just off well-trodden terrain, a retailer could rent a respectable shop for under £100.[63] With the exception of some traders on Oxford, Regent, and New Bond Streets, female vendors set up shop in the residential squares and side streets of the West End's vestries and districts: St. George Hanover Square, St. James Westminster, St. Martin's-in-the-Fields, the Strand.[64] In the 1840s, for example, Agnes Headman signed her Savile Row lease for £115 per annum.[65]

That is not to say that the West End's major thoroughfares were completely inaccessible to female beauty entrepreneurs, but that female-owned beauty businesses tended to make more fleeting appearances at affluent addresses on major commercial streets.[66] For one year in 1859, for example, Miss Eliza Drever advertised her perfumery business at 304 Regent Street.[67] But to the west, near the up-and-coming Knightsbridge area, Euphemia Bury worked as a hairdresser and perfumer through the 1850s and mid-1860s from 205 Sloane Street, having inherited the business from her father John.[68] Others lived and worked in somewhat less affluent locales north of Oxford Street, toward Marylebone. Mrs. Jane Taylor advertised her Berner Street "restorer" business in 1868 before relocating to Great Portland—deemed by one commentator to be "so unfashionable a street"—through 1876.[69] These small-scale shops seemingly remained modest compared to the levels of renown achieved by other traders, who developed the notable "haircutting temples" along the West End's major commercial byways.[70]

The mixed class and gender composition of West End beauty provisioners testifies to the area's heterogeneous character in the mid-nineteenth century. Despite enduring perceptions of the West End as an exclusively elite space, contemporary and more recent studies of London's social geographies emphasize the intermingling of both privileged and plebeian residents in urban space.[71] In 1867, one columnist insisted, "extravagant luxury is to be found in one street, and squalid misery in the next."[72] Noted another observer, "some of London's most fashionable streets" revealed the mixed social demographics of the nineteenth-century metropolis, as small side streets of main thoroughfares harbored "the saddest sights of all may be seen."[73] However, West End residents could be impervious to their less fortunate neighbors. Social commentator John Hollingshead suggested that residents "may have all hurried for years along the bright open highways, scarcely glancing at the little doorways scattered here and there between busy shops."[74] Through such doors and in the byways "of a less attractive kind," small-scale merchants served the consumer needs of the West End's mixed classes—of gentlemen and "the impoverished ladies."[75]

Anxieties over the mixed economy and social makeup of Mayfair and St. James manifested in debates over the area's principal commercial zones and particularly Regent Street, which separated high-end from plebeian space. At times, the demographic mixing that allowed the simultaneous operation of carriage trades and middle-market providers could also work to disparage female economic participation as retailers as well as consumers, by aligning female market participation with the all-too-visible "public women" of the West End. While observers criticized elite pedestrians who ignored the social differences of little alleys and courts, the diversification and capitalization of principal commercial streets in the West End provoked anxiety over the social mix in the neighborhood. Surveyor Francis Cross declared the swelling variety of shops the "greatest impediment to real improvement" in West End architecture. For Cross, the heterogeneity of shops and the character of their keepers soiled the orderly appearance of the built environment in corridors like Regent Street. "As each trade differs in itself, so does it require different accommodation," he noted. "The irregularity in all the buildings in every street or thoroughfare exhibiting in their fronts [betray] a variety of change only to be equaled by the faces of their owners."[76]

Attention to irregularities in Regent Street's commercial development extended to the diversifying character of its patrons, especially the artificial beauties who strolled along it. London's socioeconomic divides did not prevent areas in the West End from becoming spaces of sexual commerce, and the emblematic figure of the gaudily dressed, overtly made-up prostitute served as a vivid embodiment of female artifice in public space.[77] Streetwalkers and their clients moved from byways and alleys to congregate in fashionable locales, reportedly frequenting Regent Street at midday and the Haymarket after dark.[78] They promenaded through London's elite shopping zones, as depicted in one image from 1871 showing two ornately dressed prostitutes bribing the beadle to solicit in Mayfair's Burlington Arcades, home at the time to retail perfumer Georgina Hopkins[79] (Figure 1.3).

Out of this illicit social mixing emerged perceptions of the West End as potentially inhospitable to women of standing.[80] Lynda Nead notes "there were

THE BEADLE OF THE BURLINGTON.—" SOMETIMES A SOVEREIGN, AND SOMETIMES LESS."

Figure 1.3 Prostitutes Bribing a Beadle in Burlington Arcade, *The Days' Doings*, Volume 2 (May 20, 1871): 272. Mary Evans Picture Library.

many different ways in which respectable women could inhabit the streets of London," but the public woman could nonetheless be an ambiguous figure in urban space, and social commentators and male pedestrians periodically muddied if not conflated differences between streetwalkers and fashionably dressed middle-class shoppers.[81] Differentiation between classes of women turned in large part on appearance, and pedestrians, "caught up in [a] network of gazes," relied on visual codes to assess the respectability of women moving through urban space.[82] Press descriptions of the *"demimondaine"* drew visual parallels between the two forms of public women, marking their shared love of ostentatious self-fashioning and artificial beauty aids. The physical appearance of high-end prostitutes, noted physician and social observer William Acton, was "doubtless due in part to the artistic manner of the make-up by powder and cosmetics, on the employment of which extreme care is bestowed."[83] Overt self-fashioning came to signal feminine deception of the (male) beholder and led to categorical denunciations of the female offender, regardless of social standing.

Offering tips on how to distinguish respectable women from the *demi-monde*, for example, one columnist in the *Pall Mall Gazette* claimed the poorly dyed "yellow chignons" of high-class prostitutes visiting from St. John's Wood and Pimlico betrayed those carriages "that anybody may pay for."[84]

Beauty traders seemingly occupied a tenuous public status in these narratives, as they were the commercial purveyors of the contested "yellow chignons," not to speak of powder and cosmetics. To buttress their reputation, businesswomen and men relied on local trade communities developed among kin and neighbors. While economic instabilities could mean frequent relocations for financially beleaguered entrepreneurs, many beauty businesspeople—male and female—remained in the general vicinity of their old shops.[85] Traders realized, as economist Alfred Marshall would later observe, that "the success of a business depend[ed] chiefly upon the resources and the markets of its own immediate neighborhood."[86] Not only did this localism maintain the network of clientele established over years of trading, but traders also needed to cultivate relationships with wholesalers, printers, and distributors who served the same locales.[87] London's impressive size did not preclude local neighborhoods from functioning as close-knit communities bound together by class or occupation, particularly among the working- and lower-middle classes. As one longtime occupant of Soho's Pulteney Court explained, he dreaded "going into another neighborhood" as it "would be like a 'foreign country' to him."[88]

At the same time, intimate connections within trading communities could work against traders, including women, especially when local traders supported competing retailers. This was the case for the sister of Agnes Headman who took up Headman's business following her death in 1858. Agnes Headman's story illuminates the potential shortcomings of family support and the hindrances that local trade communities could pose to enterprise. Having inherited Headman's business, Headman's sister Susan Ansell failed in her initial attempts to sustain the Headman line of products and services. Ansell's commercial inexperience, coupled with her lack of connection to local networks of traders, proved detrimental when she found herself in direct competition with Headman's former assistant.

Agnes Headman, 24 Savile Row

The appearance of Agnes Headman's estate in Chancery Court proceedings in 1858 illuminates her firm's history in exceptional detail and provides some clues about the material circumstances of her less-documented contemporaries.

The location of her business, her reliance on family support and specifically that of her sister Susan Ansell, her relationship to local occupational networks including agents, and her efforts at self-promotion all contributed to the success of her hair care business. Also propelling Headman's enterprise was her skill at meeting very personal demands of female clientele attempting to achieve an artificially natural beauty. In print ads, Headman promised discreet curative and preventative services for clients suffering from balding and thinning of the hair. She offered a variety of products to the discerning lady consumer, the most popular ostensibly being "Mrs. Headman's Medicated Oil," which both promoted "a new growth in hair" and "prevent[ed] its falling off."[89] Equally lucrative was Headman's provision of hair dyes, which she promoted using the language of bodily health and wellness as a means to "remedy greyness."[90]

It was the death of her husband that led to Ann Cole's reinvention as Mrs. Agnes Headman, "Hair Restorer and Advisor to Ladies on the State of their Hair." From 1843, working out of a number of commercial locations including a brief sojourn at 21 New Bond Street, Headman claimed to have gained the patronage of London's fashionable set, the "nobility and gentry."[91] In April 1850, Headman opened a shop at No. 24 Savile Row, in close proximity to her Bond Street location but with a lower rent[92] (Map 1.1). There, Headman produced

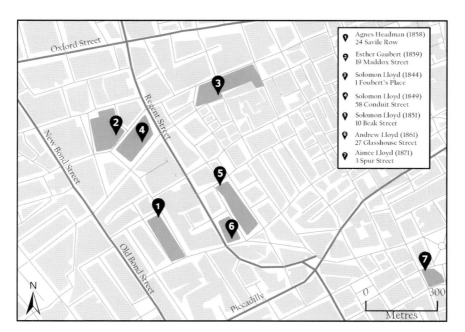

Map 1.1 Map of Regent Street and its environs (*c.*1858).

and peddled her "Darkening Fluid," "Liebig Hair-Dye," and "Blanchiretta Crème d'Amande." As the *London Times* noted, "she was [also] in the habit of performing certain processes on ladies' hair," although a sense of propriety may have prevented further descriptions of these services.[93] Savile Row was a respectable location, particularly when compared to that of local competitors who lived and worked east of Regent Street and closer to Soho's dense network of narrow and crowded streets. Many professional bachelors populated this area of Mayfair, and Headman shared her property with a young surgeon just launching his career.[94] Visitors to the respectable commercial space would consult with Headman before having their hair treated and dressed by Headman's sole lady assistant, Esther Gaubert. Meanwhile, in a separate room devoted especially to production, Headman single-handedly made up, or "compounded," her secret preparations. The only other person allowed access was an illiterate charwoman, Mrs. Bass, who washed out the bottles in an adjacent basin. When not in use, Headman kept the room locked to prevent Gaubert and other domestic servants from discerning her methods. If Gaubert endeavored to learn how to create the product or the ingredients contained therein, she would in fact renege on a binding agreement she signed at her hiring in 1853.[95]

Agnes Headman's discreet services and urban location were not the only source of her financial success. Her venture also depended upon her ability to access markets outside Savile Row, using distributive connections to multiple locations across London and beyond.[96] At mid-century, before the growth of multilocation firms, entrepreneurs could expand by selling their product through neighboring retailers or commercial agents. At a time when most commercial retailers produced only enough product to meet demand, Agnes Headman depended on independent agents, including female retailers in Dublin and Brighton, to distribute surplus goods beyond the West End. Headman not only provided goods to suppliers in seaside spa locales like Brighton and outposts in Scotland and Ireland but also acquired agents based just around the corner from her West End shop.[97] The "middling sorts" of shoppers had yet to frequent the West End in the same numbers that began to descend on the area in the 1870s and 1880s. Headman seemingly deemed it advantageous to accommodate those bourgeois and lower-middle-class consumers accustomed to purchasing beauty wares at the local chemist by selling her product through down-market agents, such as Mr. Sanger on Oxford Street and Mrs. Stevens in Chelsea.[98] Offering an alternative to a costly Savile Row consultation, Headman developed a niche in the middle market beyond Mayfair ladies by depending on a lower status of shopkeeper to sell her wares.

Headman's firm quickly unraveled after her death, however, when her sister took over the business, serving as an example of how family ties could be detrimental to sustaining enterprise. Susan Ansell was an unmarried property holder who seemingly knew little of the demands of the West End's fashionable luxury retailing trades. In this way, the Headman/Ansell case corroborates the findings of historians of enterprise who argue for the intimate relationship between commercial networks and those based on family and kinship. They concur on the centrality of family and kinship networks to mid-century commercial business ventures for both male and female traders, and their studies confirm middle-class tradespeople's dependency on relatives and spouses in conducting daily business.[99] This included the inheriting of a firm, a common occurrence among women, including London's small-scale beauty providers. From Charlotte Mintram of 7 Burlington Arcades to Ann Isidore of Bentinck Street, Marylebone, a number of widows and sisters assumed control over perfumery and hairdressing firms following the death of a loved one.[100]

Laboring alongside family was one way to improve the chance of adequate economic returns and even to gain entrance into business with little or no trading or marketing experience.[101] But these same family ties could generate problems for traders, as family interests worked for and against women's and men's commercial enterprise.[102] In the case of Ansell, who subsisted by renting out her Harley Street holdings, she had no business experience save for a brief tenure assisting her poorly sister in daily operations. Yet, when Headman died, Ansell fully assumed the operations and its holdings of just under £2,000, staking legal claims to not only the remaining stock of hair preparations but also the "exclusive" ownership of Headman's "secret of the said preparations and the recipes for the same."[103] She also moved the Mrs. Headman line to her New Bond Street residence through the 1860s, where she produced and sold the goods.[104]

Ansell's lack of experience, and particularly her lack of connection to local trade networks, seemingly made her vulnerable to local competition. Just "a few hours" after Mrs. Headman's funeral, Headman's former assistant Esther Gaubert declared her intention to leave the services of Ansell and start up a business for herself. In possession of a book of Headman's "secret recipes," Gaubert set up on Maddox Street in the immediate neighborhood of Ansell's Bond Street location[105] (Map 1.1). Aided by neighborhood merchants familiar with Headman's commercial and marketing practices, Gaubert exploited her connections to the local occupational community of perfumers, merchants, and consumers. In doing so, she exposed the limitations hindering Susan Ansell's entrepreneurial venture; she confirmed Ansell's status as a newcomer operating among West End luxury and retailing firms.

Esther Gaubert's new venture seems to have gained support from community members, the same network she had solicited for several years in the service of Agnes Headman. Having been privy to the small details of Mrs. Headman's daily operations, Gaubert simply commissioned those tradespeople who had so reliably supplied her former employer. She purchased glassware and labels— small distinctive octagonal-shaped bottles with labels of blue ink and a border of "peculiar pattern" mirroring Agnes Headman's—from the same glass men and printers who Headman employed (Figures 1.4 and 1.5). She also secured the services of Mrs. Bass, Headman's long-serving charwoman who, as before, "wash[ed] bottles and perform[ed] other menial offices."[106]

Few members of Headman's local commercial trading networks seem to have rejected Gaubert's new venture as dishonest. Those who did protest represented a higher class of commercial provider, who seemingly held a higher regard for copyright than did rough-and-ready petty entrepreneurs. This included advertisement executives at the *London Times*, who refused to insert any of

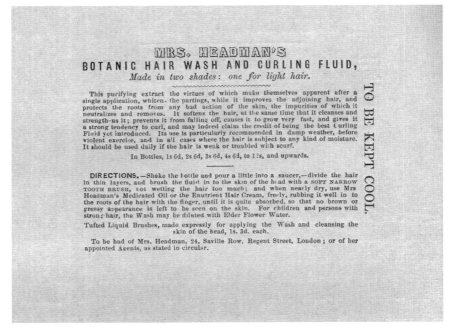

Figure 1.4 Agnes Headman's label for Mrs. Headman's Botanic Hair Wash (1858). The National Archives, UK, C15/44/A39.

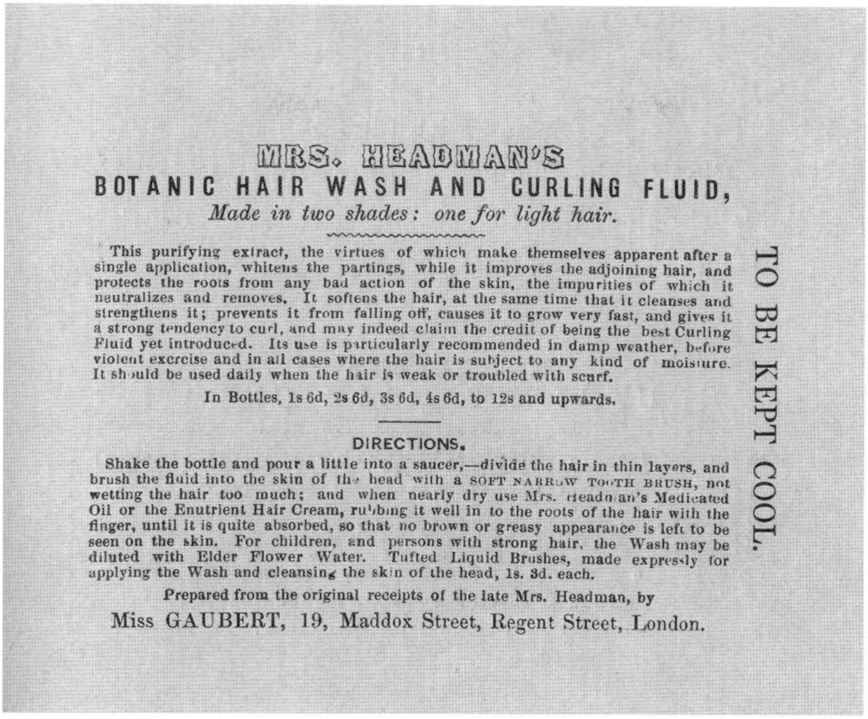

MRS. HEADMAN'S
BOTANIC HAIR WASH AND CURLING FLUID,
Made in two shades: one for light hair.

This purifying extract, the virtues of which make themselves apparent after a single application, whitens the partings, while it improves the adjoining hair, and protects the roots from any bad action of the skin, the impurities of which it neutralizes and removes. It softens the hair, at the same time that it cleanses and strengthens it; prevents it from falling off, causes it to grow very fast, and gives it a strong tendency to curl, and may indeed claim the credit of being the best Curling Fluid yet introduced. Its use is particularly recommended in damp weather, before violent exercise and in all cases where the hair is subject to any kind of moisture. It should be used daily when the hair is weak or troubled with scurf.

In Bottles, 1s 6d, 2s 6d, 3s 6d, 4s 6d, to 12s and upwards.

DIRECTIONS.

Shake the bottle and pour a little into a saucer,—divide the hair in thin layers, and brush the fluid into the skin of the head with a SOFT NARROW TOOTH BRUSH, not wetting the hair too much; and when nearly dry use Mrs. Headman's Medicated Oil or the Enutrient Hair Cream, rubbing it well in to the roots of the hair with the finger, until it is quite absorbed, so that no brown or greasy appearance is left to be seen on the skin. For children, and persons with strong hair, the Wash may be diluted with Elder Flower Water. Tufted Liquid Brushes, made expressly for applying the Wash and cleansing the skin of the head, 1s. 3d. each.

Prepared from the original receipts of the late Mrs. Headman, by

Miss GAUBERT, 19, Maddox Street, Regent Street, London.

TO BE KEPT COOL.

Figure 1.5 Esther Gaubert's label for Mrs. Headman's Botanic Hair Wash (1858). The National Archives, UK, C15/44/A39.

Gaubert's advertisements on their claims of their "fraudulent nature."[107] To the chagrin of property holder Susan Ansell, Gaubert exploited her familiarity with local occupational networks to recreate the Mrs. Headman business just around the corner from her "new" operations.

As a new retailer operating outside the bounds of the local trading community, Ansell resorted to formal avenues, and specifically London's Chancery Court, to halt Gaubert's venture. In the spring of 1858, the judge promptly overruled Gaubert's acceptance by local vendors and merchants and found in favor of Ansell. He argued that the former assistant unlawfully obtained Mrs. Headman's "secret" recipes and misrepresented her venture as part of the Headman firm. Rather than penalize Gaubert, however, Vice-Chancellor W. P. Wood cited sensitivity to the financial demands of litigation and suggested the businesswomen resolve the issue outside of formal institutions of law "on the mere question of costs."[108] They seem to have concurred, and there is no surviving evidence explaining how the two women settled the matter of "Mrs. Headman's Preparations." They undoubtedly resolved the dispute, however, as both traders continued to work as beauty providers through the 1860s. Susan Ansell produced the Mrs. Headman line from her Bond Street residence through the 1860s, moved to Holles Street near Cavendish Square, and ended her career in the 1880s on Edgware Road. Esther Gaubert appeared in 1895 as a hairdresser based on Grosvenor Street, before retiring to Twickenham. Revealingly, she refrained from publishing print advertisements following the trial, relying on trade directories and, presumably, informal publicity including word-of-mouth and reputation to sustain her venture.[109]

The Headman case illustrates how a family business crucially depended on the goodwill and cooperation of the local business community, although Ansell ultimately used legal avenues to gain redress through her family connection. Another example illuminates a different conclusion, in which family divisions, rather than community ties, undermined individual enterprise. For Aimée Lloyd, economic survival depended upon her detachment from her husband and her establishing herself independent of familial networks and hierarchies. It was the local community of traders and not Lloyd's kin that emerged as the support structure bolstering her beauty venture.

Aimée Lloyd, 3 Spur Street

Aimée Lloyd's story unfolded across the West End, to the east of Regent Street, "the boundary-line eastward of the West-End" dividing affluent from more plebeian sections of St. James parish.[110] As we have seen, the mapping of beauty traders' multiple relocations in the West End suggests the tight limits of inhabitants' knowledge of urban neighborhoods, not to mention local trade networks based on class and trader, which historian Susan Yohn dubs "multivalenced support structures."[111] No business better characterized this urban intimacy than the Lloyd family firm, whose movements over four years in the late 1840s confirmed their loyalty to a specific set of streets. Between 1847 and 1851, they relocated their perfumery business to various locations in St. James, from a small shopfront at Foubert's Place to a location on Conduit Street, followed soon after by a relocation to No. 10 Beak Street. All three shops stood within a quarter mile of one another[112] (Map 1.1).

In Foubert's Place, Lloyd's father-in-law Solomon, a lower-middle-class perfumer and hairdresser, first created the "Euxesis" formula in 1844.[113] Without the capital to develop advanced means of production, Solomon's Euxesis reportedly obtained "some small amount of repute," and "the demand for it was not great."[114] Solomon found himself in financial arrears and was remanded to debtor's prison in May of 1847.[115] It was in this period that the Lloyds's Beak Street neighbor, 18-year-old French émigré Aimée Courtois, joined the family through marriage to Solomon's son Andrew and began working in the family business. Upon his release, patriarch Solomon engaged his new daughter-in-law in the preparation and bottling of Euxesis. Laboring in the backrooms at Beak Street, Aimée manufactured "large quantities" of commercial goods for her husband and father-in-law to peddle in the hairdressing rooms.[116]

Solomon's death in 1854 put a stop to the Lloyds's frequent relocations and reconfigured not only the domestic hierarchy but also the commercial organization of the family business. Now the firm's head, Andrew Lloyd moved his wife, mother, and siblings to new premises around the corner on Glasshouse Street[117] (Map 1.1). This final move failed to advance their financial situation. Neither did it improve the tense relationship between Aimée and her spouse; allegations suggested their tumultuous relationship entered a new stage of physical violence at the Glasshouse Street shop. According to an 1867 petition for judicial separation, both Andrew and Aimée did physical harm to one another at Glasshouse Street. Andrew reportedly struck "violent blows in the face," knocked Aimée down, made "her nose bleed," used "abusive and insulting and threatening language," and "spit in her face." In one incident, Andrew was reported to have "thrown beer" over Aimée and "would not allow her to eat her dinner." For her part, Aimée allegedly kicked her husband in the stomach, causing "an injury in the abdomen" from which he never fully recovered.[118] Sources suggest that Glasshouse Street's community of milliners, lace menders, tailors, and a female hairdresser bore witness to the ferocity of the couple's domestic disputes. During one incident, neighbors heard Aimée throw "pots, bottles, tumblers"—all accoutrements of perfumery production—before reporting it to police.[119] Some months later, Aimée herself turned to police for protection, explaining that she was "afraid to go to bed" given Andrew's threats of violence.[120]

Yet the couple's intense physical and emotional altercations were not enough to establish the requisite legal grounds for divorce. It took Andrew's admitted infidelities with the Lloyds's 26-year-old shopgirl, Susannah Tarleton, for Aimée to procure a judicial separation.[121] It is possible that a neighbor or friend aided in Aimée's subsequent flight from Glasshouse Street in June 1867, as she would have needed assistance to transport the "considerable portion of the Stock in trade" that she reportedly pilfered.[122] In this way, the proximity and intimacies of urban networks implicated tradespeople in commercial but also domestic matters.

With a marketable skill, Lloyd navigated the collapse of her household and marriage and transformed into what modern business scholars term "survivalist entrepreneurs." Survivalist entrepreneurs embark on small-scale enterprise when economic and social marginalization precludes their ability to seek alternate modes of wage earning.[123] In the Victorian context, argues Kay, female survivalist entrepreneurs resembled respectable women like Aimée Lloyd; devoid of certain legal and economic privileges, they suddenly found themselves without conventional support systems of marriage and kin.[124] To avoid a loss of social standing, not to mention inferior forms of female employment like sweated labor and piecework, some women with capital subsequently ventured into London's competitive commercial arena.[125]

The threat of personal indigence was not always the primary motivation for starting a business, but this was the situation that Aimée Lloyd faced.[126] Claiming herself "[w]holly destitute" and devoid of familial or community networks, Lloyd turned to her only form of income: the production of Solomon Lloyd's Euxesis.[127] She successfully produced and sold Euxesis out of a rented room just off Leicester Square. She built on her long-standing relationships with the local occupational community from her new address in the home of a German language teacher on Spur Street, which was a mere 1,500 feet from the Glasshouse Street shop (Map 1.1). Although contemporary sources described Spur Street "as a sink of iniquity," Aimée kept the business afloat.[128] In fact, between June 1867 and the autumn of 1868, both she and Andrew Lloyd simultaneously produced competing versions of Euxesis at their respective West End manufactories. Andrew assented to this arrangement, but not before issuing a circular to neighbors that, as Aimée was manufacturing and selling the product "on [her] own account ... he would not be answerable for [her] debts." Andrew need not have worried, for Aimée's long hours in Solomon's backrooms at Beak Street seemingly paid off; of the two versions of Euxesis on the West End market, Aimée's proved the more sought-after product.

The collapse of Lloyd's family unit was not her only challenge. She soon came up against a formidable new obstacle in the form of one of London's key commercial figures: the wholesaler. Wholesalers emerged to facilitate the large-scale distribution of goods, allowing retailers to offer a greater range of wares.[129] If not working with wholesalers, retailers were obliged to maintain sufficient stocks of goods, set prices, and perform the processes of final sales: weighing, wrapping, and packaging goods. However, increases in real incomes in the

1850s meant greater consumer demand for standardized, mass-produced wares, and independent shopkeepers had to keep up with larger orders. Unable to produce sufficient surplus goods, some retailers turned to wholesalers to fill this distributive niche.[130] Wholesalers not only facilitated distribution but also accommodated the growing variety of perfumery goods increasingly stocked by the average retailer. They also assumed responsibility for the branding, packaging, and marketing of said stock, taking this job out of the hands of the retailers.[131] Given the varieties of beauty consumption, reflected in the wide range of goods, London's beauty industry was an ideal market for centralized wholesaling outfits.

The unquestionable frontrunner in London's beauty wholesaling was perfumer Robert Hovenden (Figure 1.6). The son of a Holborn-based perfumery and oils distributor, Hovenden owned and operated depots at

ROBERT HOVENDEN.

Figure 1.6 Robert Hovenden, *Hairdressers' Weekly Journal* (July 31, 1886): 493. Courtesy of © The British Library Board (Shelfmark 4238.301000).

5 Great Marlborough Street and 42 Poland Street in Soho and a manufactory near the East End at 93 City Road. His extensive self-promotion and generous financiering of trade publications like *The Hairdressers' Chronicle* was matched only by his standing as wholesaler to some of the British world's most sought-after beautifying goods.[132] As was the case for family networks, this occupational figure could be both advantageous and detrimental to individual enterprise. For Aimée Lloyd, Hovenden proved especially problematic, and she was forced to block his legal efforts to halt her production of Euxesis. Her success at deterring Hovenden's injunction was in many ways thanks to local agents, members of her West End occupational community of beauty traders and merchants who testified to Lloyd's unparalleled business reputation.

Having previously conducted business with Andrew Lloyd, Hovenden purchased 144 tubes of Euxesis manufactured by Aimée at Spur Street in June 1867. A year later, he solicited her to do further business with him "on terms of mutual interest."[133] In London's increasingly competitive market, "nineteenth-century businessmen [*sic*] faced three usual strategic options," notes historian Oliver Westall: "competition, collusion, or integration."[134] Lloyd opted for competition and refused Hovenden's offer. She subsequently found herself at odds with the metropolis' most successful perfumery wholesaler, who was in many ways the primary link between an expanding group of beauty merchants and traders.

Celebrated for his business acumen, Hovenden tried to block Aimée Lloyd from manufacturing a superior product using her "secret" processes of production. Following Andrew Lloyd's sudden death in September 1868, Hovenden turned to shopgirl Susannah Tarleton, Andrew's former lover and now executor of his estate. In 1869, he purchased Tarleton's stake in Euxesis, procured from her "the secret, on oath" to Euxesis, produced the good using Andrew's recipe, and immediately took legal action against Aimée for trademark injunction. In response, Aimée argued that "neither [Hovenden] nor Susannah Howard Tarleton nor even Andrew Solomon Lloyd during his lifetime ever knew how properly to manufacture the article as prepared by" her. Deeming it a "very inferior commodity," Aimée distanced herself from Hovenden and Tarleton's manufactures, arguing for the superiority and immutability of her version of Euxesis.[135]

Such claims could be dismissed as commercial rhetoric, crafted to gain legal advantage and formally secure Aimée's livelihood. Yet, Aimée Lloyd was not alone in her avowals of the supremacy of her product, and others corroborated her claims. In court, she produced the legal affidavits of six commercial traders with whom she conducted business, including two of her agents. In doing so, she aligned herself with male commercial traders populating her West End circle.[136] Her supporting affidavits championed not only her business acumen but also her superior personal character; they foregrounded both the economic and interpersonal trust built over years of familiarity and trade. For example, Richard Hilton, a commercial traveler working for the Lloyds since their days on Conduit Street, claimed that Andrew was never involved in the "invention and manufacturing" of Euxesis. According to Hilton, Solomon solely produced the goods up until Aimée Lloyd took over. Frederick Charles Bank, a commercial traveler from Hackney, agreed that conversations with Andrew "led him to believe" that he was not involved in Euxesis production. Furthermore, Aimée was "well kn[own]," and he attested that "she only knew the proper mode of manufacture."

> [H]ad it not been for her assiduous labour and attention in manufacturing the euxesis during her husband's lifetime and in the execution of orders for the same, the sale of euxesis would have ceased[.] [There were] frequent complaints to my knowledge being made by the various wholesale houses of the non-execution of their orders as the said Andrew Solomon Lloyd would not manufacture it some time.

George Courtice, a perfumer at 234 the Strand, championed Aimée's centrality to production, arguing that a person purchasing her Euxesis would be able to tell the difference based solely on quality. Other West End merchants, including Thomas Hill, London's leading cutler and razor maker, and William Atwell, a popular perfumer on Piccadilly, also testified to preferring Aimée's product over that of her husband and his mistress. Local perfumers and commercial travelers who swore affidavits also called into question Andrew Lloyd's fitness as the head of a respectable middle-class family. Criticizing Andrew's ability to meet normative masculine domestic roles, Hilton described how just after their marriage, Aimée "pa[id] for the furniture in the apartments they occupied" as Andrew had "no means of his own."[137]

Trial testimonies documented local businessmen's preference for Aimée's product. But they also implicitly critiqued the Lloyds' relationship and specifically Andrew's failings as both an economic and marital partner. Meanwhile, Aimée Lloyd claimed a superior work ethic, skills in production, and connections with local trade communities to legally justify her participation in the mid-century beauty business. The vice-chancellor subsequently found against Hovenden's injunction, and Lloyd continued to produce Euxesis through the nineteenth century. For Aimée, the breakdown of her family networks did not prevent her from forging new associations related to local occupational networks. The quality of her production and the stability of her intertrade relationships were the necessary means by which she staked a claim to the West End beauty and grooming market. But the shift from Lloyd's marital family to her adopted "commercial family" complicates the neat divisions separating personal from economic activity, divisions that came to increasingly define imagined private/public divides, but not the realities of Victorian enterprise through the latter half of the nineteenth century. In Lloyd's case, occupational communities were not built on economics alone and turned on familiarity, proximity, and character. Neither could economic ties transcend emotional upset, as the dissolution of Aimée's marriage—and business partnership—proved. In this way, business communities were complicated emotional and economic landscapes in which people worked and lived.

Conclusions

In the mid-century, kinship and occupational networks were integral to the success of small-scale entrepreneurs operating on the peripheries of London's luxury beauty market. In the case of Aimée Lloyd, the affidavits of local community members meant that she could circumvent legal confines by proving the social esteem and commercial support of her peers. Yet, these same networks could undermine small-scale entrepreneurial success, as was the experience of Susan Ansell. Meanwhile, distributive developments ultimately worked to the decisive advantage of businesspeople like Robert Hovenden. Through the 1860s and 1870s, Hovenden increasingly mobilized business and legal avenues in order to procure those products deemed most lucrative for his wholesaling operations.

As traders navigated the shifting terrains of expanding distributive systems, they also developed strategies for promoting their goods to a consumer public. In the years leading up to the elaborate Victorian marketing campaigns of the 1880s and 1890s, male and female small-scale providers competed with traders like Hovenden through print advertising campaigns featured in London's leading periodical publications. It would not be until the end of the nineteenth century that Victorian advertising emerged in the form of colorful billboards and handbills, markers of the visual commercial culture that came to dominate the popular imagination.[138] In the early days of an industrializing economy, there was allegedly little need for such ambitious initiatives given the proximity of producer and consumer.[139] Upon the abolition of England's advertising duty in 1853, some beauty retailers listed wares and services in modest advertisements in the popular periodical press. Ads were succinct, text-heavy, and rarely featured embellishment let alone elaborate images, trends particularly evident in Headman's case[140] (Figure 1.7). With the rise in wholesaling and the disaggregation of tasks, individual shopkeepers increasingly devoted more time to developing retailing skills, and, in particular, marketing strategies.[141] While it remained prohibitively expensive for large segments of the commercial population to place newspaper advertisements, traders like Agnes Headman, Susan Ansell, and Aimée Lloyd used advertisements in the periodical press to publicize their beauty goods and services to consuming readers.[142]

Figure 1.7 Miscellaneous Classifieds, *The Times* 22945 (March 19, 1858): 15. Courtesy of © The British Library Board (Shelfmark 1801-2009 LON LD1 NPL).

Figure 1.8 "Rossetter's Hair Restorer," *The Hairdressers' Chronicle* (June 1, 1872): iv. Courtesy of © The British Library Board (Shelfmark LOU.LON 101 [1871]).

At the same time, some retailers undertook massive advertising campaigns for products like Rowland's Macassar Oil and Atkinson's Bear Grease, with Rowland's being only the second firm in Britain to advertise a product nationally[143] (Plate 4). Following his legal defeat in the Lloyd trial, Robert Hovenden continued to build on the traditions of Rowland, Atkinson, and Alexander Ross and became one of the early promoters of female beauty aids. His advertising scheme for Rossetter's, for example, circulated visual representations of secrecy, sharing, and female bonding (Figure 1.8). One ad depicts two female confidantes conferring around a large bottle of the product. Presumably the owner of the hair tonic, a dark, longhaired female subject, proffers a single flower—representing not only the secret to her beauty, but also the naturalness of her methods — to her female visitor. The fairer if not plainer recipient reaches out in response. "It is not a dye," reads the accompanying text, which also reassures its seemingly upper-middle-class consumers that it is "the cheapest and best restorative ever used." A homely, female-centered image, the advertisement embodied an aesthetic of artificial naturalness. Its basis as a connection between friends downplayed the presence of Hovenden and a new set of commercial actors. In this way, the tradesman insinuated intimate, domestic conversation, albeit in a trade press whose readers were primarily agents and other wholesalers.[144]

Dramatic shifts in commercial advertising and the move from brief written ads to spectacular visual spectacles seems to have precluded some small-scale entrepreneurs from publicizing themselves in increasingly elaborate forms. In this way, the exclusion of under-capitalized vendors from expanded developments in marketing and promotion paralleled general trends in London's beauty trades from the late 1860s. Small-scale entrepreneurs like Ansell and Gaubert operated outside the complex distributive systems and standardized methods of production, which were adopted by leading West End firms, often headed by men. Various family perfumery firms emerged on the leading edge of this shift, and some perfumers' rapid capitalization transformed London into the site of multiple-shop beauty firms producing goods first for a national then global market.[145] The next twenty-five years also gave rise to new company formations (or incorporation) by familiar mid-century perfumers and hairdressers like Eugène Rimmel and H. P. Truefitt, whose businesses gained a global reach.[146] As we will see, these retailers, manufacturers, and wholesalers sought to confirm an expert designation, much like their professional rivals in the chemical and medical sciences. A contingent of familiar perfumers even sat as members of the London Chamber of Commerce's Chemical Trades Section beginning in 1883.[147]

Intensifying these shifts was a particularly sensational case emerging in the mid-1860s, which challenged female participation in the West End's beauty trades: the extraordinary case of Sarah "Madame Rachel" Leverson. In many ways, developments in mid-century West End commerce and beauty consumption accounted for and propelled Leverson's notoriety. This included expanded commercial development, more visible use of beauty goods, Leverson's lack of standing in the neighborhood, and her use of self-publicity through sensational law cases to advance her national stature. At the same time, the case revealed the explosive potential of a beauty businesswoman flouting the discreet conventions of the trade community and respectable society more generally. To the detriment of other small-scale beauty traders, Leverson's trials ultimately affirmed the power of a particular mode of beauty merchant, who was reputable, professional, and male.

2

Upstarts and Outliers: Sarah "Madame Rachel" Leverson

In his popular 1855 publication *The Art of Perfumery*, London perfumer G. W. Septimus Piesse (1820–1882) asserted, "[a]s an art, in England, perfumery has attained little or no distinction" (Figure 2.1). Piesse laid the blame squarely on those in the trade who "maintain[ed] a mysterious secrecy about their processes." He argued that no manufacture "could ever become great or important to the community that is carried on under a veil of mystery."[1] Piesse's sentiments reflected a position increasingly supported by London's mid-century manufacturing perfumers and hairdressers, not to mention Victorian professionals more generally. Leading traders promoted a move away from secretive processes conducted in locked backrooms in favor of rational openness in the pursuit of a "scientific" art. In this context, Piesse's position on the dangers of trade secrets was not surprising. His successful New Bond Street firm, not to mention his holding of a doctorate in chemistry, definitively situated him among a faction of professionalizing perfumers who increasingly rejected humble backroom production in favor of advanced manufacturing processes. He further promoted this openness in visual forms. Periodical press illustrations laid bare the ordered rationality of Piesse's retail showrooms (Plate 5) or the "Laboratory of Flowers," his manufacturing and exporting operations[2] (Figure 2.2).

For small-scale providers like Susan Ansell and Aimée Lloyd, however, secrets remained integral to their marketability in the West End beauty business and, it could be argued, the profitability of their ventures. Both Ansell and Lloyd went to extreme ends, so far as to turn to the courts to retain rightful ownership of their recipes for Mrs. Headman's and Euxesis products, respectively. Ansell and Lloyd were not the only mid-century commercial beauty providers in London's West End contributing to ideas about secrets and secrecy. Debates over business secrecy implicated respectable tradespeople across Mayfair and Soho—including professional male perfumers—who depended on rhetorics of secrecy

Figure 2.1 "Obituary: Septimus Piesse," *Chemist & Druggist* (November 15, 1882): 496. Courtesy of the Wellcome Library, London.

not only to attract clients but also to defend their ownership over specific trade knowledge. This was not a new development; respectable forms of trade secrets had long been valued in western business and commerce dating back to the earliest days of markets and trading.[3] Yet, for members of London's nineteenth-century beauty industry, elements of secrecy extended beyond the unique qualities of a product. The mystery of beauty compounds and processes could also enhance consumer appeal, and the more enigmatic a beauty product, the greater the possibility for significant, even miraculous effects on the customer. The reluctance of beauty providers to disclose their secrets was more than a legal precaution against commercial imposters. It also signaled claims to esoteric power, which enhanced the possibility of transformation.

If trade secrets were central to beauty providers' allure, there was also the issue of protecting the privacy—and reputations—of their customers. Historian Deborah Cohen has charted the complicated entanglements of secrecy and privacy in the nineteenth century, observing that "[s]ecrecy was privacy's indispensable handmaiden" in efforts to protect families and individuals. Privacy was "a hard-won prize" in this period, and secrets were the means to

INTERIOR OF MESSRS. PIESSE AND LUBIN'S SCENT MANUFACTORY.

Figure 2.2 "Interior of Messrs. Piesse and Lubin's Scent Manufactory," *Illustrated Weekly News* (September 20, 1862): 797. Courtesy of © The British Library Board (Shelfmark NEWS11799).

secure it.[4] The interplay between secrets and privacy had special significance in London's mid-nineteenth-century beauty business, when a number of traders exploited the two to distinguish themselves from competitors. However, a sensational 1868 case threw these strategies into question by intensifying public scrutiny of shady beauty dealers allegedly conducting disreputable operations. In it, media-driven anxieties over secrets, backroom dealings, and discretion condensed around a single, sensational female figure operating as a beauty provider on New Bond Street: Sarah "Madame Rachel" Leverson (d. 1880).[5] Leverson was a flamboyant public personality who promised to make women "beautiful, forever!" (Figure 2.3). She garnered national attention thanks to her marketing of exotic beautifying goods in Britain's major print publications. She also advertised individual services, claiming to use only herbs and essences in her procedures and not enameling processes that coated women's face, neck, and arms in bismuth or white lead.[6] "All impurities of the skin and dirt are first

Figure 2.3 Sarah "Madame Rachel" Leverson, *Illustrated Police News* 733 (March 2, 1878): 1. Courtesy of © The British Library Board (Shelfmark NEWS13104).

removed by the constant use of the bath and certain herbs," she claimed. "What I do is done by liquid and not paint."[7]

However, Leverson's controversial business practices contradicted her claims of commercial integrity and honesty. They also resulted in multiple appearances in London's criminal and civil courts between 1858 and 1878, until a five-year prison sentence definitively removed her from the public eye.[8] At her most sensational criminal trials, two 1868 appearances for deception and fraud, Crown prosecutors chipped away at Leverson's business persona and beauty secrets to expose her untrustworthiness as a commercial trader.[9] Leverson was not the only notorious beauty provider to capture the attention of the Victorian public.[10] Yet, no beauty trader elicited a more profound reaction than Leverson, and her frequent court appearances seemed to confirm doubts among critics of cosmetics about the practices of small-scale beauty providers more generally; backroom beauty was dangerous, duplicitous, and unbefitting of respectable traders *and* customers.

Leverson's trials represent particularly sensational examples of beauty trade secrets and consumer privacy gone awry.[11] Her scandals have subsequently been subject to a number of compelling treatments from feminist critics and historians, who reveal how "Madame Rachel" shaped Victorian perceptions of female beauty services and bodily secrets, aligning them with debauched efforts to entice and expose naïve female consumers. What's more, Leverson's trade practices, use of advertising, and clearly transgressive commercial dealings including pawn broking and moneylending all transpired in an iconic London space: Bond Street. As Tammy Whitlock argues, her flashy presence on the West End's most elite commercial avenue prompted public debates over the propriety of women in business.[12] Meanwhile, Elizabeth Carolyn Miller shows how exhaustive print and literary coverage detailed Leverson's intimate demands on her customers, emphasizing her dangerous manipulation of female clients' bodies.[13] This chapter builds on scholarly attention to sensation by adopting a more granular focus on the imagined and material spaces of Leverson's shop, the West End, and London more generally. This approach helps to explain Leverson's notoriety in relation to other female beauty providers who managed to operate close by or even on Bond Street, but within commercial networks that ensured their provisional respectability. Indeed, positioning a notorious figure like Leverson alongside ordinary providers confirms the significance of discreet locations and business practices, which embedded small-scale entrepreneurs in protective family or commercial networks and helped undergird their reputation in the tricky business of beauty. Furthermore, it links the public's imaginative focus on the secret, more sensational dealings transpiring in Leverson's back parlor with the historical mapping—and lived realities—of beauty traders across metropolitan space. By situating Leverson's scandals within these spatial and commercial contexts, we see that press and legal reports on sensational backroom dealings had real consequences for London's beauty and grooming industry, implicating the commercial practices of perfectly respectable beauty providers. In their defense of the trade, London's leading perfumers and hairdressers ultimately distanced themselves from modest, small-scale operations; in doing so, they also endorsed the ascendency of a particular class of professional—and reputable—manufacturing perfumer.

The Trials of Madame Rachel

Throughout the 1860s, "the celebrated Madame Rachel" advertised services as "an enameller of ladies' faces" from her shop on New Bond Street.[14] She touted goods like "Circassian Beauty Wash," "Armenian Liquid for Removing Wrinkles," and her infamous "Arabian Baths," consisting "of pure extracts of the liquid of flowers, choice and rare herbs, and other preparations equally harmless and efficacious" to improve the complexion.[15] In a self-produced twenty-four-page text *Beautiful for Ever!* Leverson rejected the deadly leads and other injurious ingredients in beauty goods, which had blighted "many young and lovely faces."[16] By contrast, she claimed that her products used natural ingredients to impart an artificial naturalness: "a brilliancy to the eyes, pearly whiteness to the teeth, and a natural colour to the lips, [with] luxuriant flowing tresses."[17] This business rhetoric was seemingly successful; in 1862, Leverson claimed she saw "so many ladies" that she could not recount whom from London's elite social set comprised her "patients."[18] By 1868, however, Leverson was the subject of two highly publicized trials that irreparably damaged her commercial and personal reputation, making "Madame Rachel" synonymous with false promises, underhanded exchanges, and female vanity (Figure 2.4).

Several comprehensive studies of Madame Rachel and the 1868 trials have examined the cultural narratives at play in what became known as the "Bond

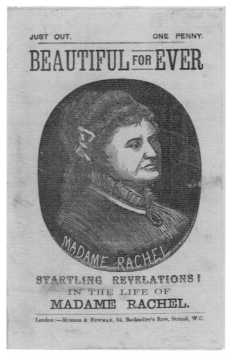

Figure 2.4 *Beautiful for Ever,* cover (n.d.). Courtesy of Lilly Library, Indiana University Library, Bloomington, Indiana.

Street Mystery." Historians like Whitlock cast Madame Rachel as a "Victorian cultural icon," situating Leverson in contemporary debates over the dangers of public life for middle-class women. For Whitlock, the 1868 trials also represent a sensational exploitation of circulating anxieties over women's new roles in the world of commerce. Leverson, she contends, was not only on trial for defrauding her clients, but also for her methods of business, including "false advertising, greed, and the immorality of specific [cosmetic] goods."[19] Expanding on the case of fraud to address questions of English national identity, Miller focuses on Leverson's brazen promotional campaigns and particularly the sexualized marketing of non-European products that prominently featured in both print media and the 1868 trials. Exoticized names like "Magnetic Rock Dew Water of Sahara for Removing Wrinkles" and Leverson's "Arabian" range "produced the illusion that the London female shopper had the entire globe at her economic disposal, all in the service of beautifying her body."[20] Leverson also made cameos in the leading literature of the day, and scholars have analyzed the appearance of her business in Mary Elizabeth Braddon's *Lady Audley's Secret* (1862) or her more elaborate connections to the "Mother Oldershaw" character in Wilkie Collins's *Armadale* (1866).[21]

These illuminating studies of the 1868 trials focus on Victorian anxieties about gender, commerce, and consumption, emphasizing critics' fears "of a fraudulent commercial culture directed at female consumers," to quote Whitlock.[22] It is also necessary to look beyond Leverson's iconic status around cosmetic consumption to highlight production, thereby bringing into view the imaginary and material spaces of her practice. Leverson was a trader and producer operating in a specific trade—London's beauty business—that was bound by particular expectations of discretion and concealment.[23] All the while, her shop stood in a significant London location, on elite New Bond Street, whose particular spatial configuration influenced her reception by customers, lawyers, and the general public.

Leverson's specific commercial and spatial practices made her a trade outsider, isolated from other male and female beauty providers. Particular details of the 1868 trials, including Leverson's trade interests, relationships to the neighboring commercial community, and descriptions of shop space reveal how sharply Madame Rachel deviated from standard practices around commercial space, consumer confidence, and businesspeople's respectability. That is not to deny that Leverson's commercial ventures hinged on duplicity, as writers like Helen Rappaport have shown.[24] She relied on puffery to attract her female clientele and almost certainly extracted some payments via blackmail and extortion.

Leverson, a Jewish woman of lower-middle-class origins, also gained notoriety because of her standing as a female beauty vendor on Bond Street in the 1860s, a location very different from most female contemporaries working in more discreet locations in Mayfair and Soho. Situated on a commercial thoroughfare that far exceeded her class origins, Leverson's conspicuousness on Bond Street highlights the centrality of commercial networks in sustaining the respectability of traders. In Leverson's case, her exclusion from mainstream networks seems to have led to her reliance on associations outside the local trading population, including pawnbrokers and merchants based in the plebeian pockets of the West End.

Some of these business connections would have been made early in Leverson's career, in the years before her move to Mayfair. Her success on Bond Street through the mid-1860s belied her much humbler origins, when she and her two daughters occupied modest premises on Clare Street in the mid-1850s. Bordered by the squalid rookeries and playhouses around Drury Lane, Clare Street was a notoriously low area in the parish of St. Clement Danes, famous for its poor costermongers and prostitutes rather than its luxury retailers.[25] Before turning to beauty goods, press reports claimed that Leverson was engaged in the second-hand clothing trade that served Drury Lane's dramatic players and poor inhabitants, an occupation typically taken on by working-class Jewish traders.[26] When she turned to "beautifying" services, the neighborhood's sordid reputation reportedly did little to deter visits from London's fashionable set. One pamphlet described how "rumours of [Leverson's] famous 'feminine beautifyings' reached higher quarters, and brought cabs to her humble 'shop' in Clare Court." Success ultimately facilitated the family's removal to "the fashionable west," to Oxford Street, a "street wide enough to accommodate 'carriages' graced with crests and coronets."[27]

Within a few years, Leverson accrued enough capital to move across the fashionable commercial geographies of the West End, relocating from Oxford Street to London's most exclusive commercial thoroughfare: New Bond Street. From their new shop, Leverson and daughters Rachel and Leonti sold goods comparable to those offered by London's most esteemed perfumers and hairdressers: washes and powders for the complexion, hair preparations, dentifrices, and mouthwashes. However, in more reputable West End shops, these wares were considered ancillary and came second to pricey luxury perfumes and hairdressing services. By contrast, doubtful goods like powders and rouges were the keystone of the "Madame Rachel" business. This overt attention to women's physical appearance was controversial and enabled critics to initially mark her off from respectable perfumers; as one prosecutor clarified in 1862, the Leverson women did not "deal in scents" but "enamel[ed] ladies' faces."[28] Promotional literature from 1863 confirms the Leversons's concentration on the complexion, skin, and less often the hair. The women listed sixty-four different products for purchase, including soaps, perfumes, rouge, dentifrices, hair dyes, and whitening washes. These goods were available by mail but also by personal consultation at Madame Rachel's Mayfair shop.

Leverson was not only a well-known trader due to her obvious presence on New Bond Street and the types of goods on offer. She also made regular, doubtful appearances in legal venues across London, which compounded her notoriety. Between 1858 and 1878, she stood as both plaintiff and defendant in more than a dozen court cases related to her business practices: extortion, deception, bankruptcy. Her most frequent, albeit unexceptional, court appearances involved efforts to avoid debtors' prison, and she appeared in bankruptcy court in 1861 and 1862. Her finances also compelled an 1862 appearance in the Court of Exchequer, where she attempted to force payment from a lady client, Mrs. Carnegie, and her husband, the Honorable Captain Carnegie.[29] Despite her guarantees of discretion and privacy for female patrons, Leverson pursued Carnegie's payment of an extraordinary bill for £938 5s.[30] In his defense, Captain Carnegie pleaded that he was unaware of his wife's "extravagant" spending of "enormous sums" and hence not responsible for her debt.[31] A jury concurred and dismissed Leverson's claim. The tables turned in her next appearance, this time in criminal court in December 1865, when a disgruntled client sued Leverson. American Aurora Knight had visited Leverson with the hopes of reducing scars stemming from a recent attack of smallpox. Shocked by the exorbitant cost and inefficacy of the treatments, Knight sought to have her bill reduced, only to find her claim dismissed by a cynical judge.[32]

The willingness of women like Knight to expose themselves to public vitriol signaled their desperation—as middle- and upper-middle-class clients—to recoup significant financial losses.[33] Both cases also brought Leverson to the attention of Britain's periodical press. Details of her sizeable profits, not to mention her propensity for catering to (and perhaps even inciting) female vanity, made her the subject of satirical lampooning but also more serious criticism.[34] However, it was not until 1868 that Leverson's infamy was confirmed, with the release of salacious details in the course of sensational court trials when she was charged with deception and fraud.[35] In many ways, the 1868 trials marked the climax of Leverson's ongoing legal problems, not to mention her vilification in

London's leading periodicals.[36] To be sure, it was her widespread reputation for profiteering from female vanity that piqued the attention of two of London's leading criminal prosecutors, who had long been monitoring Leverson. Back in 1862, during the Carnegie case, legal titans Montagu Williams and William Ballantine set their sights on Leverson's shady Bond Street practices. They reportedly sought "remand after remand" before they successfully committed "the wicked old perfume-vendor" to trial in late 1868.[37]

The 1868 trials centered on the claims of a widowed property-holder Mary Tucker Borradaile, who asserted that Leverson had promised to transform her—"a spare, thin, scraggy-looking woman"—into a resounding beauty, not to mention secure her a new spouse.[38] Lonely after the death of her husband, Borradaile sought out happiness and romance in London. Soon after Borradaile's arrival, Leverson convinced the 50-year-old that she had earned the affections of local West End bachelor, Lord Ranelagh. Surreptitious notes allegedly penned by Ranelagh—and later reprinted in London's leading daily newspapers—persuaded Borradaile to undergo some £1,400 in beautifying treatments, including treatment in Madame Rachel's "Arabian Baths." Only after Borradaile depleted her savings did Leverson's beauty treatments and Ranelagh's attentions prove false. Defying Victorian codes against public exposure, Borradaile pursued action against Leverson and turned to London's criminal courts to compensate for her financial losses. Two trials ensued, first in August (resulting in a mistrial) and then September 1868, and it was these events that garnered remarkable public attention. Ensuing press coverage was not kind to Borradaile, who figured as a naïve and pathetic dupe. "[W]holly devoid of figure," observed prosecutor Montagu Williams, "her hair was dyed a bright yellow; her face was ruddled with paint; and the darkness of her eyebrows was strongly suggestive of meretricious art."[39]

Neither was the press sympathetic to Leverson, as her daily appearances at trial marked the pinnacle of Madame Rachel's celebrity—or notoriety. Press coverage, satire, and elaborate print illustrations depicted Leverson at the helm of treacherous operations—dubbed her "Stall at 'Vanity Fair'"—profiting from the unchecked desires of fashionable female consumers (Plate 6). Scholarly treatments of the 1868 trials have focused on this public vilification of Leverson, who came to symbolize, at various junctures, the threat of female economic participation, the influx of "foreign" or Jewish traders into British markets, the vulgarity of social climbing, the perils of unbridled female vanity and consumption, and the dangers of new urban markets.[40] But Leverson was also a commercial trader operating within a specific fashionable luxury trade: the West End beauty business. The trial subsequently hinged, in part, on whether

Leverson was a perfumer or a criminal. By comparing her spaces and business practices to those of neighboring West End perfumers, we see that, at various junctures, she could be both.

Bond Street Secrets

A defining feature of trial accounts through the late 1860s was their attention to Leverson's location in urban space and specifically on London's most exclusive shopping thoroughfare, New Bond Street. Underpinning this focus was the understanding that Bond Street was not only too expensive for many female traders but also too public. But Leverson was not as unique as press depictions would have it, nor ensuing accounts that highlight her gender, trade, and ethnicity as incongruous with Bond Street commerce. Through the 1860s, businesswomen maintained a steady presence on the elite thoroughfare in a number of trades. For instance, a commercial directory from 1863 lists some fifty-one female-helmed businesses in millinery and dressmaking, in addition to bookselling, artificial flowers, and engraving.[41] Census records from 1861 show that some of these businesswomen employed female assistants, suggesting that their presence was not a short-lived anomaly but a normalized feature of Bond Street's mid-century fashionable trades.[42]

Neither was Leverson the only woman selling bodily transformation on Bond Street in this period. While not common, some female beauty providers managed inconspicuous operations through the mid-century. According to Helen Rappaport, Leverson's shop at 47a New Bond Street was previously home to Erwin Parker who sold his mother's hair tonics and pomades. "Mrs. Parker's preparations" were available to customers until some point in 1860.[43] Another Bond Street practitioner, Keturah Roberts, worked as a retail perfumer in the first half of the 1840s. Roberts shared her premises at 7 New Bond Street with a female assistant and domestic servant, before moving to Piccadilly and then into Soho and eventual obscurity.[44] Bond Street was also home to none other than Mrs. Agnes Headman—that is to say, Susan Ansell. Following the death of sister Agnes in 1858, Ansell transferred the "Mrs. Headman" business to her residence at 92 New Bond Street.[45] Through the 1850s and early 1860s, Ansell conducted business via her private dwellings; her prior class status and neighborhood connections seem to have offset any public challenges of impropriety about her new business enterprise.[46] Along with Roberts, Headman, and Leverson, women like Madame Dona SuSannah provided hair-dyeing services at 102 New Bond Street, while Ann Snelling and Mrs. H. J.

Franklin briefly advertised services in chiropody.[47] Meanwhile, Georgina Cooper
served as shopwoman for a hairdressing saloon on Old Bond Street.[48] These figures'
unremarkable standing on London's leading commercial avenue suggests it was
possible for women to discreetly manage a viable beauty business without attracting
attention from the press or leading legal experts.

If Leverson was not necessarily exceptional in her standing as a female trader
operating on Bond Street, there were, of course, many other ways that she
established a notable spatial presence—a notability that, over time, developed into
notoriety. In contrast to her neighbors, Leverson was an obvious social climber
whose advertisements for her Bond Street location signaled a promotional
flair and defiance of convention that exceeded that of other beauty traders.[49]
For Victorian observers, argues Whitlock, Leverson's advertising campaigns
through the 1860s signaled her willing participation in a "morally reprehensible
activity, [a] non-criminal 'fraud,'" which, by the 1868 trials, served to bolster the
prosecution's case.[50] Undeterred by her regular appearances in London's criminal
and civil courts, Leverson transformed them into opportunities to promote her
Bond Street firm.[51] These tactics seemed to work, and customers reportedly
flocked to her shop. According to one report in the *Saturday Review* in 1868,
"[o]n the strength of the notoriety which she has attained, Mrs. Levison [*sic*] has
beautified her shop, and the value of the paint and varnish which she bestows
on her patients may be estimated by its effects on her shutters." Apparently, the
"abundant flow of customers in Bond-street" had "to some extent reimbursed"
Leverson for her "sufferings" at the hands of the penal system.[52]

Public interest in Madame Rachel surged in 1868, obscuring the fact that Bond
Street traders had worked alongside—and seemingly tolerated—Leverson and
her commercial activities for nearly a decade. Before the trial, local merchants
seem to have been less incensed by Leverson's gender and ethnicity than by her
suspect business practices and specifically by her fraudulent personal references,
which immediately marked her as an outsider among neighboring luxury
retailers. In 1858, for example, Leverson's 16-year-old daughter Rachel was tasked
with procuring an improved location from their current Oxford-Street locale.
The Leversons entered an agreement for a two-year lease at 69 New Bond Street.
For £163 16s. per year, they rented first-floor rooms belonging to Jean Georges
Atloff, a French bootmaker. Within the week, however, Atloff realized that the
family's reference was just an Oxford Street shopman and not the property
owner. The distrustful bootmaker insisted that the family pay rent by the week
rather than quarterly.[53] That Atloff challenged the Leversons's reliability reflected
the family's considerable move from low-class trade in Clare and Oxford Streets

to New Bond Street's exclusive community of luxury traders. It also spoke to the economic untrustworthiness of an unfamiliar family—recently transplanted from a less affluent locale—who peddled beauty goods.[54]

Despite their initial experience on Bond Street, the Leversons quickly rebounded and soon welcomed a steady stream of female custom to their new location at No. 47a New Bond Street, on the corner of Maddox Street. "It was in the narrowest part of Bond Street," recounted one chronicler, "and to say that the traffic was impeded would convey but a poor idea of the congestion that retarded locomotion in that worst-built of thoroughfares."[55] To be more precise, it was the growing *female* presence around Leverson's shop that made Bond Street a traffic bottleneck.[56] While the West End was increasingly open to bourgeois feminine consumers, it could be a contested public space where ideas about propriety meant strict standards for women's behavior and appearance. This is clear in an 1863 incident at Leverson's shop, which highlights women's liminal public status in even the most exclusive of urban commercial neighborhoods. Having traveled from a family home in Blackheath, the younger Rachel procured a cab from the railway station to 47a New Bond Street. Despite having paid the fare, cabman John Denell allegedly prevented her from entering the premises. Thinking her one of Leverson's clients—and doubting her respectability as a made-up woman—he exclaimed, "I've brought one of your painted dolls, and I'll paint her eyes better than you can her cheeks." Commotion ensued for the next half hour, eventually causing "a mob to assemble" around the shop.[57] Miller rightly argues that this moment highlights popular contention over female cosmetic use and the "inferior status of women" more generally.[58] This included anxieties over the beautified female consumer moving through London's public commercial spaces; mistaken for a customer, Miss Rachel's very presence incited public disorder and destabilized the elite solemnity of Bond Street.

There were other occasions when Leverson's business disrupted the daily functioning of Bond Street luxury commerce. In December 1865, a female client—having received her bill for enameling— appeared at the shop in "such a state of excitement" that neighbors called the police.[59] Even the most straightforward of transactions could result in disorder. One *Pall Mall Gazette* columnist reported in February of the same year that a "mob" gathered around a carriage parked in front of the Bond Street shop. "On a female figure emerging from the decorator's abode," he noted, "cries were raised of 'Beautiful for ever!' 'Take care of the putty, mum!' and so on."[60]

Even in the years before these public disruptions, observers like the satirical magazine *Punch* played up on the growing traffic of elite women participating

Madame Rachel takes a Hint from the Cheap Tailors and Picture-Cleaners.

Figure 2.5 "Madame Rachel Takes a Hint," *Punch or the London Charivari* (July 12, 1862): 18. Courtesy of © The British Library Board (Shelfmark P.P.5270 [1862]).

in "base" commercial trade. Their tongue-in-cheek illustration from 1862 depicted half-aged female customers reduced to lowly laborers in Leverson's employ, adorned in sandwich boards touting her skills[61] (Figure 2.5). The illustrator especially emphasized Leverson's incompatibility with respectable Bond Street trade. The accompanying caption aligned her commercial practices with those of "Cheap Tailors and Picture-Cleaners," a reference to a low class of oftentimes Jewish traders.[62] Depicted in the satirical press as a "strong mind of the Metropolis" making "so fruitful harvest out of the weak ones," Leverson signified female disorder and indiscreet financial ambition in a fashionable trade that prized privacy above all.[63]

"The Little Back-Parlour"

In addition to flagrant self-promotion and a dubious local reputation, Leverson's commercial practices came under scrutiny, before, during, and after the 1868 trials. These practices challenged Victorian standards regulating feminine consumption, the female body in public space, and unclear divides between public and private, commercial and residential dwellings. Leverson's transgressions derived, in part, from the arrangement—and the intimacy—demanded by her small shop. Despite its elite location, Leverson's New Bond Street location was modest in design if not rent. Leverson paid the considerable sum of £250 per year, a cost she periodically struggled to meet.[64] For this, she had access to two rooms partitioned by a glass door. In the 1868 trials, prosecutors questioned the propriety of such close quarters, consisting of the long, narrow shop floor and an adjacent parlor. The parlor took on especially illicit properties in the minds of prosecutors. As the Crown claimed, "Heaven only knew what … crimes [Leverson] made her daughters perpetrate in the little back-parlour which was constantly open in New Bond-street until 12 o'clock at night."[65] There, according to press reports, "the harpies" working for the establishment in Bond Street plundered "scores of other ladies who [had] fallen into the clutches," and "only escaped ruined in pocket, tarnished in reputation—degraded, if not defiled."[66]

The shop's late-night transactions were especially unbefitting of the elite status of New Bond Street, a point underscored by prosecutors in the 1868 trials. Criticism of the Leversons's commercial hours—"until 12 o'clock at night"—reflected new ideas, in the nineteenth century, about divisions between work and home. From the 1850s, shifting demographics altered London's commercial landscape, and especially that of the West End, via the appearance of "lock-up" shops.[67] Before the mid-century, many traders both worked and lived in their commercial premises, typically residing above the shop. However, in a short span of time, some West End shops transformed into primarily commercial properties that were locked at night, hence their name.[68] This did not extend to all businesses, though, and some lower-middle and middle-class merchants seemingly did not have the means to enforce such divisions.[69] Historian Alison C. Kay has noted that some female entrepreneurs, like Aimée Lloyd, Susan Ansell, and Georgina Hopkins, fell into this category and subsequently departed from these new expectations for dividing work from home.[70] In fact, multiple uses of space—as both home and shop—long endured among retailers in central London and elsewhere.[71] However, this blurring of domestic and commercial space was an increasingly uncommon practice for successful shopowners on Bond Street, and Crown prosecutors highlighted this transgression.[72] For them, the arrangement of the shop and living spaces—compounded by the intimate nature of Leverson's work in beautifying the female body—suggested a debauched intermingling of domestic with commercial life. They demanded to know where Leverson and her daughters slept, drawing attention to Miss Rachel's admission that her mother occasionally stayed at the shop overnight.[73]

Unfortunately for the Leversons, the intimacy created by their small commercial space raised more questions about the respectability of their business. Crown prosecutors picked up on this, interpreting the shop space as circumstantial evidence of suspect practices. "The shop was a highly exceptional one," concurred Crown prosecutor William Ballantine in the 1868 trials.

> Shops of the kind had existed some centuries ago. They were places where, commencing with the perpetration of moderate frauds, other acts were done which had better not be more particularly mentioned now, except to add that the sooner such dens were rooted out of London the better.[74]

In critiquing "shops of the kind," Ballantine and the prosecution insinuated that Leverson's business was the site of commercial sex or other forms of erotic debauchery. However, neither the 1868 trials nor subsequent investigations established any real evidence of sexual impropriety at Leverson's shop; Mary Borradaile's case seemed, if nothing else, an unfortunate and very costly romantic misadventure of a lonely widow. Nonetheless, for Ballantine and other respectable observers, Leverson's venture too closely resembled shady secretive spaces—including dens of vice—that crowded an older version of London as urban labyrinth.

Secrecy and bodily privacy did play an important role in Leverson's work, although not in the way described by the Crown in their insinuations of the shop as a site of illicit erotic connection. Acutely aware of clients' desire for discretion, Leverson safeguarded her list of patrons, knowing that "ladies generally like secrecy in these cases, but not in all."[75] However, this discretion had its limits for Leverson if it meant relinquishing profits. As evidenced in the Carnegie case of 1862, Leverson periodically shamed her clients by publicizing their visits to her Bond Street shop.[76] It is quite probable that Leverson understood the power of her notoriety when she insisted that Mrs. Carnegie visit the shop, unsupervised, at 9 o'clock at night, a fact that came out in the case.[77] Other business associates described her habit of inviting disgruntled business associates back to Bond Street, where she offered "tea, … some brandy and water, and afterwards some meat."[78] Bedecked in robes with "crystals and gimcracks that crackled at her girdle," she emerged "from behind massive curtains" spouting "some phrase suggestive of 'knowing all about it.'"[79] Leverson understood that entering the liminal site of "Madame Rachel's enameling shop"—let alone witnessing her elaborate performances—instantly incriminated visitors as participants in

Madame Rachel's exploits. Once women "crossed the threshold of such places," argued prosecutor Ballantine, "[t]hey would come out with a taint upon them"[80] (Plate 7).

Testimony suggests that another distinct kind of visitor made his or her way to 47a New Bond Street that threatened the respectability of elite female patrons: business associates from "backmewsy" London, seemingly privy to Leverson's previous ventures in and around lowly Clare Street.[81] Leverson's legal appearances revealed transactions with associates operating in less affluent locales like Brewer Street on the western edge of Soho, Drury Lane, and the East End. Alienated from other West End beauty providers, Leverson seems to have relied on people like pawnbroker Sophia Stephens of Soho and boot wholesaler Thomas Austen Stack of Bethnal Green to support her firm when faced with economic difficulties.[82] To be sure, Leverson's periodic appearances at bankruptcy court and her stints in prison point to the family's cyclical pattern of wealth and financial strife, marked by transactions with questionable lawyers, pawnbrokers, and financiers.[83] Cameo appearances by these non-elite types illuminate Leverson's dependency on a lower class of trade, furthering the divide between her and her respectable Bond Street neighbors.

In her 1868 fraud trials, Crown prosecutors tried to further discredit Leverson by emphasizing her ties to activities such as pawn broking, bad credit, and moneylending. In doing so, they capitalized on associations of pawning and moneylending with low-class modes of economic exchange by Jewish traders, activities that diverged from dominant ideas about respectable commercial practice.[84] Pawning was by no means a rare occurrence, and according to Ellen Ross, there were 41,520 million pledges in London at the turn of the twentieth century.[85] By the 1860s, however, pawning was increasingly deemed a working-class practice, and the press slyly insinuated that Leverson and her daughters' reliance on it was unworthy of their elite neighbors. To be sure, some of Leverson's high-end clients balked at the pawning of their luxury items, which they "loaned" to Leverson as security on outstanding bills.[86]

Leverson also acted as a moneylender to her female clients, as women not only ran up debts but borrowed credit to cover their own bill of service. In 1868, daughter Leonti confirmed these dealings, elaborating additional illicit practices occurring in the Bond Street space. "Mamma was in the habit of lending money to ladies," she testified, and "kept her money in a cabinet in the little parlour."[87] This was of little surprise to observers of Leverson's previous trial, which revealed that Aurora James borrowed 7s. the day after receiving her bill for £100.[88] The extension of credit to customers was in no way a limited phenomenon. Yet

Leverson's lending to ladies for their own frivolous consumption underscored popular anxieties around women, consumption, and finance. Left to their own devices, critics claimed, female consumers engaged in reckless monetary transactions driven by their vanity and insatiable desires for fashion.[89]

All the while, press accounts linked her moneylending practices and purported greed to their portrayals of Leverson as a "Jewish purveyor of feminine charms."[90] A handful of successful Jewish traders, including optician Elias Solomons and jeweler Godfrey Zimmerman, conducted business on Bond Street through the mid-century, suggesting that Jewishness was not incommensurable with lucrative—and male—West End enterprise.[91] However, given Leverson's other transgressions, her ethnicity became another focal point of criticism, and her Jewishness featured prominently in Victorian press accounts. Miller has argued that the press' emphasis on Leverson's Jewishness not only played up "fears of cultural difference and otherness, but also fears associated with immigration, job competition, cosmopolitanism, and the dilution of English national identity" circulating in the 1860s.[92] Leverson's ethnicity was also central to press condemnations of her low-class economic practices, which were represented as unbefitting of her elite Bond Street location. Leading press outlets aligned questionable trade practices— like moneylending and pawning—with "Jewish" characteristics to suggest her participation in debauched trade. Alternatively, they used Leverson's ongoing associations with "low" characters to prove the futility of Leverson's attempts at social climbing. Leverson's efforts to ascend her class and spatial origins would prove fruitless as long as she maintained connections to old networks of working-class or Jewish trade.

In sum, Leverson's West End shop allegedly functioned as a meeting point between commercial worlds that catered (at least superficially) to very different classes of clientele. There is no evidence that Leverson interacted with Bond Street perfumers or other female traders like Susan Ansell and Aimée Lloyd. Instead, legal testimony and press accounts stressed Leverson's connections with low-class hawkers, pawnbrokers, and wholesalers reminiscent of her days in Clare Street.[93] More importantly, according to print outlets, it was through Madame Rachel that these ambiguous types came into contact with leading female customers from London's elite social set. These trade relations connected Leverson's business activities to a lower class of commerce, characteristic of pockets of plebeian trade in the West End, which was automatically suspect to Bond Street's vendors and eventually Crown prosecutors.

"Arabian Baths" and the Female Body

Revelations of the 1868 trials—exposing questionable practices and doubtful associations—consolidated the negative reputation of Madame Rachel's shop as a site of indiscreet if not debauched management of elite female bodies. Compounding these associations were titillating reports of a specific service, Leverson's "Arabian Baths." The Arabian Baths were a principal feature of Leverson's business, and she often prescribed multiple sessions; in 1868, Mary Borradaile reported taking over "100 of the baths" in the course of her treatments.[94] Conveniently, women could also procure Arabian Bath powders for use in their home, thereby transporting an exoticized luxury good, with its Orientalist aura, into the comforts of the domestic realm.[95] Conversely, visitors to Leverson's Bond Street shop could bathe under her direct supervision to fully benefit from its nourishing properties.

This latter practice took on illicit connotations in the 1868 trials, when rumors circulated that Lord Ranelagh had spied on Mary Borradaile while bathing, from a concealed space adjacent to the bathroom.[96] Despite denials by Leverson and Ranelagh's counsel, the story spread, even inspiring the cover illustration of a cheap print publication detailing the trial's most lurid revelations (Figure 2.6). The crude rendering depicted Madame Rachel assisting a rather young-looking Borradaile in removing her clothes, revealing her exposed calves, arms, and décolletage. Meanwhile, a concealed Ranelagh drew back the curtain—literally and figuratively—on the secretive bodily processes about to transpire. The persistence of this rumor forced Ranelagh's lawyers to issue public denials of the accusations; they even offered to have Leverson's Bond Street shop and Maddox Street home "carefully and minutely surveyed and examined by competent architects" to disprove theories of a covert apartment with its infamous bath.[97]

Fascination with Madame Rachel's baths and "covert apartments" ultimately betrayed concerns over female vulnerability in London's fashionable commercial scene. Press reports denounced ladies' ventures to unfamiliar commercial spaces managed by untrustworthy merchants like Madame Rachel, who encouraged illicit services that compromised women's respectability.[98] There is no doubt that the baths were central to Leverson's beautifying services, but the details of the bathing facilities used in the treatments remained teasingly unclear in press accounts. Trial transcripts described the shop as consisting of two rooms: a small parlor connected to the shop space. However, newspaper reports from

Figure 2.6 "Taking The Bath," *History & Trial of Madame Rachel* (1868). Courtesy of Harvard Law School Library, Historical & Special Collections.

1868 suggested the presence of bathing facilities on site, fueling the rumors of Ranelagh's illicit voyeurism.[99] Clearly evident in press accounts, as Rappaport argues, were associations between Leverson's bathing premises and *bagnios*, eighteenth-century Turkish baths that were in fact houses of assignation.[100] The nature of Leverson's services, not to mention her local reputation, encouraged suspicion about the *real* purposes of the Arabian Baths.

Complicating these discourses were conflicting reports that the baths did not take place in Leverson's shop, but in public establishments developed as municipal health initiatives aimed at London's working-class residents. According to trial records, Leverson sent at least one female client to local public baths to undergo their "beautifying treatment." In 1865, she instructed Aurora Knight, who had just recovered from smallpox, to use the baths in Argyll Place after refusing her admittance to private facilities. Knight proceeded to visit the public baths on Endell Street in Bloomsbury, a "second-class bath" even further afoot from the West End and Argyll Place.[101] By sending her female client away from Bond Street into the tangled side streets east of Regent Street, Leverson came under criticism for exposing genteel women to the dangers of the old and disordered city.

In this way, Leverson's services were especially dangerous; she enticed women by offering discreet, respectable beauty services only to expose women's bodies to what Miller terms the "public, transnational contagion" of the metropolis' working populations.[102] The trials and their coverage subsequently conjured up Victorian concerns over health and epidemics as emanating from London's old, labyrinthine geographies. Mid-century epidemics, and especially cholera, had exposed the vulnerability of the West End to the devastating effects of disease. In 1854, for example, a "terrible outbreak" of cholera spread from Soho's Broad Street water pump. The ensuing investigation found that the highest mortality was among laborers "who worked for the shops about Bond Street and Regent Street."[103] Public bathhouses sprang up across the West End to induce its laborers to meet new Victorian standards in purity and cleanliness, and it was to these facilities that Leverson reportedly directed a female client. While facilitating health and respectability, public bathhouses also figured as spatial representations of exposure to the filth and pollution of the public body.[104]

As a result, trial reports oscillated between accounts of bathing at Leverson's establishment—with its imaginative link to dens of vice—and at public baths, with their connections to the polluting influences of the city's unwashed. Whatever the location, reports of Leverson's "Arabian Baths" emphasized the exposure of the female body to the public eye, courting popular criticism.[105] The press highlighted these contradictory rumors to maintain public interest in the story, playing up the discrepancies in competing descriptions of Leverson's illicit shop space. This proved an effective tactic. "[T]he question of the bath," argued Leverson's lawyers in 1868, sufficiently condemned her commercial practices in the eyes of the public, exposing her "to ribald songs and cruel jests," not to mention "utterly and abdominally cruel" newspaper headings in leading periodicals and police sheets.[106] Fortunately for Leverson's business, all publicity was good publicity, and some female clients would not be dissuaded from their hunt for beauty nor their patronage of her services.

Perfumers versus "Perfumers"

It was Leverson's notoriety, but also her unconventional practices and services that attracted female customers from across London. Despite her exceptionality, however, there were some ways in which she resembled other metropolitan beauty traders: her widespread promotional campaigns for transformative goods and services, her assurances (however disingenuous) of consumer privacy, her deliberate courting of elite feminine patronage. Leverson's resemblance to other beauty traders became a key focus of her 1868 trials, and concluding arguments turned, in part, on her relationship to commercial practices mobilized by other beauty providers operating across London. More specifically, prosecution and defense counsels sparred over Leverson's status as a bona fide perfumer or someone involved in deceptive practices under the guise of a perfumery business.

Leverson's counsel insisted that her beautifying work sustained her family, which, according to Miller, cast her not as a greedy woman but as a maternal provider ensuring the economic sustenance of her children.[107] True, Leverson engaged in puffery, argued her lawyer, but she was not on trial for giving "her cosmetics to the world under high-sounding names." In fact, it was her customers and not Leverson who should be accountable for the huge expenses paid. "[I]f the fashionable world lent themselves to create a demand for those cosmetics," he asked, "was she to be punished for having furnished them with a supply?"[108] Prosecutors countered that Leverson was not a simple perfumer, nor was she engaged in average acts of puffery as deployed by other traders. "Competition and high sounding names there might be in all branches of trade," quipped Ballantine, but "in that of Rachel there was a quantity of worthless trash collected by her and put into bottles and sold at enormous prices." The shop, Ballantine concluded, was just a front for other deceptions and crimes; "[t]he truth was that she carried on a system of wholesale fraud under the plea of having a perfumer's shop."[109]

The jury ultimately found the prosecution's argument more convincing and rejected Leverson's standing as a perfumer. On September 25, 1868, Sarah "Madame Rachel" Leverson was found guilty of defrauding Mary Borradaile and sentenced to five years penal servitude. At sentencing, presiding Commissioner Robert Malcolm Kerr remarked "I do not recollect any case in which the obtaining of money by false pretenses, at all times a serious crime, has presented more aggravating features than this."[110] Leverson was transported to Millbank Prison to begin her sentence.[111] Meanwhile, counsel, newspapers, and critics alike celebrated the victory, condemning not only Leverson but also her New Bond Street shop, "a painted sepulchre" that housed "all the foul and filthy doings that transpired within its gilded doors."[112]

Leverson's legal designation as a fraud and not a perfumer did not prevent some journalists from continuing to characterize her as a member of London's beauty trades, bringing with it sensational associations of deceptive beauty concoctions and vulnerable female bodies. The West End's network of perfumers and hairdressers did not respond kindly to ensuing connections with Madame Rachel nor her business practices. Leverson's penchant for self-promotion—and spectacle—did not align with professional traders' promotion of their skills. Neither did her provocative public presence meet standards of discretion promoted by London's luxury retailers. In this way, the Madame Rachel trial threatened the standing of not only female traders and consumers, as Whitlock and Miller have argued, but the entire metropolitan beauty industry. At best, critics blamed London's beauty vendors for middle- and upper-class women's gaudy appearance; at worst, they drew comparisons between their perfumery shops and dens of vice.

London's leading beauty vendors subsequently asserted the respectability of their trade in the wake of the Madame Rachel scandal, as West End perfumers closed ranks against undesirable outsiders. This included a defensive response to suggestive articles in London's leading print publications. One year after the Borradaile trial, the *Pall Mall Gazette* printed an article on "The Ladies' Mile," a stretch of terrain running parallel to Hyde Park's "Rotten Row" that was notorious for the congregation of London's leading *demimondaine* or ladies of questionable repute (Plate 8). In the course of his critiques, the anonymous author noted the existence of "certain perfumers' shops at the West End notorious for enterprises not immediately connected with bloom for the lips and glitter for the eyes." These establishments, hinted the author, provided not only beauty services but also opportunities for illicit sexual connections or the purchase of pornographic images.[113]

Incensed, leading hairdresser H. P. Truefitt immediately responded to the *London Times*, one of the numerous outlets to reprint the article. In a brief missive on behalf of "every recognized perfumer," Truefitt laid into the piece, which "indicated to the initiated a well-known and infamous house, but to the general public reflects injuriously upon some of the best conducted [perfumery] establishments in London." In other words, patrons of London's houses of assignation would recognize the establishment mentioned in the *Pall Mall* article. However, general readers could incorrectly assume that other West End perfumers and hairdressers—including Truefitt—were facilitating sexual commerce.[114] A follow-up editorial in *The Hairdressers' Chronicle* entitled "Perfumers, or—What?" further bemoaned the coexistence of disreputable and reputable perfumers across London, leading to confusion among the general public. Informing readers "that such perfumers(!) do exist," the author asserted the trade's intentions to exclude unsavory "perfumers" from the benefits of trade membership.

To moralise upon such a subject may appear unsuited to our columns as a trade
journal, or we might fill our present number with a sermon upon it; but we
leave the party in the hands of our fellow-tradesmen, trusting when the secret
peeps out, that—if not justice—at least the contempt and scorn of the trade will
be awarded to the individual, and the isolation from every respectable member
of the business will perhaps be more keenly felt than any amount of legal
persecution.

With "no legal remedy" in sight, London's respectable hairdressers and perfumers
relied on traditional strategies of a localized trade: social and economic shunning
of the offender, excluding them from the professional community and the
opportunities it afforded.[115]

The Truefitt exchange highlighted the proximity of London's leading beauty
retailers to less reputable characters like Leverson, not to mention enduring
associations between vice and beauty consumption. Leverson's sensational 1868
trials reinforced these connections, and, in their critiques of Madame Rachel, the
press implicated both respectable beauty businesspeople and female customers.
Despite traders' best efforts, connections between beauty goods, vice, and illicit
sex relented long after Leverson's trials. In 1879, the chapbook *Life in London*
blamed sexual commerce on men and women who kept "an establishment to
which young girls are decoyed and surrounded with luxuries hitherto denied
them" before being "sold to a 'swell' for a big sum." The anonymous author
claimed these "'manufacturers'" could be milliners or dancing instructors, but
also "perfumers and hairdressers on a grand scale."[116] Such suspicions implicated
individual traders who beautified clients' bodies, including female entrepreneurs
whose manipulation of the female body, not to mention their sometimes
humble circumstances, could heighten public suspicions and accusations of
corruption.[117] It remains unclear, however, the extent to which beauty providers
beyond Madame Rachel did, in fact, deceive their female clientele, let alone
facilitate illicit sexual commerce.

London's perfumery and hairdressing classes were not the only professionals
to weigh in on the Madame Rachel scandal. In tandem with mid-century
consumer interest in cosmetics and hair washes and the negative coverage of
Leverson, medical professionals also criticized "secret ingredients" and their
effects on the female body. Male medical experts who critiqued the use of
injurious chemicals like bismuth and lead oxide in cosmetics were by no means
a new phenomenon.[118] However, professionalizing efforts and a recent panic
over product adulteration emboldened them, in the mid-nineteenth century, to
mount systematic attacks on beautifying products. Leading medical journal *The*

Lancet ran a series through the late 1850s on "Arsenic as a Cosmetic," where correspondents resoundingly decried arsenic's mobilization as a skin whitener.[119] Similarly, the *British Medical Journal* condemned the "enormous evil" of toilette articles, none of which could "be used with safety."[120]

Professional and scientific critiques of beauty secrets extended to Leverson's trials, and a diverse body of critics scrutinized her beautifying goods for evidence of harmful ingredients. In a general climate of concern over food and drug adulteration, a range of parties actively disputed her claims to the purity and naturalness of her products. In 1862, one disgruntled creditor—who also happened to be a chemist and druggist—claimed that Leverson had obtained, in five months, "as much bismuth as would destroy the faces of half-a-million of young ladies."[121] Further critiques appeared in periodical publications like the *Saturday Review* that detailed the ill effects of beauty treatments like those of Leverson: the "thinning hair dyed and crimped and fixed," the "lusterless eyes blackened around the lids ... perhaps the pupil dilated by belladonna."[122] The goods' secret properties, the press argued, did nothing but produce women "with cheeks daubed with stucco flaunt[ed] about in the similitude of painted jezebels"[123] (Figure 2.7). Perhaps the most organized and persistent criticism of Leverson and the secretive composition of her goods came from the prosecuting counsel, Williams and Ballantine.[124] In the 1868 trials, they grilled the younger Rachel over the composition of their wares, demanding to know the real composition of products like Jordan Water and Circassian Oil. Asserting their authenticity, Miss Rachel refused to name their commercial agent, accusing the prosecutors of wanting the firm's "professional secret to come out."[125]

Trade, medical, and legal fascination with "Madame Rachel's" wares would eventually be satisfied in a final trial appearance in 1878. Following the public spectacles of 1868 and her completion of almost four years of imprisonment, Leverson relaunched her beautifying business in late 1872 at various locations around Covent Garden and in Cavendish and Grosvenor Squares.[126] She remained active if relatively inconspicuous for almost six years, only to appear in criminal court in 1878 under charges of "unlawfully obtaining two necklaces by false pretenses."[127] Client Cecilia Maria Pearse had paid for beautifying treatments with expensive family jewels, just days before developing a severe facial rash. When she demanded that the jewels be returned, Leverson declared they had been pawned. Pearse filed charges.[128]

In the 1878 Pearse trial, the Crown sought to determine if Leverson's concoctions had in fact caused Pearse's rash, which would exempt the client from the cost of treatment.[129] An official with the Chemical Society testified that

Figure 2.7 "Stoop to Conquer," *The Tomahawk* (June 6, 1867). Hulton Archive/Getty Images.

one wash—which cost an exorbitant guinea a bottle—contained carbonate of lead, starch, fuller's earth, hydrochloric acid, and distilled water—only sixpence worth of chemicals. Furthermore, the expert alleged, Leverson's Arabian Baths were "little else than bran and water." Condemned by science, Leverson was sentenced to another five years of prison labor, but she died in 1880 before she could serve out her sentence.[130]

Conclusions

In London's nineteenth-century beauty business, traders exploited secrecy and discretion to distinguish themselves from competitors. For some female traders, intermittent advertising highlighted traders' "natural" feminine qualities, which enhanced their beautifying skills, not to mention facilitated a culture of trust. Beauty businesswomen promised secret formulas and proprietary goods, along with the assurance of discretion among women. Meanwhile, a rising contingent of successful, often male perfume manufacturers increasingly moved away from what Septimus Piesse dubbed "mysterious secrecy" to embrace a new kind of professional, public trade profile. In the wake of this shift, mysterious, esoteric bodily services took on an added air of impropriety, becoming increasingly linked with illicit and dangerous commercial practices.

Intensifying these linkages was the continued popularity of female artificial adornment in the 1860s. This popularity was not diminished by Leverson's sensational 1868 trials, when subsequent media coverage heightened already existing public concerns over the perils of self-fashioning. While it did not affect consumer interest, the explosive developments around Leverson's practices seemingly had effects on the daily trading lives of London's manufacturing perfumers, hairdressers, and beauty consultants. Undercapitalized small-scale beauty providers, whose material circumstances often situated them at the peripheries of the trade, could be implicated in public criticism; attacks on vendors' secret practices and "backroom" beauty services became a means to distinguish female and small-scale traders from an increasingly professionalized trade. Humble shop spaces, with their porous boundaries between household and business, came to represent negative markers of undercapitalized beauty providers who failed to order their lives according to Victorian expectations of domestic and commercial boundaries. That is not to say that businesswomen did not continue to work in the beauty trades, and women featured in trade listings in the 1870s and 1880s as hairdressers and perfumers. They did not, however, tend to advertise their goods and services beyond directories; nor did they stake visible claims on leading commercial thoroughfares or appear in professional trade organizations. Public vitriol reviling Leverson advanced the trade ascendency and public profile of certain manufacturing perfumers, who juxtaposed their own professionalism and respectability against Leverson's deceitful conduct.

Leverson represented an extreme precedent, as tensions around female visibility merged with circulating ideas about feminine respectability to condemn even the most renowned beauty entrepreneurs. In her exceptional case, Leverson exploited the power of secrets and privacy, which had long factored in beauty and grooming services but took on a new valence under Madame Rachel. In the course of her trials, attention to artificial adornment, women's work, and ideas about the public female body aligned to cast a shadow over London's beauty trades. Responding to unfavorable publicity, London's leading perfume manufacturers distanced themselves from the treachery and deception associated with Leverson's mode of secrecy. To counter criticisms, they bolstered their associations with the city's professional classes to promote a respectable mode of beauty business. Yet this move toward professionalization was not straightforward and could be equally fraught with uneven processes connected to gender, class, and consumers' bodies. This was especially evident as traders, and specifically London's hairdressers and barbers, navigated the introduction of a new commercial service worker to the West End: the female hairdresser.

3

Mobilizing Men: Robert Douglas and H. P. Truefitt

At a lecture at the Hanover Square Rooms in March of 1869, famed activist for female employment Emily Faithfull declared open a new "sphere of female employment in London."[1] Faithfull triumphantly reported that women, and not men, were now employed at a West End hairdresser's shop. This feat had required "a great amount of sustained effort." Hairdressing was deemed an unfit occupation for women, Faithfull later recounted, "[w]hen it was first proposed in London to employ women as hairdressers."[2] London's leading hairdressers insisted that male apprentices would never agree to work alongside female hairdressers, "and the whole establishment would be thrown into confusion." To introduce women into hairdressing, "the consent of 'the trade'" was required and such consent was not easily obtained. When applying for work at "one of the principal hairdressers in London," one would-be female apprentice was "dismissed with the simple remark that 'it would revolutionise the trade.'"[3]

Such forewarnings did not deter West End hairdresser Robert Douglas (1822–1887) from introducing female hands, and Faithfull lauded Douglas in her 1869 speech (Figure 3.1). Before their appearance at his ladies' parlor at 23 New Bond Street, one correspondent claimed, "*coiffeuses* [female hairdressers] were unheard of."[4] The previous year, in 1868, Douglas had taken on four female employees before expanding their ranks in 1870 by an additional seventeen lady hairdressers. His friend and West End neighbor H. P. Truefitt (1824–1909) also "tried the experiment" of employing women just down the street from Douglas's rooms (Figure 3.2). Despite initially muted responses from London's elite customers, Truefitt remained confident that female clients would grow to admire *coiffeuses* in light of their "extraordinary perfection" and skill. On his end, Douglas knew he would be "bitterly opposed at first," but, with ongoing perseverance, "in time his customers would come to appreciate the change."[5] In spite of public reservations, the trend in female hairdressers proliferated. By

ROBERT DOUGLAS.

Figure 3.1 "Celebrities Connected with the Trade: Robert Douglas," *Hairdressers'*
Weekly Journal (November 24, 1883): 777. Courtesy of © The British Library Board
(Shelfmark 4238.301000).

1878, according to the "Lady Correspondent" at the *Evening Telegraph*, "female
hairdressers" were "becoming numerous enough to alarm the male followers of
that agreeable profession."[6]

Trade publications reveal, however, that male workers in London's hair
trades were alarmed long before 1878, and first-wave feminist agitation over
the employment of women was not the only source of their duress. Despite
celebrations of Robert Douglas for his advanced attitudes about women, accounts
obscured the real reason that Douglas employed a female labor force; they were
cheap labor—scabs—hired following a dispute between Douglas and his male
assistants. Purportedly an advocate of female advancement, Douglas's hiring of
female hands occurred in the wake of a rebellion of lower-middle-class male
staff, mutinous over his banning of tips and gratuities.[7] Upon the departure of his
entire male staff of sixty, Douglas increasingly relied on a group who would not
demand tips on top of their weekly wages: women. He simultaneously courted
the feminist press, gaining favorable publicity by transforming questionable
labor practices into a laudable—and ultimately successful—development in the
movement for female employment.

H. P. TRUEFITT.

Figure 3.2 "Celebrities Connected with the Trade: H.P. Truefitt," *Hairdressers' Weekly Journal* (March 24, 1883): 189. Courtesy of © The British Library Board (Shelfmark 4238.301000).

Situating mid-century debates about women's work in the context of ongoing trade agitation reveals that Victorian attempts to systematically introduce female hairdressers was just one element of a complex system of gender and class that organized London's emerging beauty service sector. Concerns over the rise of the lady hairdresser were part of a much longer trajectory of trade unrest, which included debates between high- and low-class hairdressing establishments and the positioning of foreign workers as cosmopolitan "competition" for British interests. Anxieties also related to ongoing debates about the respectability of beautifying services that were playing out in the Madame Rachel trials, which unfolded in the same year that Douglas and Truefitt publicized their elaborate new spaces of feminized bodily consumption. An analysis of trade conflicts leading up to the introduction of female workers, as well as the sensational moment in which they were introduced, reveals multiple contingencies shaping the struggle for ascendency—and professional respectability—in the hairdressing industry, one of London's major urban service sectors. At play were material and imagined divisions between French, German, and British hairdressers, the East and West Ends, and women and men as they sought to consolidate the public standing of their trade.

Historian Susan Vincent argues for the fluidity of the hairdressing trades, which could be taken up by servants, a range of tradespeople, and across a variety of locations.[8] While this was certainly the case through the mid-nineteenth century, some professionalizing factions nonetheless made concerted efforts to confirm their status and respectability as London's leading hairdressers and barbers. In the same moment as the Madame Rachel scandals, a cohort of hairdressers and barbers worked to forge their legitimacy, while expanding the scale and reach of their firms via new goods, services, and the courting of female customers. This expansion required labor, however, and assistants from across London resisted what they considered to be the heightening of unfair labor practices and conditions. Hairdressers, barbers, and their employees subsequently joined "masculine-controlled organizational bodies" to bolster their interests as industry leaders and workers: trade associations, professional organizations, and benevolent societies.[9]

Despite these moves toward professionalization, the Victorian public largely dismissed the activities of British hairdressers and barbers in nineteenth- and early-twentieth-century workplace reform, much as they have been ignored in subsequent histories of Victorian labor agitation.[10] Often represented in satirical and mainstream print as effeminate and idle, London's hair workers were in fact an active if fractured group aspiring toward trade professionalization in the latter half of the nineteenth century.[11] Alienated from the masculine industrial world of work, they promoted standard trade improvements, namely professional organization via trade associations and benevolent societies. As we will see, these professional societies later rallied for improved conditions for assistants in the 1860s and 1870s, first defending their members in debates over the "natural" abilities of British versus European barbers and then resisting challenges to male trade dominance in the wake of women's introduction to the industry.

In the Cutting-Rooms

Despite a general lack of respect for London's hairdressers and barbers in the nineteenth century, the hairdressing trade had once maintained a reputable standing in the traditional guild system as the Worshipful Company of Barbers.[12] In the early modern period, hairdressers enjoyed a much higher social standing than they did later, so that elites reportedly "thought it no disgrace in that simple age to lodge in Fleet Street, or take rooms above some barber's shop."[13] According to historian Don Herzog, eighteenth-century hairdressers became representative of radical egalitarian political discourses, while being central to the "reproduction of social status" by fashioning the elaborate coiffures that marked Britain's elite ruling classes.[14] Yet in spite of their important social function, barbers and haircutters found themselves increasingly shut out of London's rapidly professionalizing circles, including the upward trajectory of their own livery brothers, the surgeons. Guild regulations through the seventeenth and eighteenth centuries curtailed barbers' ability to carry out surgical procedures, eventually limiting them to bloodletting and tooth extraction. The reputation of barbers as the inferior "profession" of the two was sealed in 1745, when the guild infamously lost more than half of its members to the Company of Surgeons, which later became the Royal College.[15]

In the following era, the Company experienced steady decline, not only in reputation, but also in professional and financial standing. By the early nineteenth century, membership in the Barber's Company no longer denoted skill or even association with the art of barbering and haircutting. Over the next fifty years, the Company increasingly found itself in financial arrears. The year 1845 saw the lowest number of freemen applying to the guild, with the admittance of only five new members.[16] Among them, few men actually practiced as barbers, most becoming members through patrilineal inheritance.[17] "[W]e never hear of any proceedings in connection with the old Hall in Monkwell Street," complained the *Hairdresser's Chronicle* in 1871, before declaring the Guild unable to provide "the means of entertainment, intellectual, moral, or physical, for those who are supposed to be its supporters"[18] (Figure 3.3). Nor did the Company administer an official guild-regulated system of apprenticeship, even though informal indenture continued to be "the rule rather than the exception" among London's hairdressers and barbers.[19] For many guild members and practicing hairdressers and barbers, it seemed that a guild connection was nothing more than a relic of the early modern past.

The decline in formal guild membership did not reflect what was in fact an overall growth in the number of metropolitan hairdressers and barbers.[20] Notoriously incomplete, census returns from 1851 registered some 2,338 hairdressers in London, outnumbering metropolitan hatters but still significantly less than the numbers of fashionable traders like tailors.[21] Neither did guild

Figure 3.3 "Barber Surgeon's Hall," by Joseph Mead (*c.*1841). Print Collector/Getty Images.

declines mean the elimination of systems of apprenticeship, a practice that remained "still almost universal" into the 1890s.[22] The continual employment of young boys was due in part to London's rapidly expanding commercial market and consumer demands that depended on a reservoir of cheap, inexperienced labor. Grooming services grew in popularity among all classes of consumer, as new modes of consumption extended notions of luxurious self-grooming beyond the elite classes. The unpredictable hours and demands of such broadening demographics compelled an even greater reliance on the large body of semiskilled apprentices and assistants. Barbers' apprenticeship periods ranged in length, with J.T. Dunk of the Hairdressers' Guild claiming "that no man can hope to learn much in less than seven years."[23] In the "high class" shops of the West End, however, apprentices were rarely taken on. "Most of the men in good trade" noted F.J. Gotty, secretary of the Journeymen Hairdressers' Trade Society, would "have [already] apprenticed in the country."[24]

For those native to London and unable to secure positions in elite firms, there seemed little choice but to train outside the metropolis or apprentice at a "low class" shop in the City, East End, or South Bank.[25] There, low levels of capitalization and the utilitarian nature of the work meant that backstage conditions could be much harsher than those experienced by West End employees. In less affluent shops, the living-in system prevailed, and groups of men, some as young as thirteen and fourteen, resided together above the saloon. Many of the boys came from workhouses that offered a "bonus" or indenture of £5 or £10 to the master, denoting the assistants' low status. Once taken on, young workers were typically left to pick up work as they could. Frequented by a regular stream of laborers, working-class shops attracted ideal customers for the inexperienced hand. Apprentices mastered shaving by "gashing the chin of the workingman," who did not "much mind what you do to them as long as you 'bring it off.'"[26] Stories abounded of the "master working man on Saturday afternoon," who cajoled young apprentices with gentle encouragements: "'Come along boy, you won't hurt me: Damn it all, you can take mine off.'"[27] After three or four years earning about 10s. per week plus board, boys graduated to a "second class business" as a "uniform" or "improver," those "young men who have been *taught the various branches of the trade*, and are seeking practice."[28]

While resembling systems of formal indenture, hairdressing apprentices were not subject to guild-approved supervisors who monitored master-apprentice relations or registered grievances from mistreated laborers.[29] Many apprentices across London reportedly found themselves in substandard situations.[30] However, conditions did not necessarily improve upon the completion of the apprenticeship period. For assistants residing in poorer shops, the permeable boundary between work and home meant that employers could demand that assistants work regardless of time of day or duration of shift. Some masters kept men working over twelve hours a day, denied breaks for meals or relieving oneself, or refused tips on services like shampooing and dyeing.[31] Hairdressing rooms were notoriously "very badly-ventilated and lighted," sometimes located in the downstairs quarters. Writing on mortality rates among hairdressers and barbers in 1892, Dr. J. T. Arlidge described "how small, confined, and laden with the waste of gas and with the breath of customers many cutting-rooms are."[32] Claiming that hairdressing's popularity among "weaker members of society" meant that tradesmen favored effeminacy, he contended that hairdressers had a higher mortality rate than other males occupied in similar urban commercial trades.[33] By the close of the nineteenth century, England's Registrar General found that hairdressers and barbers had among the highest suicide rates of all occupational categories between 1871 and 1897.[34]

The harsh material realities of assistants' lives and specifically their long working hours were due, in part, to the significance of the nineteenth-century barbershop as a site of male sociability in London's working-class neighborhoods. Aside from public houses and "cookshops," the penny barbershop was one of the few commercial spaces in London's working-class enclaves that remained open past the dinner hour. Through the summer, the shops functioned as venues for late night socializing, drinking, and gambling.[35] A member of social investigator Charles Booth's team discovered that, in a South London working neighborhood, "barbers' shops showed great activity" throughout the night, "matched only by a man staggering" along the road and some "rather gay dancing on the side walk."[36]

Masculine socializing peaked in the busy summer months, and employers brought on "odd men" to help with weekend business in low-class shops. One "House of Call" or labor board for barbers sent upward of seventy or eighty men each Saturday morning to meet the demand of the working population's free Saturday afternoons and Sundays.[37] Artistic renderings appearing throughout the nineteenth century, including George Hunt's *Sunday Morning*, captured the disorderly, mixed-class nature of the barbershop at these peak hours. While certainly exaggerated for comedic effect, the piece highlights the chaos of a weekend morning in the shop, which catered to patrons and passersby, not to mention a local animal or three (Plate 9). Even with extra help, tradesmen often had to shave and cut through the weekend without break. One small-class hairdresser estimated he worked between eighty-five and ninety-two hours a week; another estimated no less than ninety.[38] Most small-class barbers never took holidays, although one reported to have "an evening off" about "once a fortnight."[39] At the same time, steady business made for lower wages reduced to accommodate the high rate of tips. Wages were subsequently "lower in the [C]ity than in any other part of London as the work there [was] constant and the tips reach a larger amount."[40]

When London's damp winter evenings curbed late-night work, some men turned to wigmaking and artificial hairwork, an industry that surged through the mid-1860s.[41] New women's periodical publications contributed to the booming popularity of fashionable hairpieces among Britain's elite and middle classes (Figure 3.4). Between 1855 and 1868, sales of false hair increased some 400 percent. By 1870, one firm purportedly produced two tons of frizettes, or small curls, every week.[42] "[P]acks, heaps, and bales of human tresses of every length, colour, and texture" arrived daily in London's docklands, reportedly shorn from female peasants in France, Germany, and Romania. Less prized forms included "dead hair" from Italy, short tufts extracted from hairbrushes,

Figure 3.4 The Heads of Three Women Wearing Chignons Attached to Their Natural Hair (1888). Courtesy of the Wellcome Library, London.

combs, and the floors of continental cutters' shops.[43] From the docklands, wholesalers transported manufacturing hair to depots across London, many of them clustered in the City and Holborn. One 1872 inventory registered the most valuable stock of Robert Hovenden, London's leading beauty wholesaler, as £3,809 worth of manufacturing hair, which he in turn sold to West End hairdressers and wigmakers.[44] Clients who could afford custom-made pieces purchased gray hair, which they had dyed to specifically match their own tresses. Many more bought the ready-made chignons, frizettes, and fronts that crowded West End display windows, these items having typically been fashioned by poor female "street workers" or wigmakers in Soho and Clerkenwell.[45] These female laborers monopolized production due to their lower wages, and, in spite of demand, male working-class assistants found even this work to be sparse.

The intermittency of the trade, particularly for members at its lower ends, made for highs and lows for its workers, and "a large part" reportedly mitigated

unpleasant conditions via drink, gambling, and other "idleness." According to
Booth, hairdressers were "very apt to be led into gambling or drinking," the latter
being particularly problematic for barbers owing to "its accompaniment [of]
an unsteady hand."[46] Low-class barbers were notorious for their enthusiasm for
horse racing, "owing partly to the incessant talk of it in the shop and partly to the
many hours of idleness during which they … read the sporting papers." They also
had the reputation as small-scale local bookies, acting along with "tobacconists
and newsvendors … as agents on the quiet." The taking of bets—oftentimes in the
streets over the dinner hour—could work to bolster a barber's local reputation
as "always the confidant of their customers."[47] However, barbers' associations
with this type of urban, working-class activity conflicted with public perceptions
of their professional reputation. In his experiences as an employment agent for
low-class barbers, J. G. Davin surmised that temporary workers' conduct "often
lead … to a row" with employers, which damaged men's reputations in the trade
community and gradually affected their rate of placement.[48] It was in this highly
charged, competitive atmosphere that British assistants began to express fears
over the influx and alleged underhandedness of their foreign colleagues.

"Unscrupulous and Sneakish Means"

Complicating trade conditions was the widespread circulation of ideas about
the taste levels and "natural" abilities of British-born service workers in
fashionable trades like hairdressing. Commentators attributed superior taste
to non-British hairdressers, whose numbers "in the London trade [were]
very large, the majority probably being French."[49] The presumed superiority
of foreign expertise had long been a sensitive subject for Britain's hairdressers
and perfumers. Depending on the economic situation, trade leaders oscillated
between promoting foreign expertise and complaining of its harmful effects.
Out of such attitudes periodically came the invention of trade organizations,
including the founding of the British Hairdressers' Benevolent and Provident
Institution in 1831, precipitated by the "annoyance" among hairdressers when
Queen Adelaide appointed a French hairdresser.[50]

Through the 1860s and 1870s, London hairdressers continued to combat
disparagement of taste levels of British stylemakers taken up and recirculated
in Victorian popular culture. This derision manifested itself in allied trades,
notably in battles between London and Parisian dressmakers for ascendency
and the right to "set fashions."[51] Similar debates emerged in relation to fashions

in hair. While attending a "Grand Soiree" of British hairdressers in 1866, columnist Andrew Halliday noted reluctance among British tradesmen to admit foreign popularity, while trade publications expressed anger over clients' partiality for foreign hairdressers (Figure 3.5). Yet, Halliday reported that it was "whispered to [him] confidentially" that "British ladies [had] a predilection for *French* hairdressers." Noting that this was in keeping with British favor for "Italian singers, and French cooks, and Spanish dancers," Halliday downplayed British hairdressers' concerns, concluding that they did not "want protection," but merely "fair play" from the "ladies of England."[52]

Yet other forums revealed British tradesmen's very real insecurities, which were no doubt amplified by the dominance of foreign hairdressers as leading educators in the latest styles and techniques. Through most of the latter half of the nineteenth century, Le Club de la Société du Progrès de la Coiffure (est. 1863) represented the sole teaching society available to London's ambitious hairdressing assistants. On the first Tuesday of every month, members paid one shilling to attend a "grand course" in hairdressing at its headquarters in Mayfair's Charles Street, Grosvenor Square.[53] Employing a rotating schedule, three members executed a Court hairstyle on live female models, which was

Figure 3.5 A Hair-Dressing Exhibition (n.d.). Universal History Archive/UIG via Getty Images.

then subject to formal (and informal) judging by their peers. However, the official objective of La Société was not to educate low-class assistants for professional advancement, but to "give advice to Foreign Hairdressers coming to work in England"—that is, continental competition. "As its name indicates," La Société "was entirely dominated by Frenchmen [and] all the business is transacted in French." There was also a limit on British membership to La Société's executive, with no more than "'three English Members' on the Committee at a time."[54]

Such exclusionary practices drew the ire of writers at trade journal *The Hairdresser's Chronicle.* One article probing "why the Société was not more successful" opened with an apology for its simplified observations, since the columnist was "addressing many [readers] who may not be fully conversant with the English language." The language barrier proved a real impediment for many of London's assistants and meant that few British assistants attended the courses.[55] It also proved to be an issue among British board members. In one meeting of La Société's supervisory board, "the whole of the Englishmen present rose to leave the room, causing considerable confusion" after President Eugène Menard refused to translate a tabled motion into English for non-French attendees.[56]

Even in the case of assistants willing to receive their training in French, their trade standing and physical location hindered their attendance at Société gatherings, as many employers simply denied the extra hours required to travel to lessons. "If an increase in members is to be desired, and we take it for granted that is so, then a more central position should at once be sought for and obtained," noted *The Hairdressers' Chronicle* after La Société's formation. The Mayfair location precluded the attendance of assistants working in eastern and southerly neighborhoods, all of which happened to host low-class shops: Islington, Kingsland, Hackney, Borough, Southwark. The author subsequently called on the board to "select a location that the omnibuses from every part of London all travel to."[57] Not only was travel difficult, but employees in the City, South London, and East End—depicted as "never aspir[ing] to be anything higher than [a] Barber"— lived in the shop and worked too late into the night to attend sessions that ran from 9:30 to 10:45 p.m.[58] Critics subsequently denounced both the trade policies of London employers, as well as the inflexibility of La Société's French managers.

In addition to widespread distrust of French trade leaders, there emerged, from the late 1870s, extensive anti-German sentiment when they gained widespread employment in working-class barbershops in the East End.[59] Reportedly "clannish" in nature, German nationals assumed responsibility for a second purportedly "English-speaking" training institution, the International

Hair-dressers' Society (est. 1893).[60] Based in the Harmony Club at Fitzroy Square, the Society offered lessons to its 400 members every Wednesday night at 9:30 p.m.[61] While touted as an improvement on the French Société, the amenities of the new institution did not significantly differ from their French predecessors. Fitzroy Square remained a considerable distance to travel after a day's labor, and again the Society developed into a refuge for non-native hairdressers, this time of German origin. Although "all nationalities were accepted," a late-addition rule stated that no more than two English members were permitted to join the committee of seven German-born masters. While the Harmony Club represented the interests of high-end German assistants, a second club, the Concordia in Houndsditch, assisted more recent German arrivals to London's hairdressing trade community. Managed by Mr. Richter, "an old German whose English is sadly to lack, and who is also very deaf," the Club was patronized by German and Polish Jews employed in the poorest of London's East End barbershops.[62] Rarely mentioned in trade periodicals, the Club accommodated a group of émigré hairdressers and barbers operating outside of mainstream trade connections.[63]

Consumer preference for foreigners, compounded by feelings of exclusion from their professional organizations, was not the only factor contributing to enduring tensions between British and non-native tradesmen. Some employers alleged that foreign assistants had a better work ethic and subsequently made more valuable employees than their British counterparts. Even some advocates of British laborers conceded to the professionalism of non-British—and particularly German—hairdressers and barbers. "[E]ven if not as good barbers as the English (and as to this there is some difference of opinion)," wrote Charles Booth, German barbers "have the reputation of being more industrious, more cleanly, and more sober, and for these reasons even many English masters prefer them." Any German inferiority to French hairdressing skills, he added, was "share[d] with our own countrymen."[64]At the same time, this unwavering work ethic could be seen as an attempt to undercut efforts at labor improvements. Trade leaders collectively blamed non-native hairdressers for the lack of political mobilization in the hairdressing trades. Davin, being the proprietor of an employment agency for "barbers of the lower class," blamed thwarted efforts at work hour reforms squarely on Germans. He claimed that "the Englishman could work among themselves to close on Sunday" if there "were no German barbers … but now if an Englishman have [sic] to close on Sunday it would only mean that a German would fit up a shop close by and keep open."[65]

Trade publications perpetuated distrust among British tradesmen by recounting examples of underhanded business arrangements of recent émigrés. Hairdresser C. H. Cole, a self-proclaimed "Cosmopolitan," described how, after he claimed to have no vacancies, a German applicant declared, "'If you employ me, I will do three men's work, and work for less money than the others.'" "Can we wonder at the dislike, and even hatred with which Englishmen look upon foreigners," Cole demanded, "and Germans especially, who use such unscrupulous and sneakish means of getting employment?"[66]

Complaints of undercutting by foreign workers notwithstanding, the enduring popularity of continental fashions meant that non-British nationals flourished in London's hair industry. By the late nineteenth century, Booth's contemporary examination of trade directories found that, of the 1,696 master hairdressers, 518 or 31 percent were "obviously foreigners."[67] Without older forms of professional guild organization to regulate admission into the trade, foreign labor was treated as an adversarial faction working against native-born British hairdressers.[68] From 1868, trade conflicts would be further exacerbated by relationships defined by London's social geographies, as embodied in the personas of Robert Douglas in the West and his chief critic, hairdresser Edwin Creer, in the East.

From East to West

If employment in the working-class hair trades was transient and unpredictable, these same fluid qualities meant the possibility for social mobility and professional advancement. Assistants moved between London's hairdressing establishments and neighborhoods, fostering opportunities for cross-class interactions that were uncommon in other urban trades. As demand was relatively universal, the class of customers varied considerably; a client could be "a nobleman, [and] the next perhaps a neighbouring shopkeeper, while a third may possibly be a lady of title or a milliner's apprentice." This required that a hairdresser adopt chameleon-like qualities to ensure future business. Adjusting their behavior to suit an individual client meant that a hairdresser was "require[d] to be affable with all, offending none."[69] As Eugène Rimmel pointed out in his annual speech as Chair of the Hairdressers' Benevolent and Provident Institution, "the hairdresser was a gentleman and an artist; he must be so from the very nature of his business."[70]

Writing of the French scene, historian Steven Zdatny illuminates parallel conditions in which Parisian hairdressers "worked under a great diversity of conditions, from the wretched to the sumptuous."[71] In London, these conditions mapped on to very specific urban geographies, with many working-class assistants aspiring to make their way across London's imaginary East/West divide to earn high-end work in Mayfair or Knightsbridge. Numerous scholars have documented the demarcation of Victorian London as a classed landscape, divided between the plebeian East and elite West End.[72] While the hair trades seemingly aligned with this imagined terrain—with trade-oriented working-class penny barbers in the East and South juxtaposed against high-end increasingly mixed-gender hairdressing parlors in the West—the mobility of workers signaled the permeability of these geographic and socioeconomic boundaries.[73]

To do so, the profession demanded an elaborate mode of professional performance from tradesmen and the ability to adapt to the class standing of the client in the chair. The more skilled a hairdresser was at these performances, the greater the possibilities for class passing and professional success, a phenomenon that was satirized by the *Hairdressers' Weekly Journal* (*HWJ*) in 1884 (Plate 10). But frequent interactions with the upper classes could purportedly take its toll on assistants. Hairdresser Hans Hugo of Covent Garden claimed the reason tradesmen drank "a good deal at nights, and as a class live[d] rather loose lives" was due to "the fact that they mix so much with persons of a higher social class than themselves, and try to ape their ways."[74] Despite some assistants' best efforts at genteel class passing, *HWJ* ruefully noted how satirical magazines made fun of hairdressers' poor diction, "ever lashing us into fury for our murdered English."[75] Yet, instances of successful appropriations of a higher-class demeanor could facilitate a young man's move to the professional wig and barbershops of the City or the elite parlors of the West End.

Earning a placement in one of these high-end locales seemingly improved the quality of life of an assistant. In both the City and the West End, assistants could live off the premises, which made for higher wages and greater personal autonomy.[76] The varied demands of elite clientele also meant that the work was anything but monotonous. West End patrons (or "victims," as they were dubbed by one assistant) were purported to pay as much as 5s. 6d. per shave compared to the standard "ha'penny" or penny treatments in the East. "We have a gentleman who comes here thrice weekly and pays 16s. 6d. every Saturday morning for services," revealed one anonymous gentlemen's hand. "He must have a special soap and a fresh cake every time; but the expensive item is a small bottle of eau-de-cologne [*sic*], with which we spray his face over and over until the perfume is exhausted." The process took over a half hour to perform. Another customer demanded a wash of his own recipe, comprising "of bay rum, mixed with white of egg, half an ounce of French perfume, and a few drops of lemon juice." Another "society actor" demanded the assistant perform fifteen minutes of "rubbing his face after shaving" so as to "beautify the skin." A fourth "young man of fashion" requested a private room "to sleep with his face buried in fragrant foam previous to submitting his skin to the steel."[77] The work of lady's hands—that is, male hairdressers serving women—was no less attractive, garnering them access to the homes of London's most exclusive families as they attended ladies in their dressing rooms, earning up to 1s. 6d. in the process.[78]

Yet, work in the City and West End could also mean arduous backstage conditions specific to the hairdressing trades, circumstances that were often concealed by sociable niceties between hairdressers and clients. From a standard wage of 30s. to 40s. per week, a high-end gentlemen's hand often had to purchase "his own tools, razor, scissors and combs," unlike those employed in low-class shops that fell short of new standards of sanitation and hygiene. Gentlemen's hands also had "to buy aprons, and in some cases pay for their washing," which could run upward of £20 a year.[79] Despite their luxurious decors, elite haircutting rooms could also make for intolerable places of work. As the century progressed, elaborate water piping systems, necessitated by the rise of American-style shampooing, gave rise to "unexpected but prevalent evil." In even the most fashionable haircutting establishments, the drain pipes attached to elaborate sink fittings were "in direct communication with a soil pipe or other drainage apparatus" and "air of deadly character [was] directly imbibed from inhalation over the basin" or diffused throughout the cutting room.[80] Furthermore, as in London's low-end shops, the hours could be excessively long. The irregular hours specific to the social season meant that, "to oblige customers" and their employers, assistants "commenced at seven in the morning and continued till nine o'clock in the evening" every night.[81] As in the East End, shops remained open on Saturdays until midnight, only to reopen at six or seven o'clock on Sunday morning. Demands on assistants grew if neighboring shops stayed open for longer hours, forcing competitors to extend their own hours.[82]

In spite of the long hours, classified advertisements in leading trade periodicals reveal constant demand for male hairdressers in the West End and City. This westerly exodus, intensifying through the 1860s, further strained class and geographic divisions within the industry, eventually boiling over into intense competition for high-end jobs. By the mid-1860s hairdressers and barbers were, by their own account, "a profession … not only without voice, but dead at heart."

MR. CREER.

Figure 3.6 "Mr. Creer," *Hairdressers' Weekly Journal* (August 1, 1885): 490. Courtesy of © The British Library Board (Shelfmark 4238.301000).

It was out of this "offspring of necessity" that *The Hairdressers' Chronicle and Trade Journal* first appeared in November 1866 to represent "a class which, of late years, had rather descended than advanced in the social scale."[83] With the financial backing of publisher Robert Hovenden, editor Edwin Creer (1823–1897) appealed to hairdressers across London, who he claimed were "entitled to an organ of their own" that advocated for industry improvements[84] (Figure 3.6).

According to Creer, London's "hairdressing community" in the 1860s was marked by "mutual distrust," "perpetual feud[ing]," and "bitter antagonism" within its ranks.[85] Creer no doubt embellished intertrade antagonisms to draw attention to specific issues. Nevertheless, the conflicts described in the *Chronicle* pointed more generally to problems with new forms of Victorian commerce. New types of economic relationships, argued Creer and others, undermined customary trade organization and led to the deterioration of traditional relationships between *and* among employer and employees. This awareness—a cross-class phenomenon, expressed by masters and assistants alike—was overwhelmingly characterized by expressions of loss of community and the inability to organize within industry lines. Despite 1866 being one of most lucrative years in the hair trades given fashionable demands for false hair,[86] London's hair and beauty traders expressed concern that major shifts in the industry were undermining traditional business practices and relationships. The community had, according to Creer, "drawn exclusive lines between East and West," and "recognised no ability beyond certain narrow bounds of civic demarcation." What was once "a slight distinction" was now, according to Creer, "a class prejudice."[87]

If Creer represented the interests of the East, it can be argued that Robert Douglas and H. P. Truefitt stood as his contemporaries in the West, instituting the very trade developments that, at times, stoked internal antagonisms. But, outside of Creer, these shifts were more often framed as innovations rather than disruptions, and, despite his critics, Douglas enjoyed a fine reputation across the trade. Deriving from humble Scottish origins, he established himself as one of the West End's foremost high-end hairdressers and perfumers; only five years after opening his New Bond Street location in 1856, he employed twenty-eight men, one boy, and an apprentice.[88] Throughout, he claimed to promote "the interest of [his] profession and the happiness and prosperity of the families connected with it" via campaigns for improved labor conditions. This included the early closing movement, and in November 1866, Douglas, along with West-End proprietors like Truefitt, came out in support of assistants' calls for earlier hours for evenings and Sundays.[89] And yet, despite these displays of solidarity, when faced with a dissatisfied male staff in 1868, Douglas locked them out and turned to a new type of more conciliatory worker to serve his clientele: female hairdressers. In doing so, he not only introduced a new element to existing, conflicting trade factions, but definitively transformed the composition of London's beauty service industry.

"A New Phase in London"

In and of itself, Douglas's mass hiring of a female workforce in 1868 did not make for a trade "revolution" despite the claims of Emily Faithfull and others. Female hairdressers had in fact done business throughout the nineteenth century, if not earlier. Between 1849 and 1887, women made up between 2 and 4 percent of "Hairdressers and Perfumers" listed in London trade directories.[90] This is a decidedly low estimate, as feminist scholars have argued that nineteenth-century trade directories included only a small contingent of London's businesswomen.[91] It may be assumed that some women also worked in less visible roles as wives, assistants, or itinerant hairdressers privately serving clients in their homes (Plate

11). For example, "respectable elderly women," reminisced one columnist, would "call on families every month, and cut and dress the ladies' and children's hair."[92] Often widowed or never married, earlier generations of female hairdressers frequently worked without assistants. These were not young, lower-middle-class women making informed decisions to take up a "trade," but women who worked for their livelihoods. They were subsequently absent from campaigns through the latter nineteenth century to make hairdressing a "respectable" trade for the surplus of young, employable women.[93]

Regardless of precedents in female hairdressing, it became apparent that London's upper-middle-class female clients embraced the "introduction" of female hands; Douglas's move to hire female hairdressers proved a financial success, and the initiative's unsavory origins did not figure beyond the trade journals. Despite later attempts by trade leaders to limit the hiring of female hands, enthusiastic reviews from London's female shoppers seem to have defined public opinion. Coverage of Douglas's establishment inspired a flood of positive responses in not only the women's press, but also in London's mainstream publications. Some women expressed relief at being freed from the bullying of male hairdressers. Writing to the *Pall Mall Gazette*, one female correspondent recounted a story of "intimidation" at the hands of two separate male assistants at high-end establishments, who declared her to be imminently bald-headed and grey-haired. "Courageously refus[ing]" their high-priced tonics, she noted she "had always felt it derogatory to the dignity of a man that he should be … employed" as a ladies' hairdresser.[94] Writers at *The Graphic* also declared no employment to be more suitable for women than hairdressing.[95] The *Woman's Penny Paper* seconded this sentiment: "[h]air dressing is one of the most essentially womanly occupations," and ladies should subsequently "avail themselves of the deft fingers of a woman."[96] Correspondent Alice B. LeGeyt wrote to the *Lady's Own Paper* to recommend Douglas's parlor, having been "shown the establishment" by the proprietor himself.[97]

Having introduced female laborers, both Douglas and his neighbor Truefitt took the opportunity to make their business more hospitable to female clientele through the careful redesign of commercial space and the creation of rooms devoted explicitly to the "feminine." Previously, neither businessman seemingly provided private areas for female customers venturing outside the home to have their hair cut and dressed. Following other commercial trends in the West End aimed at attending to elite women, Douglas and Truefitt invited mobile, increasingly visible female consumers into refurbished spaces specifically organized to ensure propriety and privacy.

These renovation projects received extensive publicity in the periodical press via interviews and self-produced advertisements. Truefitt marked the occasion with a series of large pictorial advertisements devoted to the "extensive alterations" to his shop at 13 and 14 Old Bond Street, which "obtain[ed] a splendid suite of rooms for carrying out" a "much approved innovation."[98] The advertisement spotlighted a lady hairdresser washing the hair of an anonymous female client (Figure 3.7). With her face downward in the washbasin—a standard practice through the latter half of the nineteenth century—Truefitt's illustrated advertisement preserved the privacy of even a fictitious client-subject. This new space not only created "splendid suites" to entice women but carefully mapped gender divides onto what was only recently a firmly masculine site of sociability and service.

Figure 3.7 Advertisement for H. P. Truefitt, "Ladies' Hairdressing" (n.d.). Courtesy of John Murray Publishers.

The redesign—and feminization—of commercial space subsequently changed male clients' consumer experiences. By constructing separate entranceways for women, customers of either sex were assured they would not cross paths, as "ladies" would "not be subjected to the inconvenience of having to pass through or in fact see the gentlemen's room."[99] As the main provider of female-to-female services, Douglas went so far as to divide his two Bond Street addresses by gender: No. 23 was converted into the ladies' shop, while No. 21 was devoted exclusively to preexisting male clients. These two buildings operated independently of one another. In fact, the arrangement of the building meant that a visitor to the ladies' parlor had to "descend ... again to the ground floor" and exit on to Bond Street in order to enter the men's saloon "at the back of 21 shop."[100]

As more recent additions to London shops, some ladies' hairdressing parlors were located on the second floor directly above gentlemen's hairdressing rooms. Gendered divisions of space could be further reinforced by different decorating schemes on the two levels. At Nestor Tirard's shop at 39 Curzon Street, the decor in the main men's saloon featured a "vein marble chimney piece" and "moulded doors paper[ed] with white and brown." Increasingly luxurious fittings appeared as one moved upstairs, with "statuary marble pieces" presiding over the ladies parlor, whose rooms were "papered with paper and gilt moulding."[101] For his female clients, Douglas constructed "a waiting-room, with rich Persian carpet, beautiful fire, and a table heaped with fashionable newspapers and magazines suitable for lady-like waiting moments." In the haircutting room, women were greeted by "handsome grained panels" and "snug green curtains," which gave "a tantalising appearance to the place peculiarly suited to the supposed (or imagined) operations carried on therein."[102]

The illusion of privacy in the very public act of luxury consumption and bodily management was a primary concern for both client and shopkeeper, as it was "in private comfort" that the female consumer could "make those purchases which most conduce to individual effect." The management of space supported customer desires for discretion, despite services taking place in open, populated spaces. The "Ladies' Room" at Douglas's shop consisted of a long, wide single room marked along one side with private alcoves; each of these "very small apartments" accommodated a single female client and was "replete with every known (and to the male sex *un*known) appliance for adding lustre to the female complexion and toilet."[103] Contrasting the privacy seemingly afforded by these individual alcoves was the stately room in which they were nestled. An illustration depicted a relatively indiscreet public space, reminiscent of other

Figure 3.8 Robert Douglas's Ladies' Hair-Cutting Saloon at 23 New Bond Street in "Women at Work, No. 6: Hairdressers," *Women and Work* 12 (August 22, 1874): 2. Courtesy of © The British Library Board (Shelfmark 017160165).

nineteenth-century communal institutions like museum galleries or reading rooms (Figure 3.8). And yet, according to a female columnist, "each lady enjoys entire privacy," which seemingly protected "those who are waiting their turn catching hairs upon their clothes."[104] In spite of the grand space "furnished with every possible requisite for every branch and stage of the toilet," Douglas's room was insufficient in one respect. "The room is not large enough to accommodate the customers that flock to the saloon in the season."[105]

Gender divisions served not only to protect feminine propriety in the early days of elite female shopping but also as a means to preserve the masculine comforts typically offered to existing male patrons. Douglas's haircutting saloon for gentlemen presented "the appearance of a comfortable reading room, with large fire, green baize covered table spread with newspapers, glass gaseliers, and many other appliances for comfort." Glass panels on each wall gave the illusion of enlarged, open apartments. Similar to the lady's department, its principal features were "unique alcove boxes," paved with encaustic tile and lined with semi-opaque glass sides. Men's saloons were promoted not only as a site of luxury grooming, however, but as a space of congenial social interactions between peers. Members of Parliament and the gentry patronized Douglas and Truefitt; "to meet at Douglas's [was] nearly as common an appointment as the West-end affords." The saloon was touted as an extension of the West End's Clubland, all the while affording "every requisite likely to be required for a gentleman's hair—notably, pomades, washes, brilliantine, cosmetics, astringents, lotions, etc."[106]

Haircutting saloons' standing as markedly masculine domains meant that, prior to the introduction of the coiffeuse, many elite women commissioned house calls from a local hairdresser or relied on domestic servants to prepare all aspects of their evening *toilette*.[107] It was subsequently little surprise that, when opening his ladies' parlor, Douglas only engaged women "who [had] been lady's maids, thus having already acquired a knowledge of their business."[108] This was a savvy move on Douglas's part, as such "business" would have included not only the dressing of the hair but also the deferential manners demanded in domestic service. Not leaving it to chance, Douglas expected applicants to submit themselves to rigorous examinations that determined whether they were of "the highest character." Douglas reportedly designed five months of training in which the coiffeuse was to learn "anything more that [was] required." This was a slightly less intensive schedule than that of his neighbor Truefitt, who trained lady hairdressers in his workshops where "a moderately apt girl [was] ready to take her turn in the hair-dressing salon in six or nine months."[109]

From his initial pool of applicants, Douglas employed twenty young women who he transformed, via costume and grooming, into an ordered group of exemplary employees. "Attired uniformly in black," he demanded they be tall and "at least good-looking."[110]After dyeing their hair a uniform "nut-brown," they were "required to dress their hair according to the mode" to afford lady customers "an opportunity (which was impossible with men) of seeing how a particular fashion appears on a living model." At both Douglas's and Truefitt's shops, scheduling demands were markedly less stringent than those made on male assistants. Employees worked from 9:30 a.m to 6:30 p.m, with an hour break for dinner and a half hour for tea. In the case that an assistant worked through her dinner break, she departed early. Employees at both Douglas's and Truefitt's earned generous weekly wages of 32s. to 35s., and all overtime work was compensated.[111]

Douglas and Truefitt may not have "revolutionised the trade," but their initiatives most certainly aligned with growing attention to London's increasingly visible female hairdressers. While "not plentiful," lady hairdressers continued to "spring ... up here and there" through the 1880s.[112] Census returns from 1881 documented 3,447 male and 295 female hairdressers employed in London. Seemingly a small percentage of the trade in London, the number of female hairdressers in fact outnumbered the total number of tradesmen operating as hairdressers in major urban centers including Manchester (274) and Leeds (250).[113] Some female hairdressers were former employees of Douglas, who set up their own shops independent of male ownership and management. A notable case was Harriet Muston (b. 1858) and Dinah "Rose" Collins (1856–1945), who jointly ran a popular court hairdressing business in Mayfair for over ten years.[114] In 1880, the two set up "a tiny *atelier*" at 48 South Molton Street, adjacent to New Bond Street.[115] Within a decade, they developed such a following that "a row of ladies [would] always be found sitting against the wall … sternly refusing the ministrations of the trained assistants." Press articles described primarily aristocratic clientele, as well as stage actress Ellen Terry and "her abundance of fair hair."[116]

Muston and Collins were not the only female hands who successfully transitioned to the world of individual enterprise, as other former hairdressing assistants branched out on their own accord. In 1888, Hannah Latter (1853–1903) went into business for herself at St. George's Place, Knightsbridge after "many years' experience at Douglas."[117] The daughter of an alehouse keeper, she spent her youth like many other future lady hairdressers: working as a ladies' maid. Not long after opening her shop, Latter was "getting a reputation for hair dyes," as "rich women are in the habit of having their hair dyed." It was, by all accounts, a long and protracted process. "'I was eight hours dyeing a lady's hair, the other day'" she recalled in one interview, as "'it was coal black'" which she dyed to a "'lovely auburn.'"[118] While detailing the length of the procedure, Latter stopped short of revealing how readers could replicate the experience in their own homes. Fanny Ives of 7 Blandford Street was also known for her skills in dyeing, but offered home visits rather than working out of a commercial shop. Ives's house calls may have filled a market niche by appealing to older forms of discreet domestic service.[119]

From the late 1860s, then, the practice of women's hairdressing moved increasingly from the boudoir to the public world of fashionable consumption, providing female shoppers with access to new West End spaces, as well as new opportunities for expression via self-fashioning and bodily transformation. Elite women consumers eagerly patronized lady hairdressers, enlisting in marketing schemes reminiscent of those at men's West-End toilet clubs. At one saloon, female customers signed a monthly "contract" which offered a negligible discount but allowed women to visit their hairdresser "regularly every day to have their hair dressed." According to one source, a few did it twice a day.[120] Always the savvy businessman, Douglas issued twenty-six "shilling hair-cutting tickets" for £1, saving the buyer 6s. on the packet. According to Douglas, the scheme was a great success "especially where there are many in a family."[121]

By 1891, the collective efforts of enterprising capitalists and feminist advocates in opening new hairdressing spaces—for both consumers and employees— seemed to achieve modest advances across the trade. Of 6,002 wigmakers and hairdressers counted in 1891, 521 or some 9 percent were women.[122] Praised for its "good wages, easy hours, light work, the society of refined people, open, well-ventilated apartments, kindness and courtesy, and certainty," employment as a female hairdresser purportedly stood in stark contrast to the proletarian conditions of many men in the trade. While certainly exaggerated for popular press coverage, this rosy envisioning of female employment dramatically contrasted that of their male counterparts, who labored under exploitive working conditions that continued to define the trade into the twentieth century.

Conclusions

In late 1869, trade leaders held a "Meeting of Master Hairdressers" to decide, as a collective, whether to hire female hands. The meeting proved inconclusive, but most agreed on the inevitability of the gendered shift. At the conclusion of the three-hour meeting, attendees passed a motion that "females would ultimately be employed in the business to a large extent; and that it was useless passing any resolution in this crude shape of the movement, either approving or disapproving of it." Coincidentally, the meeting took place at the same Hanover Square rooms that had hosted Emily Faithfull earlier that year.[123]

In the end, the introduction of women into London's hairdressing service sector was not a temporary diversion from "real" labor issues, but a permanent development. Women became another group in the complex networks comprising London's hair trades: West End businessmen, British-born assistants, penny barbers, émigré laborers, and new female employees. Significant differences along class, gender, and ethnic lines meant that each group had diverse economic and personal motivations. And yet, as a whole, they collectively sought trade respectability, striving to be considered a serious component of London's laboring service classes.

In many ways, nineteenth-century trade initiatives designed to unite London's hair trades exacerbated tensions based on class, gender, and location in metropolitan space. Trade leaders including Robert Douglas, H. P. Truefitt, and Edwin Creer framed their initiatives in relational terms, blaming poor, foreign, capitalist, or female elements for the profession's demise. However, it was London's changing retail scene—and consumer tastes—that established the conditions for foreign and female laborers to "usurp" the rights of British-born assistants. The entry of women workers into hairdressing also reflected broader shifts defining London's new commercial geographies, shifts that would continue to remap the beauty and grooming trades into the early twentieth century. Despite efforts by London's hairdressers and barbers to resist the feminization of commercial trades serving the female body, a growing contingent of elite and middle-class female consumers demanded the privacy afforded by female service workers attending them. As we shall see, this demand would eventually open a new "island of opportunity" for female workers, not to mention female entrepreneurs in London's expanding beauty service sector.

At the same time, Victorian professionalizing initiatives paved the way for trade organizations, limited liability legislation, and technologies in production and distribution to widen the divisions—both spatial and symbolic—between London's small- and mid-sized ventures, employers, and employees. Successful firms led by a handful of male beauty providers, including hairdressers Robert Douglas and H. P. Truefitt, reached new levels of capitalization from the mid-century onward, leaving humble enterprises in their wake. Implicated in this were London perfumers, who transitioned into roles as leading manufacturers operating on a global scale, as exemplified in the illuminating life and career of Eugène Rimmel.

Professionalizing Perfumery:
Eugène Rimmel

In 1883, the *Hairdressers' Weekly Journal* (*HWJ*) launched an extended series praising the lives and work of "Celebrities Connected with the Trade." Introducing the column in February, editors explained their decision to highlight "personal characteristics" of "men whose names are 'familiar in our mouths as household words.'"[1] In the years that followed, the series offered biographical sketches that praised the professional achievements of a particular cohort of London's leading hairdressers and perfumers: familiar names like Robert Hovenden, Robert Douglas, and H. P. Truefitt, alongside others like wigmaker Joseph Lichtenfeld and Westminster hairdresser Walter Hopekirk.[2] While teasing some personal details about the individuals behind London's leading beauty firms, the profiles ultimately followed a standard form of Victorian biography. They focused on the professional activities of the trade's "Great Men," celebrating their contributions not only to industry but also to the public good.[3] Profiles typically opened with a tale of traders' humble origins, periodically in foreign nations, tracing their apprenticeship in leading London hairdressing or perfumery houses, to the expansion of their firms, to their establishment as fixtures in London's professional beauty organizations: trade guilds, benevolent societies, and in the pages of leading industry publications like the *HWJ*. In this way, the series anointed a small cohort of traders as industry authorities, bestowing upon them a "Celebrity" status and securing their standing as exemplars in a pivotal moment of professionalization among London's hairdressers and perfumers.

Yet, the ascendency of these traders was by no means secure, something that was evident in the need for a "Celebrity" series in the first place. A closer look at traders' individual stories reveals multiple, contested factors shaping the success of these men, while others around them tried and failed to reach such heights. This especially comes to the fore in the case of Eugène Rimmel (1820–1887), the first trader featured in the 1883 "Celebrity" series (Figure 4.1). From relatively

Figure 4.1 Eugène Rimmel (n.d.). Courtesy of The New York Public Library Digital Collections.

humble locations in St. Anne's Soho, Rimmel experienced breakout success when his elaborate perfume fountain became a hit of the Great Exhibition of 1851. Over twenty years, he developed a global brand, establishing himself as Britain's foremost manufacturer of perfumery and beautifying goods. Yet, this was not a straightforward trajectory to trade ascendency, and the *HWJ* profile revealed an important paradox. The preeminent representative of British perfumery was not, in fact, British but *French*. According to a similar profile in *The Chemist and Druggist*, Rimmel's foreignness enhanced his work. "He owes much of his reputation and success to the advantages of his dual nature and training," the columnist argued, "combining the lively imagination of the Frenchman with the sound practical knowledge of the Englishman."[4] What his natal character allegedly lacked in business acumen, he made up by mimicking the inherent characteristics of his British contemporaries. Rimmel was simultaneously continental and British, an outsider and a citizen.

Trade journal profiles emphasized the fascinating role of duality in Rimmel's business transactions and in the public professional personas that he himself cultivated. The profiles also raised the question of the multiple national loyalties among London's émigré populations. As a Frenchman living in London, Rimmel's story offers an important perspective on personal and public representations of British nationalities, reflecting the complex experiences of Europeans operating within Britain's commercial metropolis. Ultimately, Rimmel exploited the conditions of possibility fostered by multiple national loyalties to align with an explicitly British narrative of professionalization. In doing so, he established himself among a powerful contingent of West End beauty proprietors—the "Celebrities of the Trade"—who, beginning in the 1860s, expanded their businesses into multinational firms. This small cohort of successful London hairdressers and perfumers opened new locations across the British world, relocated production to larger manufactories, and moved their families to London's emerging residential suburbs.

Focusing on a single individual, Eugène Rimmel, to frame the British beauty industry's local and transnational interests also reveals the ways that space and place—on the local and national scale, with its real and imaginative possibilities— shaped perfumers' commercial practices. Historians have acknowledged the importance of "national cultural characteristics" in determining business success.[5] As historian Geoffrey Jones has observed, Rimmel's outsider status "proved no handicap to his business, and may indeed have played some role in his recognition of opportunities which others did not see."[6] Situating Rimmel in the context of London's beauty business and its commercial neighborhoods reveals the ways he mobilized his foreignness to position himself as a knowledgeable authority on continental tastes.[7] Rimmel—an urban, middle-class émigré— seemed an unlikely advocate of luxury consumption in mid-century London. As nineteenth-century commentators bristled over incoming "floods" of émigrés, Rimmel's origins represented potentially problematic connections to local and continental French networks. By focusing on ethnicity and urban space, however, we can see the ways that Rimmel aligned with British commercial practices, all the while promoting national differences in the name of competition. In the wake of heightened British nationalism, he commodified his Frenchness while definitively situating himself as a London perfumer.[8]

By highlighting his connections to urban migration networks and transnational trading communities, we also see that Rimmel's entrepreneurial success was in no way a singular effort. It depended on long-term and ongoing connections to continental family members, Soho's Francophone community, fellow tradesmen, and, in many ways, the international consuming public. Ultimately, Rimmel brought together multiple national loyalties to align with an explicitly British narrative of business success that dominated nineteenth-century economic discourses.[9] Moving through three modes of Rimmel's gradual emergence as Britain's leading perfumer—on the local, the national, and the global scale—we also see that, despite foreign origins, Rimmel participated in the global circulation of aesthetic and cultural values about "Britishness" in an era of high imperialism.

"La Petite France"

Rimmel's ties to a transnational network of perfumers, traders, and consumers began with his arrival in London as a member of Soho's nineteenth-century Francophone migration networks. In the wake of continental political unrest through the 1840s and 1850s, an influx of French, German, and Italian émigrés sought political asylum in London. Many others arrived as migrants and artisans seeking opportunity in London's manufacturing trades. London's foreign-born population subsequently surged, from thirteen thousand in the 1840s to twenty-six thousand by 1851. Foreigners settled throughout London and its suburbs, but the area around Soho's Leicester Square became, according to Jerry White, "the very epicentre of refugee life."[10]

Rimmel's father, Hyacinthe, was one such continental tradesman coming to try his hand in London. In 1830, Hyacinthe accepted an invitation from the widow of renowned London perfumer Joseph Delcroix to take over the recently deceased Delcroix's New Bond Street premises.[11] By 1834, the association was over, and Hyacinthe set up an independent business in Soho. Despite his venerable apprenticeship under some of Paris and London's most renowned perfumers, Hyacinthe spent considerable time in avoiding his creditors. As was the case for many small-scale retailing firms of the mid-century, his modest venture on Gerrard Street, Soho operated under constant threat of bankruptcy.[12]

As Hyacinthe Rimmel's case suggests, financial success was by no means guaranteed in Soho's Francophone community of artisanal laborers, including jewelers, carpenters, and engravers.[13] Featuring "many … primitive little shops," the area around Leicester Square was reportedly dominated in this period by "French families of humble and lowly position"[14] (Figure 4.2). According to another commentator, Soho's small family firms rarely lasted beyond a single generation, and contemporaries subsequently considered the "French colony"

Figure 4.2 Ryders Court and the corner of Lisle Street, Soho (n.d.). © Look and Learn / Peter Jackson Collection.

less important in business than other national groups.[15] Despite Hyacinthe's early establishment in Soho and its émigré population, he was forced to abandon two perfumery ventures. Neither produced sufficient capital to maintain 13-year-old Eugène in school at Versailles College, and in 1834, the younger Rimmel traveled to London to apprentice at the countinghouse of West Indian merchants Joseph Marryat & Sons.[16] By age 24, Eugène assumed management of the Gerrard Street firm and removed his father from all legal responsibilities relating to the London venture.[17]

Moving beyond his father's orbit of Soho's Little France and its immigrant community, Eugène's ambitions grew to encompass London's metropolitan consumers. As head of the family business, Rimmel endeavored to set up a "great laboratory of sweet scents and pretty sights."[18] This new space would prove a dramatic departure from the narrow, densely populated streets of Soho, which was home to its own less desirable smells: those of "gloomy, mildewed houses" and "flavor[s] of garlic and oil which prevail[ed] about Soho [and] betray[ed] its foreign population."[19] The district had an unsavory reputation that extended beyond its unfamiliar odors. Soho's foreignness held both an exotic and dangerous appeal for London's locally born population.[20] Rimmel subsequently took up more respectable—and trafficked—premises on the wide and stately thoroughfare, the Strand.[21] Relocation to the Strand distanced Rimmel from Soho, with its potentially dangerous associations of Frenchness. Indeed, census records from 1861 show that, of seventy-six heads of household residing on the Strand, Rimmel was the only merchant born outside of Britain. This stood in stark contrast to records of Gerrard Street, where, in 1851, almost 20 percent of its residents were born outside of England.[22] Rimmel's move subsequently marked an important first step toward the sanitization—and eventual commodification—of his foreign origins.[23]

The Strand was already home to a handful of beauty tradesmen including Robert Low, one of London's leading wholesale perfumers.[24] But Rimmel's shop at No. 96 soon outdid Low's as a lavish site of consumption and spectacle, "the centre (scenter) of the Strand."[25] A few years later, Rimmel purchased the extensive building behind the Strand residence, named Beaufort after the Duke who was its principal resident through the late seventeenth century[26] (Figure 4.3). Illustrated advertisements highlighted the striking, stately new premises, where he stored goods and set up the first perfumery manufactory in London to employ female laborers[27] (Figure 4.4). Rimmel intended the conspicuous new location to "look as if filled with gifts from Fairyland."[28] Adopting the increasingly ornate fittings of his neighbors, he displayed his soaps, perfumes, and sundries in elaborately designed plate-windows.[29] He manufactured commercial wares in the neighboring Beaufort Buildings, which held raw materials insured for some £16,000. After 1870, the storehouses' proximity to the new Thames Embankment not only associated Rimmel with metropolitan improvements but also facilitated the rapid transport of goods via the ports of London, a central transportation hub in global trade.[30]

Rimmel's resourceful distributive organization and attention to consumers' material desires generated considerable financial gain. In order to achieve professional repute, London's manufacturing perfumers like Rimmel also felt obliged to promote themselves as leaders of progress and technological development through periodicals, texts, and public lectures aimed at the consuming public. This popularization aligned with a new familiarity among Victorian readers with scientific language. London's manufacturing perfumers publicized their participation in the science of chemistry, promoting technical advances in distilling and extraction at the Great Exhibition in 1851.[31]

Figure 4.3 Eugène Rimmel's factory, 96 The Strand, and Beaufort House (1878). © City of London, London Metropolitan Archives.

Perfumers had long employed elements of organic chemistry, botany, and the pharmaceutical sciences, but the 1851 Exhibition meant unprecedented publicity for the scientific elements of perfumery, in this case the development of fruit-based ethers.[32] Perfumers also aligned themselves with scientific societies like London's Royal College of Chemistry, communicating to the public their affinity with the scientific arts. "To the chemical philosopher," noted perfumer Septimus Piesse in 1855, "the study of perfumery opens a book as yet unread," since the chemical compositions of many essential oils had yet to be defined.[33] Popular studies written by Rimmel and Piesse explained new modes of scientific perfumery, which included techniques in isolating simple odors—known as essential oils or "ottos"—that transformed material processes of perfume manufacturing.[34] They explained delicate new techniques in solvent extraction, which made for greater efficacy in distillation, and steam-powered methods meant that perfumers isolated odiferous plant and animal materials faster and in greater quantities.[35] Rimmel, Piesse, and others' scientific efforts featured in

Figure 4.4 "'Making Valentines' at Rimmel's Beaufort Manufactory," *Illustrated London News* (February 14, 1874). Courtesy of © The British Library Board (Shelfmark P.P.7611).

The British Medical Journal and *Scientific American*, leading publications of the day.[36] Exploiting public fascination with scientific advances, perfumers allied themselves with a rapidly professionalizing body of middle- and upper-class male experts: physicians, scientists, and leisured gentlemen of science.

Early on, Rimmel publicized his scientific and technological advances, and his business developments often featured in London's primary print publications. In particular, his property on the Strand became emblematic of modern modes of production. All "passers-by from afar" were reportedly aware that there was "a constant distilling going on."[37] Each vat in Rimmel's cellar held two to three gallons of his popular perfumes: Star of India, Jockey Club Bouquet, New Mown Hay. Rimmel kept at least ten thousand gallons of Ess (or "Essence") Bouquet on hand, "to be recruited as fast as they are emptied."[38] He produced cosmetiques and violet powders, contributing to the "many ton-weights" of powder "used in [the] country annually."[39] Media outlets also publicized how Rimmel sold perfumed soap and, like other manufacturing perfumers, earned one-third of his returns from its sale.[40] By the 1870s, two tons of soap were "remelted" in the Beaufort manufactory each day.[41] The "scented, polished, pleasant tablets" emerged out of "bubbling masses of brick-dust red, chocolate, or flesh-pink, which men stir[red] like soup in cauldrons."[42] Yet, despite Rimmel's insistence of the industrial sophistication of the trade, images and articles from the periodical press suggest that production did not significantly change from pre-industrial modes. As historian Laura Ugolini has argued of the Victorian clothing industry, industrialized perfumers did not necessarily rely upon "large-scale, steam-driven and mechanised units of production." Rather, individual (and often unskilled) workers were organized into small labor groups, where they performed a single menial task as part of the production process.[43]

Rimmel's move away from "La Petite France" to one of the metropolis' main thoroughfares entailed a second metamorphosis—a formal refashioning of his foreign status through his naturalization as a British citizen. In the latter nineteenth century, non-nationals were barred from owning or inheriting property.[44] To apply for citizenship, an applicant or "memorialist" obtained testimonials from property-holding British-born citizens, often from within local occupational communities. For Rimmel, this included a well-known Lombard Street perfumer, a wholesale druggist in the heart of the City, and two brothers who worked as spirit merchants and export agents on Old Bond Street.[45] In requiring British-born witnesses, the process guaranteed an applicant's social and economic ties to British traders and communities. It was, in this way, a bureaucratic necessity for Rimmel to extend his occupational networks beyond Soho's small community of Francophone merchants and businessmen.

Ultimately, Rimmel's relocation from the cramped yet cosmopolitan community in Soho facilitated his move onto the global stage of transnational commerce. As the naturalization procedures indicate, social and political imperatives—exile out of émigré neighborhoods, acquisition of citizenship, the purchase of British property—opened up economic possibilities for new levels of success. Rimmel's move meant a new public visibility of his commercial ventures and a heightened sense of his foreign tastes and expertise. His move also involved his increased participation in professional hairdressing and perfumery associations. Tributes from his fellow class of traders reveal that Rimmel's professional rise symbolized a new era defined by rationality and open communication within the community of perfumers. This contrasted with the culture of concealment that, as we have seen in Chapter 2, had defined perfume manufacturing via "a mysterious secrecy about their processes."[46] Rimmel's alignment with circulating ideas about the Victorian professional man meant that he fashioned himself a worthy participant in a worldly imperial culture.[47] This cosmopolitan standing would become increasingly important, as Rimmel became a central figure on the global stage as a leading supporter of Victorian international exhibitions.

National Spectacle and "British" Beauty

Although well known within the professional community, Rimmel first gained public renown from his participation in the Great Exhibition of 1851, one of the Victorian era's defining public spectacles. From May through October, the Exhibition captivated London with its industrial wares and technological marvels. It was also a platform from which national interests advertised their country's resources and economic successes through the display of new commodities aimed at the Victorian mass public[48] (Plate 12).

The Exhibition was the ultimate forum for industrial advances, and Rimmel exploited it fully by constructing a large perfume fountain that spouted different toilet vinegars. His display was a great success, "one of the lions of the place" according to *The Chemist and Druggist*, earning Rimmel acclaim for his "novel and ingenious" innovation and enhancing his public role as a Victorian commercial leader. For observers, the ingenuity of Rimmel's Exhibition entry was symbolic of British superiority over a global commodity market; Rimmel was, according to the reviewer, "*par excellence* the man of exhibitions"[49] (Plate 13).

More importantly, events of 1851 introduced him to London's mixed-class consuming public. Critic Anne McClintock argues that the Exhibition supported "an emerging national narrative [which] began to include the working class in the Progress narrative as consumers of national spectacle."[50] Rimmel recognized this opportunity to expand perfumery's consumer base beyond London's elite classes.[51] Located in the Transept Gallery, his fountain attracted thousands of visitors, including the Queen and her royal party, who dipped their handkerchiefs, gloves, even their hands into his "scent fountain, for cooling and perfuming apartments, &c"[52] (Plate 14). The open display of Rimmel's contraption encouraged its consumption by all types of visitors; in many ways, it democratized an expensive, previously inaccessible luxury item. Even though Europe and British India consumed more than 150,000 gallons of perfumed spirits—"eau de Cologne, essence of lavender, esprit de rose"—every year, the exhibit must have represented the first tactile experience of beautifying commodities for many working-class visitors.[53]

The Exhibition also marked a moment when Rimmel's "French artistry" came to the fore, as the spectacle and accessibility of his fountain set him apart from fellow exhibitors in Class 29 (Miscellaneous Manufactures and Small Wares). The category included London's best-known manufacturing perfumers: Charles Yardley, Francis Pears (who won the prize medal for soap), Jean Marie Farina, Alexander Rowland, Frederick Cleaver, Robert Hendrie, J. F. Grossmith, and his neighbor Robert Low[54] (Figure 4.5). While lacking spectacle, rival perfumers also aligned themselves with messages of industrial progress; this happened at a moment when the collection of raw materials central to the perfumery trade had vastly expanded due to colonization and advances in transportation.[55] As Geoffrey Jones has shown, French and British perfumers procured "a range of exotic raw materials by building supply chains which enabled a flow of natural essences from all corners of the world."[56] The industry's primary animal materials derived from species native to the colonial world: the Asian civet cat and the

CLASS 29. *Miscellaneous Manufactures and Small Wares.*

1 ROWLAND & SONS, 20 Hatton Garden, Prop.—Articles of perfumery and for the toilet ; oils, cosmetics, dentifrices, &c.

2 YARDLEY & STATHAM, 7 Vine St. Bloomsbury, Manu.—Specimens of refined scented soaps.

3 RIMMEL, F. 39 Gerrard St. Soho, and 19 Boulevard de la Gare d'Ivry, Paris.—Artificial hair. Scent fountain, for cooling and perfuming apartments, &c. Scented winter bouquets. Perfumery, &c.

4 WILLIAMS & SON, 28 Compton St. Clerkenwell, Manu.—Soaps used by cloth manufacturers, lace-bleachers, and woollen-manufacturers. Scouring soap. Mottled and yellow soap. Fancy soaps, perfumed.

5 TAYLOR, HUMPHREY, & Co. King's Rd. Chelsea.—British liqueurs distilled from foreign and English fruits, &c. Distilled waters, extracted from flowers, herbs, &c. Fancy scented soaps.

6 LLOYD, A. 10 Beak St. Manu.—The Euxesis, for shaving without soap or water.

7 LANGDALE, E. F. 83 Upper Thames St. and 52 Frith St. Soho, Manu.—Specimens of perfumes. Samples of essential oils for distillation, flavouring confectionery, and summer beverages.

8 KNIGHT, J. Old Gravel Lane, St. George's, Middlesex, Manu.—Extra pale-yellow soap, of pure and harmless

F 4

Figure 4.5 "Class 29. Miscellaneous Manufactures and Small Wares (detail)," *Official Catalogue of the Great Exhibition of the Works of Industry of all Nations* (1851). Courtesy of HathiTrust.

musk deer of northern India. Both secrete a substance that, when diluted to one thousand times its volume, featured in French and British perfumery.[57] Musk was in greater demand on the London market, and it supplied the basis of London's most popular soaps, sachet powders, and liquid perfumes.[58] Imported from China, distillers collected the substance from the navel cavities of male musk deer.[59]

International trade exhibitions enabled London's perfumers to publicize these connections to colonized markets, as exporters of manufactured commodities and importers of raw materials. Rimmel was especially aware of this. Just a few years after his 1851 successes, he became a formal representative of continental trade relations by securing a leading role as official documenter of international proceedings. By 1862, he was juror of the Perfumery Class of London's International Exhibition, which featured 232 exhibitors of perfumery.[60] He also served on juries in Dublin and Le Havre and acted as assistant commissioner at 1867's Paris Exhibition.[61] Rimmel's bureaucratic role positioned him as London's authority on international manufacturing skill and taste; he was responsible for the technical and imaginative ranking of perfumers from across the western and imperial world. As critic Catherine Maxwell notes, Rimmel staunchly defended the quality of British production in the wake of its poor international showings, reportedly owing to Britons' overreliance on essential oils.[62] "[I]nstead of wasting silver medals on Belgian, German, and Russian perfumers, whose productions were very inferior," he noted in his survey of the Paris Exhibition, "it would have been more judicious to bestow them on some really deserving British manufacturers, such as Pears, ... Cleaver, ... N. Price and S. Piesse."[63]

Firmly entrenched as London perfumery's representative to the world, Rimmel invoked his dual role as both a foreign and local figure to advocate on behalf of British production.[64] But the duality also functioned in less formal circumstances, namely his commercial advertising and self-promotion. Messages of cultural hybridity, where a foreignness was downplayed to enhance Britishness, most vividly appeared in print productions produced for Rimmel's primary patrons: middle-class and elite female shoppers.

"Natural" Beauty and Global Exchange

Over the course of Rimmel's career, female consumers became increasingly important to retailers' commercial success, as traders attempted to meet changes in the consumer desires of London's mobile middle-class women. Rimmel's ubiquitous presence in Victorian women's magazines—in advertisements and featured articles on perfumery and paper novelties—augmented his commercial success, while the periodicals served as a platform to advance new ideas about domesticity and women's role in the private sphere.[65] In 1865, he compiled the *Book of Perfumes* from a series of articles he wrote for science-minded readers of *The Englishwoman's Domestic Magazine*. This task, he told readers, demanded his transition from the masculine world of professional science to the feminized sphere of general knowledge; he "was led to emerge from the depths of [his] laboratory, and to appear thus before the public *in an entirely new character*."[66] Rendering himself a gentlemanly man of science accustomed to the solitary labor of his craft, Rimmel embraced the role of self-proclaimed educator of the gentler sex.

Gender was also the framework by which he demarcated traditional home production of cosmetic washes and perfumed vinegars from the mass manufactures of the perfumery industry. Ladies once operated "a private stillroom of their own, and personally superintended the various 'confections' used for their toilet" out of necessity. Now, he argued, technological developments in London's growing commercial industry, not to mention perfumers' role in imperial commodity flows, trumped the material resources and technologies available to women's self-production.

> [G]ood perfumers and good perfumes are abundant enough; and, with the best recipes in the world, ladies would be unable to equal the productions of our laboratories, for how could they procure the various materials which we receive from all parts of the world? And were they even to succeed in so doing, there would still be wanting the necessary utensils and the *modus faciendi*, which is not easily acquired...perfumery can always be bought much better and cheaper from dealers, than it could be manufactured privately by untutored persons.[67]

Women could not produce the same quality of goods as those professional men laboring in the imperial market; their efforts were consequently of no value.[68] In this way, Rimmel's business persona was firmly entrenched within a hierarchy that privileged masculine, middle-class values. As we will see, his insistent alignment with masculine self-made rhetoric resulted in contradictory messages to his female clients.

Despite his legal naturalization and professional activities, Rimmel remained a foreigner in the context of London's beauty business. However, this did not position him as an outsider, as he capitalized on the exotic cachet engendered by his difference. Rimmel spoke some half-dozen languages, and his continental fluency extended to business.[69] Multiple print outlets picked up on Rimmel's winning of "cosmopolitan fame for his house which it unquestionably enjoys," underscoring the worldly and sophisticated character of his commercial persona.[70] In this case, characterizations of cosmopolitanism suggested elegant pleasures and refinement, qualities bolstered by Rimmel's international commercial expansion. By 1874, the firm boasted retail branches in the City, the West End, and Brighton; export manufactories in Neuilly; and continental depots in Paris, Brussels, Antwerp, Liege, the Hague, Amsterdam, and Florence.[71] Rimmel drew consumers' attention to his geographic expansion, crafting remarkable retail goods that reflected his global span. He promoted the idea of taking exoticized unprocessed materials from the empire and quite literally distilling them down to a pure, British luxury good. By demystifying colonized resources, Rimmel transformed them into standardized British commodities fit for "civilized" consumption. His customers subsequently participated in a safe, sanitized mode of global exchange.

In doing so, Rimmel's work aligned with the rise of a new imperialism that intensified the use of British nationalist iconography in mass consumption. With the exception of soaps such as Pears and Sunlight, beauty advertising rarely featured popular nationalist allegorical figures like Britannia or John Bull, who appeared in other commercial advertising. British perfumers recognized the popular appeal of foreign imports, especially those of France. The popular preference for foreign beauty products led some London merchants to exaggerate their claims to continental knowledge. French perfumery was so much in demand that, until London-based Piesse and Lubin's introduction of "Kiss-Me-Quick," British products typically featured French names or else be "considered below par."[72] To be cosmopolitan arbiters of taste, merchants had to go beyond explicitly British commercial identities.

At the same time, Rimmel and his contemporaries avidly engaged in a cultural nationalism promoting British beauty and authenticity. Manufacturing perfumers and other beauty providers purveyed a subtle, seemingly implicit preference for a racialized beauty—that is, the alabaster complexion of an "English Rose"—that could be far less explicit than the nationalist imagery deployed in other commercial advertising for tea, bouillon, and soap.[73] For Rimmel, symbolic conceptions of nationalism were distinctly feminine.[74] According to Victorian scientific discourses, "features of the face spelled out the character of the race," and beauty represented racial purity and natural ascendency.[75]

Rimmel's most celebrated mode of publicizing such messages was his perfumed almanacs, produced annually in the Beaufort Manufactory. The editions often featured female pictorial representations relating to popular themes in art, literature, and science, such as *The Language of Flowers* (1859), *The Four Seasons* (1866), and *Heroines of French Poets* (1871). Rendered in a florid, sometimes Orientalist style, the almanacs' exoticized decorative elements underscored very western narratives of modernity and industrial progress.[76] They functioned as vivid, brightly colored advertisements for Rimmel's feature products, all the while promoting discourses of Victorian femininity and "civilized" white beauty. In the decade between 1861 and 1871, the almanacs took up an increasingly nationalist tone, depicting female representatives of European continental competitors. Whereas the 1859 *Language of Flowers* included exoticized images suggestive of broad regional differences, the 1863 edition was more explicitly organized by nation. National allegories played on cultural stereotypes relating to climate, culture, and natural physical appearance. Each of the six European nations depicted was represented by a two-month season, a flower, and an affective quality. German wild flowers, for example, depicted summer "Simplicity," while the autumn was devoted to Spain and its "Elegance" (Plate 15). Pictorial descriptions of Russia, France, and Turkey rounded out the group, depicted in an ornate, romantic form. Some female allegories betrayed darker coloring, including women of Turkey and Spain, whose black hair contrasted with the lighter pigmentation of northern European representatives. By contrast, England's springtime "Beauty" reigned in an alabaster gown, adorned by a rose coronet and blonde ringlets[77] (Plate 16).

In maintaining the fairness of "England," Rimmel projected an ethnic typology often used to position Europeans in relation to colonized subjects, while also playing into cultural tensions around the self-fashioning of British versus foreign women. Popular critics condemned female visitors from the continent for indulging in overt cosmetic use and especially French women.[78] As literary critic Amy Montz has pointed out, cultural productions like Eliza Haweis's *Art of Beauty* (1878) blamed French women's artifice on their "racial heritage rather than inferior morality," as French women "'belonged to an artistic race.'"[79] In this way, Victorian fashion criticism reflected pressing issues of national identity and cultural authenticity that was also influencing contemporary political thought.

By upholding a dichotomy between the domestic and the foreign, Rimmel endorsed ideas about British women's authenticity over artifice.[80] "England's" blond hair and fair coloring represented the unblemished morality of a nation currently overseeing the global civilizing mission. Her clear white skin and rosy cheeks were strikingly unusual in their perfection, seemingly the product of some improvements. The list of beautifying goods following immediately afterward may have confirmed readers' suspicions of artificial enhancement. The almanac's organization implicitly signaled the unlikelihood that such beauty was achieved without participating in Victorian commodity culture. The trade list detailed cosmetic goods that were not meant to dramatically alter a female consumer's appearance, but that would help her achieve the natural "English" aesthetic: perfumes, pomade, cosmetic washes like "Rimmel's Lotion for the Skin" and "Glycerine Cold Cream," toilet soaps, dentifrices (Plate 17). Rimmel's juxtaposition of nature and artifice promoted an "artificial naturalness" that, on the surface, did not challenge Victorian values of authentic British identity.[81] In other words, Rimmel's "naturalness," like national identity, was a construct; it could be learned and was increasingly achievable through the use of discreet commercial goods.

All the while, Rimmel sought to mollify popular distrust of his own foreignness and specifically his *French* origins. But his cultural duality also justified his cultural borrowing, and, in doing so, he promoted beauty consumption as a global practice of hybridization and exchange. In fact, British colonial expansion meant the extraction and exploitation of global resources and labor, and Rimmel extended such practices to female consumers and their beauty consumption. One celebratory profile recounted how Rimmel "ransack[ed] the stores of every manufacture, the vegetable, mineral, and animal kingdoms of nature, the farthest countries, from Peru to Japan, the workshops of Bohemia, Genoa, and Perth for a diversity of materials." This even included "the work of nuns in a Brazilian convent, who are accustomed to making artificial flowers entirely of the feathers of the gorgeous birds that haunt the South American forest."[82] Rimmel allegedly marshaled both the natural world and its inhabitants in his building of a commercial perfumery empire, tailored specifically to the "civilized" British consumer.

Continental Competition

Firmly ensconced in a national commercial culture, Rimmel all the while acted as patron to Soho's French émigré population. His altruism and practical philanthropy supported his well-managed personal publicity.[83] Benevolence and social welfare were central to Victorian conceptions of Christian duty and moral character. Rimmel's altruism evoked the "practical philanthropy" of Victorian social reformers, yet there was a pivotal divide separating him from his beneficiaries.[84] Rimmel had definitively moved out of the émigré population, fashioning himself as a respectable Frenchman improved by his British naturalization. But "[s]uccess in life," noted one profiler, "has not made Mr. Rimmel unmindful that there are others upon whom fortune has not smiled kindly."[85]

Rimmel's patronage of Soho's Francophone community points to inherent contradictions within his professional position as a renowned British merchant. Rimmel donated capital earned as an Anglicized version of a French businessman to London's Francophone community, especially those who had the greatest difficulty assimilating into British culture. Emblematic of self-made success, Rimmel was nonetheless sympathetic to Soho émigrés who operated at the margins of mainstream Anglo society. Rimmel solicited British support for French victims of the Franco-Prussian War in 1870–1, the Paris Commune of 1871, and widespread French flooding in 1875.[86] He also collected funds in his capacity as the president of the French Benevolent Society on Panton Street, Soho.[87] Interestingly, British trade publications were overwhelmingly accepting of the fact that "the nation which gave him birth had a prior claim on his benevolence."[88]

Rimmel recast his relationship to Soho's Francophone community as one of benevolence rather than belonging; he affirmed his loyalty to his national heritage, but also acknowledged his family's humble origins. Rimmel was responsible for at least three benevolent institutions located in Soho, yet he garnered the most publicity for his philanthropic work at the French Hospital and Dispensary in Leicester Square. The French Hospital, opening early December 1867, served "cases of destitution and distress among foreigners who have been tempted to seek their fortunes in this capital."[89] Within a year of its opening, it had treated some 4,226 members of London's Francophone community.[90] "Some of the poor creatures could not speak a word of English," wrote one journalist after a facility tour, "and one could not help thinking what a blessed thing it was for those sick exiles, practically dumb and friendless in a strange land, that they have this little oasis of home to go to in their day of need!"[91]

Rimmel's careful self-representation as an Anglicized businessman occurred at a moment of relative stability in Anglo-Francophone relations. Some scholars argue that British Francophobia lessened throughout the nineteenth century in the absence of armed conflict. It was nonetheless enforced by the two nations' economic and imperial competition through the century. London's perfume manufacturers, for example, feared the greatest economic challenge from their Parisian counterparts. France, and more specifically Paris, had been the seat of international perfumery from the late seventeenth century under the patronage of Louis XIV. Parisian tradesmen developed a guild system representing perfumers and glovemakers (*gantier-parfumeurs*), which, by the mid-eighteenth century, sanctioned some 250 masters.[92] This dominance shifted slightly when, in the face of British military blockades during the Napoleonic Wars, Parisian perfumers found themselves losing global market share to competitors in London.[93] International demand for British perfumery surged until the 1820s, thanks to the blockades.[94]

Political unrest in France throughout the nineteenth century enabled British perfumers to make significant gains in scale of production and revenues. In 1857, Britain's perfume exports were humbly estimated at £40,000 per annum; by 1862, this number had doubled.[95] London was reportedly home to approximately 151 wholesale perfumers in 1867, while 849 retail perfumers sold beauty products.[96] Meanwhile, two of perfumery's most important plant species, lavender and peppermint, were long-established in Britain, and perfumers gained an important foothold in their distillation.[97] Lavender was especially emblematic of British rural life and its traditions, and a select group of British perfumers publicized their reliance on local stills to emphasize their adherence to Old English values. "In these days of new scents," attested the shopping columnist for *The London and Paris Ladies' Magazine of Fashion*, "it is pleasant to come upon an old-fashioned perfume which reminds us of our childhood's days."[98] Manufacturers of lavender water periodically lived and worked outside of Greater London. Yet a few of London's leading manufacturers advertised their patronage of lavender stills at Mitcham in Surrey and Hitchin in Hertfordshire.[99] Despite suggestions of provinciality, these production sites were ambitious ventures, as some 112 pounds of lavender flowers were required to yield just 30 to 32 ounces of otto.[100]

British perfumery's opportunity for ascendency was short lived. Through the 1860s, as Britain was gripped in an economic slump and faced aggressive global competition, Paris maintained its standing as the de facto site of luxury beauty production, despite declines in its own exports.[101] Moreover, France was also the principal source of perfumery's raw materials; the British emphasis on local lavender production masked the fact that many of the world's perfumers relied on the south of France where orange blossoms and lavender were cultivated. This included Rimmel, who employed his father Hyacinthe to manage his extensive agricultural holdings in Nice (Figure 4.6). The south of France had first gained international attention in the seventeenth century for the quality of its commercial flower farming. By the mid-nineteenth century, over one hundred distillation houses operated in Grasse, Nice, Montpellier, and Cannes,

Figure 4.6 Interior of Eugène Rimmel's Perfume Manufactory at Nice (1865). Science History Images/Alamy Stock Photo.

"the only real garden of utility to the perfumer."[102] In one agricultural season, the houses harvested over two million pounds of orange flowers worth some £40,000, produced 700,000 lbs. of scented oils and pomades and 200,000 lbs. of rose water, and employed over ten thousand workers.[103] France was not the only contender in global exporting of odiferous materials. Turkish and Algerian firms came a close second to the production levels of continental European distilleries. British India became another important colonial producer, from where Rimmel imported "cassia, cloves, sandalwood, patchouly, and several essential oils of the andropogon genus." And, as mentioned, Asian markets—those making up the "Celestial Empire"—provided the natural basis of musk, "which, carefully blended with other perfumes, gives them strength and piquancy without being in any way offensive."[104]

From the south of France, raw materials made their way to perfumery manufacturers in London and Paris, which acted as the main transport hubs for perfumery articles "and whence these products are exported to all parts of the world."[105] Nonetheless, global consumer demand for French manufacturers meant that Paris's market share and cultural cachet for perfumery continued to grow and would do so well into the twentieth century. In the 1860s, Paris was home to double the perfumery firms of London. Annual returns yielded no less than 40 million francs; perfumery exports exceeded 30 million francs.

On top of cultural prestige, Paris was privy to important material distinctions in perfumery manufacturing. French perfumes relied on brandy or grape spirit. By contrast, British perfumers used inferior corn spirit.[106] A handful of British specialty goods that did not employ corn spirits eventually gained popularity on the continent. For the most part, however, western consumers in Europe and North America prized French over British exports.[107]

Perfuming Empire

Despite lower regard for British perfumery products in Europe and America, considerable quantities made their way to colonial markets.[108] In 1863, British India was the main recipient of British perfumery, and according to official sources, exports provided almost £22,000 in returns. Australia followed closely behind, at £18,921.[109] While Rimmel was no doubt a trade leader among London colleagues, demand for Rimmel goods on the desirable European markets is less clear. In the Beaufort manufactory, one writer observed packing cases "set as close as building bricks," destined for colonial ports in "all parts of the habitable world, from Monte Video to Calabria, from Faree [Iran] to the Fiji Islands, … from Russia to Jamaica." Missing from this catalogue were western retail markets in France, Germany, or the United States, as was seemingly the case for many of London's manufacturing perfumers.[110]

British beauty providers' subsequent dependence on colonial demand would implicate them in a range of imperial developments. This included the transmission of ideas about "British" bodily aesthetics, which circulated via advertisements, press coverage, and the goods themselves.[111] At the forefront of messages about "natural" British beauty was its fairness in complexion, a classification that took on increasingly racialized connotations from the mid-nineteenth century as it was refashioned more explicitly as whiteness. As we have seen, fairness was long privileged in British beauty culture, dating back to the early modern period.[112] In the nineteenth century, ideas about racialized differences coalesced with idealized beauty norms to definitively promote whiteness as simultaneously "natural" and superior.[113] Historian Sadiah Qureshi has highlighted the complex constitution of ethnic categories at the mid-century, showing how race was one means of categorizing human variety and was subject to debate among scholars, scientists, and the public.[114] As the century progressed, promotional schemes of London beauty brokers that privileged an unblemished whiteness came to reflect circulating ideas about racialized differences all while contributing to the production of these images and hierarchies. Such messages aligned with others codified through the latter half of the nineteenth century, when disciplines like ethnology and phrenology transformed physical characteristics into increasingly hardened taxonomies of difference based on hair, skin tone, and facial features.[115] In the context of Britain's global role as a major colonizing force, dominant beauty ideals—as natural, unblemished, and white—informed the purchasing habits of domestic consumers, before disseminating across colonial markets.

It was not only ideas about and images of beauty that made their way around the world, and British beautifying goods were also part of the dissemination of a "natural" white aesthetic. Historians have noted the ways that cultural narratives of empire and cleanliness potently aligned in the form of soap, as advertisers like Thomas J. Barratt of Pears mobilized goods' "civilizing" effects to promote their popular products.[116] Similar trends extended to other types of beautifying goods, including perfumery. In the case of Rimmel, one article reported that he sent large quantities of rose water to "all warm countries," where it became especially popular in "every part of the equatorial world."[117] But, according to *All the Year Round*, Rimmel manufactured two grades of rose water. The higher-quality product went to domestic markets, while the lower-quality product was reserved for "'darkies' [who were] fond of pouring rose-water over their heated skins [and] consequently gallons and gallons [were] sent."[118] In its denigrating and racialized characterization of imperial consumers, the account juxtaposed colonized subjects and their beauty practices against those of Rimmel's "civilized" metropolitan patrons. In the report, colonial subjects' overuse of luxury goods diverged from European consumption practices, which observers characterized as sparing and self-controlled. Hierarchies of production were allegedly developed to accommodate these racialized markets, in the form of "commoner" versus "finer" kinds of rose water.[119]

The same author positioned colonial beauty consumption as an important part of Britain's imperial civilizing mission. For them, the use of Rimmel's soap, toilet water, and rose water by colonial subjects was "the first steps in the great ladder" toward civilization.

> Toilet vinegar and rose-water, pomades and soaps, and even the more questionable adjuncts of face-powders and restorative washes, are better than the dirt and unpersonableness—in other words, the brutalisation—of savages. So that we may, without being too fanciful or far-fetched, regard [Rimmel's] house of sweet odours in the Strand as one of the agents of civilisation, helping in the great task of refining and educating to the full as much as the more serious labours of missionaries.[120]

With its characterizations of "unpersonable" "savages," the account promoted circulating narratives that linked colonial consumers' bodies to uncleanliness and barbarity. As historian Timothy Burke argues, "European visions of difference and hierarchy" often depended on such "colonial and metropolitan stereotypes" that critiqued the hygienic practices of colonized subjects and the urban poor.[121]

The depiction of the colonial consumer as "savage" functioned to diminish not only the humanity but also the power of local actors in imperial markets. Scholars have shown how beauty and hygiene products were central to colonial consumer markets through the late nineteenth and twentieth centuries. While initially marketed by virtue of their "civilizing effects," imported beautifying goods were taken up by colonial consumers as part of broader processes of self-fashioning that reflected local aesthetics and individual desires. As Burke argues, colonized subjects had considerable power as consumers, even if some western producers created goods that aligned with colonizers' rather than local consumers' needs.[122] By the twentieth century, beauty goods were increasingly developed, adopted, and mobilized to suit the interests and values of local consumers around the world.[123]

Despite the consumer power of colonial patrons, western standards of idealized beauty continued to shape many global beauty trends, including the privileging of whiteness or "fairness."[124] This was not the only legacy of nineteenth-century beauty firms, and, into the twentieth century, western and especially American multinational corporations benefitted from global commodity and cultural flows forged at the height of British imperialism. Historian Alys Eve Weinbaum and others note that "linguistic affinities and cultural continuities in the vast imperial markets constructed through centuries of British conquest" created a ready-made consumer market where American and British ideals were "easily … blended and conflated, producing an Anglo-American imperial whiteness."[125] In other words, British imperial networks laid the foundations for a global system of beauty provision into the twentieth century, which continued to produce and reproduce a beauty aesthetic that was "natural," unblemished, and white.

For the nineteenth century, there remains additional work to be done on global consumers' experiences with British beauty goods. We do know that, in the domestic context, London's beauty providers and their advocates circulated messages about the desirability of fairness and the civilizing potential of beautifying wares. Rimmel depended on imperial natural resources and, ostensibly, local colonial labor to maintain his global trade; all the while, coverage of his operations lionized specific versions of white, western beauty consumption while championing "civilizing" missions of the empire.[126] London-based beauty providers continued to promote messages about fairness well into the twentieth century, paralleling dominant messages about Britain's role as a "civilizing" force.[127] In this way, beauty brokers contributed to increasingly rigid associations of whiteness as "the norm" against which other skin tones, hair types, and physical attributes were compared.[128]

Rimmel was not the only London-based beauty provider to situate products within an imperial framework of domesticity and British civilization, while relying on colonial markets to buoy a firm's success. By the late nineteenth century, perfumery exports to colonial markets were of inordinate importance, which meant trade leaders' involvement in new regulatory bodies aimed at protecting their interests around the world. This included the London Chamber of Commerce (LCC), founded in 1881, which represented metropolitan firms against detrimental government policies and protectionism.[129] The LCC was divided into committees based on distinct trade interests. Perfumers sat on the Chemical Trades Section; there, they worked alongside London's drysalters, chemists and druggists, and chemical analysts to oversee importing and exporting of London-made perfumery and its ingredients.

British perfumers' standing on the LCC was especially important in the wake of ongoing challenges from foreign producers. Having ceded European markets to Parisian counterparts, London's manufacturing perfumers nonetheless competed with French and American imports for local and colonial market shares. Faced with growing international competition and the circulation of goods, the perfumery industry expanded upon its earlier narratives of cross-cultural exchange and exploration to include government initiatives that benefited their national industry.[130] By the time of Rimmel's death in 1887, perfumers had embarked on a protracted campaign to reduce the costs of export manufacture from London ports. Through the Perfumery Sub-Committee of the LCC, founded in 1883, they worked to reduce the duties on spirits, which had long hindered the industry and led to exorbitant fees.[131] Members representing the city's leading firms—C. A. Gosnell of John Gosnell & Co., Barrett of Atkinson & Co., Cleaver, Grossmith, Thompson of the Crown Perfumery Company—defended rights already granted to the trade in the form of bonded warehouses at St. Katharine Docks in the East End. Bonded warehouses were owned by independent tradesmen who leased manufacturing space to perfumers "whose business [was] big enough to allow them to rent such a floor." Under the supervision of a Revenue officer, the Board of Customs sanctioned the manufacture, storage, and transporting of perfumery from these sites. While this was not an ideal arrangement for London's perfumers, "[w]ithout such a concession," argued *The Chemist and Druggist*, "the British trade in perfumery would be entirely hopeless."[132]

To the detriment of small firms, however, these bonded warehouses were "in the hands of a comparatively few houses."[133] Not coincidentally, many of these bonded firms had representatives on the Perfumery Sub-Committee of the LCC: that is, board members seemingly held the monopoly on London's perfumery export trade. LCC members subsequently devoted efforts to securing their existing privileges, leaving the standing of smaller firms undetermined.[134] Notably, many of these powerful manufacturers, like Eugène Rimmel, had built their enterprises from small-scale firms, firms that were now disadvantaged in global trade. Successful, capitalist perfumers had developed colonial markets for British perfumery, which were off-limits to London's smaller providers under current regulations. Within a single generation, London's small perfumery firms had established an internal trade hierarchy that aligned with formal state policy to hinder even the lowliest of competitors—competitors that, until only recently, they had resembled.

Conclusions

From the 1880s onward, London's mid- and large-scale beauty merchants adopted an openly masculine, professional trade profile that included their shared interests in global exporting. This meant the emergence of some firms as regulatory forces, working with local and national governments to administer Britain's perfumery trade and global exports. But this did not necessarily guarantee British ascendancy on global markets.[135]

Some years later, in 1904, trade journal *The Hairdressers' Chronicle* reflected back on trade professionalization, including the marked decline of British hairdressers' and perfumers' standing. The columnist criticized London's beauty tradesmen for failing to see the real reason behind the trade's "falling off of business [beyond] the Empire's politics and commerce": the rise of the local "capitalists with unlimited resources and facilities" who wrenched "the commercial adjunct of a profession at no time, generally considered, remarkable for its comprehensive business faculty."[136] Leading London tradesmen blamed contingencies of the global market for their declining market share through the nineteenth century. Yet, according to the columnist at the *Chronicle*, it was not external elements of international trade and excise that affected British profitability; rather, it was the rise of British industrial capitalists who outpaced traditional occupational networks of small-scale barbers, hairdressers, and perfumers. The "purely professional" had taken over the beauty trades, squeezing out local representatives of the traditional trade community.

In this way, developments in the perfumery industry adhered to some conventional narratives of the second industrial revolution. Through technological innovations and improved communication and distributive systems, a select cohort of small-scale manufacturers like Rimmel developed their firms into national commercial operations. In doing so, this group of professionalizing men became part of the expanding colonial market in import and export goods. The British perfumery industry was implicated in transnational trade and commodity flows, advocating particular modes of "national" goods. However, British perfumery failed to maintain its niche in the European market through the latter half of the nineteenth century; as historians have noted, London's beauty businesses fell behind companies of other industrialized nations.[137] Not only did London-based providers face new global competition but they also experienced renewed competition from closer to home. In Paris—London's long-standing rival as Europe's most desirable site of luxury consumption—perfumery firms like Guerlain established French ascendency over the beauty market.[138] At the same time, new "Americanized" beauty services, defined by spectacle and innovation, forced British adoption of new technologies: shampoo systems, hair-brushing machines, and techniques in electrolysis and manicure.

As London's most prolific perfumer, Rimmel not only weathered nineteenth-century economic shifts but developed strategies of self-representation out of the material conditions of his business practice. However, the success of Rimmel and others like him came at a cost for his competition: smaller, less capitalized British perfumers who failed to expand their businesses at similar rates. Economies of scale and professional consolidation resulted in a decline in small-sized firms catering to individual clients. Among British consumers, successful firms like Rimmel's met general demand for perfumery and soap by the late nineteenth century. Mass-produced British beauty products were readily available in a variety of locations, from chemists to cooperatives to department stores.[139]

But businesses like that of Rimmel could no longer meet the personal needs of London's increasingly mobile middle- and upper-class female customer. The *fin de siècle* woman had renewed interest in beauty consumption and desired more than traditional manufactured offerings like soap and scent. This engendered changes in the early 1890s, when a new contingent of London-based beauty providers helped to fill the vacuum—and sense of depersonalization—created by the expansion of mid-century firms. New West End boutiques offered personal attention, unique services, and, perhaps most attractively, feminine intimacy—for taking up this niche market was a new generation of female beauty entrepreneurs.

5

Female Enterprise at the *Fin-de-Siècle*: Jeannette Pomeroy

In 1897, there was a new addition to London's *Post Office Directory*. Flanked by "Compensation Balance Makers" and "Composing Machine Makers," there appeared, for the first time, the category of "Complexion Specialist." In its inaugural appearance, the category featured just a single listing: that of Mrs. Pomeroy Ltd., operating out of 29 Old Bond Street with additional locations in Sackville Street, Liverpool, Dublin, and Cape Town.[1] This singularity testified to the standing of Mrs. Jeannette Scalé Pomeroy (1862?–1938) as London's de facto "authority on the subject of the complexion and of the art of beauty in general" (Figure 5.1). Across multiple shop locations, "Mrs. Pomeroy" sold "hygienic complexion treatments," a personal line of toilet preparations including Pomeroy Complexion Purifier and Pomeroy Astringent Tonic Lotion, and "the best" liquid rouge "both from the point of colour and hygiene."[2] She was also one of London's first electrolysis operators, adept at the removal of "superfluous hair, moles, birth marks."[3] From the mid-1890s, "Mrs. Pomeroy" stood at the forefront of London's new tide of small boutique businesses offering explicitly feminized services, for women by women. At the height of her success, she saw a turnover of £21,000 a year and employed eighty female assistants.[4]

By the spring of 1906, however, a confusing series of developments saw the simultaneous operation of not one but two distinct locations on Old Bond Street claiming the name "Mrs. Pomeroy." The complex scenario of Mrs. Pomeroy impersonating "Mrs. Pomeroy" began when Scalé, having sold and exited from her financially embarrassed company "Mrs. Pomeroy Ltd.," decided to launch a new business—under the name of Mrs. Pomeroy. She took out an advertisement in London's *Daily Mail* in which she dissociated herself from her former operations in light of "her intention to carry on business as a complexion specialist for herself."[5] Scalé proceeded to open a new Bond Street complexion business— just "four doors from [her former] premises—under the name of

JEANNETTE POMEROY.
Photo by Lafayette.

Figure 5.1 "A Chat with Mrs. Pomeroy," *Hearth and Home* 16, no. 405 (February 16, 1899): 589. Courtesy of © The British Library Board (Shelfmark LOU.LON 351 [1899]).

Mrs. Jeannette Pomeroy."[6] For several weeks, in the spring of 1906, two distinct businesses claiming to be run by "Mrs. Pomeroy" served London's elite female clientele. Before long, the new owners of Mrs. Pomeroy, Ltd. applied for a court injunction against Jeannette Scalé.[7] In December 1906, the trial came before the Court of Chancery, when the firm of Mrs. Pomeroy Ltd. charged that its trademark had been infringed upon by Scalé who was, of course, the former owner of the company.

A focus on the confounding case of multiple Mrs. Pomeroys reveals the opportunities—and enduring contingencies—shaping the efforts of a new cohort of beauty businesswomen operating in *fin de siècle* London. In this moment, challenges of scale and production materialized but so did new possibilities for businesswomen, particularly in the luxury beauty trades. "Beauty culturists" like Scalé, alongside Anna Ruppert (1864?–1896), Eleanor Adair (b. 1867), Frances Hemming (1872–1934), and others, capitalized on consumers' dissatisfaction with impersonal, manufactured goods by offering new "artisanal" boutique services like manicure, complexion care, and electrolysis. These women mobilized an opening in London's luxury beauty services by appealing to female shoppers via intimacy and trust, positioning themselves as deeply personal alternatives to modern mass production. In this way, beauty businesses like Scalé's on Bond Street came to represent an "'island' of opportunity" and specifically what historian Pamela Sharpe terms an "expanding niche of economic opportunity for women."[8] A specialized commercial community marked by its location as well as by the elite status of its patrons, Bond Street's beauty businesses offered growing opportunities for female enterprise rather than the decline sometimes described in histories of industrial development.[9] Rather, technologies particular to the *fin de siècle* heralded lucrative prospects for a new cohort of middle-class beauty businesswomen.[10] They exploited elements of modern celebrity culture, expanding global mobility, and new modes of individual reinvention to stake a claim in London's competitive beauty scene.

These ventures nonetheless faced challenges in the form of long-held ideas regulating the sale and consumption of beauty goods, ideas that periodically limited the possibilities for successful female enterprise. Anxieties over truthfulness, trickery, and respectability extended into the *fin de siècle* and continued to inform public opinions of beautifying businesses, including those run by women. Despite the enhanced public presence of women like Jeannette Scalé, the role thus demanded the careful creation of a feminine business persona in order to thrive in the emerging niche market in the West End's beauty trades. The cultivation of these commercial identities turned, in part, on innovative technologies of self-fashioning that emerged at the *fin de siècle*, technologies that Jeannette Scalé took full advantage of.[11] In just over a decade, she transformed herself from Jeannette Shepherd, the daughter of financially besieged Methodist Episcopal missionaries from Ohio living in India, into Jeannette Jobbins, the young bride and mother of two small sons, in flight from Darjeeling and her terminally ill husband. Her next appearance was as Jeannette Scalé, the optimistic émigré to London and new bride to a cabinet upholsterer from Camberwell, South London. Her final role was that of Mrs. Jeannette Pomeroy, arguably the West End's most enterprising and visible beauty businesswoman, whose empire extended across Britain and its colonies, from Dublin to Cape Town. It was in the legal decision over the rights to this final incarnation that Jeannette Shepherd Jobbins Scalé Pomeroy met her match. On December 13, 1906, the Chancery justice ruled against her, taking away her right to the Pomeroy name and granting it to the limited company that she herself had founded in 1896.

This was a devastating loss. As a fictional personality trading as "Mrs. Pomeroy," Scalé dominated the late-nineteenth-century West End beauty market. But her accusers attested that the feminine figure of "Mrs. Pomeroy," who provided intimate beauty secrets and bodily regimens, was merely "a myth, a convenient name for the business."[12] Certainly, it obscured key factors that challenged Scalé's public presentation as a genteel woman of business. In fact, Jeannette Scalé/Pomeroy was not a widow, as claimed of Mrs. Pomeroy, but had a real (second) husband who worked for her. She was American and was not privy to exoticized Indian beauty secrets as her advertisements proclaimed. She was ambitious, materialistic, and had overt economic ambitions "unbefitting" her sex. As we shall see, she disliked her elite female clients tremendously, and she resented the work, ultimately wanting as little to do with clientele as possible. To fashion a sufficient aura of respectability and perhaps with an eye to convenience as well, Scalé subsequently produced, reproduced, and circulated the fiction of "Mrs. Pomeroy" by exploiting new means of self-presentation available in the modern urban context.[13] She was not alone in these ventures, laboring alongside a cohort of enterprising women at the *fin de siècle* who fashioned consumer bodies, but also unique business personas in their quest to infiltrate the rapidly modernizing West End scene.

The Rise of the Beauty Culturist

"London, or to speak more truly, the West End of London, is the city of beautiful women, and why?" posed a columnist in 1896. "Because there, as a rule, one sees woman at her best—well dressed, well coiffée [*sic*], and with due care paid to every detail of her person and toilet."[14] The presence of fashionable women—and men—in London's West End was not a new phenomenon. Through much of the nineteenth century, London's upper-middle and elite classes converged on Mayfair in search of the finest luxury goods and services. In the 1850s and 1860s, this included patronage of hairdressers like H. P. Truefitt and Robert Douglas, but also less savory characters including Sarah "Madame Rachel" Leverson. By the 1870s, as Erika Rappaport has shown, the expansion of commercial "pleasure zones" and the subsequent opening of the West End to "middling sorts" further bolstered London's fashionable trades.[15] Yet, despite this alleged democratization of the West End, Old and New Bond Streets remained an exclusive refuge for the high-end consumer[16] (Figure 5.2). Popular print publications like 1906's *Olivia's Shopping and How She Does It* perpetuated these elite associations among

Figure 5.2 "On Bond Street," by Charles Dana Gibson (1896). The Minneapolis College of Art and Design.

readers and metropolitan visitors. "[T]he neat way one avoids knocking into a duke," "Olivia" informed them, "the price one has to pay for a toque—these must convince the ordinary mortal that Bond Street is for the elect."[17]

The West End also remained the most desirable site for luxury beauty businesses, as the affluent classes stayed faithful to expensive beauty regimens despite enduring criticisms of cosmetic practices. This aligned with new ideas emerging at the *fin de siècle* promoting the cultivation of healthy, attractive bodies among both men and women. As historian Ina Zweiniger-Bargielowska has shown, the late nineteenth century saw the elaboration of a commodified body culture, in which the physical form garnered new levels of appreciation, but also heightened attention from health and commercial providers.[18] Despite this, new ideas about the healthy active body did not fully supplant enduring Victorian attitudes toward "artificial" manipulation. While innovative beauty technologies appeared in the *fin de siècle* market, long-standing messages about the moral, virtuous origins of inner attractiveness persisted into the twentieth century.[19]

Standing at the crossroads of enhanced public attention to the healthy body and enduring critiques of artificiality was a new mode of *fin de siècle* beauty provider, the most successful of whom operated in the West End.

This was particularly the case on Bond Street, where male beauty providers, unlike some small-scale providers in more humble locales, consistently did good business throughout the nineteenth century. However, by the end of the nineteenth century, new ideas about beautiful female bodies and expanding scales of production among professional classes of perfumers meant that the gender configurations of Bond Street beauty businesses began to shift. At the *fin de siècle*, many major perfumery firms relocated their manufacturing operations to London's suburban perimeters, which yielded them greater space for enhanced production of mass quantities of beauty goods.[20] This meant that Bond Street's small constituency of beauty providers declined in numbers; by 1905, beauty businesses made up only 5 percent of trade on the street, an all-time low since 1841.[21] However, this decrease opened up new opportunities for small-scale boutique beauty providers, including a significant number of women who now made up the ranks, some 45 percent of Bond Street beauty vendors.[22] These beauty businesswomen set up shop on and around the thoroughfare as "complexion specialists," "electrolycians," "manicurists," and "beauty culturists." As a new class of West End beauty provider, they offered unique skill sets to affluent female clients seeking out discreet yet effective bodily services that departed from the increasingly standardized, depersonalized wares of perfumers, druggists, and hairdressers. This new generation of female "beauty culturists" established lucrative enterprises by foregrounding their feminine expertise, tailored specifically for genteel clients of the fairer sex.[23]

Fin de siècle beauty culturists staked commercial claims across London's West End, catering to growing consumer demand for new services and technologies, but also the personalized care that only individuals could provide. This included Helen Cavendish at 120 New Bond Street who offered elaborate electrical beauty services and Helen Best at 524 Oxford Street who specialized in the removal of superfluous hairs.[24] In 1896, Fanny Forsythe, aka Mrs. Frances Hemming, opened a beauty salon on South Molton Street, from where she developed the successful Cyclax line of complexion "remedies" and services.[25] From 1905, Eleanor Adair advertised a lucrative shop for "LADIES ONLY" at 92 New Bond Street, where she touted her popular Ganesh Facial Strap service, which consisted of linen bindings lain to form a tight-fitting mask[26] (Figure 5.3). Ostensibly shaping and firming the face, the treatments foreshadowed techniques later employed by both Helena Rubinstein and her rival Elizabeth Arden at the height of twentieth-century spa culture.[27] Unfortunately, the treatments prevented the client from

Figure 5.3 Advertisement for Eleanor Adair's Ganesh System (1912), BH1352. Courtesy of AdAccess Digital Collection, John W. Hartman Center for Sales, Advertising & Marketing History, David M. Rubenstein Rare Book and Manuscript Library, Duke University.

engaging in polite (or any) conversation with their lady attendant, so some more talkative or sociable female clients may have resorted to the services of Madame DeMedici at 120 New Bond or Miss Mabel Manners at 31 New Bond Street.[28]

Other women worked at the behest of one of Bond Street's "new" limited liability corporations and subsequently did not appear in trade directory listings. For example, H. P. Truefitt procured the services of the purported "originator of the 'Manicure' system," New York native Mary E. Cobb, for his "American Manicure Saloon."[29] She was replaced by another American, Lydia Carmichael, who soon had "more work than she [could] do."[30] Within the year, Carmichael teamed up with husband Melville at his chiropody business at 158 New Bond Street.[31] Not all women worked in the employ of limited firms, and traders like Madame Ducamp of Portland Place independently operated manicure salons

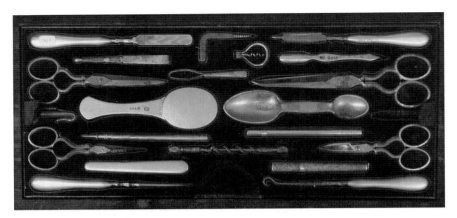

Figure 5.4 Tools including Cuticle Remover by F. P. (*c*.1875). Courtesy of the Metropolitan Museum of Art, New York.

from the late 1880s onward. From 1891, manicurists had their own listing in the *Post Office Directory*; by 1915, forty-eight manicurists appeared, all but six of them women[32] (Figure 5.4).

It was not only through their physical presence that London's beauty businesswomen transformed consumers' relationship to beauty and their bodies. Many beauty culturists also launched ambitious advertising and marketing campaigns that promoted new messages about respectable feminized beauty consumption. Beauty culturists took out illustrated advertisements in leading women's periodicals, often in addition to other, more public forums. From her arrival in London in 1891, American beauty culturist-cum-author Anna Ruppert circulated interviews, advertisements, and texts to promote herself as much as her services in "preserving beauty"[33] (Figure 5.5). Her public lectures on topics like "A Womanly Woman; How to Become One, How to Preserve the Gentle Appearance of a Pretty Woman" complemented services offered out of her shop at 89 Regent Street.[34] In addition to these forms, Ruppert managed a correspondence column in *Hearth and Home* through 1893, from which she proffered advice on a range of topics from graying hair to wrinkles to flabby skin.[35] Ruppert was not the only beauty culturist who appeared across multiple textual registers at the end of the nineteenth century.[36] Health lecturer and editor Ada S. Ballin (1862–1906) promoted her theories on aging—along with her commercial services—via her periodical, *Womanhood*, which functioned as a platform for her beauty business from 1898 until her untimely death in May 1906.[37] As we will see, Jeannette Scalé was herself a prolific advertiser, proving especially adept at the "advertorial," newspaper pieces that initially

Figure 5.5 Anna Ruppert, *Chemist & Druggist* (January 20, 1894). Courtesy of the Wellcome Library, London.

read as objective reporting but were carefully designed to promote the subject's business—and only her business.[38]

Perhaps the most valuable form of self-promotion, produced by Ruppert, Scalé, and others, was the self-authored beauty book, a platform from which culturists could insist that "[b]eauty can be made as well almost, as born."[39] These texts followed conventional forms of didactic beauty guides in legitimating the pursuit of beauty as a worthy task of self-improvement and feminine duty.[40] There was, however, a twist; the anti-aging tonics, unguents, and beauty services were exclusively available from the author, whose advertisements typically closed out the manual. Texts like Ruppert's 1892 publication *Dermatology: A Book of Beauty* offered a range of beauty advice, much of which could be advanced via the purchase of Ruppert's "Skin Tonic," as backmatter adverts loudly proclaimed.[41] Meanwhile, Jeannette Scalé mailed copies of *Beauty Rules* to correspondents through the late 1890s, while Miss Sanders of Maddox Street touted her *Practical Face Treatment and Natural Beauty* from 1903 onward.[42]

In these texts, specialists advanced unique theories of beauty and rejuvenation, while promoting narratives about women's right to self-improvement; authors took seriously the centrality of appearance to the new generation of modern women. It was a "very real, by no means imaginary grievance," wrote Sanders, when "any woman in any station of life" experienced "the loss of good looks."[43] In the textual arena of commercial beauty books, the pursuit of youth and beauty was a critical venture, and authors established themselves as guides for female readers—and consumers—through this important journey.[44] In doing so, female beauty culturists positioned themselves as experienced guides bestowing hope onto clients and readers alike. "The modern beautifier steps in," declared an 1898 *Daily Mail* column, "and contradicts her female clients, bidding them not despair ... [for] receding chins, hollow cheeks, dull eyes, double chins, indeed facial defects of all sorts need exist no longer."[45]

The new cohort of beauty culturists could not have "stepped in" at a more opportune time, according to some columnists, who argued that the stakes of attaining beauty and youth were especially high for British women of the *fin de siècle*. Recent sociocultural shifts gave rise to women's enhanced public role, evidenced by their independent movement through urban space, growing political responsibilities, and expanded economic pursuits.[46] As one fictional "business woman" wrote, turn-of-the-century advances were transformative in more ways than one, and the enterprising woman now required a "bright and attractive appearance." She insisted that "[w]rinkles and blemishes on [a working woman's] complexion may have quite a deleterious effect upon her position from a business point of view, while in many instances the appearance of grey hair has been known to disqualify a woman from obtaining a coveted post."[47] Following this logic, the pursuit of youth and beauty was not a vanity but a necessity, given new social and economic responsibilities for middling and elite British women.[48] Theirs was not the "foolish and detrimental crusade" of previous generations, argued another column, but the "slough of despond [to] emerge ... in a fair and happy country, permeated by beauty specialists, whose whole lives are devoted to [ladies'] embellishment."[49] Aligning themselves with broader political and social reforms for elite and middling women, columnists and beauty providers alike situated their commercial services within a movement toward the advancement of their sex, promoting beautification as an imperative rather than an indulgence (Figure 5.6).

To complement their textual strategies, *fin de siècle* beauty culturists like Eleanor Adair and Jeannette Scalé advanced a number of innovative new techniques to beautify middling and elite female clients. Alongside traditional

Figure 5.6 "Titivating," from "My Lady's Evening in London, by Mrs. Aria" in George Sims, ed., *Living London Volume II* (London: Cassell, 1902), 186. Courtesy of University of California Libraries.

offerings like tonics and astringents, technologies in facial massage and dynamic electrical processes set them apart from previous generations of beauty providers.[50] Despite their novelty, these techniques aimed to produce a similar aesthetic as seen in an earlier era in beautifying trends: a white, unblemished countenance, signaling the sustained emphasis on and privileging of fairness. Lightness of skin long denoted a woman's distancing from the laboring classes, and fair aesthetics typified idealized western tastes through the eighteenth and nineteenth centuries.[51] However, the pursuit of whiteness took on new meanings at the *fin de siècle* in relation to shifting understandings of race as a means of categorizing human variety.[52] Scholars have shown how increasingly rigid conceptualizations of racial classification took hold in this era of high imperialism, advancing messages of codified differences based on skin tones and complexion. This periodically circulated in the form of commodities, and some advertising turned on representations of racial and ethnic difference to advance ideas of British imperial hegemony.[53] That is not to say that race became a stable category, and its meanings remained contingent, variable, and subject to debate. The expanding influence of scientific, eugenic, and commercial discourses on racial difference nonetheless imbued beauty culturists' privileging of whiteness with more explicitly racialized implications. What Kathy Peiss terms "the aesthetic dimension of racism," including "gradations of skin color [and] textures of hair" was especially potent in the context of Britain's role as a "civilizing" colonial force, and London's beauty providers were key participants in the transmission of aesthetic "ideals" from their base in the imperial metropolis.[54]

This included London's beauty businesswomen, who participated in the commercial cultivation of whiteness as providers of goods and services that enhanced the fairness of customers' complexions. From their shops in the cosmopolitan capital, they promoted and perpetuated the construction of white skin as "natural," consolidating long-circulating beauty aesthetics that privileged lightness over darkness.[55] Consumers' desires to meet these aesthetics subsequently informed the design of some beautifying products, including those that featured familiar—and deleterious—ingredients. This included goods expressly formulated to lighten the skin, such as those of Anna Ruppert who, according to critic Michelle Smith, originally classified her skin tonic as a "Face Bleach" when promoting it for the American market.[56] Concerns over lead paint and bismuth subsequently persisted into the late nineteenth century, via sustained critiques decrying the use of complexion tonics and powders owing to their potentially toxic ingredients. This particularly extended to whitening wares, and mercury, arsenic, and lead remained central ingredients in some of the leading complexion products of the day[57] (Plate 18). This does not seem to have stemmed their popularity, however, and whiteness of skin remained a dominant feminine aesthetic among British consumers well into the twentieth century until a shift to the tanned, "healthy" physiques that came to characterize interwar bodily trends.[58]

The novelty of new techniques at the *fin de siècle*, alongside enduring public distrust of potentially injurious beauty remedies meant that commercial beauty providers undertook considerable efforts to forge their legitimacy. London's complexion specialists did so via their multilateral, multi-medium offensives, employing advertising technologies of the latter half of the nineteenth century that transformed beauty goods into "systems of spectacular representation."[59] Beauty culturists mobilized both visual and discursive tools, tailoring articles, advertisements, and hybrid "advertorials" in Britain's periodical press to introduce the latest technologies.[60] This included the exhaustive detailing of tonics, facial massage, and electricity, which served to demystify beautifying and antiaging processes for the public, including potential clients.[61] In this way, beauty culturists emphasized revelation, drawing back the curtains on commercial beauty treatments to encourage readers' movement from the textual register—from the written word—into urban commercial shops.[62] At the same time, these promotional messages foregrounded feminine secrets, intimacy, and discretion, situating their shops and services as respectable sites of tacit female self-fashioning and beautification.

Despite their enthusiastic efforts, traders and consumers alike continued to operate under the careful scrutiny of social commentators, medical experts, and the general public.[63] Beauty culturists were left to navigate the fine line between promoting respectable modes of beauty services while providing female customers that which they desired: transformative experiences that enhanced their appearance. This required prudence, however, and despite the development of innovative beauty promotions, technologies, and services in the *fin de siècle* market, enduring messages about the inner origins of beauty continued to have currency.[64] To successfully marshal these multiple, contradictory discourses, a beauty culturist required considerable tact and business savvy, qualities seemingly possessed by the West End's industry leader, Mrs. Pomeroy.

Mrs. Pomeroy's Debut

When Jeannette Jobbins Scalé appeared in the West End in 1895, launching her practice as "Mrs. Pomeroy—complexion specialist," the new wave of female beauty culturists was just coming into being. Initially, Scalé rented office space in Chancery Lane, "which she used as a postal address and for practicing massage."[65] In less than a year and with no prior commercial experience, she moved the business to 29 Old Bond Street. For an inexperienced female entrepreneur to have so quickly established herself on Bond Street was not as exceptional as previously believed. This was due in part to Bond Street's shifting stature; through the 1880s, critics complained that the avenue had lost some of its old cachet and was "mostly tenanted by shopkeepers or let out in apartments," with "the tide of fashion, flowing uninterruptedly westward" to Knightsbridge.[66] True to this observation, Scalé's premises at 29 Old Bond Street had housed, since 1861, two (unrelated) tailors, a live-in employee, and a hat maker. But despite its purported degeneration in the wake of London's expanding westerly sites of consumption and spectacle, Bond Street remained for many women a symbol of elite associations and activities, a spatial representation of metropolitan female society—"the Mecca of the fashionable feminine," according to one female columnist.[67]

By 1896, Scalé's socio-geographic (not to mention symbolic) relocation had paid off, and she registered her business as a limited liability corporation, drawing five of the necessary seven shareholders from family and friends.[68] Yet Scalé omitted the newly acquired "Ltd." from marketing and advertising campaigns. "'Ladies do not like limited companies,'" she explained in the 1906 trial. "'They think there are men there who may get into the secret of their little foibles.'"[69] Commencing the Pomeroy fiction, Scalé understood that she and her female competitors owed their success to the provision of more discreet, intimate services neglected by larger, long-established firms, which were increasingly looking to the mass market.[70] Intimate bodily services no longer denoted indecency as they had for their mid-century predecessors like Sarah "Madame Rachel" Leverson. Mrs. Pomeroy was, according to print campaigns, "an honest woman who would candidly tell her sister-women the truth about their complexions."[71]

Her shops further bolstered Mrs. Pomeroy's place as purveyor of feminine specialties. The shops, noted one observer, offered a "perfumed atmosphere, the implements of silver and ivory gleaming amidst the paper packets tied with pale tinted ribbons, express[ing] the frivolities feminine in this bower."[72] Corresponding with Douglas's and Truefitt's initiatives launched some thirty years earlier, a careful demarcation of space defined her shop on Old Bond Street. Print illustrations appearing in *Cassell's Magazine* in 1902 highlighted private booths for individual clients, which protected elite ladies from the prying eyes of passersby, including male observers (Figure 5.7). Male visitors featured prominently in one of Mrs. Pomeroy's more creative advertorials, in which a fictitious columnist "Ohnely A. Mann" claimed to be "impressed with the efficiency" of Mrs. Pomeroy's operations. He noted several separate rooms "fitted up for … treatment by electrolysis." A "bright, airy" atmosphere, in which "[e]verything is sweet, pure, and fresh" brought the clean privacy of home into the commercial sphere.[73] For those still too reticent (or rich) to visit her West End location, Mrs. Pomeroy made personal visits to clients' homes, where "Mrs. Pomeroy [knew] at once what course to recommend."[74]

Treatments at the Bond Street shop furthered the personal connections between provider and client, including a degree of physical intimacy only recently expanded outside the private domains of the boudoir or bath. Mrs. Pomeroy's treatments combined beauty techniques of the Victorian era with technologies emerging at the *fin de siècle*. According to a female columnist in the *Daily Mirror*, the standard visit included facial steaming "which emitted a most refreshingly aromatic odour"; a facial massage "in the American manner, with a pad of chamois leather"; the application of Pomeroy's famous "Skin Food" "by means of a dainty little square of lawn, which was immediately thrown away"; a light misting of tonic "which fell like a soft summer shower upon [the client's] upturned face"; and an optional application of a "soupçon ... a tiny touch of rouge which Mrs. Pomeroy never provides unless asked to do so." The routine, foreshadowing the modern facial, differed in one important respect; an "application of electricity" followed the "Skin Food," the current being "very gentle, and the effect produc[ing] nothing more dreadful than a prickly sensation." At Mrs. Pomeroy's shop, female clientele forged intimate, physical bonds with female employees, making visible the private practices of self-grooming and bodily care. As seen in a 1903 image from the *Daily Mirror*, seated "at her feet," the client submitted to the "excessively tender touch" of Mrs. Pomeroy and her beauty specialists[75] (Figure 5.8).

AT THE MANICURIST'S.

Figure 5.7 "At the Manicurist's," from "My Lady's Afternoon in London, by Mrs. Aria" in George Sims, ed., *Living London Volume I* (London: Cassell, 1902), 44. Courtesy of University of California Libraries.

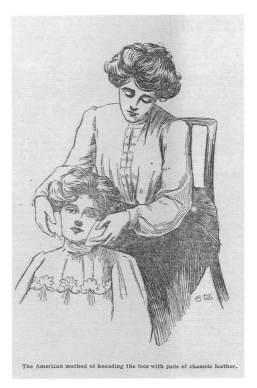

The American method of kneading the face with pads of chamois leather.

Figure 5.8 "The American Method," in "The Experiences of a Pilgrim of Seventeen in Search of Prettiness: The Hunt after Beauty," *The Daily Mirror* (December 10, 1903): 11. Courtesy of © The British Library Board (Shelfmark MLD4).

Feminine discretion and intimacy were not exclusive to Mrs. Pomeroy's venture, but her ubiquitous advertising campaigns enabled her to stand out among her competitors, both male and female. Mrs. Pomeroy sponsored lavish marketing campaigns that rivaled long-established industry leaders like Rimmel and Pears.[76] In addition to print ads in periodicals ranging from *Hearth and Home* to the *London Times*, she printed circulars and gave innumerable interviews on beauty and women's work.[77] Like those of Ruppert, her advertisements featured attractive visual elements that were increasingly popular in the *fin de siècle*, including self-portraits that supported her self-presentation as a discreet lady who espoused an unostentatious beauty. She even sponsored a design competition for amateur artists in 1899, which solicited "hundreds of very good designs" for her Bond Street windows.[78] Mrs. Pomeroy embraced aggressive, expensive campaigning with the hope "that regular customers become established in their patronage that so much costly advertising would not be necessary."[79]

While Mrs. Pomeroy's campaigns espoused traditional forms of feminine gentility, their success depended on cultural forms emerging in the *fin de siècle*, namely the culture of celebrity. As Smith has observed, celebrities from the world of West End theater like Ellen Terry and Sarah Bernhardt increasingly appeared in late-nineteenth-century beauty advertisements, standing as "exceptional examples of older women as icons of emulation"[80] (Figure 5.9). Mrs. Pomeroy and other beauty culturists mobilized celebrity in a slightly different manner, situating themselves as the subjects of emulation while offering unprecedented degrees of intimacy and connection. In doing so, Mrs. Pomeroy and her contemporaries reflected consumer desires back on to their potential customers, producing what theater historian Joseph Roach terms "public intimacy," or the humanization of "glamorous icons" by way of "provocative glimpses of their vulnerabilities."[81] Through advertisements, Mrs. Pomeroy's mode of public intimacy encouraged a demure feminine sociability, marketing a respectable space for women to exchange bodily secrets.[82]

Via advertisements, the telling of secrets and sharing of intimacies unfolded even before a client visited Bond Street. In one print advertisement, Mrs. Pomeroy courted readers' sympathy by focusing on her widowhood, conveniently omitting details of her second marriage; "my husband died and left me with two children, and as I wanted my two little sons to have the benefit of a good education, I knew I must work that they might have it."[83] In detailing private tragedies, Mrs. Pomeroy did not only seek to gain the trust of her female customers. She also justified her commercial participation, as widowhood remained one of the viable means for bourgeois women to conduct respectable business, at least in the opinion of male commentators. "A woman in the middle ranks, when cast on her own exertions, has two courses before her," wrote John Milne in 1870. "Either she may endeavor to gain the means of subsistence in a way in some measure fitting her previous station in life; or, unable to do this, she may leave that status to join the ranks below. In either case she has many formidable hardships to encounter."[84] Mrs. Pomeroy's alleged widowhood separated her from disreputable, self-interested providers. Following the success of her venture, she made it known that she no longer needed the money and labored for the sake of her female clients (one self-commissioned article declared her "a woman of wealth … [r]ich beyond the dream of avarice").[85] Advertisements worked to endear the Pomeroy character to an elite female clientele by reinforcing her respectability and middle-class values. But they also situated her business activities within a conservative bourgeois gender framework.[86]

Figure 5.9 Ellen Terry for Koko for the Hair (1896). Courtesy of the John Johnson Collection, Bodleian Libraries, Beauty Parlour 2 (26b).

The character of "Mrs. Pomeroy" also aligned the cosmopolitanism of *fin de siècle* London with the conservative nationalism of Britain's new imperialism. The character had no ostensible nationality, although the press alleged eastern influences, processed and adapted to British use. "[Mrs. Pomeroy's] idea [of beauty]," wrote one reporter, "is a product of Indian occultism and ... is to beautify the face by suggestion." These theories derived from her "years in India, where she was born and where she learned how to direct the mind so that it may have an influence over all physical defects."[87] Mrs. Pomeroy, who personally promoted her time in British India, was just one of many non-British beauty entrepreneurs exploiting imperial connections to position themselves as purveyors of foreign, exotic products. In marketing schemes, Mrs. Pomeroy, Eugène Rimmel, Anna Ruppert, and other non-British traders fostered what Iveta Jusová terms "the potential to produce new hybridities in liminal spaces" by aligning their exoticized origins with the demands of the genteel British consumer.[88] Despite these evocations of heterogeneity, Mrs. Pomeroy, like her peers, catered to a homogenized "British" beauty aesthetic: a "non-look," allegedly natural, fresh, unadulterated, and white.

Despite her conservative self-fashioning, Mrs. Pomeroy's advocacy of female employment went beyond the norms of conventional femininity. A profile in *Hearth and Home* declared her to be an enthusiast "in all women's work," and she claimed that "every woman would be the happier and the better for working, and moreover, by starting a business she could lend a helping hand to her less fortunate sisters by giving them work."[89] Gendered restrictions on employment apparently forced her to choose the beauty trade rather than higher professions. Indeed, Mrs. Pomeroy "would have been a lady doctor" but turned her sights toward complexion care when "[her] parents [would not] permit it."[90] Mrs. Pomeroy's critique of limited female opportunity may have resonated with elite and educated women, whose own employment aspirations may have been constrained by dominant gender expectations. Even in her cautious deviations from elite class and gender norms, Mrs. Pomeroy attempted to initiate an intimate dialogue with London's increasingly mobile upper-class woman.

Jeannette Pomeroy v. Jeannette Scalé

Scalé's careful enactment of the "Mrs. Pomeroy" character not only endeared her to London's upper-middle-class female shoppers. It also functioned to conceal her genuine distaste for the work. In a letter to her sister dated February 1903, Jeannette Scalé expressed dismay over the end of a holiday in the countryside. "I must go back to London on Monday and be Mrs. Pomeroy again," she lamented. "I hope to find a capable woman to train and relieve me."[91] That winter marked Scalé's eighth year of conducting business as "Mrs. Pomeroy." In spite of financial success and a transnational following, Scalé often expressed a desire to leave the business and become, at various junctures, a painter, a singer, or an art teacher.[92] Yet she never found the "right moment" to abandon her role, lest she risk her personal cachet among London's elite shoppers and their patronage of the Mrs. Pomeroy brand.

In the course of her performance as "Mrs. Pomeroy," Jeannette Scalé employed commercial and technological developments specific to the period in order to efface her economic ambitions and business savvy. All the while, she evoked vendor–patron relations based on trust and intimacy, assuring the resilience of traditional market relationships in the modern city, despite wide-scale cultural change. The communication of this intimacy depended on a very public form of dissemination, via the commercial reproduction and distribution of multiple "Mrs. Pomeroys." More specifically, Scalé mobilized new developments in photography and portraiture, technologies refined in the late nineteenth century, to facilitate marketing schemes that constantly replicated her image. This, in turn, created in its viewers a misperception that they *knew* Mrs. Pomeroy on intimate, personalized terms.[93]

In fact, Jeannette Scalé was quite personally different from her portrayal of Jeannette Pomeroy. Judging from correspondence with her mother, Jeannette Shepherd Hauser, and her sister, Miriam Hauser Rosser, Scalé was unwaveringly ambitious, business-minded, and "unfeminine."[94]

Having grown up as the daughter of Methodist Episcopal missionaries in Darjeeling, India, Scalé married a local art instructor named Jobbins in the early 1890s, yearning for a career in the visual arts or music. The marriage was "intensely unhappy," and Scalé soon left both India and her husband, departing for England with her two young sons. Following after her, Jobbins died en route to London in 1895.[95] As was the case with the Mrs. Pomeroy character she was soon to create, Scalé was a widow—but only for a month. In the first letter to her mother following the death of her husband, she wrote "you will be astounded at my news following so soon after what may have seemed to you sad news, [but] I am to be married and that so soon as Wednesday," a mere eight days later. Her second husband was Bernard Scalé, a "thoroughly English" cabinetmaker and "a partner in a large house Furnishing Business" who she met "when [she] went to buy the Furniture when [she] first went to [England]."[96] With no training or prior experience in the complexion business, the pair turned her first husband's life insurance settlement into the modest Chancery Lane operations. They adopted the name Pomeroy from a "family name on [her] mother's side," related to military notable General Seth Pomeroy, who was "well known in the history" of the United States.[97]

To enact the role of a respectable woman of business, Jeannette Scalé systematically concealed key details about her personal situation from her clients and the media. The most notable discrepancy from the Pomeroy public narrative was the presence of the very alive second husband, Bernard. The lower-middle-class Bernard was in fact central to behind-the-scenes daily management of Mrs. Pomeroy, Ltd. His letters describe no less than nine-hour days as company director, "simply overwhelmed with work" if not literally the piles of letters received daily from female correspondents, estimated at 125 a day.[98] "Life here passes very quickly," he wrote to Jeannette's sister Miriam, "the 'strenuous life' at the office from 9.30 to 6.30 then a walk home a very quiet meal all by myself or a stroll or some writing in bed." The office at Bond Street was "crowded from opening to closing & at the office in Sackville [too]." Bernard, along with six assistants, could "scarcely keep up" with "correspondence, bookkeeping & [the] order[s] department."[99] As an alleged "widow," Jeannette circumvented any distrust of a female-managed beauty enterprise when she was in fact putting her husband to work as her second-in-command.

Bernard's work was not restricted to Mrs. Pomeroy's Bond Street location. The Pomeroy empire included satellite offices in Glasgow, Birmingham, Liverpool, Dublin, Johannesburg, and Cape Town, South Africa.[100] Jeannette frequently traveled to oversee new branches and "get all the money back, invested there,"[101] which, in cases like Cape Town, amounted to over 5,000 American dollars.[102] She did not, however, travel in character as Mrs. Pomeroy. "In each Branch," explained Scalé's mother to Miriam, "the leading lady manager must be for the time 'Mrs. Pomeroy' & no one must expect to see the real head of a great business like this, for it is a great business."[103] As a consequence, a multitude of "Mrs. Pomeroys" proliferated around the world, as ordinary assistants took on the role in satellite locations in Britain and beyond.

While this clearly opened up opportunities for women across the empire, in all of Scalé's copious personal correspondence, she never addressed the condition of the female sex, its potential limitations over her entrepreneurial activities, or the gender conventions regulating her participation in the late-Victorian beauty market. What did interest her was her own family's social mobility. Via Bond Street, Scalé and her family moved into London's upper middle classes, embracing the social and economic expectations befitting such status. At the turn of the century, at the height of the company's success, Scalé moved her family into a large home in St. John's Wood. An affluent suburb in northwest London, "the knowledge that many houses … [were] inhabited by actors and painters bestow[ed] on it a glamour of a sort."[104] The Scalés mixed with London's upper classes, "making new friends and doing some entertaining" or accepting invitations addressed to "Mrs. Pomeroy."[105] She also enrolled her

Figure 5.10 Electrolysis from Arthur Bass Moler, *The Manual on Barbering…* (Chicago?: The Author, 1905), 132. Courtesy of the Library of Congress.

two young sons in a private boarding school near "The Bungalow," her country home in Herefordshire (no doubt allowing more frequent socializing with London's elite).

Her rise in the ranks came at a cost; Scalé despised the work of being London's leading beauty culturist. Despite the personal intimacy projected onto clients by the character of "Mrs. Pomeroy," correspondence from Scalé's mother suggests that she "hate[d] Bond St & all the women patients with their vanities." According to her mother, writing home to Miriam during a stay in London, Scalé found herself doing "electrolysis nearly all day, which trie[d] her eyes," and made "her almost frantic"[106] (Figure 5.10). She was the only expert in the shop "who ventured on the delicate operation of removing moles," adding to her workload.[107] Furthermore, Scalé resented "her own necessity to be so smart & dressed up all the time when [at the shop]." Decked out in the finest of conservative feminine fashions, she was constantly battling to "reduce her figure" and "improve her appearance," judging herself "no advertisement for her business."[108]

During her tenure as Mrs. Pomeroy, Scalé also grew increasingly impatient with the vain and self-absorbed, anxious habits of the leisured class. Even with "seven or eight operators" at their Bond Street location, "the chairs [were] full nearly all the time, & often a number of ladies waiting." Wrote her mother, "appointments are made for days beforehand, & the women have to be on hand or [lose] their turn."[109] The company received the daily pile of letters with "the correspondence … growing all the time."[110] Noted Jeannette Sr., "a good deal of them can be answered by forms, but those that come … are often more puzzling. Some women are so silly or vain or stupid or expect a lotion that will turn them into Venuses & many have real distress that one must advise as carefully as a doctor would."[111]

Scalé's American origins undoubtedly colored her perception of British class culture, as elements of class resentment combined with her social ambitions. Scalé was part of *a fin de siècle* influx of American businesspeople, entrepreneurs, and travelers who flocked to London's fashionable West End.[112] Unlike other parvenus, however, Scalé's personal correspondence allows us to see her intent to plunder, and not just join, London's wealthy classes through the provision of her services. Writing to her mother in the early days of business, she claimed to "have found a gold mine in English womens pocket [*sic*]."[113] The public character of Mrs. Pomeroy may have been stripped of her national identity, but Scalé considered herself "all-American" when it came to her unfaltering determination to succeed in business; in her own words, she was "a chip off the old block [who would] not give in and shall work on," with a sense of "perseverances [*sic*] and pluck [to] make a living."[114]

Despite Scalé's negative views of her clientele, commercial success ultimately demanded the fostering of a certain type of retail relationship that prized intimacy between vendors and shoppers. Significantly, the intensity of vendor–patron relations in London's beauty businesses stood in contrast to general concerns in this period about the breakdown of commercial relationships. The end of the nineteenth century saw an expansion of shopping in new—and alienating—ways. In London, this meant the opening of new commercial areas west of Mayfair, in Knightsbridge and Bayswater. Anchoring these new districts were universal providers—which would become the modern department store—that offered new forms of shopping experiences to London consumers.[115] However, this expansion reportedly came at a price. Department stores, with their promotion of leisurely browsing, clearly labeled prices, and an army of shop assistants, allegedly encouraged shoppers' move away from traditional small-scale shops.[116] For some critics, this meant the breakdown of traditional vendor–patron relationships, as shoppers no longer knew—or trusted—their local retailer. This story of deteriorating commercial relations subsequently gained traction among some historians of nineteenth-century commerce, who argued that a "modernizing turn" saw the alleged "triumph of anonymous consumer relations."[117]

Ongoing intimacy between London's *fin de siècle* beauty culturists and their customers defy this trend, suggesting that, when it came to the body, elite and middling consumers continued to rely on personal connections with local Mayfair providers (Figure 5.11). This aligns with arguments from historians like Margot Finn and Michael Winstanley, who argue that personal interactions of a

Figure 5.11 "Removing Wrinkles with the Electric Roller," *The Daily Mirror* (December 15, 1903): 11. Courtesy of © The British Library Board (Shelfmark MLD4).

"moral market" persisted well into the twentieth century.[118] In 1915, for example, independent shops and not department stores "were the site of 82 per cent of all retail trade transacted from a fixed address."[119] Despite the rise of new retail institutions like the department store, they argue, most shoppers across classes continued to depend on older forms of trustworthy retail relationships to fulfill their consumer needs and desires.

However, in the case of Scalé, her personal, intimate relationships with clients were based on deceit; in this way, her story complicates arguments about the endurance of traditional forms of the "moral market." Mobilizing new "modernizing" developments, Scalé fabricated, marketed, and successfully passed off a commercial alter ego, which clients not only accepted but also *trusted*. All the while, her persona functioned to mask her very real distaste for the social group she served and necessarily imitated. In the mid-century, potentially fabricated commercial identities and self-promotion of women like Sarah Rachel Leverson had been a source of distrust and prosecution. However, by the end of the century, Scalé's case seems to suggest a new acceptance, or at least increasingly lenient standards, of middle-class women entrepreneurs and their marketing schemes. By creating and performing a commercial character at the *fin de siècle*, Scalé carved out an elite niche for herself and her female competitors, positioning them against the increasingly impersonal corporate scene. While this seemingly made for a persistence in "moral market" transactions, it was the "modernizing turn" that enabled new conditions of possibility for middle-class beauty businesswomen, who crafted fanciful—and false—commercial identities to advance their business.

Beauty on Trial

But just how viable were these performative possibilities for women in the context of London's increasingly regulated commercial scene? To tackle this question, we must return to the legal proceedings of 1906, between Old Bond Street's Mrs. Pomeroy, Ltd. and its impersonator next door.

For unknown reasons, Jeannette Scalé's business and marriage collapsed in 1906, forcing her to sell Mrs. Pomeroy, Ltd. to new owners in May of that year. However, Scalé had no intention of abandoning London's lucrative West End beauty scene. Instead, she opened a new shop—just down the road from her old premises—in August 1906. To promote her new business, Scalé characteristically launched a multi-medium marketing campaign, using the Pomeroy name despite having sold her limited company. When citing her misuse of "Mrs. Pomeroy" in the service of her new business, trial reports listed no less than "advertisements, address plates, and labels, door-plates, removal notices, circulars, and business cards and documents … pamphlets, [and] letters."[120] The new owners of "Mrs. Pomeroy" promptly filed suit over the use of the company name.

The trial convened on December 11, 1906 before Mr. Justice Parker in London's Chancery Division. Over the four-day hearing, the plaintiffs portrayed Jeannette Scalé as everything Mrs. Pomeroy was not; they ransacked her private life to expose a callous businesswoman who thought nothing of abandoning her family or deceiving her customers if it meant financial gain. Their case included a careful outlining of Scalé's questionable activities over her last days at the company, including attempts "to induce staff to call her Mrs. Pomeroy" rather than Mrs. Scalé and having "a copy of the customers' names made for her."[121] Yet Scalé's female staff had nothing but high praise for their employer and corroborated her position as a reputable employer throughout the trial. When cross-examined, three of Scalé's "beautiful electrolysers" described "referring affectionately to their absent chief as 'Mrs. P' and 'Mrs. Pom'" and *not* Mrs. Scalé, as the plaintiffs maintained.[122]

But her employees could not counter what was perhaps the most damning evidence, the disintegration of her marriage to Bernard and their hasty separation. The plaintiffs depicted the split as a means for Jeannette to further her reckless economic ambitions "despite the fact that there were no differences between herself and Mr. Scalé."[123] According to plaintiffs' counsel, their separation was merely a means to "carry on … trade, business, profession or occupation as she thought proper, without interference from her husband." Furthermore, the breakdown of her marriage meant she was "entitled to abandon her name of Scalé and adopt such name as, in her opinion, might be best suited to the interests of such business."[124]

When called to the stand, Scalé relied on skills central to her daily performance as "Mrs. Pomeroy," those of consummate charm and personality. Her clever retorts elicited frequent laughter from court spectators, including one instance when she offered to "beautify" the leading counsel for the plaintiffs. In keeping with her performance as the discreet proprietress of an exclusive establishment, Scalé resisted discussing her marital matters, stating that she "did not want to disclose [her] private affairs."[125] When pressed during cross-examination, she admitted her anxiety over the separation, having "wanted to be separated three years ago [in 1903], but [she] could not be separated till Jan. 15 [*sic*], because things had not come to a crisis," before asking "won't you get off this subject?"[126] Countering claims of callousness, Scalé's description of the separation—"a very serious step to take"— conveyed the gravity of such a move for a mother of two who was only precariously holding on to middle-class status.[127] At one point "during her cross-examination," according to the *Daily Mirror*, "the witness burst into tears."[128]

Her case was dealt a significant blow by Bernard in his turn on the stand. According to him, the separation came about after a single "serious difference of opinion" in 1903, yet he was allowed to stay married to Jeannette "because until [January 1906] he was earning money." Neither family correspondence nor Company records sufficiently explain the sudden financial collapse of Mrs. Pomeroy, Ltd. in 1906. We do know that Bernard was suddenly unable to assist in daily operations, and only then did Jeannette's lawyer suggest, "it would be much better for Mrs. Pomeroy not to be controlled by [him] in any way."[129] When asked if he himself desired the separation, Bernard, in a final blow to Mrs. Pomeroy's reputation, replied no.

"The Defendant [Scalé] is so much identified with the business," her counsel had argued at the first of the four sessions, "that she is *Mrs. Pomeroy*."[130] Scalé herself testified, "she had always regarded herself and the Company as being identical."[131] But for Scalé, the real stakes of *Mrs. Pomeroy, Ltd. v. Scalé* was not the threat to her identity or sense of selfhood; it was the potential nullity of the Pomeroy fiction and its accompanying marketing schemes. Justice Parker recognized this in his decision following four days of testimony. While authorized to "introduc[e] an exception" to the common law in order "to avoid the hardship which would otherwise fall upon [the individual Scalé]," Parker looked instead to the interests of Mrs. Pomeroy's female clients.[132] He saw no feasible way for Scalé to continue in the beauty business as Mrs. Pomeroy without confusing (and subsequently deceiving) women shoppers.[133] In spite of her admirable attempts at what Parker termed "self-preservation," the judge ruled against Scalé; she was barred from commercial use of "Pomeroy."[134] This was no small matter given the power of the Mrs. Pomeroy fiction. Justice Parker acknowledged as much, noting, "the very fact that both parties consider that my decision in this case is so important, is a tribute to the position that *Mrs. Pomeroy* held in the Company."[135]

While we know that both the legal community and general public were made aware of Scalé's real name, the extent of the damage done to the Mrs. Pomeroy fiction over the course of the trial remains unclear. Despite extensive and damning press coverage (including one headline in the *Daily Mirror* that asked, "When is Mrs. Pomeroy Not Mrs. Pomeroy?"[136]) it seems that Scalé experienced no public defamation in the aftermath of the trial. Painfully obvious, though, was the fact that Scalé's success depended far more on the Pomeroy fiction than "her own personality" as she had testified in court.[137] Scalé's new business failed, and she once again closed shop on Old Bond Street in late December 1906. Putting what she termed "her failure" behind her, Scalé opened two more West End complexion businesses between 1907 and 1909, one optimistically named "Hope."[138] But intermittent letters to family described "dark clouds" and "fiendish anxiety" as Scalé "[hung] on by the skin of [her] teeth." By November 1910, she contracted out her electrolysis services to competitor Helen Best and took up cheap rooms on Oxford Street. With mounting debts, however, "the chief aim of life" became "circumvent[ing] the law & the bailiff."[139] She departed from London the following year.[140] As for Mrs. Pomeroy Ltd., the company continued operations without their namesake, encouraging women to "Pomeroy" themselves well into the 1940s.[141]

Conclusions

In the context of London's modernizing retail scene, Jeannette Scalé and other West End beauty providers exploited consumer dissatisfaction with the impersonal nature of "modern" retailing at the *fin de siècle*. Identifying new needs being unmet by professionalized beauty businesses, female entrepreneurs like Adair and Carmichael challenged the anonymity of the expanding urban scene by catering to the individual female consumer. At the same time, this growing anonymity facilitated the creation of elaborate business personas, defined by self-promotion and performance and not, as was the case in earlier moments, by personal and family reputation.[142] In the case of Mrs. Pomeroy, a commercial persona became a powerful tool in circumventing dominant expectations of feminine respectability, expectations that continued to shape conditions of female beauty enterprise. Unfortunately for Jeannette Scalé, this well-crafted personal fiction—engendered by opportunities specific to the *fin de siècle*—did not survive the legal challenge from Mrs. Pomeroy, Ltd. After years of firm ascendancy over London's flourishing beauty market, it seemed that Mrs. Pomeroy had finally met some estimable competition: herself.

While some of Jeannette Scalé's West End contemporaries fared better than their neighbor, others experienced their own precipitous declines. Among success stories, beauty maven Eleanor Adair expanded her business through the early twentieth century, eventually opening a branch in New York City at which she hired a young Canadian, Elizabeth Arden, to staff the front desk. Back in London, the number of manicurists and electrolysis operators continued to expand into the interwar period, and businesswomen like Helen Cavendish saw the thriving of their enterprises alongside a more general expansion of modern beauty culture. This commercial profitability did not extend to all, and some beauty businesswomen faded into obscurity after listing operations in London's commercial directories for only a year or two. Mirroring the experience of Scalé, other traders experienced more sensational collapses, including Anna Ruppert who found herself charged under Ireland's Pharmaceutical Act in 1893 for selling arsenical compounds.[143] A survey of the variable experiences of London's female beauty culturists thus suggests that the late nineteenth and early twentieth centuries remained a period of potential liminality, as women's work continued to tread the bounds of respectability defining both female beautification and independent business pursuits.[144]

That is not to say that the *fin de siècle* did not give rise to important new opportunities for London's beauty businesswomen. At the same time, the failure of traders like Jeannette Scalé harkened back to an earlier period of female beauty enterprise and specifically the mid-century trials of "Madame Rachel" Leverson. While Leverson signaled a move away from "backroom" business in the wake of trade professionalization, Mrs. Pomeroy represented a triumph of the small-scale entrepreneur in response to corporate mass beauty. And yet, despite the considerable years separating their cases, these women's stories highlight the enduring challenges facing small-scale entrepreneurs, including women, in London's modern beauty industry. This would change, however, with the next generation of beauty businesswomen—women like Helena Rubinstein—who exploited modern twentieth-century ideas about femininity, beauty, and mass consumption to irrefutable success.

6

From Beauty Culturists to Beauty Magnates: Helena Rubinstein

In July 1911, an Anglo-American socialite was called before a London court. Louise Winterfeldt (1863–1914), the wife of a prominent German-American banker, stood charged with "enticing away" a British beauty worker to a better life across the Atlantic. The conflict started during one of Winterfeldt's annual trips from her home on New York's Fifth Avenue to London, for the season. In 1908, her visit included treatments at a West End beauty boutique administered by shop worker Dora Isabel Stock (1882–1979). Winterfeldt took a liking to Stock. Before returning to New York, the socialite proposed to take the worker to America and offered her London employer, Mrs. Titus, £150 per month for three months of Stock's labor. Three months later, when Stock remained in the United States as Winterfeldt's personal secretary, Titus brought a suit for damages against the American socialite to recoup the lost labor of her prized "complexion girl."

Mrs. Titus was none other than Helena Rubinstein (1872–1965), embroiled in a very public lawsuit some years before her rise to the status of global beauty magnate (Figure 6.1). Testifying under—and perhaps concealed by— her married name, Rubinstein described her early struggles in establishing a London business before its transformation into a successful venture raking in some £16,000 per year. She simultaneously defended the importance of laborers like Stock to dubious legal authorities, emphasizing the time and skill invested in training the "girls" only to lose them to a better opportunity in America. These revealing details from the 1911 trial provide an evocative glimpse into the early experiences of a woman who went on to become one of the greatest beauty entrepreneurs of the twentieth century. But it also foregrounds the importance of transnational consumers like Winterfeldt and service workers like Stock as part of a network of players propelling London's beauty and fashion industries through the early twentieth century. The entangled histories of female

Figure 6.1 Helena Rubinstein (n.d.). Hulton Archive/Getty Images.

entrepreneurs, clients, and laborers—embodied in the figures of Rubinstein, Winterfeldt, and Stock—reveal the complex transatlantic and commercial networks that allowed for the relatively unhindered ascent of individual businesswomen in Edwardian London's beauty scene. Developments specific to this period saw the substantial growth in sustained transatlantic travel between London and New York, particularly among a wealthy contingent of bourgeois elites. The fashionable pursuits of these mobile high-class consumers extended to bodily services and provisions, including those offered by London beauty experts and their workers. In this way, female providers, clients, and laborers participated in an expanding commercial nexus that served the bodily desires of mobile transatlantic consumers, many of whom considered London the pinnacle of a particular mode of fashionable modernity.

Devoting attention to three distinct historical actors and their relationship to London's twentieth-century beauty scene moves us away from depictions of Rubinstein's work as a singular example of innovative female enterprise and achievement, isolated from the broader commercial contingencies and contexts in which she operated. This approach subsequently complicates more conventional depictions of Rubinstein's entrepreneurial "origin stories," which titillated both the court gallery in 1911 and modern readers exploring the history of the cosmetics industry and its "trailblazers." Historians and bloggers alike have devoted well-deserved attention to some of the first "highly successful women entrepreneurs" like Rubinstein. Of course, Rubinstein was not simply an entrepreneur, but a leading *beauty* entrepreneur. Documentary and biographical projects highlight the beauty mogul's role in transforming gendered perceptions of beauty consumption, "usher[ing] in the 'new woman' of the 1920s—young, independent, and in every way equal to men."[1] Most recently, this includes attention to her competitive relationship with leading rival Elizabeth Arden, an international magnate of Canadian descent who figured as a consistent source of conflict—and motivation—throughout much of Rubinstein's career. Celebratory projects bolster a common story in entrepreneurial history; they argue that specific innovators reinvented their respective industry through equal parts hard work and originality, which set them apart from fellow trade members.[2] What makes recent depictions like Broadway's *Warpaint* (2017) particularly compelling, of course, was that the innovators were not one but *two* dynamic women competing to revolutionize the western beauty industry.

There is also a geographic dimension to many biographies and documentaries, which maintain that Rubinstein's independent development of a synonymous, internationally recognized brand took hold following her breakout success in New York City from 1914, when her American triumphs guaranteed global ascendency.[3] In doing so, some histories of Rubinstein replicate a common theme in entrepreneurial histories of the twentieth century: a geographic focus on the United States as the principal site of innovation, enterprise, and triumph. Biographies maintain that it was through her move to America—and abandonment of humble colonial markets—that Rubinstein developed the sufficient cultural and economic capital to fulfill her entrepreneurial vision.[4]

Transatlantic movement in the nineteenth and twentieth centuries undoubtedly offered new opportunities for women's social and economic mobility, capitalist ventures, and enterprise. To be sure, Rubinstein's renown was guaranteed by her successes on the American market after 1914. Yet, Rubinstein was also a citizen of a British imperial world who had to develop substantive relationships to deeply localized commercial scenes to first establish her reputation.[5] This is especially clear in her time in London, where Rubinstein adopted a number of established business practices already employed by her competitors who dominated the late-nineteenth-century commercial scene, including women like Jeannette Scalé. In this way, a survey of Rubinstein's time in London reveals that her commercial strategies represented a continuity in the beauty industry rather than the dramatic break depicted in biographic takes, including productions like *Warpaint*. Rubinstein offered discreet, respectable services to London's elite classes, providing treatments in facial massage and skin care that echoed those available on Bond Street from the 1890s. She amplified her associations with cosmopolitanism, balancing her foreignness with carefully curated self-promotion linking her to feminine respectability. She worked within a deeply localized urban setting, depending on the reputation of the West End to bolster her respectability, while she navigated—and attempted to infiltrate—the rarefied world of the Edwardian carriage trades (Plate 19).

Rubinstein's efforts in London also suggest the capital's enduring status as a preeminent site of fashionable internationalism, as she integrated into a service sector tailored to the bodily needs of a powerful cohort of elite, mobile consumers. London was a single albeit significant node within a constellation of western fashion capitals that flourished in the early twentieth century: Paris, Berlin, New York. Expanded networks of travel between these sites offered new opportunities for the reinvention of beauty providers, customers, and service people, as we will see in the experiences of Rubinstein, Winterfeldt, and Stock, respectively. Each woman engaged in processes of self-making as they moved between London and New York in particular, the latter soon if not already eclipsing the former as the Anglo world's most dynamic urban center. By the second decade of the twentieth century, such reinventions increasingly became a choice rather than a necessity, as new conceptions of women's public visibility made for the growing celebration of female entrepreneurs like Rubinstein as part of a cadre of successful international businesswomen. However, these increasingly common celebrations of entrepreneurs like Rubinstein functioned, at times, to obscure their debts to earlier generations of beauty businesswomen in London, not to mention their reliance on the concealed labor of women like Dora Stock to buoy their enterprise.

Melbourne to Mayfair: Helena Titus Rubinstein

Rubinstein, her clients, and her workers were bound by long-standing conditions specific to London's commercial beauty scene, while benefitting from developments of the twentieth century that facilitated new modes of global mobility, reinvention of the self, and the growing visibility—and acceptance—of ambulatory, ambitious female enterprise. This included Rubinstein's courting of new modes of cosmopolitanism to bolster her commercial reputation. By the early twentieth century, the sanitizing efforts undertaken by previous generations of foreign-born beauty brokers did not apply to Rubinstein, who actively fashioned herself a "woman of the world" with the goal of enlightening British women on the subject of beauty.

Rubinstein's "foreign" allure derived from Polish origins, having been born into a middle-class Jewish family in Krakow in 1870. By 1903, Rubinstein had immigrated to Melbourne to live with extended family, where she launched her first beauty venture. As an outsider in Australia, Rubinstein quickly adapted her foreignness to her advantage; the "archetypical rootless cosmopolitan" transformed cultural differences into a selling point, just as Eugène Rimmel and Jeannette Scalé had done before her.[6] However, unlike earlier generations of traders, Rubinstein made no attempts to cater her goods and services to Anglo sensibilities. Instead, she claimed to have directly transported her "Russian Cream Valaze" products "to the Commonwealth" from her Viennese home, where she designed the goods alongside the mysterious and "eminent Russian Skin Specialist" Dr. Lykuski. At the same time, she declared there was "no mystery clouding and deluding the sense about the character" and efficacy of her skin food, which protected Australian women's complexions from "the oft times trying climates." Developing local publicity campaigns and a lucrative mail-order trade, Rubinstein's Melbourne operations paralleled strategies of small-scale entrepreneurs in London, but in a settler colonial context. She capitalized on these imperial associations, aligning Australian women with those from New Zealand, Canada, and America who sent "equal praise and appreciation" to the "dainty young agent of Valaze."[7]

Soon enough, Rubinstein set her sights on more lucrative metropolitan markets. As a soon-to-be naturalized Australian citizen and an imperial subject, Rubinstein looked first to the British capital in 1905 before venturing to Paris or New York.[8] As historian Angela Woollacott argues, travel to the imperial metropole was a means for young Australian women to pursue economic goals without transgressing social conventions regulating feminine ambition.[9] Although twentieth-century London was a site of potential opportunity, it could also prove challenging for newcomers and residents alike. It was little surprise, then, that Rubinstein's foray into the metropolis proved a daunting task, at least as she recalled it in her 1966 autobiography, *My Life for Beauty*. London was, in her opinion, "the richest, the gayest, the most elegant capital in the world."[10]

It was also notoriously exclusive, and Rubinstein had no contacts in London's beauty industry nor its social set. Rubinstein subsequently embarked on a scouting mission to discern her prospects in the British scene. The Bond Street that Rubinstein first experienced in 1905 may have been dominated by Jeannette Scalé and her contemporaries, but it was a different space from that inhabited by Susan Ansell and Sarah Rachel Leverson some forty years earlier (Figure 6.2). While the thoroughfare retained its reputation as a site of elite consumption, the areas around Bond Street had reportedly undergone a downturn at the end of the nineteenth century. But now, "[g]ood style" businesses sprung up in place of "very dingy" establishments. New development replaced plebeian courts "and corners where there used to be small tenements occupied by a rather rough population."[11] By 1905, Bond Street and its environs were a modern commercial district populated primarily by traders and shoppers. During her tour of Europe

Figure 6.2 "Oxford Street from Bond Street," by Rose Barton (1898). Lordprice Collection/Alamy Stock Photo.

that year, Rubinstein took on the latter role and "experiment[ed] by having had treatments at every salon in Bond Street."[12]

It would be another three years before Rubinstein could accrue sufficient capital to sustain a successful business in London. Challenges arose on a number of familiar fronts, including affording Mayfair's exorbitant rents, integrating into the existing service sector, and attracting female clientele while maintaining the discretion and respectability demanded by these same women. In the face of such conditions, recalled Rubinstein, friends in Australia advised against the expansion, claiming that Londoners would "slaughter" her.[13] Rubinstein rejected these warnings, returning to Britain in 1908 to obtain prime commercial space. Reminiscing in later life, she described a protracted process characterized by daily walks "from one street to another" through Mayfair, the location in which she had to settle "if [she] wanted the 'carriage trade.'"[14] She eventually secured a stately Georgian town house two blocks west of Bond Street, at 24 Grafton (Figure 6.3). Featuring four floors and twenty-six rooms, the rent—"several thousand pounds

Figure 6.3 Designs for a Salon for Helena Rubinstein, 26 Grafton Street, by Erno Goldfinger (1926). Courtesy of Royal Institute of British Architecture, London.

per annum"—far exceeded her means.[15] Rubinstein subsequently resorted to strategies of earlier entrepreneurs by living on the third floor of the "Maison de Beauté Valaze" for her first few years in London. As late as 1911, Rubinstein, her husband, two sons, and two servants shared the attic apartment. All the while, she produced her goods in its basement.[16]

When Rubinstein sought out her Grafton Street location, she almost certainly followed examples set by other West End female operatives, an indebtedness that does not figure in her autobiographical recollections. "Complexion Specialists" had featured in trade directories from 1897, when Jeannette Scalé appeared as its first and only affiliate. By 1908, directories advertised twenty complexion specialists clustered in and around Bond Street, all but two of them women.[17] This growth reflected, in part, shifting attitudes about the roles and lives of women in public. As we have seen, the *fin de siècle* saw the rise in women's public visibility, characterized by their growing access to new forms of work, political expression, leisure, and unencumbered movement through public space, including urban sites of consumption.[18] Expanded sociocultural opportunities allegedly made for a new significance in women's outwardly appearance. In response, a new generation of socially mobile women increasingly sought out beauty aids to enhance their public presence.[19]

Despite these new attitudes toward commercial beauty, Rubinstein initially struggled, and her business failed to turn a profit for the first two years of operation.[20] Throughout, she remained acutely aware of her "outsider" status, in terms of her ethnicity but also her alienation from local trade networks. In London, unlike Melbourne, "all doors seemed closed except to a select few," and it became her own loneliness that "gave [her] impetus." This alienation also extended to her relationship with clients, with London's smart set being very different from the middle-class women who supported her Australian trade.[21] Although reluctant, there was some evidence of overt beauty consumption among London elites, with one observer describing "coquettish grand-mothers in rouge and coloured hair, looking at age as a hateful hag, with debutantes round and rosy trying to be serious and severe."[22] Yet, despite slow shifts toward beauty consumption, London's elite women continued to veil their beautifying activities in secrecy.[23] Visitors to Rubinstein's salon were reportedly "anxious that [their] friends should know nothing of [their] visit." Rubinstein recalled how British ladies waited "with [their] veil lowered" around the corner in Bruton Lane until Grafton Street emptied of pedestrians. "More than once," she quipped, "I wondered what would have happened if any two of my furtive visitors had stepped simultaneously from their carriages and recognized each other."[24]

In spite of their misgivings, local and visiting elites eventually flocked to her shop. This was due in part to Rubinstein's extensive advertising, but also her offer of exclusive—and initially free—beautifying services which ingratiated her with the city's elite female shoppers.[25] Services resembled those offered by Rubinstein's London predecessors and contemporaries, including Mrs. Pomeroy and Eleanor Adair: electrolysis, facial massage, and complexion treatments. Complementing these services was Rubinstein's signature Valaze line, which featured the original Beautifying Skinfood but, by 1915, expanded to include some forty-four items including Herbal Soap, Blackhead and Open Pore Cure, Face Powder, and Lip Lustre.[26] Rubinstein also developed services that targeted dermatological "problems," which involved a "scientifically studied" designation of clients' skin—dry, oily, or otherwise—before receipt of individually tailored services and products.[27] Despite her insistence on the naturalness of her interventions and the importance of holistic approaches to dermatological health, Rubinstein also reportedly remedied ladies' wrinkles via paraffin injections and offered "face peeling" in more extreme cases; such services understandably did not feature in print advertising campaigns.[28] While she discouraged heavy use of makeup in her promotional materials, Rubinstein also developed color cosmetics and persuaded leading clients like Margot Asquith to experiment with rouge "to dramatise her remarkable features."[29] With elite patronage firmly secured, Rubinstein came to charge upward of ten guineas for twelve treatments.

While Rubinstein's goods and services echoed those of her London-based competition, she further distinguished herself by foregrounding her cosmopolitan connections to a global network of western fashion capitals. As we will see, the early twentieth century saw the development of an "imagined community" of fashionable elites who, through expanded technologies of travel, patronized leading goods and services in Paris, Berlin, New York, and London. Rubinstein's early English print campaigns firmly situated her within this cosmopolitan milieu, portraying her as a globe-trotting connoisseur of all things beauty. Following "acclaim … by thousands of clients on the Continent," Rubinstein brought her scientific approach and international experience to London, having allegedly traveled the world on the hunt for beauty so that her elite customers did not have to. Following her tours, she elected the "new and unique" approaches of the Viennese school as "(practised nowhere else in England)." Rejecting the "French" approach of "accepting ugliness as a fact and concealing it as deftly as possible," the Viennese system tackled "dermic defects" in a "rational" way, relying on "scientific measures which restore and maintain the skin in a perfect and healthy condition."[30] In this way, Rubinstein resembled Rimmel by positioning herself as a foreign arbiter of taste for her beauty consumers, but with an important distinction; unlike Rimmel, Rubinstein's goods and services were not Anglicized but deliberately and unapologetically foreign, turning on Vienna's widespread reputation as the "dermatology capital" of the early-twentieth-century world.[31]

The strategy seems to have worked. After initial losses, Rubinstein transformed her London business into a lucrative British firm, buoying her professional and personal circumstances. By 1909, she made £12,823 per year in the sale of preparations and another £10,905 for in-house treatments.[32] To achieve this, she had sufficiently distinguished herself from other London complexion specialists, maximizing her cosmopolitan worldliness for twentieth-century consumers who prized her knowledge of international commercial beauty cultures. This translated into familial advancement, and her firm's success allowed her to purchase separate residential property in London's suburban belt by 1912. As Scalé had done just a few years earlier, Rubinstein relocated her family to the suburbs—modest Richmond and not wealthy, "pleasure-seeking Putney," as she later claimed—before turning her attentions to Paris and New York in the following years.[33]

The London Look: Louise Winterfeldt

Biographies highlight the individual efforts of Rubinstein in establishing her London business before crossing the Atlantic in 1914 for even greater triumphs. This story of singular success—made in America—ignores broader trends in global fashionable consumption, and it is important to situate Rubinstein's business within transatlantic commercial networks fueling global economies of the early twentieth century. Historian Kristin Hoganson points to the development of a "fashionable world" at the turn of the century, which forged an "imagined community" of elite western shoppers and producers across major fashion cities: London, Paris, New York, Berlin.[34] While the American market promised certain financial advantages, elite consumers moved fluidly through a range of global settings, soliciting traders and service providers across fashionable urban nodes.

The global mobility of fashionable consumers—including beauty patrons— is exemplified in the movements of Louise Winterfeldt, the Rubinstein client and, ultimately, defendant charged with absconding with a "complexion girl"

(Figure 6.4). Winterfeldt was the wife of German banker Hans Winterfeldt, who headed up American operations for famed Berlin banking outfit Speyer. Her ascent to the upper reaches of New York society concealed a more complicated backstory that included class and geographic mobility, engendered by multiple marriages and a steady accrual of social and cultural capital. Born Annie "Louise" Druce in 1863, Winterfeldt spent her early years laboring for her victauler-father in the Manor Hotel in Datchet, Buckinghamshire. In August 1887, aged twenty-four, she entered into her first marriage to a local jockey. Following his death two years later, Louise married once if not twice more before meeting Berlin-born Hans Winterfeldt under unknown circumstances. By 1905, Louise and Hans were en route to New York where they married in November of that year, celebrating with a nuptial dinner of lamb medallions and kingfish filets at the Waldorf Astoria.[35]

MRS. LOUISE WINTERFELDT

Figure 6.4 Mrs. Louise Winterfeldt, *The Charlotte News* (July 10, 1911): 8. Courtesy of Newspapers.com.

In the years that followed, the Winterfeldts made regular appearances in the *New York Times's* society columns, lauded for their philanthropic and social activities but also for Mrs. Winterfeldt's fashion sense.[36] In addition to residences on Fifth Avenue, on the Hudson River in the wealthy suburb of Scarborough, and on Paris's Rue d'Artois, the couple made annual trips for the London season. As Woollacott has shown, London's "pull" came from its importance in "the publishing, art, educational, reform, theatrical, musical, scientific, medical, legal, and political worlds."[37] But it was also a site of consumer and urban pleasures, and the Winterfeldts and other travelers buoyed the city's international fashion scene and its attendant service sector via their patronage of the finest in accommodation, dining, fashion, and bodily services.[38]

To be sure, London's service sector depended on the yearly influx of international elites to sustain their operations. The season followed a relatively fixed schedule, and the time of year subsequently dictated the pace of business.[39] Travelers from around the world descended on London through the spring and into the summer, with the city operating as an imperial entrepôt hosting intellectuals, aristocrats, and students from across the empire.[40] This cohort also included a notable contingent of Americans, who, in the early twentieth century, deigned London a desirable fashion capital where their own standing could be enhanced. The widow of an American diplomat, Rebecca Insley Casper, observed in 1912 how "sailings from New York during the summer season [with] a thousand persons, spending on an average two hundred pounds each, start every week for European ports."[41] This included Britain, where links could be made to an esteemed Anglo past, one characterized by venerable pedigrees to which parvenu Americans sought access.

Upon arrival in Edwardian London, elite Americans depended on social connections and economic influence to sustain their position among established networks of British nobility. This approach was bolstered by Edward VII himself, who reportedly "brought to court the cosmopolitan society he had long made fashionable away from the court," which included a special penchant for visitors from the United States.[42] Insley Casper noted the king's favoring of "American women" in particular, with "the American ambassador ... so thoroughly persona grata that it gave all Americans presented there an enviable status they did not receive elsewhere."[43] This standing had its limits, however, and Americans did not always have the lineage nor the history to make meaningful inroads into the social hierarchies dictating the London season. What they lacked in heredity, they reportedly made up for with money, and transatlantic travelers conveyed their right to belonging through their readily accessible wealth. As Insley Casper observed, in a chapter devoted exclusively to "American Money,"

> [T]here is no more absurd illusion in existence than the idea that Americans were ever really welcomed into the inner circle of court life in any monarchical country, or that American women ever conquered there by beauty, charm, or intellectual gifts alone... No, no, they had to bring money, more of it than their rivals could muster, and spend it more ingeniously, more amazingly, than their rivals dared.[44]

Wealth was the key to social and cultural capital for American visitors. "What is Money," waxed Insley Casper, "but the symbol and instrument of conquest, and the only one that could be used?"[45] The Edwardian season subsequently gained a reputation for being especially extravagant, owing to the tastes of the king as bolstered by American funds.

To sustain the lavish displays of wealth for which they became known, American interlopers subsequently relied on the services—and skill—of London's existing commercial providers.[46] International elites turned to the London carriage trades to help them act but also *look* the part of worthy season-goer; in doing so, they tapped into an infrastructure of British service providers who helped them secure the material trappings demanded by high-class London life. The London season sustained many of the city's dressmaking, millinery, and beauty businesses as part of a fashionable global network linking western capitals.[47] This renewed veneration of London style also corroborated the British capital's standing as a preeminent space of urban luxury consumption and culture at the *fin de siècle* (Figure 6.5). London was, according to Rubinstein, "the world center of thought, taste, money, and beauty."[48] As a growing cadre of elite global travelers like Louise Winterfeldt engaged in what Hoganson terms "upper-class internationalism," Rubinstein and other London-based traders benefited from this boom in transatlantic consumption by a global class of people with means.[49]

Elite travelers like Winterfeldt signaled their belonging to national and international networks via their choices in dressmakers, styles, and services.[50] In soliciting London-based firms, American visitors attempted to establish their worth in the carefully calibrated hierarchies underpinning the British aristocracy. "[H]ow was [the Old World] to be conquered by the New" posed Insley Casper, "except by Money, for more splendid homes and entertainments, by gowns of more costly material, and more of them, by the conscious superiority which these bring to the woman[?]" For American visitors, fashion was power,

"TOWN LIFE."
In Bond Street

After the black & white drawing by Edward King.

Figure 6.5 "'Town Life' in Bond Street" (n.d.). Culture Club/Getty Images.

providing arrivistes like Winterfeldt the "courage to look down her nose at a duchess!"[51]

Processes of consumer self-making also turned on beautifying services offered by Rubinstein and her competitors. Fashionable toilettes demanded a sufficiently beautified body, from carefully coiffed hair to a clear, white complexion. While London's complexion specialists, including Rubinstein, worked to ingratiate themselves with British clients, they also relied on steady trade from visitors for the season like Winterfeldt. Wealthy Americans were keen to fashion themselves in the vein of elite English ladies and solicited the help of Rubinstein, Pomeroy, and others to do so. Rubinstein and other London-based beauty brokers subsequently courted foreign custom, while benefitting from looser cultural attitudes toward overt beautification shared by non-British consumers visiting from the United States, France, and beyond.[52]

To do so, Rubinstein mobilized her international experiences to connect with a cohort of worldly consumers who, like her, circulated just outside the most exclusive circles of elite London life. In doing so, both Rubinstein and American elites contributed to London's prewar cosmopolitan scene, participating in what historian Judith Walkowitz characterizes, in part, as "a pleasurable, stylized form of imaginative expatriation, associated with privileged mobility." And yet, foreign beauty experts and American consumers were not fully cosmopolitan in their pursuits, in their resistance to its other potential associations: as "a debased condition of deracination, hybridity, displacement, and racial degeneration."[53] Instead, Rubinstein, Winterfeldt, and others strove for belonging within an entrenched classed hierarchy, mobilizing the cachet of elite global internationalism to engender belonging among traditional English gentility.

American Ambitions: Dora Isabel Stock

If beauty providers and clients like Rubinstein and Winterfeldt depended on the internationalism of Edwardian London's commercial beauty scene, there was an additional element that tied the industry more firmly to local, working-class influences in production and retailing: female laborers who worked in increasingly visible beauty ventures. While Rubinstein was the public face of her business, it was the labor of working- and lower-middle-class complexion "girls" that sustained her firm. This included Dora Stock, the subject of the 1911 trial, who was a prized member of Rubinstein's team before her turn to Winterfeldt— and global networks of elite Anglo-American wealth—and departure for New York City. Stock's case reveals that it was not only businesspeople and elite customers who moved fluidly in and out of London through the season. Through her, we see alternate possibilities for transatlantic pursuits among more humble actors populating the fashionable service sector. In Louise Winterfeldt's quest to embody the part of an elite Anglo beauty, she opened up possibilities for a laborer who possessed specialized bodily expertise. In this way, transatlantic fashionable communities could engender opportunities for a range of women and even lower-middle-class "complexion girls." Stock subsequently attempted to take advantage of these new transnational pursuits available to modern, mobile women of the early twentieth century, albeit to mixed success.

Before becoming the focus of a transatlantic legal drama, Dora Stock was one of a number of young British women who, in the early twentieth century, entered London's fashionable urban service sector. As Edwardian beauty businesspeople rose in stature and prominence, they expanded their workforces to include greater numbers of working- and lower-middle-class female service staff. This manifested in different modes of occupation across the beauty trades, examples of which suggest increasingly rigid distinctions between the production and service sectors. For the former, the late nineteenth century saw a clear rise in young women taking up work behind the scenes in manufacturing operations around London. Evidence from the 1881 census, for example, suggests the growing presence of working-class and lower-middle-class women and girls filling production positions as "Perfumers" or, more accurately, "Chemical Manufacturers." Expanding commercial perfumery operations like those of Breidenbach & Co. employed growing ranks of women to work on simple production lines in the manufactory setting.[54] The rising dependency on feminized production labor continued into the twentieth century, coming to the fore in photographic evidence documenting John Gosnell & Co.'s 1900 move from Upper Thames Street to impressive new premises on Blackfriars Road. Seemingly orchestrated to show off their new facilities, images also highlighted rows of uniformly attired female workers producing large quantities of goods like Cherry Tooth Paste.[55] Echoing promotional materials by Rimmel in the 1870s, traders foregrounded their mobilization of female laborers as a testament to their progressive manufacturing practices and processes.[56]

Manufacturing labor dramatically departed from beauty service provision, yet it was nonetheless part of the growing range of economic possibilities increasingly available to a feminized *fin de siècle* workforce. As is the case for working-class chemical manufacturers, details about the lives and work conditions of late-nineteenth- and early-twentieth-century "complexion girls" are difficult to acquire, as their labor was often underpaid and discreet by design. This is the case for Dora Stock, and there is little information about her early life before working for Rubinstein. Records suggest she was the youngest of three unmarried daughters of a Croydon draper with no experience in the beauty business, having previously been employed as "a milliner or something like that."[57] Despite this, Rubinstein hired Stock on March 21, 1908, when the 26-year-old signed a three-year contract. Like other "complexion girls" Stock reportedly underwent arduous training to learn Rubinstein's methods. She did well despite the rigors of the process, with Stock proving a model employee unlike many of her fellow apprentices. Three weeks after her arrival, she was allowed to "work on the poorer clients." Reportedly "a person of tact, with a very pleasant manner," Stock soon "became popular" with patients.[58] Rubinstein was fortunate. Competent assistants were apparently hard to find, and she purported to "engage … lots of" complexion workers before discharging them "because they were useless."[59] It took another eight months for Rubinstein to find four other suitable complexion workers to labor alongside Stock. Eventually Rubinstein had five complexion girls on staff, supported by "three typists, three girls making up preparations, and a lady doctor."[60]

Despite the training and labor demanded by the position, salaries were not necessarily commensurate with complexion girls' skill. When initially employed, most assistants earned 5s. per week "unless they paid a premium" to Rubinstein. Over time wages could range from 7s. 6d. per week to 15s. in the second year to £1 in the third. At the time of Stock's departure for America she made 12s. 6d. per week. This stood in stark contrast to the net profit the "girls" reportedly earned for Rubinstein, which could allegedly range between £20 and £60 per week per assistant. These payments took the form of cash, and in contrast to earlier generations of beauty transactions, Rubinstein avoided potential conflicts over indebtedness and unpaid fees by refusing credit-based transactions.[61]

While salaries were not necessarily high, work as an assistant opened up a number of other possibilities beyond financial remuneration. Day-to-day life in the shop is difficult to reconstruct, since, as we have seen, many beauty entrepreneurs worked to conceal the labor that went into beautification. However, there exists some evidence of the "backstage" conditions of a beauty shop, including ways that the work forged connections between shop assistants and a cohort of cosmopolitan, well-connected clientele. Historian Steven Zdatny points to the 1952 novel *Madeleine Grown Up* to illuminate experiences of a young female manicurist employed at London's Savoy Hotel in the 1920s, near the former site of Eugène Rimmel's flagship store.[62] In her reminiscences, author Madeleine Henrey paints a loosely fictionalized portrait of her time as an entry-level assistant in the hotel's manicure and beauty parlor. Henrey details a deeply feminized atmosphere of service work interspersed with sewing, singing, and smoking in the employee cubbyholes.[63] Most notably, the manicurists' days also involved endearing themselves to elite clients: businessmen, bored wives, showbiz moguls, low-ranking royalty. "The ones from New York are the most generous," observed Henrey, "the financiers, the theatre people, and men in the clothing trade."[64] Henrey herself received lavish gifts, invitations to private theater boxes, dinners, and tips before finally securing the ultimate connection: an engagement to one of her former clients, a newspaper man who whisked her away from a life of service work to one as a middle-class wife.

Henrey's fictional account emphasized the romantic rather than financial advantages of beauty service work, but the position also seems to have engendered a number of economic possibilities for unmarried female workers. This was the case for Stock, who, via her work in Rubinstein's salon, first met Louise Winterfeldt. During the 1908 season, the year of Rubinstein's London opening, Stock was responsible for twenty-six of Winterfeldt's thirty-six treatments. It is unclear how or when the two women came to their arrangement, but when it came time for Winterfeldt to return to New York, she proposed to bring along the complexion girl. Rubinstein agreed, given the pecuniary benefits of the exchange; Winterfeldt paid Rubinstein £150 per month for Stock's services, securing a steady flow of income for the businesswoman. While Stock initially served as her beauty provider—a traveling, transatlantic complexion girl—she eventually received an offer to become Winterfeldt's personal secretary. What began as a beauty service job in London transformed into a possibility for personal and economic advancement, something the daughter of a Croydon draper earned through hard work but also via possibilities engendered by new transatlantic opportunities for mobile working women (Figure 6.6).

If New York City offered Stock the opportunity for reinvention and self-making, there exists scant evidence of these experiences. The 27-year-old arrived at Ellis Island via *the Teutonic* on January 14, 1909, but we know little of her early reactions to America.[65] It was sufficiently positive, however, for her to break her arrangement with Rubinstein by mid-March and elect not to return home after

Figure 6.6 "In Upper New York Bay," Cunard Steamship Company (*c*.1904). Courtesy of The New York Public Library Digital Collections.

the three-month US engagement. Writing to Rubinstein on March 14, Stock explained that Winterfeldt "likes me so much that she would like to keep me as a secretary" and hoped her former employer would "not mind me deserting [her]." In addition to the financial benefits of working with Winterfeldt—"£250 a year, all expenses paid, and three months' holiday a year to go to England"— she also indicated genuine appreciation for her new home. "New York suits me so well," she wrote, observing, "I am getting quite fat."[66] By the following year, census records show Stock residing in a thirty-two-person boardinghouse on East 41st Street, populated by other unmarried women laboring across New York City in a range of occupations: secretaries, librarians, teachers.[67] This proved a short-lived arrangement, however, and in October 1910, Stock accompanied Winterfeldt and her daughter across the Atlantic in first-class accommodations on *the Lusitania*.[68] By the summer, she would be the subject of the contentious lawsuit over her responsibility—or lack thereof—to Rubinstein.

The paucity of information about Stock's time in New York speaks to disparities in class and power that defined her employment and thus her overseas experiences. A stint in America may have offered relative freedom, novelty, and opportunity, but all were linked to the desires and demands of Stock's two distinct employers: Rubinstein and Winterfeldt. Complicating matters was the fact that her employers' relationship hinged on misunderstandings of the terms and conditions of Stock's engagement. Rubinstein had not considered a scenario in which Stock would not return to London; possibilities for transatlantic reinvention were seemingly limited to those with means, like Rubinstein or Winterfeldt. Meanwhile, Winterfeldt expressed surprise at Stock's lack of agency over her employment options, intimating that she did not know that Stock was bound to Rubinstein and had to give notice of termination; she "thought only servants did that."[69] Subject to the whims of these misperceptions and miscommunications was Stock. Her work as a beauty service provider established the conditions of possibility for social and geographic advancement, only to have them withdrawn when it became inconvenient for both sets of employers. Her access to transatlantic fashionable communities was contingent on her ability to serve, be it London-based beauty culturists or Anglo-American clients.

Titus at Trial

The intersecting stories of the beauty businesswoman, the elite transatlantic traveler, and the complexion girl converged in a London courtroom in the summer of 1911. The trial unfolded over a single day, July 1, at London's King Bench Division. Rubinstein, the plaintiff, Winterfeldt, the defendant, and Stock, the subject, took turns on the stand, to the delight of the court gallery and journalists alike. In her bringing of the trial, Rubinstein became yet another British beauty expert who found herself defending—and exposing—her practices and profits to a curious court. Notably, the trial reveals previously unknown details of Rubinstein's early business that depart from the beauty magnate's own accounts in later autobiographies, written after her success was secured. Instead, in 1911, Rubinstein was just one of a long line of London beauty specialists who had to prove the legitimacy of her work to the court, despite having brought the charges on her own accord.[70]

Rubinstein's case hinged on the notion that Stock was difficult to replace, and the beauty culturist had lost money during the 1909 season when her complexion girl failed to return from New York. Winterfeldt countered that she knew nothing about the arrangement between Rubinstein and Stock and thus could not be held fiscally responsible for any losses incurred. The trial turned when Winterfeldt's lawyers submitted a forensic analysis of Rubinstein's account books. Rubinstein initially resisted such details being entered into evidence, arguing, as had Sarah Leverson and Jeannette Scalé before her, that they compromised the privacy of her female clients. An accountant nonetheless examined the records, before testifying that, rather than lose money in 1909, Rubinstein had secured steady business. In fact, she had raked in some £10,905 for services and £12,823 in sales between March 14 and September 30, 1909.[71] "[F]inancially," the counsel asserted, "it did not matter one brass farthing to Mrs. Titus whether Miss Stock stayed in America or returned to London."[72] Judgment passed for Winterfeldt; the case was dismissed.

Unlike the Madame Rachel or Mrs. Pomeroy trials, neither Rubinstein's business nor Winterfeldt's reputation seem to have suffered in the aftermath of public scrutiny. Nonetheless, Louise Winterfeldt seems to have shifted her relationship to cosmopolitan fashionable circles after July 1911. Concerned over public attention to the trial, Winterfeldt told the *New York Times*, "I was really afraid to come home after the things that had been printed in the London papers." She seemingly came out on top, however, even securing the "Title of Best Dressed Woman" owing to the stylish outfits she donned on the stand.[73] The new title pleased Winterfeldt, but she was less enamored with London's fashionable scene and its provisioners. "There seems to be an impression over there," she wryly observed, "that if you come from America you have plenty of money and it is easy to obtain a share."[74] Winterfeldt went to court to prove otherwise, defying moneyed Americans' reputation for loose purse strings in their desires to fit in with London's smart set. In doing so, she guaranteed the Winterfeldt fortune and kept it out of the hands of Rubinstein or other allegedly opportunistic commercial types.[75]

Trial revelations do not indicate why Rubinstein pursued the case against Winterfeldt given the growing profitability of her Grafton Street firm. To be sure, financial motivations—and specifically the less assured standing of Rubinstein's early London operations—may have propelled the case. What is clear is that Rubinstein's revelations of initial precarity implicate her in a longer history of London's beauty businesswomen who battled economic uncertainty, periodically accompanied by public scrutiny at trial. This connects more broadly to a common tendency to depict Rubinstein as singularly successful, which downplays those contingencies and conditions of small-scale enterprise that were also experienced by predecessors like Jeannette Scalé and Anna Ruppert. In this way, Rubinstein's early experiences in London point to processes of *integration* before *individuation*, as she navigated an atmosphere of small-scale boutique enterprise already populated by other entrepreneurs, customers, and workers. Rubinstein mobilized existing strategies based on cosmopolitan internationalism to fashion herself a citizen of the world, not tied to any one urban market. Her movement in and out of London opened her up to a new world of consumers, as she built a globally-recognized business, thus forging her international status—and success—as part of established western fashion systems. Primarily characterized as an American success story, Rubinstein's was, more accurately, a transnational tale turning on mobile female protagonists who were forced to establish themselves in deeply localized commercial milieus like the West End beauty scene.

Social and local contingencies also shaped the lives and fortunes of female laborers who found themselves employed by increasingly respectable—and visible—Edwardian beauty businesswomen. Precarity took on new dimensions for complexion "girls" like Dora Stock, who were subject to the whims of employers and clients alike. Opportunities for reinvention in new urban settings remained bounded by the conditions of Stock's class and labor, a fact made clear by the post-trial termination of her American sojourns. Trial testimony suggests Stock was understandably upset at the idea of losing her position in New York, pleading to Rubinstein through tears in May 1909 that "[y]ou know my circumstances, and what this splendid offer means to me." Stock further claimed that she was "willing" to come home to London, "but of course [she didn't] want to."[76] Stock did come home, for the 1911 hearing, but her reaction to and movements after the trial are unclear.[77] She does not seem to have resumed working for Rubinstein or Winterfeldt, even when the former opened her first New York salon in 1915 just a few blocks from Stock's former boardinghouse.[78] Records show that Stock did return to the United States in mid-December 1915, although a 1979 death recorded in Cheltenham implies that her return to New York was temporary rather than triumphant.[79]

Stock's fading from the historical record signals an important shift in cultures of concealment that, as we have seen, defined London's beauty businesses from the mid-nineteenth century onward. Unlike in previous decades, Rubinstein was not relegated to the margins of the industry owing to her gender, scale of operation, or location in London space. In fact, Edwardian London was home to a growing cadre of visible female beauty experts, who openly and actively courted customers free from the censure of previous generations. Buoyed in part by the growing internationalism that transformed both the buying and selling of beauty goods, women like Helena Rubinstein continued to carefully manage their print and promotional campaigns, but were ultimately celebrated rather than slandered for their business acumen. That is not to say, however, that all elements of the industry were transformed. Cultures of concealment continued to operate, extending to a new contingent of female subjects: the laborers working in these increasingly famous businesswomen's employ. The concealment of lower-class laborers was not a new development, but now worked in tandem with businesswomen's ascent into the public eye as respectable proponents of female enterprise. While Rubinstein continues to appear in best-selling biographies, Dora Stock's exceptional appearance at the King's Bench in 1911 offers a fleeting glimpse into the experiences and thwarted opportunities of one of hundreds of beauty workers. In this way, Stock's story stands as a reminder of the precariousness of women's positions in London's modern beauty business, albeit in new forms determined by social status, which dictated the economic opportunities—or lack thereof—available to beauty workers laboring behind the scenes. Workers' historical marginality is subsequently replicated in contemporary accounts of Rubinstein's success, which obscure the collective, backstage labor that propelled her ascent.

Conclusions

If Dora Stock fell victim to classed contingencies of Edwardian London's beauty industry, the ensuing success of businesswomen like Helena Rubinstein signaled alternate pursuits and possibilities available to enterprising women of sufficient economic stature. With luck and business savvy, women like Rubinstein forged increasingly viable—and visible—businesses in cultivating white, bourgeois consumer bodies. In doing so, beauty businesswomen betrayed meaningful connections to their nineteenth-century predecessors as much as distinct departures as daring innovators of the modern era. When situated within longer histories of commercial beauty provision, we see how very similar entrepreneurial conditions could produce both failures—in the case of Jeannette Scalé—and successes—in the case of Helena Rubinstein—depending on small variations in circumstance. This alignment connects with the broader aims of this study, which offers alternative chronologies that situate moguls like Rubinstein as part of a longer lineage of beauty providers.[80] By positioning conventional "founders" of the modern beauty business in London's urban settings, we see how historical precedents underpinned the marketing and commercial strategies of entrepreneurs like Rubinstein. And by resituating twentieth-century success stories like those of Rubinstein in the longer history of British—and global—beauty, we foreground the diverse and previously concealed group of traders and laborers who propelled the development of the local commercial scene, as supported by the most humble of participants like complexion girl Dora Stock.

Entrepreneurs like Rubinstein also benefited from later developments specific to the interwar period, which saw the significant expansion of the luxury market in beauty. By the early 1920s, the global beauty industry was a coherent and lucrative business with a broad base of female consumers.[81] The period also saw unprecedented expansions of scale made possible by technological developments and production techniques of the 1920s and 1930s. Future moguls, along with French and American innovators like Eugène Schueller of L'Oréal and Charles Revson of Revlon, capitalized on scientific innovations and experimentalism to offer new, safer products to growing constituencies of female consumers. In this way, Rubinstein's success was also contingent upon industrial and technological developments specific to the twentieth-century market, which she exploited to her benefit. And yet, her initial foray into a modern western market meant careful planning and marketing for a unique group of local consumers, in this case, London's elite female customers. Despite the expanding scale engendered by new developments of the twentieth-century, Rubinstein appreciated the specificities of localized commercial geographies and explicitly catered to the demands of their inhabitants.

In this way, the tendency to depict magnates like Rubinstein as singularly successful and innovative downplays the contingencies and conditions of small-scale enterprise, conditions understood far too well by the unsuccessful beauty traders featured in this book. Singular, celebratory histories of entrepreneurs can have an effacing effect, glossing over the realities—and labor—of establishing and maintaining an early beauty business. Feminist scholars in Britain and America have compellingly highlighted this trend and other ways that gender continues to shape the study of business history.[82] And yet, the celebration of individual twentieth-century female entrepreneurs remains a popular—and problematic— narrative in some histories of women and business.[83] To be sure, successful female entrepreneurs like Rubinstein who triumphed in the modern western beauty business deserve special attention. Yet, these accolades come at the cost of undermining the contributions of other male and female entrepreneurs—the vast majority of them—who were undercapitalized and unsuccessful, not to mention the broader networks of labor that sustained their enterprise, as vivified in subjects like Dora Stock.

Rubinstein and others mobilized shifting modern attitudes toward commercial beauty, as well as the growing internationalism of the western fashion scene, to forge significant beauty enterprises that flourished well into the twentieth century. But we cannot forget the foundations of these businesses, as laid by those individual entrepreneurs who made up London and other cities' nineteenth-century beauty industries, some of whom are the subjects of this study. Unlike Rubinstein, the experiences of some of the protagonists of *The Business of Beauty* were not resoundingly successful. Their stories represent those on the peripheries of an earlier moment in London trade operating under threat of insolvency, misfortune, and failure. When considered in the spatial and commercial context of London's burgeoning beauty business—and juxtaposed against more successful counterparts like Rimmel, Douglas, and Truefitt—the experience of these concealed traders and laborers points to a gendered pattern of commercial development of an urban luxury trade, more often characterized by concessions than innovation among small-scale businesspeople, including some women. As we have seen, small-scale traders were nevertheless a significant element of a localized commercial atmosphere that propelled certain members to considerable economic success and eventual expansion beyond the local trade community and into global markets. In this way, their efforts and those of British service workers contributed to the rise of entrepreneurs like Rubinstein, whose British operations were built on the work of London's male and female beauty entrepreneurs and laborers in the latter half of the nineteenth century. While histories of the beauty industry typically encourage us to look to twentieth-century developments as the beginnings of the modern business, it is perhaps in its more distant past that we can see the foundations of contemporary beauty culture.

Epilogue

If Helena Rubinstein developed into one of the twentieth century's leading beauty entrepreneurs, modern London acted as a launch pad for her extraordinary career. However, her British experiences were admittedly short lived, and her subsequent flight to the United States with the outbreak of the Great War meant expanded opportunities for consumption, capitalization, and, ultimately, success. She was not alone in thriving on the American market. Along with French purveyors, American beauty producers capitalized on a new twentieth-century attention to the healthy body, which included its transformation via the unconcealed consumption of elaborate commercial goods. This soon spread across global markets, and the century gave rise to a new type of bodily consumer culture, in which women's and men's bodies were further imbued, for better and for worse, with messages about race, national health, fertility, and power. Across locales, beauty consumption, and especially that of women, moved definitively from the backroom into the public domain, as earlier strategies of consumer and commercial concealment gave way to bold new aesthetics and the tools and technologies required to attain them. As a result, beauty and other bodily consumption transitioned from the realm of vanity to necessity, a move advocated years earlier by London-based beauty culturists but one that arguably did not take hold until the interwar period.[1]

While Rubinstein and her American contemporaries confidently strode into the twentieth century expanding their businesses and cultural capital, the same cannot necessarily be said of their British counterparts. The diminishing status of British beauty firms is part of a broader story about the shifting fashionability of London versus Paris and New York; the disruption of the Great War and an ensuing "flow of creative talent" into the United States, as seen in the case of Rubinstein; the "scale and dynamism" of US markets; and the expansion of international firms that took precedence—and hold—over smaller companies.[2] Arguably, it was also linked to British beauty brokers' longstanding dependency on particular repertoires of bodily consumption and selling that emphasized discretion and concealment, trends that continued to define the national industry into the early twentieth century. Shifting consumer desires for more visible, active engagement with obvious interventions—color cosmetics, massage and calisthenics, heady perfumes—thus demanded a reworking of existing commercial profiles of traditional British beauty traders and their firms.

Many of Britain's professional classes who had once dominated the London beauty trades failed to align with new, twentieth-century demands for fresh, bold products; it was perhaps this aesthetic shift that contributed to the relocation or shuttering of some of the metropolis' leading perfumery, grooming, and beauty firms. This trend accelerated through the interwar period, and the closure of many familiar Victorian beauty businesses appeared throughout the *London Gazette* into the 1970s. John Gosnell & Co., managed in the early twentieth century by Ralph P. Gosnell, went into liquidation in 1933 before being bought and moved to Lewes, East Sussex.[3] Representatives of the Rowland firm of Macassar Oil fame advertised into the late 1940s before ceasing operations in 1954.[4] R. Hovenden and Sons was a listed exhibitor at the 1947 British Industries Fair, but sources suggest the company was voluntarily wound up in 1956 before being dissolved in May 1969; Robert Douglas (Bond Street) Limited was liquidated that same year.[5] J. Grossmith and Son Ltd. operated until 1973, when company members were invited to attend a General Meeting to wind up operations[6] (Figure E.1).

As Geoffrey Jones has shown, British beauty firms did not always shut their doors in the twentieth century. However, they did not always keep up with the growing internationalism of twentieth-century global beauty, which entailed shifts from relatively localized markets in western capitals to international demand for "mega-brands" hawked by the likes of Procter & Gamble and the Anglo-Dutch company Unilever.[7] Localized British firms came to depend on national custom, sharing the domestic market with powerful brands based in the United States and France.[8] In the late 1930s, for example, Jones shows that some six hundred local British beauty firms operated alongside successful foreign operations, with thirty of these having "significant turnover."[9] This included firms like Yardley and new cosmetic companies like Gala of London, which garnered success by offering relatively affordable, refillable lipsticks during the Second World War[10] (Figure E.2). Yardley eventually became the foundation for British American Cosmetics (BAC), a subsidiary of British American Tobacco that operated through the 1970s and 1980s. By 1984, however, its diverse offerings were offloaded to Beecham, which increasingly turned its attention to pharmaceuticals.[11]

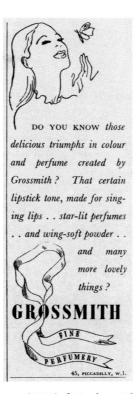

Figure E.1 Grossmith Perfumery (1947). f8 Archive/Alamy Stock Photo.

In some cases, then, traditional British beauty firms joined the new breed of global corporations via firm acquisitions. In 1914, for example, Lever Brothers teamed with A. & F. Pears to expand the latter's scope as a leading global provider of soap and toiletries.[12] Some years later, in 1957, Unilever made a bid for minority holdings in nineteenth-century firm J. & E. Atkinson's. They subsequently oversaturated the market with Atkinson's goods, transforming them from luxurious to mass-produced wares.[13] In the case of Rimmel, the firm remained in the family through much of the twentieth century before a postwar takeover by Robert and Rose Caplin. It transferred ownership a number of times before being acquired by Coty International in 1996.[14] The Rimmel example suggests that even some traditionally powerful British firms could not avoid their co-opting by formidable global operations, which represented the future of twenty-first-century beauty businesses. While firms like Coty eventually promoted Rimmel items through brash campaigns for the "London Look," their interests extended far beyond the British context to implicate a global network of beauty firms and consumers.

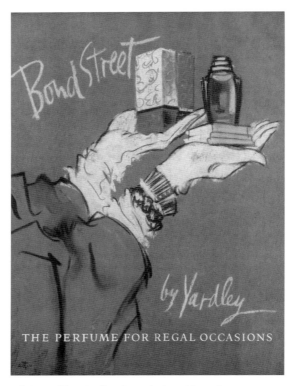

Figure E.2 "Bond Street," by Yardley (1953). Apic/Getty Images.

Global Beauty

Britain's twentieth-century industry also underwent significant shifts in their relationship to colonial holdings and markets, when a global cohort of beauty consumers challenged traditional "natural" aesthetics, disrupting the exclusivity of "British beauty" to make it their own.[15] Despite challenges, the period after the First World War saw some expansion of western-style beauty goods from capitals like Paris and New York to a worldwide network of customers.[16] This eventually transformed the movement of global beauty commodity flows, as consumers beyond western markets emerged as some of the driving forces compelling new goods and services in an increasingly global beauty scene. This took a range of forms and aesthetics, which included phenomena like the "Modern Girl," an important new mode of femininity emerging in the interwar period. Defined by her consumption of beauty and fashion, as well as her rejection of conventional gender roles as a wife or mother, the Modern

Girl appeared in various incarnations across twentieth-century Africa, Asia, Europe, and North America. Scholars including Alys Eve Weinbaum show that their shared interwar aesthetic transcended national boundaries. The Modern Girl's "elongated, wiry, and svelte body" was also "elegantly polished, carefully scrubbed, and meticulously sprayed" via new technologies of the self related to interwar standards of beauty but also hygiene.[17] This shared aesthetic—across multiple locales—signals the relationship between beauty advertising and the production or contestation of "national racial formation[s]" on the local and global levels.[18] Advertisements from four continents reveal the fluidity of global representations of femininity and race via beauty consumption and advertising.[19]

Through the twentieth century, soap, lotions, and perfumes moved from a British tool of "civilization" via cleanliness into consumer necessities integral to the self-definition of global consumers. This extended to women's use of cosmetics, which engendered new types of self making for customers around the world. This was, however, a contested process. In the case of Zimbabwe, historian Timothy Burke argues that cosmetics were at the center of complex debates over the "role of women in African communities."[20] Some urban workers who challenged dominant social norms regulating women's roles outside the home signaled this via their cosmetic use, often in the face of intense criticism.[21] Despite this censure, some women in Zimbabwe used "consumer choices"—including the purchase of cosmetics—to express "new possibilities for social autonomy and freedom" through an "identification with modernity."[22] While some British brands were implicated in these expanded consumer markets, twentieth-century marketing and selling of beauty could also be a local experience, involving new producers and consumers beyond traditional sites in the west, including Britain and its fashion capital.

The twentieth century saw not only economic shifts in beauty markets but also important transformations in conceptions of beauty and the body that challenged racialized beauty ideals often promoted by traditional firms. In the modern period, some advertising expanded beyond limited representations—and celebrations—of a white, Anglo beauty to include a range of aesthetics. According to historians, these expanded beauty aesthetics—and consumption of goods that supported them—could function as an important means of resisting and remaking conventional western beauty standards.[23] For example, historian Priti Ramamurthy argues that, for a short time in pre-independence India of the 1920s and 1930s, the aforementioned Modern Girl became a gendered symbol through which some women established Indian distinctions from British colonizers. The "bobbed hair, dark lipstick, mascara, and long, painted nails" of leading Anglo-Indian actresses were often complemented by local style elements: bindis, lace saris, and pearls. The Modern Girl was an aesthetic hybrid, a symbol of a specifically Indian modernity that distinguished herself from western forms that had long dominated beauty ideals.[24]

Following the Second World War, there were further challenges to idealized modes of white feminine beauty from across the Anglo world. This periodically took the form of another mode of beauty consumption beyond the buying of goods: performance and pageantry. In the Anglo-Caribbean context, historian Rochelle Rowe shows how twentieth-century beauty contests were central to the construction of new notions of nationhood via the promotion of particular types of local femininity. By celebrating "a brown feminine ideal," argues Rowe, a Caribbean middle class sought to challenge colonial systems in the years before and after decolonization.[25] The performance of beauty in local and national competitions became crucial to forging racialized identities in the decolonized Caribbean world, as a means of challenging "colonialism and othering."[26] However, there could be limits to these processes, which replicated historical patterns of reifying particular racialized and gendered types as ideal, resulting in the "institutionalization of brown middle-class beauty as national motif in the Caribbean."[27] Exceptions existed, however, including Claudia Jones's organization of the "Carnival Queen" pageant at London's first Caribbean Carnival in 1959, which spotlighted black femininities and signaled the radical possibilities of the pageant to resist "racist beauty politics."[28] In these cases, beauty aesthetics that privileged whiteness—not to mention the goods that supported them—no longer represented a national ideal, let alone the needs of modern British beauty consumers. And yet, the promotion of particular forms of idealized beauty could still function to constrain and limit definitions of "cultured modern femininities," argues Rowe, creating new sets of "racialized paradigms of beauty."[29]

British Beauty Enterprise

The twentieth-century beauty industry expanded not only in terms of international markets and beauty aesthetics but also in opportunities and power afforded to its entrepreneurs, and especially women. This was due, in part, to the ongoing feminization of trades like hairdressing through the twentieth century and, with it, growing possibilities for female service providers and entrepreneurs. Susan Vincent notes that, as a trade, hairdressing almost doubled in size between

1921 and 1931, with more than five times the women present than in previous decades.[30] And yet, male hairdressers sustained their trade dominance despite this increase in women. In Britain, this was embodied in the rise of figures like Vidal Sassoon (1928–2012) who opened his first location at 108 New Bond Street in 1954. As historian Kim Smith demonstrates, Sassoon helped propel a postwar resurgence of the "Mayfair Masters" who became world-renowned for their avant-garde services in hairstyling. While they counted relatively few women among their ranks, male hairdressers instilled London's West End with a renewed sense of cool, as elite and middling customers traveled great lengths to secure their services.[31]

Male ascendency was not guaranteed across the trade, and this same postwar moment gave rise to a small but significant cohort of black female beauty entrepreneurs in Britain.[32] This included Trinidad-born Carmen England (1909–1991), who launched her South Kensington salon, Carmen Colonial Hairdressers, in 1955.[33] Two years later, celebrated pianist (and former pupil of England) Winifred Atwell (1914–1983) opened her own firm in Brixton to great acclaim[34] (Figure E.3). According to Smith, Atwell made the move to 39–41 New Bond Street in 1960, taking up across the street from Sassoon's second location.[35] England also moved west, to Piccadilly Arcade, in 1971.[36] The establishment of beauty schools further advanced the visibility and expansion of black British beauty enterprise. This included the Madame Rose Academy of Beauty Culture in East Ham and, from 1958, the Roy Lando School in North London, with further institutions established through the next decade.[37] In this same moment, trade debates raged over a color bar maintained by a number of white British salon owners who refused to accommodate black customers.[38] The opening of black-owned salons thus afforded not only economic opportunity but also the conditions of possibility for forging commercial spaces—and communities—for black clientele, while defying the racist policies of the day.[39] By the 1970s, notes historian Tanisha C. Ford, "black women's hair care … was one of the most financially lucrative industries for black women."[40]

The endurance of particular modes of individual British beauty enterprise was also apparent in those who, beginning in the late 1970s, promoted a move away from "big business" to embrace personalized, eco-friendly beauty wares. Environmentally conscious alternatives of the 1980s and 1990s represented new ways to shuck the impersonal offerings of modern corporate beauty. This was most famously exemplified in the work of Anita Roddick (1942–2007), who promoted her goods as an alternative to mass-produced wares, targeting women who wanted to beautify themselves using natural, ethically produced items

Figure E.3 Services at Winifred Atwell's Salon in Brixton (April 30, 1957). Lee Tracey/ BIPs/Getty Images.

(Figure E.4). When she launched The Body Shop in Brighton in 1976, Roddick was at the forefront of a global movement toward responsible, sustainable beauty products. She promoted these values via a rhetoric of radical transparency, claiming complete openness about ingredients, production processes, and the beautifying effects (or lack thereof) of her offerings.[41] But she also articulated her position in relation to gender, in language that could have come directly from promotional material for Mrs. Pomeroy. Writing in 1991, Roddick observed:

> The industry is now controlled by men, even though, ironically, it was founded by a handful of powerful women … Helena Rubinstein, Elizabeth Arden, Coco Chanel and Estée Lauder. Most of the cosmetics houses they set up are now no more than baubles in a string of multinational companies. The businessmen who run them betray little grasp of the fact that the notions they are trading in—age, beauty, self-esteem—are more often than not an emotional powder keg for their customers.[42]

Figure E.4 Anita Roddick Outside a Body Shop Store on Oxford Street (n.d.). Christopher Pillitz/Alamy Stock Photo.

In developing her company, Roddick criticized "the business world" as "hard and uncaring and detached from human values."[43] Instead, Roddick argued that "'business practices would improve immeasurably if they were guided by 'feminine' principles—qualities like love and care and intuition."[44] Geoffrey Jones shows that, to put these practices into effect, Roddick relied exclusively on women to helm her early franchises, as "[w]omen wanted products with benign ingredients produced by a company run by women and with an understanding of women."[45] Like her *fin de siècle* precursors, Roddick positioned herself as an intimate feminine alternative to mass-manufactured, impersonal beauty goods and depended on a feminized labor force to do so. Messages about transparency and reliability continue to characterize the Body Shop's marketing into the twenty-first century, despite the fact that Roddick sold the firm to the world's largest cosmetic company, L'Oreal, shortly before her death in 2007, a development that no doubt shifted the nature of operations.[46]

British Beauty Today

While some notable British businesswomen developed goods and services for female clients, luxury spaces devoted to masculine, elite grooming continued to flourish in the heart of London's West End through the twentieth century.[47] Bespoke services from perfumers and hairdressers like Floris and Truefitt survived consumer movements away from London through the mid-century by appealing to longstanding elite patronage, as well as aspirational shoppers and tourists (Figure E.5). Continental and US fashions may have been highly desired, but the goods and services offered by stalwarts in St. James's and Mayfair allegedly transcended trendiness; their wares were timeless and not subject to the whims of a fickle modern consumer. This brand loyalty buoyed certain beauty firms through twentieth-century slumps, with companies like Floris operating into the present day, advancing a particular mode of exclusive British style. The onus on luxury heritage brands left a few key firms to represent traditional British beauty goods. It is perhaps this deeply local, exclusive appeal that accounts for the ways that British perfumery, grooming, and cosmetics continued to attract local consumers, while large-scale global beauty corporations came to dominate the postwar beauty business.

Despite lulls in the twentieth century, British beauty is once again on the rise. Recent trends in the contemporary beauty business have meant a further

Figure E.5 Floris Shop Interior, 89 Jermyn Street (1974). © City of London, London Metropolitan Archives.

revitalization of national heritage brands, operated by some of the leading firms of the nineteenth century. In this era of powerful global corporations, British brands have gained renewed attention by promoting their unique histories and bespoke production for the discerning luxury shopper, invoking longstanding messages of exclusivity and rarity. Some of these companies have subsequently moved from the forefront of nineteenth-century efforts to standardize Victorian beauty production into an alternate role, in which they offer discreet alternatives to mass-manufactured twenty-first-century wares. This includes descendants of the Grossmith family who repurchased the firm in 2009 and recreated scents first developed by their forebears. With the support of leading perfumery expert Roja Dove, the Brooke family relied on original recipes to regenerate a luxury perfumery firm, now available at stockists like Fortnum & Mason and Harrods.[48] In 2013, Atkinson's also relaunched its historical line with heritage-inspired scents including The Nuptial Bouquet and 24 Old Bond Street.[49] The discretion and prestige of heritage brands are once again prized in a beauty market that is arguably oversaturated with corporate-made goods. By reviving their traditional formulations for modern consumers, these firms are deeply relevant to a twenty-first-century British beauty scene.

The renewed relevancy of elite firms may suggest an ongoing relegation of British beauty consumption to those with means, but this is simply no longer the case. In Britain and around the world, bloggers, influencers, and new cohorts of experts celebrate beauty culture and services in all its multiple forms. The rise of online registers like the beauty forum and tutorial democratizes commercial beauty in new ways, across consumers of varying ethnicities, classes, races, and genders. No longer do customers slink around corners to avoid detection from passersby, as they did in the early years of Helena Rubinstein's Grafton Street operations. Instead, beauty consumers deeply engage in virtual communities and markets that grant access to the latest goods, techniques, and reviews with the click of a button. Rather than promote the homogenizing tendencies of historical beauty ideals and aesthetics, new networks of independent beauty businesspeople foreground the imaginative possibilities of beauty consumption, with its opportunities for transformation and transgression. Underpinning these messages are beauty experts' attempts to meet consumers' desires to feel the most beautiful they can be. It is here, perhaps, in the *desires* that underpin commercial beautification that links can be made to the practices of the past. Whether it was to meet dominant standards or to satisfy very personal expectations of the self, British consumers have long sought to manipulate their appearance and turned to beauty and grooming aids to do so. The history of these aids—and the people who discreetly provided them—ultimately tells a story about modernity, urban life, gender, and the self. Most importantly, it illuminates the centrality of beauty to Britons' lives, even if they did not care to admit it.

Plate 1 Six Stages of Mending a Face, by Thomas Rowlandson (1792). Courtesy of the Metropolitan Museum of Art, New York.

Plate 2 Alexander Ross's Ornamental Hair and Perfumery Warehouse, Bishopsgate (1816). Guildhall Library & Art Gallery/Heritage Images/Getty Images.

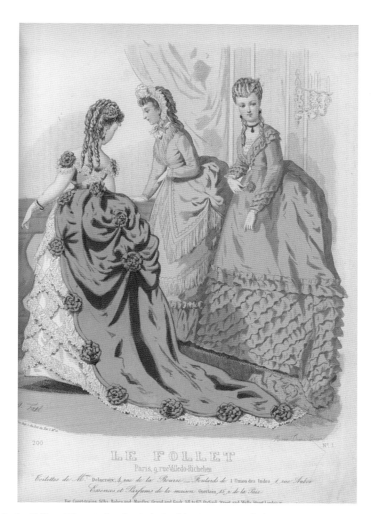

Plate 3 *Le Follett*, Pl. 700, by G. Fath (n.d.). Courtesy of The New York Public Library Digital Collections.

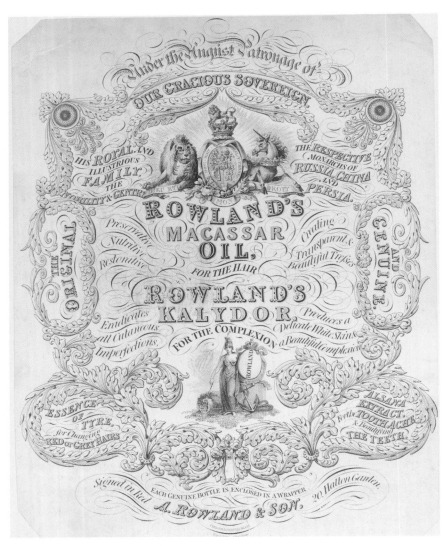

Plate 4 Rowland's Macassar Oil (n.d.). Courtesy of the John Johnson Collection, Bodleian Libraries, University of Oxford, Beauty Parlour 2 (48).

Plate 5 Piesse and Lubin (1862). Courtesy of the John Johnson Collection, Bodleian Libraries, University of Oxford, Beauty Parlour 3 (20).

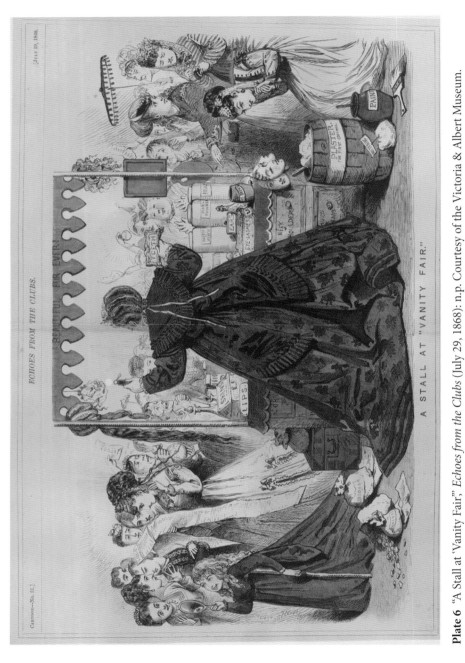

A STALL AT "VANITY FAIR."

Plate 6 "A Stall at 'Vanity Fair'", *Echoes from the Clubs* (July 29, 1868): n.p. Courtesy of the Victoria & Albert Museum.

Plate 7 "Rachel—and her Children!" *The Censor* (June 27, 1868): n.p. Courtesy of the Victoria & Albert Museum.

Plate 8 High Society, Rotten Row, Hyde Park, by Carlo Bossoli (n.d.). Fine Art Photographic Library/CORBIS/Corbis via Getty Images.

Plate 9 "Sunday Morning," after George Hunt (c.1825). Courtesy of the Wellcome Library, London.

Plate 10 "Days with Celebrities. Our Barber," *Hairdressers' Weekly Journal* (March 8, 1884): 154. Courtesy of © The British Library Board (Shelfmark 4238.301000).

Plate 11 A Woman at Her Dressing Table Having Her Hair Dressed by a Female Assistant (n.d.). Courtesy of the Wellcome Library, London.

Plate 12 The Crystal Palace from the Northeast during the Great Exhibition of 1851, by Louis Haghe, Joseph Nash, and David Roberts (1854). Wikimedia Commons.

Plate 13 Great Exhibition, Transept Gallery (1851). © Historical Picture Archive/CORBIS/Corbis via Getty Images.

Plate 14 Rimmel's Perfume Fountain (1851). Science History Images/Alamy Stock Photo.

Plate 15 "Germany," Rimmel's Perfumed Almanack (1863). Courtesy of the John Johnson Collection, Bodleian Libraries, University of Oxford, Beauty Parlour 4 (4a).

Plate 16 "England," Rimmel's Perfumed Almanack (1863). Courtesy of the John Johnson Collection, Bodleian Libraries, University of Oxford, Beauty Parlour 4 (4a).

Plate 17 Back Cover, Rimmel's Perfumed Almanack (1863). Courtesy of the John Johnson Collection, Bodleian Libraries, University of Oxford, Beauty Parlour 4 (4a).

Plate 18 Aspinall's Neigeline Skin Lotion (*c*.1890). History of Advertising Trust/
Heritage Images/Getty Images.

Plate 19 "Helena Rubinstein," by Paul Helleu (1911). Wikimedia Commons.

Appendix I

While representing only a small sample of London's nineteenth- and early-twentieth-century beauty providers, the following individuals feature in *The Business of Beauty* and worked in the British perfumery, hairdressing, and grooming trades:

Adair, Eleanor (b. 1867): A complexion specialist, Adair ran a lucrative business in London's West End from the 1890s into the early twentieth century. Her business first appears in trade directories in 1905, when she operated out of 92 New Bond Street. Adair was a prolific advertiser who took out full-page illustrated ads for goods like her "Ganesh" facial strapping system, as well as tonics and creams. According to Victoria Sherrow, Adair was the first to hire a young Canadian, Elizabeth Arden (1878–1966), as a "complexion girl" and receptionist in her New York branch.

Ansell, Susan (1813–1887): Sister to Agnes Headman, Ansell was a never-married property owner of "independent means," suggesting that she supported herself through inheritance. She resided at 7 Harley Street before taking up Headman's business after her death in 1858. By 1869, Ansell relocated the business from 92 New Bond Street to 29 Holles Street, Cavendish Square. In 1881, the census records her as providing "Advice for ladies, esp. hair" from 16 Edgware Road.

Arden, Elizabeth (1878–1966): Born into a farming family outside of Toronto, Arden relocated to New York City where she eventually worked her way up to the role of "treatment girl" and receptionist for the American operations of Eleanor Adair, the London-based contemporary and competitor of Mrs. Jeannette Pomeroy. By 1909, she and a partner launched their own venture on Fifth Avenue, New York's counterpart to Bond Street with its exclusive shops serving a lucrative carriage trade. In 1922, a decade after launching her New York firm, she opened her first London shop at 25b Old Bond Street. Arden also set up a small laboratory in Coach and Horses Yard, Bond Street, where she manufactured her own beautifying wares. Arden received considerable returns from her Bond Street shop, which remained in the same location until her death in 1966.

Atkinson, James (1782–1853): Atkinson was a hairdresser and perfumer who was especially renowned for his bear's grease pomade. He founded his London firm in 1799 at 9 High Street Bloomsbury; by 1814, he was located at 44 Gerrard Street; by 1832, he had relocated to 24 Old Bond Street. When joined by brother Edward in 1831, the firm rebranded as "J.&E. Atkinson's" and expanded their wholesale operations. Subsequent generations sustained the firm through the nineteenth century, with help from manager Eugene Barrett. After closing in the 1950s, the firm relaunched in 2013 with a shopfront in the Burlington Arcades.

Ballin, Ada Sarah (1862–1906): Health lecturer and editor Ada S. Ballin promoted her theories on beauty—along with her commercial services—via her periodical, *Womanhood*. This functioned as a platform for her London-based beauty business from 1898 until her untimely death in May 1906. Ballin's fall from a window at her Portland Square home was ruled accidental.

Boehm, Gustav (1827–1900): Born in Offenbach am Main, Boehm was a German-based soapmaker and manufacturer of toilet specialties. In 1880, the British government passed a soap duty on foreign manufactures, forcing Boehm to establish a branch manufactory in the City to bypass the tax. In doing so, he became the first to bring transparent glycerine soap to Britain. From 1887 to 1890, he was an elected member of the Reichstag. He was profiled in the *Hairdressers' Weekly Journal*'s "Celebrities Connected with the Trade."

Breidenbach, Francis Henry (1813–1871): A Prussian national, Breidenbach assumed control of his father-in-law's perfumery firm upon his marriage in 1836, which he developed into a major London operation. By 1847, Breidenbach became a naturalized subject. He died by drowning in Brighton in early 1871; an inquest ruled it accidental. Following his death, his wife Emily Ann (1817–1893) managed ten employees at their 157 New Bond Street location. She did so into the 1880s, supported by son Reginald.

Breidenbach, Reginald Blackwell (1863–1923): Son of Francis Henry, R. B. Breidenbach was a member of the Perfumery Committee of the London Chamber of Commerce in 1898. Upon his death in 1923, he left an estate of some £21,593.

Bury, Euphemia (1798–1867): Daughter of Chelsea perfumer John Bury (d. 1850), Bury was a never-married perfumer who operated a business at 205 Sloane Street from 1854. She supported her nephew Frederick, who she took on as an apprentice. Records also suggest that Bury assisted a niece living near the slums in St. Giles. Bury's niece was named for her.

Carter, John (b. 1836): Born into an agricultural family in Willingdon, Carter apprenticed as a hairdresser to Mr. Walker of Brighton in 1850. At 19, he relocated to London and worked at a number of locations, including that of a Mrs. Clark (possibly Mary Ann Clark, hairdresser at Great Suffolk Street, Borough). In 1861, he took over the business of Honey and Skelton at 17 Fleet Street, which was advertised as "formerly the Palace of Henry VIII and Cardinal Wolsey." In 1863, he became one of the first hairdressers to introduce hairbrushing by machinery, which required significant renovations to the shop. A president of the Hairdressers' Provident and Benevolent Institution, he was profiled in the *Hairdressers' Weekly Journal*'s "Celebrities Connected with the Trade."

Clarkson, Willy (1861–1934): Born William Berry Clarkson, he was London's leading theatrical wigmaker and supplier through the late nineteenth and early twentieth centuries. Clarkson learned the craft from his family before expanding his business to become chief supplier to the West End's leading theaters. Clarkson was also renowned for his work for fancy dress balls, serving, among others, Edward VII as the "Royal Perruquier and Costumier." A master of disguises, Clarkson was well known for his role in a number of well-publicized pranks involving costume.

Cleaver, Frederick (1807–1872): Cleaver was the son of William Cleaver (1774–1852) and Hermina Yardley (1781–1845), a marriage that united two of London's great perfumery families. Frederick launched his own venture in 1841 under the name F. S. Cleaver & Sons. He exhibited manufactures at the Great Exhibition of 1851, with the aid of thirty-two employees.

Colin, Alfred (c.1835–1891): Born in l'Aisne, France to a leatherworker, Colin trained in Paris and emigrated to London in 1862 as a haircutter's assistant. He went into business with London hairdresser Henri Proust at 233 Regent Street, although this dissolved acrimoniously by 1870 (see *Colin v. Proust*). Colin co-founded La Société du Progrès de la Coiffure before serving as its president for over sixteen years. He also featured in the *Hairdressers' Weekly Journal*'s "Celebrities Connected with the Trade." He left effects of £502 upon his death.

Collins, Dinah "Rose" (1856–1945): Never married, Collins was the daughter of an undertaker's attendant. Records suggest she was among Douglas's first female employees, apprenticing in 1871 at age 15. Along with Harriet Muston, she opened a small hairdressing salon in 1880 at 48 South Molton Street, Mayfair. By 1901, Collins had left the partnership and moved to Aldershot, where she continued to work as a court hairdresser.

Creer, Edwin A. O. (1823–1897): A hairdresser, barber, and wigmaker, Creer worked out of a modest shop in Stepney, a poor neighborhood in East London. Creer grew up in an equally poor but westerly area of Marylebone. Taken on as an apprentice in his late teens under master hairdresser Samuel Crouch of Islington, he set out on his own in 1846. He depended on family support to run the shop; he and his wife Louisa lived with six adult children, four of whom worked as "assistants in the business" or "assistant hairdressers." The eight members of the Creer family shared accommodations at 589 Commercial Road with, among others, a rope maker and his wife. Creer was not only a tradesman but also an important organizer among hairdressers and barbers, advocating for the early closing movement via his establishment and editorship of the *Hairdressers' Chronicle* in November 1866. He was also a member of the Hairdressers' Association and onetime Master of the Hairdressers' Guild.

Delcroix, Joseph (d. 1826): French-born Delcroix operated a firm at 158 New Bond Street, as well as a distillery in Grasse, France. Upon his death in 1826, his widow invited Hyacinthe Rimmel (b. 1796) to take over management of the firm.

Douglas, Robert (1822–1887): Born in Scotland, Douglas relocated to London as a young man to work under the famous theatrical hairdresser Wilson in the Strand. After establishing his own business in North Audley Street, he soon moved to 21 and 23 New Bond Street where his firm became one of the first to cater to female customers by employing lady hairdressers. He also ran an operation in Leadenhall Street and a manufactory in Carnaby Street. He participated in the Great Exhibition of 1851 and the International Exhibition of 1862. A member of the Benevolent and Provident Institution and a Freemason, he was profiled in the *Hairdressers' Weekly Journal*'s "Celebrities Connected with the Trade."

Floris (firm): Originally established in 1730 at 89 Jermyn Street, the firm continues to this day in the same location. From 1878 onward, the shop was operated by Mary Anne Floris (1848–1936) and her husband James R. D. Bodenham (1845–1929).

Gaubert, Esther Mary Ann (1825–1905): Gaubert was the daughter of a Golden Square jeweler, himself a descendant of goldsmiths based in London. Gaubert worked as an assistant to Agnes Headman until her employer's death in 1858. After a legal battle with Susan Ansell, Gaubert launched her own business as a hair restorer, employing her sister Charlotte as an assistant. Working initially out of 19 Maddox Street, Gaubert's business relocated to 81 Grosvenor Street from 1862. She advertised in trade directories until 1890 and appeared as late as the 1901 Census as a "Ladies Hair Cutter."

Gosnell, John (d. 1832): John Gosnell & Co. dated its origins to 1677. By 1760, it established itself on the London scene as a purveyor of cosmetics and soap to the city's elites. Gosnell's descendants maintained the firm from the mid-nineteenth century from their location on Lombard Street. In this period, their Cherry Blossom line generated significant business. They registered as a limited liability company in 1898 and moved to expanded locations on Blackfriars Road in 1900. The firm operates today in Lewes, East Sussex, as John Gosnell & Co. Ltd.

Grossmith, John Lipscomb (1843–1921): Son of John Grossmith, manufacturer of perfumes, toiletries, and cosmetics in Cannon Street who exhibited manufactures at the Great Exhibition of 1851. John Lipscomb inherited the company upon his father's death in 1867, operating out of Piccadilly Street. By the late nineteenth century, the firm moved into fancy soap making and manufacturing. In 1919, it became a limited company. The Company was recently relaunched by family who recreated Grossmith's original "Oriental" perfumes including Shem-el-Nessim and Phul-Nana.

Headman, Agnes (*c.*1808–1858): aka Anne Headman, aka Ann Cole. From 1849, Headman operated as a perfumer and consultant on women's hair at No. 24 Savile Row before moving to 92 New Bond Street. Upon her death in 1858, her sister Susan Ansell took over operations.

Hendrie, Robert (*c.*1779–1862): A manufacturing perfumer, Hendrie operated a shop in Tichborne Street for almost fifty years. He exhibited

manufactures at the Great Exhibition of 1851. Employees included
Osborne, Bauer, and Cheeseman, who went on to establish their own
successful perfumery business following his death.

Hewson, William: A hairdresser, Hewson operated out of 104 Cromer
Street. In 1866, along with Robert Douglas, H. P. Truefitt, John Marsh,
and William Wilcox, he became a vice president of the Hairdressers'
Sunday Closing Movement Association.

Hopekirk, Walter (1822–1897): Born in Edinburgh, Hopekirk worked as
an assistant under Unwin, founder of the Hairdressers' Philanthropic
Society. Working out of Westminster Bridge Road, Hopekirk also ran
a branch in the reconstructed Crystal Palace at Sydenham. A Mason,
he was vice president of the Hairdressers' Provident and Benevolent
Institution, onetime Master of the Hairdressers' Guild, and featured in
the *Hairdressers' Weekly Journal*'s "Celebrities Connected with the Trade."
In 1883 he was elected a councillor in the new borough of Croydon.

Hopkins, Sarah (b. 1801): Hopkins operated a perfumery business out of
6 Burlington Gardens from the early 1840s. Her daughter Georgina (b.
1831) took over the firm from the late 1860s, advertising her company in
trade directories until 1883.

Hovenden, Robert (1830–1908): Hovenden was born to Robert Hovenden
(1803–1872), wholesale perfumer of 57 Crown Street, Finsbury. Upon
taking over the business, Robert the younger substantially expanded
its scope. By 1872, as Stephanie Jones has shown, Hovenden operated
branches at 85 City Road, 5 Great Marlborough Street, 41 & 42 Poland
Street, and 27 Glasshouse Street. In that same year, he joined the
Worshipful Company of Barbers. Hovenden worked alongside his sons
Charles William (1864–1927) and Robert George Hovenden (1856–
1937). He left effects of £134,324 upon his death.

Ives, Fanny: Ives operated a hairdressing salon on Blandford Street,
Marylebone, through the late nineteenth and early twentieth centuries.
She was celebrated for her skills in hair dyeing.

Latter, Hannah (1853–1903): The daughter of an alehouse keeper, Latter
spent her youth like many other future lady hairdressers: working as
a ladies' maid. She parlayed this experience into a position at Robert
Douglas's. In 1888, she went into business for herself at St. George's Place,
Knightsbridge. Not long after opening her shop, Latter was "getting a
reputation for hair dyes" for "rich women are in the habit of having their
hair dyed."

Leverson, Sarah "Madame Rachel" (d. 1880): aka Sarah Rachel Russell or Sarah Rachel Levison. Born into unknown circumstances, Leverson lived in a common-law relationship with Philip Levison and two daughters from a previous marriage, Rachel and Leonti. They ran a second-hand clothing store in Clare Street before relocating westward, to Mayfair, to open a new beautifying business. Leverson was a profligate self-promoter, taking out advertisements, self-publishing beauty books, and refashioning herself as a high-class lady about town. After a number of court appearances, she was charged with defrauding Mary Borradaile in 1868. She was found guilty and served five years, primarily in Millbank Prison. Upon her release in 1872, she reestablished her beauty business, serving customers from Duke Street, Grosvenor Square. In 1878, she was charged again with fraud, found guilty, and died in prison in 1880.

Lichtenfeld, Joseph (b. 1848): A native of Danzig, Prussia, Lichtenfeld emigrated to London in 1866 where he worked with theatrical wigmakers. He in turn became a renowned wigmaker who was widely celebrated for his creations and boardwork. In 1873, he established a long-running shop at 39 Great Castle Street. He penned a number of tracts including *Principles of Physiognomical Hairdressing* (1880) and *Principles of Modern Hairdressing* (1881). He was a member of the Hairdressers' Association and president of the Hairdressers' Provident and Benevolent Institution, as well as a Freemason. He was profiled in the *Hairdressers' Weekly Journal*'s "Celebrities Connected with the Trade."

Lloyd, Aimée (b. 1828): Born in France as Aimée Courtois, she married her neighbor Andrew Solomon Lloyd in July 1852 at St. Pancras Parish Chapel. After her 1867 divorce, Aimée relocated to 3 Spur Street where she remained until at least 1881. The firm remained there into the early twentieth century, when the street was renamed Panton.

Lloyd, Andrew Solomon (1829–1868): Born to Solomon and Mary Ann Lloyd in Westminster, Andrew worked as a manufacturing perfumer producing his father's Euxesis waterless shaving cream. In 1852, he married French-born neighbor Aimée Courtois, taking over the business from his father. By the mid-1860s, Andrew began an affair with shopgirl Susannah Howard Tarleton. Andrew and Aimée divorced in 1867. Andrew died in September 1868 leaving effects under £100 to Tarleton.

Lloyd, Solomon (1783–1854): Originally from Shropshire, Solomon opened a business in the West End as a perfumer and hairdresser before developing an early form of the Euxesis formula. He exhibited manufactures at the Great Exhibition of 1851. Despite this, Solomon was plagued by indebtedness and spent time in London's debtor prisons before passing the business on to his son and daughter-in-law.

Low, Alfred (1843–1901): Son of Robert Low Jr., Alfred was born at 330 the Strand. Taking up a partnership with his father in the 1860s, he worked alongside Robert Haydon as "Messrs. Low, Son, and Haydon" until the early 1880s. In 1881, he became one of the first London perfumers to establish a branch factory in New York. As was the case with his father and grandfather, he was a member of the Livery of the Barbers' Company, as well as a vice president of the Hairdressers' Provident and Benevolent Institution. He was profiled in the *Hairdressers' Weekly Journal*'s "Celebrities Connected with the Trade." On his death, he left effects of £19,497.

Low, Robert (*c*.1801–1874): Son of Robert Low (*c*.1766–1848), a Master of the Barbers' Company, Low was a perfumer at 330 the Strand. Taking over from his father in 1828, Low expanded his family's wholesale perfumery and soapmaking business. Through most of the nineteenth century, the firm produced a popular version of Brown Windsor Soap, submitting manufactures to various international exhibitions, including the 1851 Exhibition and the International Exhibition of 1862. Like his father, Robert Low became a Master of the Barbers' Company.

Marsh, John: Marsh ran a hairdressing establishment at 175 Piccadilly. In 1866, along with Robert Douglas, H. P. Truefitt, William Hewson, and William Wilcox, he became a vice president of the Hairdressers' Sunday Closing Movement Association.

Muston, Harriet (b. 1858): Never married, Muston was the daughter of a farm laborer and worked from a young age as a parlor maid in Warwickshire. In the 1870s, she took a position at Robert Douglas's firm as a female hairdresser. In 1880, she left Douglas's to open her own hairdressing salon with Dinah "Rose" Collins at 48 South Molton Street, Mayfair.

Nevers, Marie: Nevers worked as a perfumer out of a shop at 218a Regent Street. She advertised in London's *Post Office Directory* in 1856.

Pears (firm): Founded by Andrew Pears (*c*.1770–1845), the firm became a leading producer of British soap. Andrew launched the business via a barbershop on Gerrard Street in 1789. By 1835, Andrew's grandson Francis (1813–1875) joined the firm, which was renamed A. & F. Pears. The firm exhibited manufactures at the Great Exhibition of 1851. In 1864,

Thomas J. Barratt (1841–1914) joined the company, married Francis's daughter Mary (1844–1916), and adopted new strategies in marketing and production. This included elaborate advertising campaigns, many of which advanced messages about imperial Britain's alleged racial and cultural superiority. In 1917, Lever Brothers, producers of Sunlight soap, acquired the Pears brand.

Piesse, George William Septimus (1820–1882): Author, philanthropist, and manufacturing perfumer, Piesse was one part of the successful perfumery house Piesse and Lubin, located at 2 New Bond Street from 1855. He trained as an analytical chemist prior to his career in perfumery and earned a PhD from University College, London. British-born, Piesse authored a number of definitive texts, including *The Art of Perfumery* (1855), *Chymical, Natural, and Physical Magic* (1858), and *The Laboratory of Chemical Wonders: A Scientific Melange* (1860). At his death, Piesse left personal effects to the tune of £12,699.

Pomeroy, Jeannette Shepherd Hauser Scalé (1862?–1938): Born in Uttar Pradesh, India to American missionary parents, Scalé married art teacher William Henry Jobbins in 1889. En route to London, Jobbins died, leaving Scalé a widow. She promptly established a complexion business in Savile Row in 1895, marrying James Bernard Scalé soon after. With his assistance, she moved the business to 29 Old Bond Street, working as "Mrs. Pomeroy." She soon had branches in Birmingham, Dublin, Johannesburg, and Cape Town. In 1906, she sold the company and found herself in court over legal use of the Pomeroy name. Upon losing that case, she lived with her mother and sons in Indiana, Ohio, and New York. In 1922, she was deported back to Britain by US authorities, where she died in Dartford, Kent in 1938.

Rainford, Violet (1871–1927): Electrolysis operator and manicurist, Rainford ran a business at 33 Old Bond Street from 1910. Working alongside her daughter Adjah, Rainford left effects of £1,221 at her death.

Rimmel, Eugène (1820–1887): Born in Paris, Rimmel relocated to London in 1833, when the widow of perfumer Joseph Delcroix of New Bond Street offered the position of firm manager to his father Hyacinthe Mars Rimmel (b. 1796). Hyacinthe thereafter established his own business on Gerrard Street, Soho, in London's "Little France." After apprenticing with East India Company merchants, Eugène took over the perfumery business and expanded it across Britain and eventually its colonies. In the late 1850s, Rimmel moved to 96 the Strand, opening additional retail outlets in Brighton, Paris, Rome, Antwerp, Liege, the Hague, Amsterdam, and Florence. He cofounded the French Benevolent Society and the French Hospital in Leicester Square. He also served on the British Hairdressers' Benevolent and Provident Institution.

Rolland, Olivier (1829–1890): Professional pseudonym of Isidore Ville. Born in Viviers, Ardèche, France, Ville came to London in 1851 where he worked at his brother-in-law M. Olivier Rolland's shop at 68 Park Street, which he later inherited. In the years that followed, Ville became one of Britain's most renowned and sought-after ladies' hairdressers. He was a member of La Société du Progrès de la Coiffure, the Hairdressers' Guild, and the Benevolent and Provident Institution. He also worked with Rimmel on the Committee of the French Benevolent Society. In 1890, Ville died by what papers dubbed "Sensational Suicide." Sheriffs for the County of London attempted to execute a warrant for arrest, when Ville escaped to an upstairs office where he died by gunshot to the head. He was profiled in the *Hairdressers' Weekly Journal*'s "Celebrities Connected with the Trade."

Ross, Alexander (d. 1819): Ross was a perfumer and hairdresser who operated an "Ornamental Hair and Perfumery Warehouse" at 119 Bishopsgate Street from the late eighteenth century. He self-published *A Treatise on Bear's Grease* in 1795. His son (1798–1849) and grandson (1825–1904), both named Alexander, continued these traditions with the release of such texts as *Recollections of an Ex-Maniac! And Other Tales* (1858), *The Tale of a Hair* (1868), and *The Black Wizard: A Wonderful Toilet Tale* (1874). The firm exhibited manufactures at the Great Exhibition of 1851.

Rowland, Alexander (*c.*1783–1861): Purveyor of the famed Macassar Oil from his Hatton Garden shop, Rowland was a prolific advertiser. He was also an author, penning a number of texts like *An Essay on the Cultivation and Improvement of the Human Hair* (1809) and *A Practical and Philosophical Treatise on the Human Hair* (1814). His son Alexander William also aided in the business.

Ruppert, Anna (1864?–1896): Ruppert, an American complexion specialist operating at 89 Regent Street, also offered a series of West End lectures in the early 1890s to which she invited attendees "to convince fathers, mothers and husbands that 'she is not a Rachel or cosmetic artiste.'" Despite her assertions, she was prosecuted by the Pharmaceutical Society of Ireland in 1893 for selling a tonic containing a "corrosive sublimate."

In a subsequent suit by one of her female agents, the prosecution proclaimed that if Ruppert "had endeavoured to emulate Madame Rachel [they did] not think she could have been more successful." Her business never recovered, and she went on to a career in the theater, to mixed reviews. She died of consumption in 1896.

Sanders, Miss: Sanders (possibly Emmeline) of Maddox Street touted her *Practical Face Treatment and Natural Beauty* from 1903 onward. She participated in print debates over proper massage techniques, and readers as far away as New Zealand were introduced to Miss Sanders's method ("the circles should be small, but as the fingers sweep back to the starting point they must sink well into the flesh").

Taylor, Jane: Taylor advertised her hairdressing business at 90 Great Portland Street in London's *Post Office Directories* between 1868 and 1875.

Truefitt, H. P. (1824–1909): H. P. Truefitt was nephew of William Francis Truefitt, who first opened a barbershop around Covent Garden in 1805. By 1849, Henry Paul ran his own shop in the Burlington Arcades. Truefitt developed a number of innovations, including a "Toilet Club" to which patrons paid an annual subscription for haircutting services. By 1880, he formed a limited liability company worth £72,000. He was the author of *New Views on Baldness* (1863) and a member of the Hairdressers' Association. He was also president of the Benevolent and Provident Institution and was profiled in the *Hairdressers' Weekly Journal's* "Celebrities Connected with the Trade."

Wilcox, William: A hairdresser, Wilcox operated out of 36 Glasshouse Street. In 1866, along with Robert Douglas, H. P. Truefitt, John Marsh, and William Hewson, he became a vice president of the Hairdressers' Sunday Closing Movement Association.

Yardley (firm): Founded in 1770 by Samuel Cleaver (1750–1805), the family perfumery business passed to Samuel's sons upon his death. It was subsequently taken over by two of the sons' father-in-law William Yardley in 1823. Under new management, as Yardley & Statham, the firm submitted manufactures to the Great Exhibition of 1851. Having been located in Bloomsbury, a Yardley shop opened at 8 New Bond Street in 1910 to great success.

Appendix II

The following excerpt from Robert Kemp Philp's 1853 *Shopkeeper's Guide* suggests the quantity and range of goods available from perfumers and fancy soap makers in the mid-nineteenth century:

English Pomatum, of various Perfumes—

    Otto of Rose

    Jessamine

    Orange

    Millefleur

    Violet

    Bergamot

    Lemon

    Marrow

    Rose

    Jamaica, &c.

    Castor Oil Pomatum

Hair Oils of every Odour—

    Rose (Red)

    Rose (Pale)

    Jasmine

    Millefleurs

    Violette

    Bouquet

    Citron

    Bergamot, &c.

Preparations for the Hair—

    Macassar Oil

    Ditto, smaller sizes

    Pomade de Macassar

    Curling Fluid

Russia Oil
Prince's ditto
Curling Cream
Marrow Oil
Circassian Cream (best)
Ditto (common)
Devereaux's Curling Fluid
Devereaux's Oil of Columbia
Dr. Verdigon's Oil of Persia
Stiracias, or Italian Oil
Bandoline for fixing the Hair
Noisettine

Bear's Grease—

Bear's Grease, in Fancy Pots
Ditto, Otto of Rose scented
Bear's Grease (in Bottles)
Bear's Marrow (ditto)

Soaps in Packets—

Real Old Brown Windsor
Second Quality, ditto
Third quality, for Family use
Johnstone's Patent White Windsor
White Windsor
Montpellier
Marine
Floating
Silica
Lavender
Rose
Vegetable
Camphor
Almond
Verbena
Sandal Wood
Palm Oil
Anti-Cholera
Rondeletia

Shaving Cakes, Best Quality, (in Wrappers)—

Transparent
Almond
Military and Naval
Camphor
Amber, &c.
Cocoa Nut Oil
Common Shaving Cakes, various Colours
Medallion Shaving Cakes

Fancy Soaps, squares, extra Scented—

Vegetable
Cocoa Nut
Almond (brown)
Ditto (white)
Camphor
Sultana
Violet
Lavender
Otto of Rose
Jessamine
Coronation
Palmyrene
Abyssinian
Bandana
Naples
Musk
Rondeletia
Transparent, &c.

Oriental Soap Tablets, without angles, Scented with

Verbena
Sandal Wood
Almond
Honey
Lavender
Otto of Rose

Orange
Millefleur
Vegetable, &c.

Shaving Soaps, in Pots

Ambrosial Shaving Cream
Ditto, in Marbled Pots
Genuine Naples Soap
Pasta del Castagna, &c.

Soaps, Windsor, &c.—

White Windsor
Patent Windsor
Brown Windsor
Old Brown, Superior
Pink Windsor
Palm Soap
Marine Soap
Almond
Vegetable, &c.
Castile Soap, French and English
Honey Soap, in Squares
Honey Soap, in Tablets
Isle Of Wight Sand Ball Soap
Hair Powders

Perfumes for the Handkerchief—

Espirits, Essences, Extracts, and Eaux, of every Perfume
Mouseline
Jasmine
Ambergris
Violette
Fleur d' Orange
Tubereuse
Muguet
Amaranthe
Marechalle
Rose

Millefleurs
Bergamot, &c.
Citronella Rosae
Ambrosial Essence
Bouquet d'Amour
Spring Flowers
Extract of Wild Flowers
Lily of the Valley
Sweet Pea
Extract of Moss Rose
Extract of Roses
Essence of Roses
    Magnolia
    Verbena
    Rondoletia
    Hovenia
    Geranium
    Mignonette
    Sweetbriar
    Eglantine
Bouquet des Dames
    du Roi
    de Florence
    Militaire
Eau Aromatique de Montpellier

Court Perfumes—

Victoria Bouquet
Prince Albert's ditto
Prince of Wales's ditto
Princess's ditto
Princess Alice's ditto
Princess Helena's ditto
Prince Alfred's Perfume
Adelaide ditto
Royal Sovereign ditto
Duke of York's
Duke of Wellington's

Duke of Buccleugh's
Coronation Bouquet
Court Bouquet
Bouquet d'Orsay
Vegetable Essence
Extract of Flowers
New Perfume
Fragrant Perfume
Carnation Bouquet
Eau de Portugal
Military Bouquet
Bouquet de la Republique de 1848

Lavender Water—

Lavender Water
Treble Distilled
Concentrated Essence Lavender
Musk Lavender
Sweet Scented ditto
Perfumed ditto

Hair Washes, for Cleansing and Beautifying the Hair—

Vegetable Extract
Extract of Roses
Botanic Extract
Honey Water
Smyrna Extract of Rose
Marlborough Water

Distilled Waters—

Orange Flower Water
Rose Water
Elder Flower Water
Eau de Cologne
Hungary Water

Smelling Salts, &c.—

Pungent Salts

Preston Salts, in Stoppered Bottles
Inexhaustible Salts
Godfrey's Salts
Aromatic Salts of Vinegar
Sel Aromatique de Vinaigre à la Rose
Eau de Luce
Aromatic Vinegar

Tooth Powders, &c.—

Charcoal
Camphor Chalk
Prepared Chalk
Camphor Tooth Powder
Imperial
Rose
Pearl
White Rock
Duchess of York's Tooth Powder
Prince of Wales's ditto
Persian Dentifrice
Coral ditto
Thompson's Myrrh ditto
Athenian ditto
Circassian ditto
Ceylon Tooth Powder
Malabar ditto
Botanic Dentifrice
Dr. Verdigon's Vegetable Tooth Powder
Vegetable Tooth Paste
Devereaux's Odonto
Antiseptic Charcoal
Circassian Opiate
Butler's Tooth Powder
Trotter's ditto
Ruspini's Dentifrice and Tincture
Dr. Verdigon's Alsana Extract, a cure for the Tooth Ache

Cosmetics—

> Patent Naples Cream
> Bloom of Roses
> Bloom of Ninon de l'Enclos
> Carmine, in Packets
> Face Powder
> Pearl Powder
> Rouge, in Pots
> Blanc de Perle, in Pots
> Milk of Roses
> Lip Salve
> Otto of Rose, Lip Salve
> Cold Cream
> Rose Cream
> Almond Cream
> Almond Paste
> Honey Paste
> Devereaux's Kalydor Lotion
> Devereaux's Paté au Miel
> Crême de Sultane
> Mother o' Pearl White
> Pommade pour les Moustaches,
>   Noir et Brune
> Pommade Divine

Genuine Essential Oils—

> Otto of Roses
> Neroli
> Sandal Wood
> Cedrat
> Citron
> Cinnamon
> Nutmeg
> Mace
> Citronella
> Clove
> Cassia
> Lemon

Bergamot
Thyme
Rosemary
English Lavender
French Lavender
Verbena, &c.

Hair Dyes—

Devereaux's Poudre Unique
Devereaux's Essence of Tyre
Devereaux's Vegetable Dye
Devereaux's Eau Vegetal
Devereaux's Turkish Dye
Sicilian Water
Verdigon's Persian Water

Fashionable Perfumers generally keep the following kinds of
FANCY BRUSHES AND COMBS
In Wood.—At per dozen.

Hair Brushes of every variety of pattern and quality, from 6s. to 120s.
Clothes Brushes of all sizes and patterns, with or without handles, from
     6s. to 66s.
Hat Brushes of all descriptions, 4s. to 12s.
Flesh Brushes, with or without handles, 14s. to 36s.
Curl Brushes, 8s. to 16s.
Bandoline Brushes, 8s. to 18s.
Whisker Brushes

Brushes in Bone and Ivory.

Hair Brushes, Ivory, from 10s. to 20s. each
Tooth Brushes, in Bone, Second quality, 24s., 36s. 42s., 48s. per gross
Tooth Brushes, in Bone, first quality, 60s., 66s., 72s., 84s. per gross
Tooth Brushes, in Ivory, 14s., 16s., 18s. per dozen
Tooth Brushes, in sets, Bone, 24s. per dozen sets
Comb Brushes, 3s., 4s., 6s., 8s., 12s., per dozen
Nail Brushes, 3s., 4s., 6s., 8s., to 60s. per dozen.

Shaving Brushes.

Second Quality, 2s., 2s. 6d., 3s. 6d., 6s. per dozen

First Quality, ground hair, 4s., 6s., 8s., 12s., 18s. per dozen

Badger Hair, 16s., 21s., 24s., 36s., 42s. per dozen

Sadler's Brushes, &c.

Horse Brushes, from 15s. to 70s.

Spoke ditto … 24s. to 42s.

Water ditto … 18s. to 60s.

Bitt ditto … 10s. to 14s.

Boot-top ditto … 14s. to 16s.

Dish ditto … 18s. to 24s.

Plate ditto … 4s. to 20s.

Shoe Brushes 32s. to 84s. per doz. sets

Shaving Boxes.—At per dozen.

In Wood … 2s. 6d. to 18s.

Metal … 4s. to 12s.

Glass with Plated Covers 16s. to 36s.

Combs—

Dressing Combs of every quality and description, in Tortoise-shell, Ivory, Horn, Boxwood, and German Silver, at all prices.

Horn—At per dozen.

Ornamental Braid Combs, 12s. to 24s.

Braid ditto 2s. 6d. to 12s.

Tail ditto 4s. to 12s.

Side ditto 8d. to 4s.

Band ditto 2s. 6d. to 6s.

Pocket ditto 1s. 6d. to 12s.

Ditto (in Metal) 6s. to 12s.

Shell—

Ornamental Braid Combs 42s. to 160s.

Braid ditto 18s. to 96s.

Tail ditto 18s. to 42s.

Side ditto 3s. to 21s.

Band ditto 8s. to 12s.

Pocket ditto 18s. to 48s.

Ivory Small Tooth Combs—

At per dozen.
Bastards from 1*s*. 6*d*. to 8*s*.
Dandrif 2*s*. to 12*s*.
Superfine 3*s*. to 18*s*.
Extra Superfine 4*s*. to 36*s*.
Imperials 6*s*. to 18*s*.

Hair, &c.—

Hair—Crop, Ladies' Ringlet and Band, from 18*s*. to 48*s*. per lb.
Partings (Silk), at per Inch 6*d*. to 8*d*.
Partings (Skin), from 1*s*. to 1*s*. 3*d*.
Crowns (Silk), each 1*s*. 6*d*. to 2*s*.
Crowns (Skin), each 2*s*. to 2*s*. 6*d*.
Galloons per piece from 2*s*. 6*d*. to 3*s*. 6*d*.
Wig Ribbon 3*s*. 6*d*. to 8*s*.
Net (Cotton), per yard, from 2*s*. 6*d*.
Net (Silk), from 6*s*. to 7*s*.
Weaving and Sewing Silk, per oz., 2*s*. 3*d*. and 2*s*. 6*d*.
Scalp Snaps, per dozen 3*s*. 6*d*.
Metallic Springs, per dozen 18*s*. 21*s*.
Elastics, per dozen 2*s*. 6*d*.

Miscellaneous—

Bleaching Liquid
Bleaching Liquid (Hudson's)
Court Plaister
Court Plaister in Books Tricoloured
Court Plaister, India Rubber, &c.
Curling Irons
Dragon's Root for the Teeth
Dressing Cases, Japanned
Dressing Cases, Mahogany
Essence of Jamaica Ginger
Essence of Peppermint
Gold Beater's Skin
Hair Rollers

Hair Pins, per lb.

Hair Pins, per doz. Boxes and Papers

Horse Hair Gloves, &c. for Rheumatism

Ivory and Metal Comb Cleaners

Oil Silk Bags, for Sponges

Oil Silk Bathing Caps

Pastils, per dozen

Pastile Burners

Plate Powder

Pot Pourri

Powder Boxes, Tin Japanned

Powder Boxes, Wood

Powder Bags

Razors, Black

Razors, Ivory

Razors, Shell

Salt of Lemons

Saucers, Pink, Blue, Crimson, Green, &c.

Scent Bags

Scented Fruit for Scenting Drawers

Scented Powders all sorts for drawers

Scouring Drops

Swan Puffs

Toothpicks (French), in Boxes

Tongue Scrapers—Shell, Ivory, and Silver

Tonquin Beans, per oz.

Tonquin Musk in Packets

Turkey Sponge, per lb.

Vanilla, per oz.

Walking and Riding Sticks

Permanent Ink for writing on Linen with preparation

Ditto without preparation

Notes

Introduction

1 "Real Mysteries of Paris and London," *All the Year Round* (October 27, 1860): 69–72.

2 Eliza Lynn Linton, "The Girl of the Period," *Saturday Review* 25, no. 646 (March 14, 1868): 340. See Valerie Steele, *Fashion and Eroticism: Ideals of Feminine Beauty from the Victorian Era to the Jazz Age* (New York: Oxford University Press, 1985), 128–32.

3 The development of the cultural values that regulated nineteenth-century beauty consumption had a long trajectory, ramping up with the Romantic renunciation of overt paints and powders in the early nineteenth century. Through the 1830s, cosmetics and beauty goods remained widely available, but their use was driven underground as they came to be understood as duplicitous and dangerous. Carolyn Day, *Consumptive Chic; a History of Beauty, Fashion, and Disease* (London: Bloomsbury, 2017), 92; and Richard Corson, *Fashions in Makeup: From Ancient to Modern Times* (London: Owen, 1972), 295.

4 Nineteenth-century commentary on the poisonous effects of beauty wares is too plentiful to list in full. Illustrative medical examples include "Arsenic for the Million," *Lancet* (December 15, 1860): 592; "Hair-Washes," *Lancet* (August 15, 1868): 228; Lead-Poisoning from the Use of Cosmetics," *British Medical Journal* 2, no. 1075 (August 6, 1881): 231; "Poisonous Cosmetics," *British Medical Journal* 1, no. 474 (January 29, 1870): 115; and "Poisonous Cosmetics," *British Medical Journal* 2, no. 1704 (August 26, 1893): 480–1. See Alison Matthews David, *Fashion Victims: The Dangers of Dress Past and Present* (London: Bloomsbury, 2015), 20–4. On the emphasis on "natural" beauty via late nineteenth-century beauty regimens, see Michelle J. Smith, "Beauty Advertising and Advice in the *Queen* and *Woman*," in *Women, Periodicals and Print Culture in Britain, 1830s–1900s: The Victorian Period*, ed. Alexis Easley, Clare Gill, and Beth Rodgers (Edinburgh: Edinburgh University Press, 2019), 218–31.

5 See, for example, William and Robert Chambers, "Beautiful for Ever," *Chambers's Journal of Popular Literature, Science, and Art* 82 (July 22, 1865): 449–52; and J. Scoffern, "Beautiful for Ever," *Belgravia: A London Magazine*, 5 (June 1868): 227–36.

6 I am indebted to Katie Hindmarch-Watson for her insights into discretion and consumption. For more, see her forthcoming book from University of California Press.

7 In *The History of Sexuality, Volume I*, Michel Foucault critiques the "repressive hypothesis," the notion that the Victorians promoted silences around sex and

sexuality. Instead, he argues, by prohibiting and regulating sexuality, the Victorians actually proliferated and multiplied these discourses. According to Foucault, the belief in the repressive hypothesis was as much a reflection of twentieth-century observers who wanted to see themselves as sexually "liberated" as it was their Victorian subjects. Foucault, *The History of Sexuality, Volume I*, trans. Robert Hurley (New York: Vintage Books, 1978).

8 Two such examples are Teresa deLauretis, *Technologies of Gender: Essays on Theory, Film, and Fiction* (Bloomington: Indiana University Press, 1987); and Ann Laura Stoler, *Race and the Education of Desire: Foucault's* History of Sexuality *and the Colonial Order of Things* (Durham, NC: Duke University Press, 1995).

9 See, for example, Paul Deslandes's forthcoming study of male beauty from the University of Chicago Press; Erika D. Rappaport, *Shopping for Pleasure: Women in the Making of London's West End* (Princeton, NJ: Princeton University Press, 2000); and Ina Zweiniger-Bargielowska, *Managing the Body: Beauty, Health and Fitness in Britain, 1800–1939* (Oxford: Oxford University Press, 2010). On the interwar period, see Justin Bengry, "Courting the Pink Pound: *Men Only* and the Queer Consumer, 1935–39," *History Workshop Journal* 68, no. 1 (October 2009): 122–48; Paul Deslandes, "Selling, Consuming, and Becoming the Beautiful Man in Britain: The 1930s and 1940s," in *Consuming Behaviors: Identity, Politics and Pleasure in Twentieth-Century Britain*, ed. Erika D. Rappaport, Sandra Trudgen Dawson, and Mark J. Crowley (London: Bloomsbury, 2015), 53–70; Matt Houlbrook, "'The Man with the Powder Puff' in Interwar London," *Historical Journal* 50, no. 1 (March 2007): 145–71; and Alys Eve Weinbaum et al., eds., *The Modern Girl around the World: Consumption, Modernity, and Globalization* (Durham, NC: Duke University Press, 2008).

10 Gareth Shaw, "The European Scene: Britain and Germany," in *The Evolution of Retail Systems, c. 1800–1914*, ed. John Benson and Gareth Shaw (Leicester: Leicester University Press, 1992), 29.

11 The concept of "self-fashioning" is extensive and well-explored in scholarship but originates in Stephen Greenblatt, *Renaissance Self-Fashioning, from More to Shakespeare* (Chicago, IL: University of Chicago Press, [1980] 2005), 2. On technologies of self-fashioning, see Jennifer Craik, *The Face of Fashion: Cultural Studies in Fashion* (London: Routledge, 1993).

12 See also Steele, *Fashion and Eroticism*, 118–20.

13 See, for example, Jessica P. Clark, "Clever Ministrations: Regenerative Beauty at the *Fin de Siècle*," *Palgrave Communications* 3, no. 47 (2017): n.p.

14 Kathy Peiss, *Hope in a Jar: The Making of America's Beauty Culture* (New York: Metropolitan, 1998). On the United States, see also Philip Scranton, ed. *Beauty and Business: Commerce, Gender, and Culture in Modern America* (New York: Routledge, 2001).

15 Morag Martin, *Selling Beauty: Cosmetics, Commerce, and French Society, 1750–1830* (Baltimore, MD: Johns Hopkins University Press, 2009).

16 Holly Grout, *The Force of Beauty: Transforming French Ideas of Femininity in the Third Republic* (Baton Rouge: Louisiana State University Press, 2015), 7.

17 Amy Montz, "Dressing for England: Fashion and Nationalism in Victorian Novels" (PhD dissertation, Texas A&M, 2008), especially chapters 2 and 3; and Steele, *Fashion and Eroticism*, 6–7.

18 Mikiko Ashikari, "The Memory of the Women's White Faces: Japaneseness and the Ideal Image of Women," *Japan Forum* 15, no. 1 (2003): 55–79; Geoffrey Jones, *Beauty Imagined: A History of the Global Beauty Industry* (London: Oxford University Press, 2010); and Weinbaum et al., eds., *Modern Girl around the World*.

19 Jessica P. Clark, "Buying Beauty: Female Beauty Consumption in the Modern British World," *History Compass* 14, no. 5 (May 2016): 206–17.

20 For the nineteenth century, see Jessica P. Clark, "'Will You Give Me Your Opinion?': Mundane Beauty in the *Englishwoman's Domestic Magazine*, 1860–1875," *Victorian Periodicals Review* 52, no. 3 (Fall 2019): 540–65; Catherine Maxwell, *Scents and Sensibility: Perfume in Victorian Literary Culture* (Oxford: Oxford University Press, 2017); Arthur Marwick, *Beauty in History: Society, Politics and Personal Appearance c. 1500 to the Present* (London: Thames and Hudson, 1988); Galia Ofek, *Representations of Hair in Victorian Literature and Culture* (Basingstoke: Ashgate, 2009); Christopher Oldstone-Moore, "The Beard Movement in Victorian Britain," *Victorian Studies* 48, no. 1 (2005): 7–34; Steele, *Fashion and Eroticism*; Susan Vincent, *Hair: An Illustrated History* (London: Bloomsbury, 2018); and Susan Walton, "Squalid Impropriety to Manly Respectability: The Revival of Beards, Moustaches and Martial Values in the 1850s in England," *Nineteenth-Century Contexts* 30, no. 3 (2008): 229–45.

For the early modern period see, for example, Holly Dugan, *The Ephemeral History of Perfume: Scent and Sense in Early Modern England* (Baltimore, MD: Johns Hopkins University Press, 2011); Edith Snook, *Women, Beauty, and Power in Early Modern England: A Feminist Literary History* (London: Palgrave Macmillan, 2011); Edith Snook, "Beautiful Hair, Health, and Privilege in Early Modern England," *Journal for Early Modern Cultural Studies* 15, no. 4 (Fall 2015): 22–51; and Alun Withey, *Technology, Self-Fashioning and Politeness in Eighteenth-Century Britain: Refined Bodies* (London: Palgrave Macmillan, 2016).

For the twentieth century, see, for example, Timothy Burke, *Lifebuoy Men, Lux Women: Commodification, Consumption, and Cleanliness in Modern Zimbabwe* (Durham, NC: Duke University Press, 1996); Carol Dyhouse, *Glamour: Women, History, Feminism* (London: Zed Books, 2010); Tanisha C. Ford, *Liberated Threads: Black Women, Style, and the Global Politics of Soul* (Chapel Hill: University of North Carolina Press, 2015); Rochelle Rowe, *Imagining*

Caribbean Womanhood: Race, Nation and Beauty Competitions, 1929–70
(Manchester: Manchester University Press, 2013); Rowe, "'Glorifying the Jamaican
Girl': The 'Ten Types—One People' Beauty Contest, Racialized Femininities and
Jamaican Nationalism," *Radical History Review* 103 (2009): 36–58; Kim Smith,
"Strands of the Sixties. A Cultural Analysis of the Design and Consumption of the
New London West End Hair Salons, *c.*1954–1975" (PhD dissertation, University
of East London, 2014); Weinbaum et al., eds., *The Modern Girl around the World*;
Zweiniger-Bargielowska, *Managing the Body*; and Zweiniger-Bargielowska, "The
Making of a Modern Female Body: Beauty, Health and Fitness in Interwar Britain,"
Women's History Review 20, no. 2 (2011): 299–317.

21 Day, *Consumptive Chic*; and Smith, "Beauty Advertising."

22 Deslandes, forthcoming; and Paul Deslandes, "The Male Body, Beauty and
Aesthetics in Modern British Culture," *History Compass* 8, no. 10 (2010): 1192.
See also Bengry, "Courting the Pink Pound"; Deslandes, "Selling, Consuming, and
Becoming the Beautiful Man in Britain"; and Houlbrook, "'Powder Puff.'" The field
continues to expand. See, for example, Bloomsbury's forthcoming *Cultural History
of Beauty* series and Alun Withey's forthcoming history of beards.

23 James Vernon, *Distant Strangers: How Britain Became Modern* (Berkeley: University
of California Press, 2014), 7.

24 Lynda Nead, *Victorian Babylon: People, Streets, and Images in Nineteenth-Century
London* (New Haven, CT: Yale University Press, 2000), 67. See also Sharrona Pearl,
About Faces: Physiognomy in Nineteenth-Century Britain (Cambridge, MA: Harvard
University Press, 2010), chapter 1.

25 Nead, *Victorian Babylon*, 66–7; Sadiah Qureshi, *Peoples on Parade: Exhibitions, and
Anthropology in Nineteenth-Century Britain* (Chicago, IL: University of Chicago
Press, 2011), 38–46; and Vernon, *Distant Strangers*, 14.

26 Qureshi, *Peoples on Parade*, 38–44.

27 On visual legibility, see Judith R. Walkowitz, "Going Public: Shopping, Street
Harassment, and Streetwalking in Late Victorian London." *Representations* 62
(Spring 1998): 1–30.

28 Christopher Breward, *The Hidden Consumer: Masculinities, Fashion, and City Life,
1860–1914* (Manchester: Manchester University Press, 1999), 1–2.

29 For Britain, fashioning of the modern body is typically attributed to the twentieth
century and especially the interwar period. See note 9. On the significance of
bodies as productive sites of historical study, see Kathleen Canning's germinal essay
"The Body as Method? Reflections on the Place of the Body in Gender History," in
Gender History in Practice: Historical Perspectives on Bodies, Class, and Citizenship
(Ithaca, NY: Cornell University Press, 2006), 168–89.

30 Vernon, *Distant Strangers*, 39.

31 Steele, *Fashion and Eroticism*, especially chapters 7 and 11; and Zweiniger-
Bargielowska, *Managing the Body*, 4–5.

32   Deborah Cohen, *Family Secrets: Living with Shame from the Victorians to the Present Day* (London: Viking, 2013).

33   Stephanie M. H. Camp, "Black Is Beautiful: An American History," *Journal of Southern History* 81, no. 3 (August 2015): 690; and Camp, "Making Racial Beauty in the United States: Toward a History of Black Beauty," in *Connexions: Histories of Race and Sex in North America*, ed. Jennifer Brier, Jim Downs, and Jennifer L. Morgan (Urbana: University of Illinois Press, 2016), 113–26. On beauty and historical constructions of race, see, for example, essays in Bloomsbury's forthcoming *Cultural History of Beauty*, Volume V; Sharon Block, "Early American Bodies: Creating Race, Sex, and Beauty," in *Connexions: Histories of Race and Sex in North America*, ed. Jennifer Brier, Jim Downs, and Jennifer L. Morgan (Urbana: University of Illinois Press, 2016), 85–112; Jennifer L. Morgan, *Laboring Women: Reproduction and Gender in New World Slavery* (Philadelphia: University of Pennsylvania Press, 2004), 14–16; Charmaine Nelson, *Representing the Black Female Subject in Western Art* (New York: Routledge, 2010); Kimberly Poitevin, "Inventing Whiteness: Cosmetics, Race, and Women in Early Modern England," *Journal for Early Modern Cultural Studie*s 11, no. 1 (Spring/Summer 2011): 59–89; and Rowe, *Imagining Caribbean Womanhood*.

34   For discussions of beauty culture, race, and empire, see, for example, Burke, *Lifebuoy Men, Lux Women*; Kay Heath, *Aging by the Book: The Emergence of Midlife in Victorian Britain* (Albany: State University of New York Press, 2009), chapter 6; Anne McClintock, *Imperial Leather: Race, Gender and Sexuality in the Colonial Contest* (New York: Routledge, 1995), chapter 5; Anandi Ramamurthy, *Imperial Persuaders: Images of Africa and Asia in British Advertising* (Manchester: Manchester University Press, 2003), chapter 2; Rowe, *Imagining Caribbean Womanhood*; and Weinbaum et al., eds., *The Modern Girl around the World*.

35   On Victorian London as a heterogeneous, multi-ethnic city, see Qureshi, *Peoples on Parade*, especially 34–8 and 44–6. See also the work of Caroline Bressey, including "The Black Presence in England and Wales after the Abolition Act, 1807–1930," *Parliamentary History* 26 (2007): 224–37; Panikos Panayi, *Immigration, Ethnicity, and Racism in Britain, 1815–1945* (Manchester: Manchester University Press, 1994); and Laura Tabili, *Global Migrants, Local Culture: Natives and Newcomers in Provincial England, 1841–1939* (Basingstoke: Palgrave Macmillan, 2011).

36   Christopher Breward, Edwina Ehrman, and Caroline Evans, *The London Look: Fashion from Street to Catwalk* (New Haven, CT: Yale University Press, 2004), 4. On the concept of fashionable "world cities," see David Gilbert, "From Paris to Shanghai: The Changing Geographies of Fashion's World Cities," in *Fashion's World Cities*, ed. Christopher Breward and David Gilbert (Oxford: Berg, 2006), especially 10–16.

37 See, for example, Leonore Davidoff, *The Best Circles: Society Etiquette and the Season* (London: Cresset Library, 1986); and Kristin Hoganson, "The Fashionable World: Imagined Communities of Dress," in *After the Imperial Turn: Thinking with and Through the Nation*, ed. Antoinette Burton (Durham, NC: Duke University Press, 2003), 260–78.

38 Breward et al., *London Look*, 7.

39 Christopher Breward, *Fashioning London: Clothing and the Modern Metropolis* (Oxford: Berg, 2004), 11.

40 On Victorian London as a classed landscape, see Nead, *Victorian Babylon*; Judith R. Walkowitz, *City of Dreadful Delight: Narratives of Sexual Danger in late-Victorian London* (Chicago, IL: University of Chicago Press, 1992); and James Winter, *London's Teeming Streets, 1830–1914* (London: Routledge, 1993).

41 Rappaport, *Shopping for Pleasure*; and Michael Winstanley, *The Shopkeeper's World, 1830–1914* (Manchester: Manchester University Press, 1983), 2.

42 Breward, *The Hidden Consumer*; and Ariel Beaujot, *Victorian Fashion Accessories* (London: Berg, 2013). On clubs, see Amy Milne-Smith, *London Clubland: A Cultural History of Gender and Class in Late Victorian Britain* (New York: Palgrave Macmillan, 2011).

43 On Old Bond Street, St. James's Street, and Savile Row in the early nineteenth century, see Breward et al., *London Look*, 18–20; and Breward, *Fashioning London*, 30. On fashionable masculine geographies in London and beyond, see Breward, *The Hidden Consumer*; David Kuchta, *The Three-Piece Suit and Modern Masculinity: England 1550–1850* (Berkeley: University of California Press, 2002); David Shannon, *The Cut of His Coat: Men, Dress, and Consumer Culture in Britain, 1860–1914* (Dayton: Ohio University Press, 2006); and Laura Ugolini, *Men and Menswear: Sartorial Consumption in Britain, 1880–1939* (Burlington, VT: Ashgate, 2007).

44 According to an unsubstantiated story, Truefitt created the first lipstick. "It was a salve for the lips, the recipe for which guaranteed that, if properly made, it would 'last two years without losing its colour.' The colour was made from cochineal." Ivor Halstead, *Bond Street* (London: Barcliff, 1952), 97.

45 *Post Office London Directory, 1856* (London: W. Kelly, 1856), 541–2.

46 See Deslandes, forthcoming; and Breward, *Hidden Consumer*. The late nineteenth century saw the opening up of new fashion pleasure zones to women in Knightsbridge and Bayswater, west of Mayfair. On this, see Rappaport, *Shopping for Pleasure*.

47 Laurel Flinn, "Social and Spatial Politics in the Construction of Regent Street," *Journal of Social History* 46, no. 2 (Winter 2012): 364–90.

48 Breward, *Fashioning London*, 60–1.

49 Breward, *Fashioning London*, chapter 3.

50 Breward et al., *London Look*, 36–7; and Breward, "Sartorial Spectacle: Clothing and Masculine Identities in the Imperial City, 1860–1914," in *Imperial Cities: Landscape,*

Display and Identity, ed. Felix Driver and David Gilbert (Manchester: Manchester University Press, 1999), 244–51.

51   Margaret Skelton assumed the business from 1854 onward. It was celebrated for being the onetime palace of Cardinal Wolsey, advisor to Henry VIII. *Post Office London Directory* (London: W. Kelly, 1854, 1857, 1859). See "A Fine Day in Fleet Street," *Fraser's Magazine* 29 (January 1844): 72.

52   Alison Adburgham, *Shops and Shopping, 1800–1914: Where and in What Manner the Well-Dressed Englishwoman Bought Her Clothes* (London: Allen & Unwin, [1964] 1981), especially chapter 10; Jacky Susan Bratton, *The Making of the West End Stage: Marriage, Management and the Mapping of Gender in London, 1830–1870* (New York: Cambridge University Press, 2011), chapter 1; Lynne Walker, "Vistas of Pleasure: Women Consumers of Urban Space in the West End of London, 1850–1900," in *Women in the Victorian Art World*, ed. Clarissa Campbell Orr (Manchester: Manchester University Press, 1995), 70–85; Walkowitz, *City of Dreadful Delight*; Walkowitz, "Going Public"; and Tammy Whitlock, *Crime, Gender, and Consumer Culture in Nineteenth-Century England* (Burlington, VT: Ashgate, 2005), 22–4.

53   On the Port of London as imagined and sartorial space, see Breward, *Fashioning London*, 55–7.

54   Jones, *Beauty Imagined*, 26–9; and Eugénie Briot, "From Industry to Luxury: French Perfume in the Nineteenth Century," *Business History Review* 85 (Summer 2011): 273–94.

55   Jones, *Beauty Imagined*, 27.

56   On the United States, see Peiss, *Hope in a Jar*, chapters 4 and 5. On France, see Grout, especially chapter 6. See also Jones, *Beauty Imagined*, chapter 4.

57   Alison C. Kay, "Retailing, Respectability and the Independent Woman in Nineteenth-Century London," in *Women, Business and Finance in Nineteenth-Century Europe: Rethinking Separate Spheres*, ed. Robert Beachy, Béatrice Craig and Alastair Owens (Oxford: Berg, 2006), 153.

58   Whitlock, *Crime, Culture, and Consumer Culture*, 72.

59   See, for example, Takahiro Ueyama, *Health in the Marketplace: Professionalism, Therapeutic Desires, and Medical Commodification in Late-Victorian London* (Palo Alto, CA: The Society for the Promotion of Science and Scholarship, 2010).

60   David, *Fashion Victims*, 22–4. See also Aviva Briefel, "Cosmetic Tragedies: Failed Masquerade in Wilkie Collins's *The Lady and the Law*," *Victorian Literature and Culture* 37, no. 2 (2009): 463–81; Laurence Talairach-Vielmas, *Moulding the Female Body in Victorian Fairy Tales and Sensation Novels* (Burlington, VT: Ashgate, 2007), especially chapter 9; and James C. Whorton, *The Arsenic Century: How Victorian Britain Was Poisoned at Home, Work, and Play* (New York: Oxford University Press, 2010), 273–8. On the United States, see Gwen Kay, *Dying to Be Beautiful: The Fight*

for Safe Cosmetics (Columbus: Ohio State University, 2005); and Peiss, *Hope in a Jar*, 21–2 and 41–3.

61 George Robb, *White-Collar Crime in Modern England: Financial Fraud and Business Morality, 1845–1929* (Cambridge: Cambridge University Press, 1992), 4.

62 John Benson and Laura Ugolini, "Introduction: Historians and the Nation of Shopkeepers," in *A Nation of Shopkeepers: Five Centuries of British Retailing* (London: I.B. Tauris, 2003), 6–7.

63 For the American context, see Karen Halttunen, *Confidence Men and Painted Women: A Study of Middle-Class Culture in America, 1830–1870* (New Haven, CT: Yale University Press, 1982).

64 Gareth Shaw, "The Evolution and Impact of Large-Scale Retailing in Britain," in *The Evolution of Retail Systems, c. 1800–1914*, ed. John Benson and Gareth Shaw (Leicester: Leicester University Press, 1992), 135–65; and Rappaport, *Shopping*, 11. On retailing, see David Alexander, *Retailing in England during the Industrial Revolution* (London: Athlone, 1970); and James B. Jefferys, *Retail Trading in Britain, 1850–1950* (Cambridge: Cambridge University Press, 1954). On the department store, see Geoffrey Crossick and Serge Jaumain, eds., *Cathedrals of Consumption: The European Department Store, 1850-1939* (Aldershot: Aldergate, 1999); Heinz-Gerhard Haupt, "Small Shops and Department Stores," in *The Oxford Handbook of the History of Consumption*, ed. Frank Trentmann (New York: Oxford University Press, 2012), 267–88; William Lancaster, *The Department Store: A Social History* (London: Leicester University Press, 1995); William R. Leach, "Transformations in a Culture of Consumption: Women and Department Stores, 1890–1925," *Journal of American History* 71, no. 2 (September 1984): 319–42; Mica Nava, "Modernity's Disavowal: Women, the City, and the Department Store," in *Modern Times: Reflections on a Century of Modernity*, ed. Mica Nava and Alan O'Shea (London: Routledge, 1996), 38–76; and Rappaport, *Shopping*, especially chapter 5.

65 Margot C. Finn, *The Character of Credit: Personal Debt in English Culture, 1740–1914* (New York: Cambridge University Press, 2003), 89–98. See also Whitlock, *Crime, Culture, and Consumer Culture*, 30–2 and 95–7. Finn and others have asserted that our conceptions of increasingly impersonal market interactions fail "to convey the tenor of exchange relations in either domestic settings or the market." Finn, *Character of Credit*, 21.

66 Finn, *Character of Credit*, 320.

67 John Benson and Laura Ugolini, "Introduction," in *Cultures of Selling: Perspectives on Consumption and Society since 1700* (Aldershot: Ashgate, 2006), 19; Margot C. Finn, "Working-Class Women and the Contest for Consumer Control in Victorian County Courts," *Past & Present* 161 (1998): 116–54; Erika D. Rappaport, "'A Husband and his Wife's Dresses': Consumer Credit and the Debtor Family in

England, 1864–1914," in *The Sex of Things: Gender and Consumption in Historical Perspective*, ed. Victoria de Grazia with Ellen Furlough (Berkeley: University of California Press, 1996), 163–87; and Rappaport, *Shopping*, 53. For an earlier moment, see Elizabeth Kowaleski-Wallace, *Consuming Subjects: Women, Shopping, and Business in the Eighteenth Century* (New York: Columbia University Press, 1997), 86–9.

68   On the latter, see Benson and Ugolini, "Introduction," in *Cultures of Selling*, 10.

69   These categories come from Robb, *White-Collar Crime in Modern England*, 5.

70   On the importance of personality to enterprise, see Jennifer Aston, *Female Entrepreneurship in Nineteenth-Century England: Engagement in the Urban Economy* (London: Palgrave, 2016), 64.

71   Benson and Ugolini, "Introduction," in *A Nation of Shopkeepers*, 3.

72   On enterprise, interpersonal relations, and emotion, see Robin Holt and Andrew Popp, "Emotion, Succession, and the Family Firm: Josiah Wedgwood & Sons," *Business History* 55, no. 6 (2013): 892–909. See also Andrew Popp, *Entrepreneurial Families: Business, Marriage and Life in the Early Nineteenth Century* (London: Pickering & Chatto, 2012).

73   For women in business, see Aston, *Female Entrepreneurship*; Hannah Barker, *The Business of Women: Female Enterprise and Urban Development in Northern England, 1760–1830* (Oxford: Oxford University Press, 2006); Katrina Honeyman, "Doing Business with Gender: Service Industries and British Business History," *Business History Review* 81, no. 3 (Autumn 2007): 471–93; Honeyman, *Women, Gender and Industrialisation in England, 1700–1870* (New York: St. Martin's Press, 2000); and Alison C. Kay, *The Foundations of Female Entrepreneurship: Enterprise, Home and Household in London c. 1800–1870* (London: Routledge, 2009). See also Stana Nenadic, "Gender and the Rhetoric of Business Success: The Impact on Women Entrepreneurs and the 'New Woman' in Later Nineteenth-Century Edinburgh," in *Women's Work in Industrial England: Regional and Local Perspectives*, ed. Nigel Goose (Hatfield: Local Population Studies, 2007), 269–88; and Pamela Sharpe, *Adapting to Capitalism: Working Women in the English Economy, 1700–1850* (New York: St. Martin's Press, 1996). For more on the American case, see Wendy Gamber, *The Female Economy: The Millinery and Dressmaking Trades, 1860–1930* (Urbana, IL: University of Chicago Press, 1997); Wendy Gamber, "A Gendered Enterprise: Placing Nineteenth-Century Businesswomen in History," *Business History Review*, Gender and Business 72, no. 2 (1998): 188–217; Peiss, *Hope in a Jar*; Kathy Peiss, "'Vital Industry' and Women's Ventures: Conceptualizing Gender in Twentieth Century Business History," *Business History Review*, Gender and Business 72, no. 2 (1998): 219–41; Philip Scranton, "Introduction: Gender and Business History," *Business History Review*, Gender and Business 72, no. 2 (1998): 185–7; and Joan W. Scott,

"Comment: Conceptualizing Gender in American Business History," *Business History Review*, Gender and Business 72, no. 2 (1998): 242–9.

74 This does not refer to the concept of "emotional messiness," which, as Holt and Popp point out, raises issues of historicization. See Holt and Popp, "Emotion, Succession, and the Family Firm," 894.

75 Monique Scheer, "Are Emotions a Kind of Practice (And Is That What Makes Them Have a History)? A Bourdieuian Approach to Understanding Emotion," *History and Theory* 51 (May 2012): 193–220.

76 Aston, *Female Entrepreneurship*, 6–9; and Kay, *Foundations*. See also Kay, "A Little Enterprise of Her Own: Lodging-House Keeping and the Accommodation Business in Nineteenth-Century London," *The London Journal* 28, no. 2 (2003): 41–53; Kay, "Retailing, Respectability"; and Nenadic, "Gender and the Rhetoric of Business Success."

77 This aligns with strategies developed by historians of female enterprise in nineteenth-century Britain. See Aston, *Female Entrepreneurship*; and Kay, *Foundations*.

78 As historians like Andrew Popp compellingly argue, intimate studies of individual, everyday enterprise are essential if we are to sufficiently account for the role of humanity in economic life. Popp, *Entrepreneurial Families*, 2.

79 Ruth Brandon, *Ugly Beauty: Helena Rubinstein, L'Oreal, and the Blemished History of Looking Good* (New York: HarperCollins, 2011); Jones, *Beauty Imagined*, 59–60; and Lindy Woodhead, *War Paint: Madame Helena Rubinstein and Miss Elizabeth Arden: Their Lives, Their Times, Their Rivalry* (London: Virago, 2003).

1 "Backmewsy" Beauty: Agnes Headman and Aimée Lloyd

1 Ansell v. Gaubert A.39 (1858) The National Archives (hereafter TNA), C 15/444/A39. Surname misspelled as "Ganbert."

2 Divorce Court File, Lloyd v. Lloyd (June 13, 1867) TNA J 77/75/457. Forename misspelled as "Amiee Lloyd."

3 Alfred Marshall, *Principles of Economics, Volume I* (London: Macmillan, 1890), Book 6, chapter 4.

4 On women in business, see Pamela Sharpe, "Lace and Place: Women's Business in Occupational Communities in England, 1550–1950," *Women's History Review* 19, no. 2 (2010): 283–306; and Alison C. Kay, *The Foundations of Female Entrepreneurship: Enterprise, Home and Household in London c. 1800-1870* (London: Routledge, 2009), 124. See also Jennifer Aston, *Female Entrepreneurship in Nineteenth-Century England: Engagement in the Urban Economy* (London: Palgrave, 2016); Hannah Barker, *The Business of*

Women: Female Enterprise and Urban Development in Northern England, 1760–1830 (Oxford: Oxford University Press, 2006); Katrina Honeyman, *Women, Gender and Industrialisation in England, 1700–1870* (New York: St. Martin's Press, 2000); Alison C. Kay, "A Little Enterprise of Her Own: Lodging-House Keeping and the Accommodation Business in Nineteenth-Century London," *The London Journal* 28, no. 2 (2003): 41–53; Alison C. Kay, "Retailing, Respectability and the Independent Woman in Nineteenth-Century London," in *Women, Business and Finance in Nineteenth-Century Europe: Rethinking Separate Spheres*, ed. Robert Beachy, Béatrice Craig, and Alastair Owens (Oxford: Berg, 2006), 152–66; Nicola Phillips, *Women in Business, 1700–1850* (Woodbridge: Boydell Press, 2006), 258; and Pamela Sharpe, *Adapting to Capitalism: Working Women in the English Economy, 1700–1850* (New York: St. Martin's Press, 1996), 4–5 and 151.

5   Fiorenza Belussi and Katia Caldari, "At the Origin of the Industrial District: Alfred Marshall and the Cambridge School," *Cambridge Journal of Economics* 33 (2009): 343. See also Alfred Marshall, *Industry and Trade* (London: Macmillan, 1919); and Giacomo Becattini, "The Industrial District as a Creative Milieu," in *Industrial Change and Regional Development: The Transformation of New Industrial Spaces*, ed. Georges Benko and Michael Dunford (London: Belhaven Press, 1991), 102–14.

6   On the potentially antagonistic relationship between independents and large-scale retailers in the late nineteenth century, see Gareth Shaw, "Evolution & Impact of Large-Scale Retailing in Britain," in *The Evolution of Retail Systems, c. 1800–1914*, ed. John Benson and Gareth Shaw (Leicester: Leicester University Press, 1992), 160–2.

7   Geoffrey Jones, *Beauty Imagined: A History of the Global Beauty Industry* (New York: Oxford University Press, 2010), 15–19 and 350.

8   Jones, *Beauty Imagined*, 18; and Jonathan Reinarz, *Past Scents: Historical Perspectives on Smell* (Urbana: University of Illinois Press, 2014), 71–2. On London's perfume trades in the sixteenth and seventeenth centuries, see Holly Dugan, *The Ephemeral History of Perfume: Scent and Sense in Early Modern England* (Baltimore, MD: Johns Hopkins University Press, 2011), 142–9.

9   Kim F. Hall, *Things of Darkness: Economies of Race and Gender in Early Modern England* (Ithaca, NY: Cornell University Press, 1995). See also David Bindman, *Ape to Apollo: Aesthetics and the Idea of Race in the Eighteenth Century* (London: Reaktion Books, 2002); Sharon Block, "Early American Bodies: Creating Race, Sex, and Beauty," in *Connexions: Histories of Race and Sex in North America*, ed. Jennifer Brier, Jim Downs, and Jennifer L. Morgan (Urbana: University of Illinois Press, 2016), 85–112; Jennifer L. Morgan, *Laboring Women: Reproduction and Gender in New World Slavery* (Philadelphia: University of Pennsylvania Press, 2004), 14–16; Kimberly Poitevin, "Inventing Whiteness: Cosmetics, Race, and Women in Early Modern England," *Journal for Early Modern Cultural Studies* 11, no. 1

(Spring/Summer 2011): 59–89; Roxann Wheeler, *The Complexion of Race: Categories of Difference in Eighteenth-Century British Culture* (Philadelphia: University of Pennsylvania Press, 2000); and Kathryn Woods, "'Facing' Identity in a 'Faceless' Society: Physiognomy, Facial Appearance and Identity Perception in Eighteenth-Century London," *Cultural & Social History* 14, no. 2 (2017): 144–7.

10   Edith Snook, "'The Beautifying Part of Physic': Women's Cosmetic Practices in Early Modern England," *Journal of Women's History* 20, no. 3 (Fall 2008): 12. See also Frances E. Dolan, "Taking the Pencil Out of God's Hand: Art, Nature, and the Face-Painting Debate in Early Modern England," *PMLA* 108, no. 2 (1993): 224–39; Annette Drew-Bear, "Cosmetics and Attitudes towards Women in the Seventeenth Century," *Journal of Popular Culture* 9, no. 1 (1975): 31–7; Annette Drew-Bear, "Face Painting Scenes in Ben Jonson's Plays," *Studies in Philology* 77, no. 4 (1980): 388–401; Annette Drew-Bear, "Face Painting in Renaissance Tragedy," *Renaissance Drama* 12 (1981): 71–93; Laurie Finke, "Painting Women: Images of Femininity in Jacobean Tragedy," *Theatre Journal* 36, no. 3 (1984): 356–70; Shirley Nelson Garner, "'Let Her Paint an Inch Thick': Painted Ladies in Renaissance Drama and Society," *Renaissance Drama* 20 (1989): 123–39; Patricia Phillippy, *Painting Women: Cosmetics, Canvases and Early Modern Culture* (Baltimore, MD: Johns Hopkins University Press, 2006); Will Pritchard, "Masks and Faces: Female Legibility in the Restoration Era," *Eighteenth-Century Life* 24, no. 3 (2000): 31–52; and Dosia Reichardt, "'Their Faces Are Not Their Own': Powders, Patches and Paint in Seventeenth–Century Poetry," *Dalhousie Review* 84, no. 2 (2004): 195–214.

11   See Paul Deslandes's forthcoming study of male beauty from the University of Chicago Press.

12   Carolyn Day, *Consumptive Chic: A History of Beauty, Fashion, and Disease* (London: Bloomsbury, 2017), 93–5.

13   Kathryn Ledbetter, *British Victorian Women's Periodicals: Beauty, Civilization, and Poetry* (New York: Palgrave Macmillan, 2009), 133–4.

14   See, for example, Mrs. Alexander Walker, *Female Beauty: As Preserved and Improved by Regimen, Cleanliness and Dress* (London: Thomas Hurst, 1837); "Crinoline and Cosmetics," *Punch* (October 3, 1863): 135; "Fraudulent Faces," *Punch* (January 9, 1864): 19; "Fashionable Forgery," *Punch* (July 23, 1870): 42; and "Finishing for Faces," *Punch* (April 20, 1878): 172.

15   Alison Adburgham, *Shops and Shopping, 1800–1914: Where and in What Manner the Well-Dressed Englishwoman Bought Her Clothes* (London: Allen & Unwin, [1964] 1981), 115; Ros Ballaster, Margaret Beetham, and Sandra Hebron, *Women's Worlds: Ideology, Femininity, and the Woman's Magazine* (London: Macmillan, 1991); and Margaret Beetham, *A Magazine of Her Own?: Domesticity and Desire in the Woman's Magazine, 1800–1914* (London: Routledge, 1996).

16   See, for example, *The Habits of Good Society: A Handbook for Ladies and Gentlemen* (New York: Carleton, 1863), 132; Kathy Peiss, *Hope in a Jar: The Making of*

America's Beauty Culture (New York: Metropolitan, 1998), 57; and Holly Lynn Grout, *The Force of Beauty: Transforming French Ideas of Femininity in the Third Republic* (Baton Rouge: Louisiana State University Press, 2015).

17 Amy Montz, *Dressing for England: Fashion and Nationalism in Victorian Novels* (PhD dissertation, Texas A&M, 2008), chapter 3; and Peiss, *Hope in a Jar*, 43–4.

18 Jessica P. Clark, "'Will You Give Me Your Opinion?': Mundane Beauty in the *Englishwoman's Domestic Magazine*, 1860–1875," *Victorian Periodicals Review* 52, no. 3 (Fall 2019): 540–65. See also Patricia Anderson, *The Printed Image and the Transformation of Popular Culture, 1790-1860* (Oxford: Clarendon Press, 1991), 150–1; Ledbetter, *British Victorian Women's Periodicals*; Laurence Talairach-Vielmas, *Moulding the Female Body in Victorian Fairy Tales and Sensation Novels* (Burlington, VT: Ashgate, 2007), 150; and Tammy Whitlock, "A 'Taint Upon Them': The Madame Rachel Case, Fraud, and Retail Trade in Nineteenth-Century England," *Victorian Review* 24, no. 1 (1998): 46.

19 Day, *Consumptive Chic*, 97–8; and Michelle J. Smith, "Beauty Advertising and Advice in the *Queen* and *Woman*," in *Women, Periodicals and Print Culture in Britain, 1830s-1900s: The Victorian Period*, ed. Alexis Easley, Clare Gill, and Beth Rodgers (Edinburgh: Edinburgh University Press, 2019), 225–9.

20 "A Rival to Madame Rachel," *Fun* (December 30, 1865): 158. See also Valerie Steele, *Fashion and Eroticism: Ideals of Feminine Beauty from the Victorian Era to the Jazz Age* (New York: Oxford University Press, 1985), 121–32.

21 *The Handbook of the Toilette. By the Author of "Familiar Hints on Sea-Bathing," The Handbook of Cookery…* (London: W. S. Orr, 1839), 48; and Lola Montez, *The Arts of Beauty* (London: James Blackwood, Paternoster Row, 1858), 25. See also Corisande, "Aids to Beauty," *Illustrated Household Journal and Englishwoman's Domestic Magazine* (May 1, 1882): 115. On the history of cosmetics, see Maggie Angeloglou, *A History of Make-Up* (New York: Macmillan, 1970); Jones, *Beauty Imagined*; Gwen Kay, *Dying to Be Beautiful: The Fight for Safe Cosmetics* (Columbus: Ohio State University Press, 2005); Peiss, *Hope in a Jar*; Teresa Riordan, *Inventing Beauty: A History of the Innovations That Have Made Us Beautiful* (New York: Broadway Books, 2004); and Philip Scranton, ed., *Beauty and Business: Commerce, Gender, and Culture in Modern America* (New York: Routledge, 2001).

22 See, for example, Samuel Beeton, "Health and Beauty," *Englishwoman's Domestic Magazine*, Volume III (1867): 266; and Mrs. White, "Chapter on Pigments, Patches, &c.," *Englishwoman's Domestic Magazine* (April 1, 1854): 385.

23 Tammy Whitlock, *Crime, Gender, and Consumer Culture in Nineteenth-Century England* (Burlington, VT: Ashgate, 2005), 62.

24 On Ross, see Deslandes, forthcoming.

25 Susan J. Vincent, *Hair: An Illustrated History* (London: Bloomsbury, 2018), 39–40.

26   Whitlock, *Crime, Gender, and Consumer Culture*, 111–12. See also Christine Bayles
     Kortsch, *Dress Culture in Late Victorian Women's Fiction: Literacy, Textiles, and
     Activism* (Farnham: Ashgate, 2009), 62; and Steele, *Fashion and Eroticism*, 130.

27   See "Questionable Faces," *London Society*, Volume XVI (London: 217 Piccadilly
     W, 1869): 511–12; and John Scoffern, "Beautiful for Ever," *Belgravia: A London
     Magazine*, Volume V (June 1868): 229. For scholarly discussions of "making
     up," see Richard Corson, *Fashions in Makeup: From Ancient to Modern Times*
     (London: Owen, 1972); Whitlock, "A 'Taint,'" 33; and Neville Williams, *Powder
     and Paint: A History of the Englishwoman's Toilet, Elizabeth I – Elizabeth II*
     (London: Longmans Green, 1957).

28   Mary Elizabeth Braddon, *Lady Audley's Secret* (London: Tinsley Bros., 1862); and
     Wilkie Collins, *Armadale* (London: Harper, 1866), originally published in the
     Cornhill Magazine (November 1864–June 1866). See also L. T. Meade, *The Sorceress
     of the Strand* (London: Ward, Lock, 1903); and Charlotte M. Yonge, *Love and
     Life: An Old Story in Eighteenth Century Costume* (London: Macmillan, 1880). For
     scholarly treatments, see Rebecca Kling, "'It Is Only Colour That You Want': *Lady
     Audley's Secret* and Cosmetics as Discursive Fantasy," *Victorian Periodicals Review*
     50, no. 3 (Fall 2017): 560–84; Katherine Montwieler, "Marketing Sensation: *Lady
     Audley's Secret* and Consumer Culture," in *Beyond Sensation: Mary Elizabeth
     Braddon in Context*, ed. Marlene Tromp, Pamela K. Gilbert, and Aeron Haynie
     (Albany: State University of New York Press, 2000), 50–1; Elizabeth Carolyn Miller,
     "'Shrewd Women of Business': Madame Rachel, Victorian Consumerism, and L.T.
     Meade's *The Sorceress of the Strand*," *Victorian Literature and Culture* 34 (2006): 313;
     Miller, *Framed: The New Woman Criminal in British Culture at the Fin de Siècle*
     (Ann Arbor: University of Michigan Press, 2008); Talairach-Vielmas, *Moulding the
     Female Body*; and Whitlock, "A 'Taint.'"

29   Angeloglou, *A History of Make-Up*, 94–7; Miller, "'Shrewd'"; Talairach-Vielmas,
     Moulding the Female Body; and Whitlock, "A 'Taint,'" 33.

30   For other national beauty industries, see Morag Martin, *Selling Beauty: Cosmetics,
     Commerce, and French Society, 1750–1830* (Baltimore, MD: Johns Hopkins
     University Press, 2009). On French ascendancy in the *fin de siècle*, see Jones, *Beauty
     Imagined*, chapter 1.

31   Adburgham, *Shops and Shopping*, especially chapter 10; Erika D. Rappaport,
     Shopping for Pleasure: Women in the Making of London's West End (Princeton,
     NJ: Princeton University Press, 2000); Lynne Walker, "Vistas of Pleasure: Women
     Consumers of Urban Space in the West End of London, 1850–1900," in *Women
     in the Victorian Art World*, ed. Clarissa Campbell Orr (Manchester: Manchester
     University Press, 1995), 70–85; Judith R. Walkowitz, *City of Dreadful
     Delight: Narratives of Sexual Danger in Late-Victorian London* (Chicago,
     IL: University of Chicago Press, 1992); Walkowitz, "Going Public: Shopping, Street

Harassment, and Streetwalking in Late Victorian London" *Representations* 62
(Spring 1998): 1–30; and Whitlock, *Crime, Gender and Consumer Culture*, 22–4.

32 "A Rival to Madame Rachel," *Fun* (December 30, 1865): 158.

33 "Advertisement," *Chemist and Druggist* (January 15, 1874): 15. On Rimmel, see
chapter 4; and Jones, *Beauty Imagined*, 18–20.

34 Jessica P. Clark, "Grooming Men: The Material World of the Nineteenth-Century
Barbershop," in *Gender and Material Culture in Britain since 1600*, ed. Hannah
Greig, Jane Hamlett, and Leonie Hannan (London: Palgrave Macmillan, 2015),
104–19.

35 *Post Office London Directory, 1891* (London: W. Kelly, 1891), 1882; *Post Office
London Directory, 1897* (London: W. Kelly, 1897), 1805; and *Post Office London
Directory, 1903* (London: W. Kelly, 1903), 2692.

36 Jones, *Beauty Imagined*, 24; and Deslandes, forthcoming.

37 Floris Account Books, private collection. Goods included Almond Cream,
Glycerine, Naples Soap, Pâte au Miel, Toilet Vinegar, Violet Oil, and Honey Tablets.

38 An exception occurred when George Eliot complained to feminist Barbara Leigh-
Smith Bodichon about her dissatisfaction with glycerine soap she purchased at a
shop on Oxford Street. George Eliot, "Letter from George Eliot to Barbara Leigh-
Smith Bodichon, January 18, 1872," in *The George Eliot Letters, vol. 9: 1871–1881*,
ed. Gordon S. Haight (New Haven, CT: Yale University Press, 1978), 539.

39 For further discussion of Breidenbach, see chapter 4.

40 William John Loftie, *Kensington Picturesque & Historical* (London: Leadenhall
Press, 1888), 111–12. On Scarsdale House, see Adburgham, *Shops and
Shopping*, 165.

41 "Breidenbach's Perfumery: Cash Book" (July 1869–February 1871) in Records
Relating to Breidenbach's Perfumery, Croydon Museum and Archives Service,
AR165/1.

42 The half-crown Percy used to pay was bad, but the Crown found her not guilty
of coining offences. *Old Bailey Proceedings Online*. See www.oldbaileyonline.org,
accessed May 21, 2011, May 1858, trial of Georgiana Percy (22) (t18580510-525).

43 Like Percy, Watts passed a bad coin. *Old Bailey Proceedings Online*. See www.
oldbaileyonline.org, accessed December 21, 2011, June 1864, trial of Charlotte
Watts (19) (t18640606-583).

44 Max Beerbohm, "A Defence of Cosmetics," in *The Yellow Book: An Illustrated
Quarterly* 1 (London: E. Matthews & J. Lane, 1894): 65. For examples of support
for visible cosmetic use from respectable sources, see *Beauty and How to Keep
It* (London: Brentano's, 1889); Jane Francesca, Lady Wilde, "The Laws of Dress,"
Burlington Magazine (May–June 1881); Baroness Blanche Staffe, *My Lady's
Dressing Room*, trans. Harriet Hubbard Ayer (New York: Cassell, 1892); *Beauty: Its
Attainment and Preservation* (New York: Butterick, 1890); and *The Art of Being*

Beautiful: A Series of Interviews with a Society Beauty (London: Henry J. Drane, 1902). For a scholarly consideration of many of these texts, see Corson, *Fashions in Makeup*, chapter 16.

45 "Skin-Deep Beauty," *The Daily Mirror* (July 12, 1906): 4. For considerations of male beauty in the twentieth century, see Paul Deslandes, "Selling, Consuming, and Becoming the Beautiful Man in Britain: The 1930s and 1940s," in *Consuming Behaviors: Identity, Politics and Pleasure in Twentieth-Century Britain*, ed. Erika D. Rappaport, Sandra Trudgen Dawson, and Mark J. Crowley (London: Bloomsbury, 2015), 53–70; Paul Deslandes, "The Male Body, Beauty and Aesthetics in Modern British Culture," *History Compass* 8, no. 10 (2010): 1191–208; and his forthcoming book from University of Chicago Press.

46 *Post Office London Directory, 1857* (London: W. Kelly, 1857). This tally also includes perfumery distillers and *eau de Cologne* importers.

47 See W. A. Jackson, *The Victorian Chemist and Druggist* (Princes Risborough: Shire, 1981), 17.

48 Aston, *Female Entrepreneurship*, 6–9; and Kay, *Foundations*, 51–2. See also David Foster, "Albion's Sisters: A Study of Trade Directories and Female Economic Participation in the Mid-Nineteenth Century" (MPhil dissertation, University of Exeter, 2002); Edward Higgs and Amanda Wilkinson, "Women, Occupations and Work in the Victorian Censuses Revisited," *History Workshop Journal* 81, no. 1 (Spring 2016): 17–38; and Bridget Hill, "Women, Work, and the Census: A Problem for Historians of Women," *History Workshop Journal* 35 (Spring 1993): 78–94.

49 I have compiled a database of 943 female beauty providers operating in London between 1815 and 1915. This data derives from trade directories; trade journals; periodical press coverage and advertisements; census data; and fire insurance records.

50 The Court of Chancery serves a special role in the history of women in business. Notes Nicola Phillips, "Chancery was … important for women, whose legal status under the common law was limited, but also central to the regulation of many business practices." Nicola Phillips, *Women in Business, 1700–1850* (Woodbridge: Boydell Press, 2006), 70.

51 The average number of "Retail Perfumers" listed in this category per year between 1852 and 1870 was 71.

52 This geographic concentration is evident in listings for "Retail Perfumers" in the *Post Office London Directory* from 1840 to 1870.

53 Hannah Barker and Karen Harvey, "Women Entrepreneurs and Urban Expansion: Manchester 1760–1820," in *Women and Urban Life in Eighteenth-Century England: "On the Town,"* ed. Rosemary Sweet and Penelope Lane (Burlington, VT: Ashgate 2003), 114. See also Kay, *Foundations*, 51–2; Foster, "Albion's Sisters"; Hill, "Women, Work, and the Census," 78–94; and Gareth Shaw and Allison Tipper, *British Directories: A Bibliography and Guide to*

Directories Published in England and Wales 1850–1950 and Scotland 1773–1950 (London: Mansell, 1996), 22. Aston points out the relative affordability of advertising in trade directories. See Aston, *Female Entrepreneurship*, 7–9.

54 Kay, *Foundations*; and Aston, *Female Entrepreneurship*.

55 Aston, *Female Entrepreneurship*; and Jennifer Aston and Paolo Di Martino, "Risk, Success, and Failure: Female Entrepreneurship in Late Victorian and Edwardian England," *The Economic History Review* 70, no. 3 (2017): 837–58.

56 Honeyman, *Women, Gender, and Industrialisation in Britain*, 51–71. See also Stana Nenadic, "Gender and the Rhetoric of Business Success: The Impact on Women Entrepreneurs and the 'New Woman' in Late Nineteenth-Century Edinburgh," in *Women's Work in Industrial England: Regional and Local Perspectives*, ed. Nigel Goose (Hatfield: Local Population Studies, 2007), 272–3.

57 J. G. L. Burnby, "Women in Pharmacy," *Pharmaceutical Historian* 20, no. 2 (1990): 6; and Ellen Jordan, "'The Great Principle of English Fair-Play': Male Champions, the English Women's Movement and the Admission of Women to the Pharmaceutical Society in 1879," *Women's History Review* 7, no. 3 (1998): 381–410.

58 On gender and start-up capital, see Aston, *Female Entrepreneurship*, 57; Lynn Hunt, *The Middling Sort: Commerce, Gender, and the Family in England, 1680–1780* (Berkeley: University of California Press, 1996), 145; Kay, *Foundations*, 25 and 42–3; and Whitlock, *Crime, Gender and Consumer Culture*, 72.

59 "Classified Advertisements," *The London Times* 21866 (October 7, 1854): 11. On maintaining a firm, see Aston, *Female Entrepreneurship*, 47. For a complete list of suggested goods when launching a perfumery shop, see Appendix II from Robert Kemp Philp, *The Shopkeeper's Guide* (London: Houlston and Stoneman, 1853), 97–101.

60 Kay, *Foundations*, 76; and Aston, *Female Entrepreneurship*. See also Kay, "Retailing."

61 For the American case, see Susan Yohn, "The Primacy of Place, Collaborations, and Alliances: Mapping Women's Businesses in Nineteenth-Century Brooklyn," *Journal of Urban History* 36, no. 4 (2010): 418.

62 Kay, *Foundations*, 76. On Regent Street and Piccadilly as desirable retailing locales, see E. Beresford Chancellor, *Liberty and Regent Street* (London: Liberty, 1927); Hermione Hobhouse, *A History of Regent Street: A Mile of Style* (Chichester: Phillimore, 2008); and Whitlock, *Crime, Gender and Consumer Culture*, 23.

63 David Alexander, *Retailing in England during the Industrial Revolution* (London: Athlone, 1970), 199.

64 Of the 255 female traders operating between 1840 and 1870, four appeared on Oxford Street, six on Regent Street, and seven on New Bond Street.

65 Ansell v. Ganbert A.39 (1858) TNA C 15/444/A39. A rental price for locations like Headman's remained affordable into the 1860s. In 1865, hairdresser Jean Marie Tirard and his wife took over No. 39 Curzon Street for the same annual rate that

Headman paid some twenty years earlier. "Lease for 21 years, counterpart," Henry White Hitchins and Jean Nestor Marie Tirard for 39 Curzon Street, Mayfair, Middlesex (June 26, 1865) London Metropolitan Archives (hereafter LMA) O/108/014/001.

66 Two exceptions are hairdressers and perfumers Clara Terry and Martha Dean, who operated on Regent Street from 1862 to 1872 and from 1865 to 1872, respectively. Beauty businesswomen's more discreet locations in London diverge from Aston's findings on businesswomen working in a variety of trades in Birmingham and Leeds; there, businesswomen established operations on the cities' leading commercial thoroughfares. Aston, *Entrepreneurship*, 75–6, 106–7.

67 *Post Office London Directory, 1859* (London: W. Kelly, 1859), 1781.

68 John Bury died in 1850. Euphemia's brother Alfred Bury (1817–1892) also worked as a perfumer at Exeter Change. *Census Returns of England and Wales, 1841*, class HO107, piece 687, book 3, Civil Parish Chelsea, County Middlesex, Enumeration District 1, folio 8, p. 9, www.ancestry.co.uk; and *Census Returns of England and Wales, 1861*, class RG 9, piece 168, folio 70, p. 69 and class RG 9, piece 37, folio 50, p. 2, www.ancestry.co.uk.

69 Anonymous, "A Season with the Dressmakers, or the Experience of a First-Hand," *The English Woman's Journal* 12, no. 69 (1863): 184; *Post Office London Directory, 1868* (London: W. Kelly, 1868); *Post Office London Directory, 1875* (London: W. Kelly, 1875); and *Post Office London Directory, 1876* (London: W. Kelly, 1876).

70 "Real Mysteries of Paris and London," *All the Year Round* (October 27, 1860): 69–72. In her study of businesswomen in Birmingham and Leeds, Aston found that "almost without exception," female-run operations were "small firms employing fewer than fifty people." Aston, *Entrepreneurship*, 46. On the shift to larger premises by London retailers, see Whitlock, *Crime, Gender and Consumer Culture*, 32–3.

71 P. J. Atkins, "The Spatial Configuration of Class Solidarity in London's West End, 1792–1939," *Urban History Yearbook* 17 (1990): 50; and Laurel Flinn, "Social and Spatial Politics in the Construction of Regent Street," *Journal of Social History* 46, no. 2 (Winter 2012): 364–90.

72 William and Robert Chambers, "Pauperism in the Metropolis," *Chamber's Journal of Popular Literature, Science and Arts* (London: W. and R. Chambers, 1867): 344.

73 Francis Cross, *Hints to All about to Rent, Buy, or Build House Property* (London: J. K. Starling, 1851), 102. See also Emily Constance Baird Cook, *Highways and Byways in London* (London: Macmillan, 1902); and Christopher Breward, *Fashioning London: Clothing and the Modern Metropolis* (Oxford: Berg, 2004), 62–3.

74 John Hollingshead, "Near Regent Street," in *Ragged London in 1861* (London: Smith, Elder, 1861), 113.

75 Asserted Emily Constance Baird Cook, "Other byways there [in the West End] are ... of a less attractive kind; the byways where dwell the 'poor relations,' so to speak, of the Aristocracy and the 'Smart Set'; the impoverished ladies whose sense of propriety would lead them to dwell even in a wheelbarrow, could that wheelbarrow only be drawn up on the fashionable side of the street!" Cook, *Highways and Byways*, 177.

76 Cross, *Hints to All about to Rent*, 118.

77 Whitlock, "A 'Taint,'" 33. See also Angeloglou, *A History of Make-Up*, 107; and [Donald Shaw], *London in the Sixties* (London: Everett, 1908), 203.

78 Lynda Nead, *Victorian Babylon: People, Streets and Images in Nineteenth-Century London* (New Haven, CT: Yale University Press, 2000), 65; Walker, "Vistas," 75; and Chancellor, *Liberty and Regent Street*, 7.

79 Christopher Breward cites an 1894 account by Augustus Sala who caught sight of a Regent Street shopkeeper's mannequin, "highly rouged ... with ... very long silky lashes" noting "[w]hether she was the pride and ornament of a hairdresser's or a staymaker's shop, I can scarcely recall to mind." As Breward concludes, "Sala's mannequin merely reflected the warmer bodies available for purchase only several minutes' walk away." See Breward, *Fashioning London*, 62–3 and 30–2; and Morris B. Kaplan, *Sodom on the Thames: Sex, Love, and Scandal in Wilde Times* (Ithaca, NY: Cornell University Press, 2005), 33. On the development of arcades as venues for luxury consumption, see Whitlock, *Crime, Gender and Consumer Culture*, 23–6. Hopkins inherited the firm from her mother Sarah, who worked at 6 Burlington Arcades from at least 1841. See *Kelly's Directory of Chemists and Druggists for 1869* (London: W. Kelly, 1869); *Post Office London Directory, 1876* (London: W. Kelly, 1876); *Post Office London Directory, 1880* (London: W. Kelly, 1880); and *Census Returns of England and Wales, 1883*, class RG11, piece 127, folio 8, p. 9, www.ancestry.co.uk.

80 Fergus Linnane, *London's Underworld: Three Centuries of Vice and Crime* (London: Robson Books, 2003), 199.

81 Nead, *Victorian Babylon*, 63–4; Walkowitz, "Going Public," 7, 15–16; and Rappaport, *Shopping*, 7, 45–6.

82 Nead, *Victorian Babylon*, 65–6.

83 William Acton, *Prostitution*, ed. Peter Fryer (New York: Praeger, 1969), 51. Quoted in Linnane, *London's Underworld*, 213.

84 "Ladies' Mile," *Pall Mall Gazette* 1302 (April 15, 1869): 5. On the "Ladies' Mile," see Linnane, *London's Underworld*, 199.

85 On the American case, see Yohn, "The Primacy of Place, Collaborations, and Alliances," 419.

86 Marshall, *Principles of Economics*, 506.

87 To what degree these relationships deteriorated in the wake of bankruptcy remain
    unclear. However, debt and insolvency were common occurrences in mid-century
    commercial trade. Margot C. Finn, *The Character of Credit: Personal Debt in
    English Culture, 1740–1914* (New York: Cambridge University Press, 2003);
    George Robb, *White-Collar Crime in Modern England: Financial Fraud and
    Business Morality, 1845–1929* (Cambridge: Cambridge University Press, 1992), 27;
    and Whitlock, *Crime, Gender and Consumer Culture*, 97–9.

88 Hollingshead, "Near Regent Street," 121.

89 "Classifieds," *The Lady's Newspaper* 427 (March 3, 1855): 142. In light of her
    primarily female clientele, Headman at one point offered "Juvenile Cream, a
    valuable preparation expressly for Children's Hair." See "Classifieds," *The Lady's
    Newspaper* 229 (May 17, 1851): 280.

90 "Advertisements," *The Lady's Newspaper* 427 (March 3, 1855): 142.

91 "Classifieds," *The Lady's Newspaper* 171 (April 6, 1850): 194.

92 Alexander, *Retailing in England*, 199, quoted in Kay, *Foundations*, 76.

93 "Vice-Chancellors' Courts, April 30," *London Times* 22982 (May 1, 1858): 11.

94 *Census Returns of England and Wales, 1851*, class HO107, piece 1485, folio 365,
    p. 27, www.ancestry.co.uk.

95 Ansell v. Ganbert A.39 (1858) TNA C 15/444/A39.

96 Headman's reliance on multiple agents in mixed locations across the city is not
    to be mistaken with multiple retailing. Andrew Alexander, Gareth Shaw, and
    Deborah Hodson, "Regional Variations in the Development of Multiple Retailing
    in England, 1890–1939," in *A Nation of Shopkeepers: Five Centuries of British
    Retailing*, ed. John Benson and Laura Ugolini (London: I. B. Tauris, 2003), 130. See
    also Gareth Shaw, "The Study of Retail Development," in *The Evolution of Retail
    Systems, c. 1800–1914*, ed. John Benson and Gareth Shaw (Leicester: Leicester
    University Press, 1992), 10–12.

97 On Brighton, see "Advertisements," *The Lady's Newspaper* 427 (March 3,
    1855): 142. For St. Leonards, see "Advertisement – R. Hempsted, Dispensing
    Chemist," *Osborne's Stranger's Guide and Directory to Hastings and St. Leonards*
    (Hastings: Osborne, 1854). See also Adburgham, *Shops and Shopping*, 51–2.
    On the opening of "multiples" in affluent spa towns, see Shaw, "Evolution &
    Impact," 139.

98 On the influx of middling consumers from the 1870s onward, see Christopher
    P. Hosgood, "Mrs. Pooter's Purchase: Lower-Middle-Class Consumerism and
    the Sales, 1870–1914," in *Gender, Civic Culture and Consumerism: Middle-
    Class Identity in Britain, 1800-1940*, ed. Alan J. Kidd and David Nicholls
    (London: Manchester University Press, 1999), 146; and Whitlock, *Crime, Gender
    and Consumer Culture*, 24.

99   Aston, *Female Entrepreneurship*; Mary Prior, "Women and the Urban Economy," in *Women in English Society*, ed. Mary Prior (London: Methuen, 1985), 108; and Robert Beachy, Béatrice Craig, and Alastair Owens, "Introduction," in *Women, Business, and Finance in Nineteenth-Century Europe: Rethinking Separate Spheres*, ed. Robert Beachy, Béatrice Craig, and Alastair Owens (Oxford: Berg, 2006), 2. For the American case, see Yohn, "The Primacy of Place, Collaborations, and Alliances."

100   Charlotte Mintram advertised her business from 1845 to 1857, having inherited it after the death of her husband William. Following the death of her husband Marchand, Ann Isidore ran the family hairdressing business for two years, from 1849 to 1850, after which son Charles assumed control.

101   For example, Sarah Broady operated her mid-century perfumery business "Broady & Co." out of her aunt and uncle's home in Belgravia, from where she also peddled glass and china goods. *Census Returns of England and Wales, 1851*, class HO107, piece 1477, folio 99, p. 26, www.ancestry.co.uk; and *Post Office London Directory* (London: W. Kelly, 1844–52).

102   On the eighteenth century, see Katrina Honeyman, "Doing Business with Gender: Service Industries and British Business History," *Business History Review* 81 (Autumn 2007): 476.

103   "Letters of Administration for Ann Cole otherwise Headman" (March 11, 1858) Principal Probate Registry. There was no other party to take up the business, save for another sister, Mary, who lived with her husband and children in Lambeth.

104   *Post Office London Directory, 1869* (London: W. Kelly, 1869), 1762. Ansell resided at No. 92 New Bond Street.

105   Using an address book once belonging to Agnes Headman, Gaubert posted black-edged circulars—"to denote that [she was] in mourning" for Mrs. Headman—which directed customers to her "new" Maddox Street location.

106   Ansell v. Ganbert A.39 (1858) TNA C 15/444/A39.

107   Ansell v. Ganbert A.39 (1858) TNA C 15/444/A39.

108   "Vice-Chancellors' Courts," *The London Times* 22982 (May 1, 1858): 11.

109   Gaubert died in 1905. *Post Office London Directory, 1895* (London: W. Kelly, 1895), 1887; *Census Returns of England and Wales, 1871*, class RG10, piece 98, folio 17, p. 27, www.ancestry.co.uk; *Census Returns of England and Wales, 1901*, class RG13, piece 1187, folio 62, p. 18, www.ancestry.co.uk; and General Register Office, *England and Wales Civil Registration Indexes* (London: General Register Office, July-August-September 1905), 11.

110   "Regent Street in the Season," *Penny Illustrated Paper* 390 (March 20, 1869): 185.

111   Yohn, "The Primacy of Place, Collaborations, and Alliances," 419.

112 "Answer of Lloyd," Lloyd v. Lloyd (June 13, 1867) TNA J 77/75.

113 "Bill of Complaint," Hovenden v. Lloyd 1869 H59 (1869) TNA C 16/572/H59, 4.

114 "Answer of Aimée Lloyd," Hovenden v. Lloyd 1869 H59 (1869) TNA C 16/572/H59, 1.

115 Margot Finn explains how rapid commercialization and economic growth, compounded by a series of national economic downturns, made for a rise in imprisoned debtors during this period, including the likes of Solomon Lloyd. See Finn, *The Character of Credit*, 109–10.

116 For more on gendered division of commercial space, see chapter 2.

117 Hovenden v. Lloyd 1869 H59 (1869) TNA C 16/572/H59. Until 1858, Glasshouse Street was known as Marylebone Street.

118 "Answer of Respondent," Petition for Judicial Separation, Lloyd v. Lloyd (July 31, 1867) TNA J 77/75. See A. James Hammerton, *Cruelty and Companionship: Conflict in Nineteenth-Century Married Life* (New York: Routledge, 1992).

119 "Answer of Respondent," Petition for Judicial Separation, Lloyd v. Lloyd (July 31, 1867) TNA J 77/75. On neighbors as witnesses to marital violence, see Ellen Ross, *Love and Toil: Motherhood in Outcast London, 1870–1918* (New York: Oxford University Press, 1993), 84–6.

120 "Answer of Respondent," Petition for Judicial Separation, Lloyd v. Lloyd (June 13, 1867) TNA J 77/75.

121 On judicial separation and divorce in the mid-nineteenth century, see Gail Savage, "'The Wilful Communication of a Loathsome Disease': Marital Conflict and Venereal Disease in Victorian England," *Victorian Studies* 34, no. 1 (Autumn 1990): 35–54. See also Allen Horstman, *Victorian Divorce* (New York: St. Martin's, 1985); and Mary Poovey, *Uneven Developments: The Ideological Work of Gender in Mid-Victorian England* (Chicago, IL: University of Chicago Press, 1988), 51–88.

122 "Answer of Respondent," Petition for Judicial Separation, Lloyd v. Lloyd (June 13, 1867) TNA J 77/75.

123 Sociologists distinguish two modes of survivalist entrepreneurship: value entrepreneurship and disadvantaged entrepreneurship. Value entrepreneurs launch their ventures for nonmonetary reasons, including social status, domestic responsibilities, or concepts of self. Disadvantaged entrepreneurs are businesspeople who resort to self-employment because they can earn more than in wage and salaried employment. See Ivan Light and Carolyn Rosenstein, *Race, Ethnicity, and Entrepreneurship in Urban America* (Hawthorne, CA: Aldine de Gruyter, 1995), 213–14; Robert L. Boyd, "Race, Labor Market Disadvantage, and Survivalist Entrepreneurship: Black Women in the Urban North during the Great Depression," *Sociological Forum* 15, no. 4 (December 2000): 647–70; and Boyd, "Black Retail Enterprise and Racial Segregation in Northern Cities Before the 'Ghetto,'" *Sociological Perspectives* 53, no. 3 (Fall 2010): 397–417.

124 Kay, *Foundations*, 124–5.

125 John Duguid Milne, *Industrial Employment of Women in the Middle and Lower Ranks* (London: Longmans, Green, 1870), 129. See also Kay, *Foundations*, 11.

126 Shifting family economies and networks of extended relatives could also compel women's entrance into the beauty business, as was the case for the aforementioned Euphemia Bury. Fifty-eight years old and never married, Bury took up her father's perfumery and hairdressing business in the mid-1850s, not long after his death. Taking on her two nephews as apprentices, it is possible that Bury assisted if not supported two additional nephews and a niece living near the slums in St. Giles. Bury's 13-year-old niece shared her name. *Census Returns of England and Wales, 1841*, class HO107, piece 687, book 3, Civil Parish Chelsea, County Middlesex, Enumeration District 1, folio 8, p. 9, www.ancestry.co.uk; *Census Returns of England and Wales, 1861*, class RG 9, piece 168, folio 70, p. 69 and class RG 9, piece 37, folio 50, p. 2, www.ancestry.co.uk; and *Post Office London Directory* (London: W. Kelly, 1857–65).

127 In most cases, it remains unclear how women decided to produce particular beauty products. When Patience Boughton (1819–1893) opened her business in the wake of her silk-mercer husband's death, she devoted her attention to "fancy" soap production. Given the popular circulation of homemade receipts, it is possible that she had previously produced the soap on a smaller scale for home use. *Census Returns of England and Wales, 1851*, class HO107, piece 1499, folio 66, p. 1, www.ancestry.co.uk; and *Census Returns of England and Wales, 1861*, class RG 9, piece 126, folio 54, p. 12, www.ancestry.co.uk.

128 [Donald Shaw], *London in the Sixties, with a Few Digressions. By One of the Old Brigade* (London: Everett, 1908), 49.

129 Nancy Cox, *The Complete Tradesman: A Study of Retailing, 1550–1820* (Aldershot: Ashgate, 2000), 188–9.

130 James B. Jeffreys, *Retail Trading in Britain 1850–1950* (London: Cambridge University Press, 1954), 11–14.

131 There was some overlap between wholesaling and retailing in nineteenth-century Britain, which has raised problems of definition for historians. This study assumes that, in this period of retail development, the two categories were not mutually exclusive and overlap occurred. Shaw, "Retail Development," 12.

132 "Celebrities Connected with the Trade. No. 20 – Robert Hovenden," *The Hairdressers' Weekly Journal* (July 31, 1886): 492–3.

133 Hovenden commissioned the June shipment from Aimée, yet Andrew attempted to procure the payment for the goods. "Hovenden v. Lloyd," *Weekly Notes* Volume V (London: Incorporated Council of Law reporting for England and Wales, 1870), 205–6.

134 Oliver M. Westall, "The Competitive Environment of British Business, 1850–1914," in *Business Enterprise in Modern Britain, from the Eighteenth to the Twentieth Century*, ed. Maurice W. Kirby and Mary B. Rose (London: Routledge, 2004), 207.

135 1869 Deposition, Hovenden v. Lloyd 1869 H59 (1869) TNA C 16/572/H59. See also "Hovenden v. Lloyd," *Weekly Notes*, 206.

136 On male merchants' "paternalistic sensibility" see Wendy Gamber, *The Female Economy: The Millinery and Dressmaking Trades, 1860–1930* (Urbana, IL: University of Chicago Press, 1997), 160.

137 Hilton went on to reveal that Andrew had covertly sold Euxesis after Solomon's death, hiding the profits from his newly widowed mother and siblings. 1869 Deposition, Hovenden v. Lloyd 1869 H59 (1869) TNA C 16/572/H59.

138 Whitlock, "A 'Taint,'" 40; and Whitlock, *Crime, Gender and Consumer Culture*, 89–93. See also Blanche B. Elliot, *A History of English Advertising* (London: B.T. Batsford, 1962); Lori Loeb, *Consuming Angels: Advertising and Victorian Women* (New York: Oxford University Press, 1994); Henry Sampson, *History of Advertising: From the Earliest Times* (London: Chatto and Windus, 1874); and E. S. Turner, *The Shocking History of Advertising!* (London: Michael Joseph, 1952).

139 Alexander, *Retailing in England*, 5.

140 See, for example, "Classifieds," *The Lady's Newspaper* 229 (May 17, 1851): 280; "Classifieds," *The Lady's Newspaper* 427 (March 3, 1855): 142; and "Miscellaneous Classifieds," *The London Times* 22945 (March 19, 1858): 15. See also Whitlock, *Crime, Gender and Consumer Culture*, 89–90.

141 Alexander, *Retailing in England*, 164.

142 On the expense of advertising, see Kay, "Retailing," 153. On businesswomen's advertising in Birmingham and Leeds, see Aston, *Entrepreneurship*, 115–20. There are many examples of advertisements by these three women, but for Headman see "Classifieds," *Lady's Newspaper* 427 (March 3, 1855): 142. For Ansell, see "Miscellaneous Classifieds," *London Times* 22945 (March 19, 1858): 15. For Lloyd, see "Advertisements & Notices," *Pall Mall Gazette* (March 9, 1872): 15. On Victorian advertising, see Thomas Richards, *The Commodity Culture of Victorian England: Advertising and Spectacle, 1851–1914* (Stanford, CA: Stanford University Press, 1990), 6; and Loeb, *Consuming Angels*.

143 See Richard Daniel Altick, *The Presence of the Present: Topics of the Day in the Victorian Novel* (Columbus: Ohio State University Press, 1991), 64; and Gillian Dyer, *Advertising as Communication* (New York: Routledge, 1982), 30.

144 "Rossetter's Hair Restorer," *Hairdressers' Chronicle* (June 1, 1872): iv. On the general growth in advertising aimed at women, see Richards, *The Commodity Culture of Victorian England*, 1–7; Walkowitz, *City of Dreadful Delight*, 46–50; and Whitlock, *Crime, Gender and Consumer Culture*, 90.

145 Jones, *Beauty Imagined*, 18–20 and 34.

146 Jones, *Beauty Imagined*, 34.

147 Chemical Trades Section Minute Books (July 10, 1883) LMA, CLC/B/150/MS16583.

2 Upstarts and Outliers: Sarah "Madame Rachel" Leverson

1 G. W. Septimus Piesse, *The Art of Perfumery* (Philadelphia, PA: Lindsay and Blakiston, [1855] 1857), 29–30. On Piesse, see Catherine Maxwell, *Scents and Sensibility: Perfume in Victorian Literary Culture* (Oxford: Oxford University Press, 2017), 23–6.

2 "The Manufacture of Perfumery," *Illustrated Weekly News* (September 20, 1862): 797.

3 S. R. Epstein, "Craft Guilds, Apprenticeship, and Technological Exchange in Pre-Industrial Europe," in *Guilds, Innovation, and European Economy, 1400–1800*, ed. S. R. Epstein and Maarten Prak (New York: Cambridge University Press, 2008), 77.

4 Deborah Cohen, *Family Secrets: Living with Shame from the Victorians to the Present Day* (London: Viking, 2013), iii and xiv.

5 Leverson appears under a variety of names across sources. For a discussion of this, see Helen Rappaport, *Beautiful for Ever: Madame Rachel of Bond Street – Cosmetician, Con-Artist, and Blackmailer* (Ebrington: Long Barn Books, 2010), postscript.

6 "Enameling" was the process of painting the face with a hard-drying lotion to conceal discolorations and whiten the skin. It was made up by suspending zinc oxide, pearl-white (bismuth oxychloride), or the more deleterious lead carbonate in water. See Arnold James Cooley, *The Toilet in Ancient and Modern Times: with a Review of the Different Theories of Beauty and Copious Allied Information, Social, Hygienic, and Medical* (London: Robert Hardwicke, 1866), 306; and Rappaport, *Beautiful*, 40–2.

7 "Leverson v. Carnegie," *London Times* 24277 (June 20, 1862): 11.

8 On the 1878 trial, *Old Bailey Proceedings Online*. See www.oldbaileyonline.org, March 2008, accessed April 29, 2008, April 8, 1878, trial of Sarah Rachel Leverson (t18780408-428). See also "Police," *London Times* 29187 (February 25, 1878): 11; "Central Criminal Court," *London Times* 29202 (March 14, 1878): 11; "Central Criminal Court," *London Times* 29226 (April 11, 1878): 11; "Central Court Case," *London Times* 29227 (April 12, 1878): 11; and "A Fashionable Judge," *Penny Magazine* 872 (April 20, 1878): 253.

9 *Old Bailey Proceedings Online*. See www.oldbaileyonline.org, March 2008, accessed October 30, 2008, August 17, 1868, trial of Sarah Rachel Leverson (t18680817-721); and March 2008, accessed October 30, 2008, September 21, 1868, trial of Sarah Rachel Leverson (t18680921-830).

10 One female trader's deception extended not only to her fraudulent goods but also to her gender; she was, in fact, a man. Madame Rosalie Coupellé appealed to sufferers of "Baldness, Weak or Grey Hair, Whiskers," peddling her Parisian Pomade via mail order from various London locales: Gray's Inn, Soho's Newman Street, and finally Bedford Square. Coupellé eventually proved to be a middle-aged

male charlatan, and the business came to a halt with the mid-century prosecution of Dr. De Roos (real name Samuel Barker) for "quackery" under Britain's new medical regulation act. See "The 'Manly Vigour' Advertising Firm," *Association Medical Journal* (May 3, 1856): 371.

11 The Leverson case parallels American developments and in particular anxieties around the emergence of an upwardly mobile urban middle class. See Karen Halttunen, *Confidence Men and Painted Women: A Study of Middle-Class Culture in America, 1830–1870* (New Haven, CT: Yale University Press, 1982). On crises of confidence in interwar Britain, see Matt Houlbrook, *Prince of Tricksters: The Incredible True Story of Netley Lucas, Gentlemen Crook* (Chicago, IL: University of Chicago Press, 2016).

12 Tammy Whitlock, "A 'Taint' Upon Them: The Madame Rachel Case, Fraud, and the Retail Trade in Nineteenth-Century England," *Victorian Review* 24, no. 1 (Summer 1998): 29–52; and Whitlock, *Crime, Gender, and Consumer Culture in Nineteenth-Century England* (Burlington, VT: Ashgate, 2005).

13 Elizabeth Carolyn Miller, *Framed: The New Woman Criminal in British Culture at the Fin De Siècle* (Ann Arbor: University of Michigan Press, 2008); Miller, "'Shrewd Women of Business': Madame Rachel, Victorian Consumerism, and L.T. Meade's *The Sorceress of the Strand*," *Victorian Literature and Culture* 34, no. 1 (2006): 311–32; and Rappaport, *Beautiful*.

14 "Miscellaneous," *John Bull* 2, no. 203 (February 28, 1863): 104; and "Law and Police," *John Bull* 2, no. 128 (September 21, 1868): 605.

15 *Extraordinary Life & Trial of Madame Rachel at the Central Criminal Court, Old Bailey, London, …*(London: Diprose and Bateman, 1868), xi; and Madame Rachel, *Beautiful for Ever!* (London: Madame Rachel, 47a New Bond Street, 1863), 16–17. On advertising and puffery, see Whitlock, "A 'Taint,'" 45; E. S. Turner, *The Shocking History of Advertising!* (London: Michael Joseph, 1952), 112–23; and Blanche B. Elliot, *A History of English Advertising* (London: B. T. Batsford, 1962), 165.

16 *Beautiful for Ever!*, 11; and Miller, "'Shrewd Women of Business,'" 325.

17 *Beautiful for Ever!*, 20.

18 "Leverson v. Carnegie," *London Times* 24277 (June 20, 1862): 11.

19 Whitlock, "A 'Taint,'" 40; Miller, "'Shrewd Women of Business,'" 327; and Miller, *Framed*.

20 Miller, *Framed*, 95.

21 See, for example, Miller "'Shrewd Women of Business'"; Lisa Niles, "Owning 'the Dreadful Truth'; or, is Thirty-Five Too Old? Age and the Marriageable Body in Wilkie Collins's *Armadale*," *Nineteenth-Century Literature* 65, no. 1 (June 2010): 65–92; Rappaport, *Beautiful*, 85–7; and Laurence Talairach-Vielmas, *Moulding the Female Body in Victorian Fairy Tales and Sensation Novels* (Burlington, VT: Ashgate, 2007).

22 Whitlock, "A 'Taint,'" 29. Talairach-Vielmas positions the "Beauty parlour and female boudoir as 'main loci of fraud.'" Talairach-Vielmas, *Moulding the Female Body*, 150.

23 Whitlock does gesture to the presence of a Mrs. Osch selling beauty goods at Piccadilly and St. James's Street, but does not fully explore Leverson's relationship to other London beauty businesses, focusing instead on luxury consumption and retailing more generally. Osch did not appear in any advertising or directories from the period. Whitlock, "A 'Taint,'" 31, 33, 40.

24 Rappaport, *Beautiful*.

25 Walter Thornbury, "The Strand (northern tributaries): Drury Lane and Clare Market," in *Old and New London: Volume 3* (London: Cassell, Petter & Galpin, 1878): 36–44. See also Henry Mayhew, *London Labour and the London Poor*, Volume I: London Street Folk (London: Charles Griffin and Co., 1851); and Rappaport, *Beautiful*, 7–11.

26 In his autobiography, Crown Prosecutor William Ballantine claims to have met Leverson before her economic ascent "in one of the worst haunts of the metropolis" working in an "occupation that was not infrequently brought to the attention of magistrates." He considered her "one of the most filthy and dangerous moral pests that have existed in my time and within my observation." William Ballantine, *Some Experiences of a Barrister's Life* (London: R. Bentley, 1898), 230. On the characterization of second-hand clothing as a Jewish trade, see Charles Dickens Jr., "Jews," in *Dickens' Dictionary of London* (London: The Author, 1879), n.p.

27 *History and Trial of Madame Rachel or Beautiful For Ever* (London: William Swift, 1868), 2.

28 "Singular Charge of Fraud against Viscount Milton," *Bell's Life in London* (May 4, 1862): n.p.

29 Rappaport, *Beautiful*, 60–5.

30 In an 1858 trial, Miss Rachel claimed that during the season her weekly takings were around £15 and her weekly stock was worth £30 to £40. See "The Piccadilly Papers. A Day at the Old Bailey," *London Society* XIV (London: Office, 1868): 380; and "Leverson v. Atloff," *London Times* 23146 (November 9, 1858): 8.

31 "Enamelling with Vengeance," *Bell's Life in London* (June 22, 1862): 3. See also Erika D. Rappaport, "'A Husband and His Wife's Dresses': Consumer Credit and the Debtor Family in England, 1864–1914," in *The Sex of Things: Gender and Consumption in Historical Perspective*, ed. Victoria de Grazia with Ellen Furlough (Berkeley: University of California Press, 1996), 163–87; Rappaport, *Shopping for Pleasure: Women in the Making of London's West End* (Princeton, NJ: Princeton University Press, 2001), chapter 2; Margot C. Finn, "Women, Consumption and Coverture in England, c. 1760–1860," *Historical Journal* 39, no. 3 (1996): 703–22; and Finn, *The Character of Credit: Personal Debt in English Culture, 1740–1914*, (New York: Cambridge University Press, 2003), 41–50.

32 See, for example, "Law and Police," *John Bull* 2 (December 23, 1865): 350. On
    Knight see "Marlborough Street," *London Times* 25367 (December 13, 1865): 11.
    Quoted in Whitlock "A 'Taint,'" n. 23. See also "Marlborough Street," *London Times*
    25373 (December 20, 1865): 11; Miller, "'Shrewd Women of Business,'" 315; and
    Rapapport, *Beautiful*, 82–3.

33 This aligns with Angus McLaren's findings that blackmail victims were most often
    in severe pecuniary strife when they "went public." At that point, middle-class
    victims had nothing to lose. Angus McLaren, *Sexual Blackmail: A Modern History*
    (Cambridge, MA: Harvard University Press, 2002).

34 Whitlock, "A 'Taint,'" 29–31.

35 *Old Bailey Proceedings Online*, See www.oldbaileyonline.org, accessed April
    29, 2008, August 17, 1868, trial of Sarah Rachel Leverson (t18680817-721). For
    retrospective accounts of the trial by its key players, see Montagu Williams, *Leaves
    of a Life Being the Reminiscences of Montagu Williams, Q.C.* (London: Macmillan &
    Co, 1890); and Ballantine, *Some Experiences.*

36 Whitlock argues that the 1868 trials marked a turning point in press
    representations of Leverson, which "shifted from a shopkeeper catering to female
    vanity to an evil, witchlike swindler duping her gullible prey." Whitlock, "A
    'Taint,'" 29.

37 Williams, *Leaves*, 225.

38 Williams, *Leaves*, 127.

39 Williams, *Leaves*, 227.

40 Whitlock, "A 'Taint,'"; Miller, *Framed*; Rappaport, *Beautiful*; Talairach-Vielmas,
    Moulding the Female Body.

41 *Post Office London Directory, 1863* (London: W. Kelly, 1863).

42 Susanna Chafer, unmarried dressmaker at 52 New Bond Street, employed
    fourteen assistants, two apprentices, and one boy. Susan Ansell's neighbor,
    Elizabeth Gile, was an unmarried milliner and dressmaker at 93 New Bond Street
    who employed thirteen assistants. Milliner Jenny Ashe employed two women and
    shared her lodgings with a female staymaker and her assistant, meaning that six
    unmarried businesswomen lived and worked at 36 New Bond Street. See *Census
    Returns of England and Wales, 1861*, class RG 9, piece 44, folio 12, p. 8; *Census
    Returns of England and Wales, 1861*, class RG 9, piece 40, folio 3, p. 8; and *Census
    Returns of England and Wales, 1861*, class RG 9, piece 44, folio 12, p. 3, www.
    ancestry.co.uk.

43 Rappaport, *Beautiful*, 43. See, for example, Classified Advertisements, *London
    Times* 23534 (February 4, 1860): 11.

44 *Census Returns of England and Wales, 1841*, class HO107, piece 734, Book 1, Civil
    Parish St George Hanover Square, County Middlesex, Enumeration District 1,
    folio 14, p. 21, www.ancestry.co.uk; *Post Office London Directory, 1845* (London: W.
    Kelly, 1845); and *Post Office London Directory, 1847* (London: W. Kelly, 1847).

While not entirely clear, records suggest that Roberts gave up the business to marry and settle in Kensington.

45 Ansell lived at this address from at least 1849. *Post Office London Directory* (London: W. Kelly, 1849–68); and *Census Returns of England and Wales, 1861*, class RG 9, piece 40, folio 39, p. 7, www.ancestry.co.uk.

46 See chapter 1.

47 For Dona, see *Post Office London Directory, 1862* (London: W. Kelly, 1862), 1579; and *Post Office London Directory, 1863* (London: W. Kelly, 1863), 1626. For Snelling, see *Post Office London Directory, 1863* (London: W. Kelly, 1863), 1528. For Franklin, see *Post Office London Directory, 1857* (London: W. Kelly, 1857).

48 She worked alongside siblings William and Fanny. See *Census Returns of England and Wales, 1861*, class RG 9, piece 44, folio 12, p. 22, www.ancestry.co.uk.

49 According to one critic, her regular advertising in London's periodical press "beat … Rowland of old with his Kalydor in puffing." *Extraordinary Life & Trial*, iv.

50 Whitlock, "A 'Taint,'" 45. "No doubt, attractive advertisements were published," noted the trial judge in 1868, "which led many credulous persons to become her customers." *Extraordinary Life & Trial*, 101.

51 Leverson lost the Carnegie case in 1865 and the Borradaile case in 1868, yet she cited press coverage of each trial to substantiate the efficacy of her products.

52 *Saturday Review*, n.d. Quoted in *Extraordinary Life & Trial*, 119.

53 Atloff reportedly "preferred a reference to her tradespeople." "Leverson v. Atloff," *London Times* 23146 (November 9, 1858): 8. See also Rappaport, *Beautiful*, 34–7.

54 "Leverson v. Atloff," *London Times* 23146 (November 9, 1858): 8. See also Rappaport, *Beautiful*, 34–6.

55 [Donald Shaw], *London in the Sixties, with a Few Digressions. By One of the Old Brigade* (London: Everett, 1908), 238.

56 On Bond Street traffic in the 1860s, see Alison Adburgham, *Shops and Shopping, 1800–1914: Where and in What Manner the Well-Dressed Englishwoman Bought Her Clothes* (London: Allen & Unwin, [1964] 1981), 104.

57 "Police," *London Times* 24513 (March 23, 1863): 11.

58 Miller, "'Shrewd Women of Business,'" 323. See also Rappaport, *Beautiful*, 78–9.

59 "Marlborough Street," *London Times* 25367 (December 13, 1865): 11.

60 "Occasional Notes," *Pall Mall Gazette* 14 (February 22, 1865): 6. Cited in Rappaport, *Beautiful*, 79.

61 Whitlock, "A 'Taint,'" 29.

62 "Madame Rachel Takes a Hint," *Punch or the London Charivari* (July 12, 1862): 18.

63 "Man about Town," *Sporting Gazette* 304 (June 10, 1868): 507.

64 *Extraordinary Life & Trial*, 44–5, 95.

65 Prosecutors dramatically claimed they "would not attempt to paint the picture of that little back-parlour, when Rachel there instigated the forgeries and acted as the go-between in the carrying on of the intrigues." *Extraordinary Life & Trial*, 99.

66 *The Daily Mail*, n.d. Quoted in *Extraordinary Life & Trial*, 113.

67 Adburgham, *Shops and Shopping*, 149–50.

68 David Alexander, *Retailing in England during the Industrial Revolution* (London: Athlone Press, 1970), 185–9.

69 Leverson lived at the Bond Street shop until her rental of a residence at 50 Maddox Street, Mayfair in September 1866. Williams, *Leaves*, 227.

70 On women's mobilization of such arrangements, see Alison C. Kay, "'A Little Enterprise of Her Own': Lodging-House Keeping and the Accommodation Business in Nineteenth-Century London," *London Journal* 28, no. 2 (2003): 41–53.

71 Jennifer Aston found distinct geographic differences in businesswomen's living arrangements, with 12 percent of Birmingham businesswomen residing away from their firms versus 50 percent in Leeds. Aston, *Female Entrepreneurship in Nineteenth-Century England: Engagement in the Urban Economy* (London: Palgrave, 2016), chapter 5.

72 On distinctions between domestic and commercial space, see Finn, *The Character of Credit*, 26; Elizabeth Kowaleski-Wallace, *Consuming Subjects: Women, Shopping, and Business in the Eighteenth Century* (New York: Columbia University Press, 1997), 82–6; and John Tosh, *A Man's Place: Masculinity and the Middle-Class Home in Victorian England* (New Haven, CT: Yale University Press, 1999), 17–19.

73 *Extraordinary Life & Trial*, 68, 75. Prosecutors also inquired as to the whereabouts of Leverson's husband, who reportedly lived at 25 King Street, Soho Square. He and Leverson were, according to Miss Rachel, "not on very good terms."

74 *Extraordinary Life & Trial*, 96.

75 "Leverson v. Carnegie," *London Times* 24277 (June 20, 1862): 11. At the insolvency hearing in 1861, for example, she claimed that to produce her list of clients would "ruin her profession." *London Times* 24081 (November 13, 1861): 11.

76 Leverson refused to visit Carnegie at her home in Belgrave Square, forcing Carnegie to venture to Bond Street. There, she underwent four treatments to minimize scarring on her décolletage and ultimately offered Leverson "the rings off of her fingers" to pay for the by-all-accounts successful treatment. "Enamelling with Vengeance," *Bell's Life in London* (June 22, 1862): 3.

77 Judith R. Walkowitz has detailed a case in which a judge warned a milliner's assistant that "no respectable woman would be found on Regent Street at nine in the evening." This was in 1887, some twenty-five years after the Carnegie case, in which Carnegie called for treatment at midnight and stayed until 2 o'clock in the morning. See "Leverson v. Carnegie," *London Times* 24277 (June 20, 1862): 11. On Regent Street in the late 1880s, see Walkowitz, "Going Public: Shopping, Street Harassment, and Streetwalking in late Victorian London," *Representations* 62 (Spring 1998): 9.

78 "Marlborough Street," *London Times* 25155 (April 10, 1865): 11.

79 *London in the Sixties*, 238.

80 *Extraordinary Life & Trial*, 96.

81 One of the few positive treatments of Leverson painted her Clare Street days as an idyllic time. See *History and Trial*, 2.

82 Stephens frequently featured in press reports, which suggests that she did regular business with Leverson. Stack acted as Leverson's surety after her first 1868 trial. In the hearing, he explained he had known Leverson since 1853, but did not account for how they met. "Singular Charge of Fraud against Viscount Milton," *Bell's Life in London* (May 4, 1862): n.p.; and no title, *London Times* 26389 (March 19, 1869): 12.

83 Ambiguity over Leverson's financial standing played into Crown strategy at the 1868 trials. In their closing, the Crown alleged that "When first [Leverson] knew Mrs. Borradaile she owed half a year's rent, but the money now obtained not only enabled her to pay that rent, but to furnish in a most costly manner a house in Maddox-street." Leverson challenged their arguments in open court. Frustrated, she complained that the Crown swore "that I am a poor distressed woman in his evidence, and not able to pay my rent. Now [they] swear that I am a rich woman." *Extraordinary Life & Trial*, 95, 102.

84 See Melanie Tebbutt, *Making Ends Meet: Pawnbroking and Working-Class Credit* (Leicester: Leicester University Press, 1983); and Finn, *The Character of Credit*, 78–80.

85 Ellen Ross, *Love and Toil: Motherhood in Outcast London* (London: Oxford University Press, 1993), 46.

86 On the pawning of Borradaile's trousseau lace, see *Extraordinary Life & Trial*, 12.

87 *Extraordinary Life & Trial*, 74.

88 "Marlborough Street," *London Times* 25373 (December 20, 1865): 11.

89 Rappaport, "'A Husband and His Wife's Dresses,'" 165–8; and Rappaport, *Shopping*, chapter 2.

90 *Extraordinary Life & Trial*, 119. Also quoted in Whitlock, "A 'Taint,'" 36; and Miller, "'Shrewd Women of Business,'" 315.

91 *Post Office London Directory* (London: W. Kelly, 1851, 1861, 1863, 1867).

92 As Miller notes, "the Jewish Madame Rachel signified not the threat of the colonial 'Other,' but the threat of racial otherness *within* the national body, as imagined in the 1860s press." Miller, "'Shrewd Women of Business,'" 315 and 325.

93 Leverson and Rachel the younger also had connections in the East End, where they purchased "castor oil, olive oil, attar of roses, bismuth (11*l.* worth), orris root, lavender oil, white and yellow wax, oils of bergamot and lemon, and various assorted oils and essences." No title, *London Times* 24146 (January 18, 1862): 9.

94 *Extraordinary Life & Trial*, 11, 38.

95 "As the author possesses all the necessary preparations for the purpose [of Arabian baths], and as they do not take any longer time to prepare than an ordinary bath," wrote the Leversons in *Beautiful for Ever!*, "ladies can have them at their own residences, with all the comfort and luxury of an Eastern bath, and without the slightest inconvenience to themselves." *Beautiful For Ever!*, 24.

96 *Extraordinary Life & Trial*, 8; and Miller, "'Shrewd Women of Business,'" 315.

97 On the third day of trial, Kerr shot down Seymour's suggestion that jurors be taken to the premises, as "he never before heard in a criminal case of an application for a view." *Extraordinary Life & Trial*, 56; and "Madame Rachel," *London Times* 26174 (July 11, 1868): 12. The Leversons moved to Maddox Street in September 1866. It was, according to *Life and Times*, "gaudily furnished." *Extraordinary Life & Trial*, 99, quoted in Whitlock, "A 'Taint,'" 45. For Miss Rachel's account of Maddox Street, see *Extraordinary Life & Trial*, 68.

98 On the perceived dangers of unfamiliar commercial milieus for women, see Walkowitz, "Going Public," 5.

99 The lack of a bath countered Borradaile's claims that Leverson had convinced her that Ranelagh had "fallen in love with her" having "seen her while taking a bath." *Extraordinary Life & Trial*, 8.

100 Rappaport, *Beautiful*, 93–8. On London's early modern bagnios, see J. J. Keevil, "The Bagnio in London 1648–1725," *Journal of the History of Medicine and Allied Sciences* 7, no. 3 (1952): 254. For Victorian models, see Fergus Linnane, *London: The Wicked City: A Thousand Years of Prostitution and Vice* (London: Robson Books, 2003); and Roy Porter and Lesley A. Hall, *The Facts of Life: The Creation of Sexual Knowledge in Britain, 1650–1950* (New Haven, CT: Yale University Press, 1995), 22.

101 On Knight, see "Marlborough Street," *London Times* 25373 (December 20, 1865): 11; Miller, "'Shrewd Women of Business,'" 315; and Rappaport, *Beautiful*, 82–3. In 1868, Borradaile described how Leverson also sent her a few blocks west to bathe at Mrs. Hicks's premises on Davis Street, the public bath built by the parish of St. George Hanover Square. On Mrs. Hicks, see Williams, *Leaves of a Life*, 128; and *Collins' Illustrated Guides to London and Neighborhood* (London: William Collins, 1871), 181.

Even when Leverson's shop accommodated the bathing of female clients in the late 1870s, her facilities seemed of rather humble design. When Cecilia Pearse appeared at Leverson's shop to complain that her husband noticed treatment-induced inflammation, Leverson "pulled a bath from under the bed, and said [she] had better have it there and then." "Trial of Madame Rachel," *Birmingham Daily Post* 6164 (April 11, 1878): 8; and Rappaport, *Beautiful*, 231.

Bathing on site was by no means a reliable experience. One unnamed lady "lost" her jewelry in 1878, having left it in a changing room at the shop while she underwent her beauty regimen. Based on findings by John Juxon, Helen Rappaport argues that this unnamed client was Mrs. Arthur Esdaile, who subsequently attempted to prosecute Leverson for theft. Esdaile reportedly claimed that Leverson's Bond Street shop and Mrs. Hicks's Davies Street baths functioned as meeting places for upper-class women and their working-class lovers: "stable boys, out-of-work footmen, even army deserters." Williams, *Leaves*, 248; and Rappaport, *Beautiful*, 93–8.

102 Miller, "'Shrewd Women of Business,'" 315.

103 Henry Whitehead, *The Cholera in Berwick Street* (London: Hope, 1854), 2.

104 In the nineteenth century, bathing was a contested practice defined by one's class standing and gender. See Seth Koven, *Slumming: Sexual and Social Politics in Victorian London* (Princeton, NJ: Princeton University Press, 2004), 39–42. For a nineteenth-century account of the new Metropolitan Baths, see "The Metropolitan Baths," *Illustrated London News* 950 (December 18, 1858): 584, also quoted in Richard Corson, *Fashions in Makeup: From Ancient to Modern Times* (London: Peter Owen, 1972), 333.

105 On Borradaile and the public gaze, see *Extraordinary Life & Trial* 30, 60, 104; and Whitlock, "A 'Taint,'" 41.

106 *Extraordinary Life & Trial*, 83.

107 Miller, "'Shrewd Women of Business,'" 317; and *Extraordinary Life & Trial*, 75.

108 *Extraordinary Life & Trial*, 76–7.

109 *Extraordinary Life & Trial*, 94–5.

110 "Central Criminal Court, Sept. 25," *London Times* 26240 (September 26, 1868): 9.

111 Rappaport, *Beautiful*, 192.

112 "The Spider and the Fly," *Reynolds's Newspaper* 946 (September 27, 1868): 5, quoted in Rappaport, *Beautiful*, 169.

113 "The Ladies' Mile," *Pall Mall Gazette* 1302 (April 15, 1869): 5. For associations between female businesses and houses of ill-repute, see Whitlock, "A 'Taint,'" 41. On Victorian pornography, see Sharon Marcus, *Between Women: Friendship, Desire, and Marriage in Victorian England* (Princeton, NJ: Princeton University Press, 2007), 140.

114 "'The Ladies' Mile,'" *London Times* 26415 (April 19, 1869): 6.

115 "Perfumers, or—What?" *Hairdressers' Chronicle* 3, no. 31 (May 1, 1869): 48.

116 *Life in London by a Town Traveller* (London: 4, Ludgate Circus Buildings, 1879), 4–5.

117 The most notable instance of this arose in the late 1880s and 1890s, when London Metropolitan Police cracked down on massage parlors allegedly fronting for houses of assignation. These initiatives also implicated female entrepreneurs working as manicurists; files from 1904 reveal that police categorized their businesses as "similar in character to 'massage' places." See Julia Laite, *Common*

Prostitutes and Ordinary Citizens: Commercial Sex in London, 1885–1960
(London: Palgrave Macmillan, 2012), chapter 3; Takahiro Ueyama, *Health in the
Marketplace: Professionalism, Therapeutic Desires, and Medical Commodification
in late-Victorian London* (Palo Alto, CA: The Society for the Promotion of Science
and Scholarship, 2010); and "Bylaws: London County Council. Registration of
Massage Establishments," TNA PRO HO 45/10912/A56.145/25.

118 Tanya Pollard, "Beauty's Poisonous Properties," *Shakespeare Studies* 27
(1999): 187–210.

119 See, for example, "Arsenic as a Cosmetic," *The Lancet* 70, no. 1770 (August 1,
1857): 127; "Arsenic as a Cosmetic," *The Lancet* 70, no. 1771 (August 8, 1857): 155;
"Arsenic as a Cosmetic," *The Lancet* 70, no. 1772 (August 15, 1857): 181; and
"Arsenic as an Irritant to the Skin," *The Lancet* 70, no. 1776 (September 12,
1857): 281–2.

120 "The Week," *British Medical Journal* (June 22, 1861): 660. See also "The Uses and
Dangers of Cosmetics," *The Standard* 13889 (February 8, 1869): 3. Publications
like *The Ladies' Treasury* warned of the dangers of bismuth, yet in doing so
detailed the process by which to transform salt of bismuth into whitening
"pearl powder." See, for example, "The Toilette," *The Ladies' Treasury* (January
1, 1864): 30; "The Toilet," *The Ladies' Treasury* (March 1, 1864): 94; "The Toilet,"
The Ladies' Treasury (September 1, 1864): 286; and "Beauty Column," *The Ladies
Treasury* (November 1, 1876): 678. Despite medical campaigns, correspondence
columns suggest women's willingness to risk their health for beauty. See
Jessica P. Clark, "'Will You Give Me Your Opinion?': Mundane Beauty in the
Englishwoman's Domestic Magazine, 1860–1875," *Victorian Periodicals Review* 52,
no. 3 (Fall 2019): 540–65.

121 "Latest Law Intelligence," *John Bull* 2 (January 18, 1862): 128. See also
"Miscellaneous," *London Times* 24146 (January 18, 1862): 9.

122 Eliza Lynn Linton, "La Femme Passé," reprinted in *Modern Women and What Is
Said of Them* (New York: J. S. Redfield, 1868), 351. See also "Beautiful for Ever,"
The Tomahawk: A Saturday Journal of Satire (July 18, 1868): 22.

123 "Beauty Not without Paint," *Punch* (April 19, 1862): 154. See also "Saying by Our
Sage on the Streets," *Fun* (May 24, 1862): 100; "The Trials of Beauty," *Punch* (July 5,
1862): 7 and "Review of the Season," *Punch* (August 16, 1862): 63.

124 Williams, *Leaves*, 225.

125 For more on Miss Rachel's cross-examination, see *Extraordinary Life & Trial*, 71;
and Whitlock, "A 'Taint,'" 39.

126 She reopened her business following her release from Woking Prison in April
1872. Setting up first in Drury Lane, she later appeared at Duke Street, followed
by three rooms on the first floor of 153 Great Portland Street. See "Classifieds,"
The Era (October 8, 1865): 1411; *Beautiful for Ever!*, 15; Whitlock, "A 'Taint,'" 44;
Miller, "'Shrewd Women of Business,'" 313; and Rappaport, *Beautiful*, 198–9.

127 *Old Bailey Proceedings Online*. See www.oldbaileyonline.org, accessed April 29, 2008, April 8, 1878, trial of Sarah Rachel Leverson (t18780408-428).

128 Rappaport, *Beautiful*, chapter 11.

129 The composition of Leverson's formulae became the lynchpin of the trial; prosecutors resorted to new trends in commissioning independent scientific professionals, reportedly unavailable to them in 1868.

130 "Police," *London Times* 29187 (February 25, 1878): 11. Sabina Pilley, a domestic servant in Leverson's service, verified the composition of Leverson's cosmetics. See "Central Criminal Court," *The Times* 29226 (April 11, 1878): 11.

3 Mobilizing Men: Robert Douglas and H. P. Truefitt

1 "General News," *Trewman's Exeter Flying Post* 5364 (March 31, 1869): 6.

2 Emily Faithfull, *Three Visits to America* (Edinburgh: David Douglas, 1884), 304.

3 Emily Faithfull, "Needleworkers v. Society," *Victoria Magazine* I (May–October 1863): 357. See also "What Are Women Doing?" *English Woman's Journal* 7 (1861): 52.

4 "The Present Fashions in Hair," *The Graphic* 26 (May 28, 1870): 603.

5 "Women at Work, No. 5. By Our Special Commissioner. Hairdressers," *Women and Work* 12 (August 22, 1874): 2.

6 Quoted in "London Gossip," *Freeman's Journal and Daily Commercial Advertiser* (June 27, 1878): 7.

7 Douglas initially fired senior hands, which led all hands, both junior and senior, to give notice. "Trade Misunderstanding," *The Hairdressers' Chronicle* (hereafter *THC*) 2, no. 22 (August 1, 1868): 5; and "Mr. Douglas and His Assistants," *THC* 2, no. 23 (September 1, 1868): 5.

8 Susan Vincent, *Hair: An Illustrated History* (London: Bloomsbury, 2018), 72–3.

9 Alison C. Kay, "Retailing, Respectability and the Independent Woman in Nineteenth-Century London," in *Women, Business and Finance in Nineteenth-Century Europe: Rethinking Separate Spheres*, ed. Robert Beachy, Béatrice Craig, and Alastair Owens (Oxford: Berg, 2006), 153.

10 Histories of hairdressing and barbering have tended to focus on the continental context and specifically developments in Britain's most formidable competitor: France. See Michael Kwass, "Big Hair: A Wig History of Consumption in Eighteenth-Century France," *American Historical Review* 111, no. 3 (2006): 631–59; and Steven Zdatny, *Fashion, Work, and Politics in Modern France* (New York: Palgrave, 2006). This is changing, however, with forthcoming work by Alun Withey. See also Don Herzog, *Poisoning the Minds of the Lower Orders* (Princeton, NJ: Princeton University Press, 1998); Herzog, "The Trouble

with Hairdressers," *Representations* 53 (Winter 1996): 21–43; Jessica P. Clark, "Grooming Men: The Material World of the Nineteenth-Century Barbershop," in *Gender and Material Culture in Britain since 1600*, ed. Hannah Greig, Jane Hamlett, and Leonie Hannan (London: Palgrave Macmillan, 2015), 104–19; and Vincent, *Hair*.

11 On effeteness and idleness, see J. T. Arlidge, *The Hygiene, Diseases, and Mortality of Occupations* (London: Percival, 1892), 176–7.

12 Austin T. Young, *The Annals of the Barber-Surgeons of London, Compiled from Their Records and Other Sources, by Sidney Young, One of the Court of Assistants of the Worshipful Company of Barbers of London* (London: Blades, East, & Blades, 1890), iv; "Barbers' Company," *THC* 5, no. 83 (June 3, 1871): 56; and William Andrews, *At the Sign of the Barber's Pole* (Cottingham, Yorkshire: J. R. Tutin, 1904), 8.

13 Andrews, *At the Sign of the Barber's Pole*, 8.

14 See Herzog, *Poisoning the Minds*; and Herzog, "The Trouble with Hairdressers," 26. For contemporary accounts of the early modern barbershop, see Charles Manby Smith, *The Little World of London. Or, Pictures in Little of London Life* (London: Arthur Hall, Virtue, 1857), 22–3.

15 On England's early modern barber-surgeons, see Margaret Pelling, "Appearance and Reality: Barber-Surgeons, the Body and Disease," in *London 1500–1700: The Making of the Metropolis*, ed. A. L. Beier and Roger Finlay (London: Longman Group, 1985), 82–112. Alun Withey's forthcoming history will be the most comprehensive study, to date, of this shift.

16 Young, *Annals of the Barber-Surgeons of London*, 259.

17 In this period, new categories of retailing men infiltrated guild ranks. Robert Hovenden was one such member. By 1890, there was a single female freewoman of the Barbers' Company, although this did not denote participation in the hair trades. See Young, *Annals of the Barber-Surgeons of London*, 260.

18 "Building on Old Foundations," *THC* 5, no. 96 (September 2, 1871): 78.

19 Charles Booth, ed., *Life and Labour of the People in London: Population Classified by Trades, Volume VIII* (London: Macmillan, 1896), 308. On nineteenth-century declines in guild membership and apprenticeship, especially as they related to women, see Alison C. Kay, *The Foundations of Female Entrepreneurship: Enterprise, Home, and Household in London, c. 1800–1870* (London: Routledge, 2009), 23–5.

20 There were some perceived and material differences that separated hairdressers from barbers, which will be discussed in Alun Withey's forthcoming monograph.

21 General Register Office, *Fourteenth Annual Report of the Registrar-General of Births, Deaths, and Marriages in England* (London: Eyre and Spottiswoode, 1855), 148.

22 The Charles Booth Archive at the London School of Economics and Political
    Science, Notebook B160, Hairdresser & Wigmaker Interviews. "Notes on general
    visits to hairdressers, 6 January [1896]: interview with Mr. J. T. Dunk, hairdresser,
    member of the Hairdressers' Guild, 221 Brompton Road, 9 January [1896]," p. 68.

23 Booth Archive, B160, p. 68.

24 Booth Archive, B160, "Interview with Mr. F. J. Gotty, secretary of the Journeymen
    Hairdressers Trade Society, 16 December [1895]," p. 65.

25 Booth Archive, B160, "Interview with Mr. J. G. Davin, hair parlour proprietor, 2
    February [1896]," p. 91.

26 Booth Archive, B160, p. 80.

27 Booth Archive, B160, p. 91.

28 "Wanted, Improvers!" *THC* 5, no. 101 (October 7, 1871): 85. Emphasis theirs.

29 The famous theatrical wigmaker Willy Clarkson refused to complete Charles
    Booth's industrial survey on the grounds that he "really [did] not think it would
    be at all advantageous to" him. The Booth surveyor—remarking that Clarkson had
    "difficulty in keeping with the factory act regulations as his hours are very great"—
    insinuated that fears of industrial regulation kept him from participating. See
    Booth Archive, B160, p. 73. For more on Clarkson, see Angus McLaren, "Smoke
    and Mirrors: Willy Clarkson and the Role of Disguises in Inter-War England,"
    Journal of Social History 40, no. 3 (2007): 597–618.

30 For parallels with the French hairdressing trades, see Zdatny, *Fashion*, 28–30.

31 "The Master Hairdressers and Ourselves," *THC* 1, no. 2 (December 1, 1866): 6; and
    Booth Archive, B160, p. 79. According to the *OED*, "shampoo" did not function as
    a noun until 1838. First developed in New York, Alfred Tugwell of Scarborough
    purportedly introduced the process to Britain in the late 1870s. The closest British
    example was an egg wash employed at toilet clubs serving undergraduates in
    Oxford. "Celebrities Connected with the Trade. No. 15—Alfred John Tugwell,"
    Hairdressers' Weekly Journal (hereafter *HWJ*) 3, no. 106 (May 17, 1884): 315.

32 Arlidge, *Hygiene, Diseases, and Mortality*, 177.

33 Arlidge, *Hygiene, Diseases, and Mortality*, 176–7.

34 General Register Office, *Supplement to the Fifty-Fifth Annual Report of the Registrar-
    General for England and Wales. Volume 55* (London: Eyre and Spottiswoode,
    1897), liii.

35 Gambling was not the only illegal activity at the barbershop. James Greenwood
    discovered that at least one barbershop on Little Swallow Street, Soho also
    functioned as a front for an illegal Sunday drinking hole. On Greenwood's
    "uncomfortable, frowsy little den," see "A 'Sly House' on Sunday," in *In Strange
    Company: Being the Experiences of a Roving Correspondent* (London: Vizetelly,
    [1873] 1883), 108–15.

36 Charles Booth, ed. "Inner South London," in *Life and Labour of the People in London, Volume IV* (New York: Macmillan, 1902), 189.

37 Booth, ed., *Life and Labour of the People in London, Volume VIII*, 277.

38 Booth Archive, B160, p. 79; and Booth Archive, B160, p. 87.

39 Booth Archive, B160, p. 79.

40 Booth, *Life and Labour of the People in London, Volume VIII*, 275. In utilitarian shops, which charged approximately 2d. or 3d. for a haircut and 1d. for a shave, the wage of a live-in assistant ranged between 6s. and 14s. per week. Booth Archive, B160, p. 59.

41 Booth Archive, B160, p. 87.

42 Cecil Willett Cunnington, *Handbook of English Costume in the Nineteenth Century* (London: Faber and Faber, 1959), 517. Quoted in Galia Ofek, *Representations of Hair in Victorian Literature and Culture* (Burlington, VT: Ashgate 2009), 37.

43 James Greenwood, "The Human Hair Market," in *In Strange Company: Being the Experiences of a Roving Correspondent*, 124–8.

44 The 1872 returns reveal Robert Hovenden's total capital at £36,000. The stock in manufacturing hair was matched only by the combined worth of perfumery and foreign perfumery, some £2,453. The haircutting or "trimming" department was valued at £696. See Stephanie Jones, "R. Hovenden & Sons, Ltd.," *Business Archives* 56 (1988): 29.

45 "Employment of Women," *THC* 10, no. 253 (June 17, 1876): 93. For a literary treatment of a former theatrical wigmaker, see Miriam Ross, *Against Tide: A Story of a Poor Street Arab* (London: John Dicks, 1871), 89–92.

46 Booth Archive, B160, p. 88.

47 Charles Booth, ed., *Life and Labour of the People in London, Final Volume: Notes on Social Influences and Conclusion* (London: Macmillan, 1903), 56.

48 Booth Archive, B160, p. 91.

49 Booth Archive, B160, p. 58.

50 In 1867, Institution membership included "about thirteen perfumers, eleven brush and comb makers, six hair merchants, and about seventy hairdressers, and a few others connected with this trade." By 1877, there was a 10 percent decline in membership, down from an already paltry 103 members. In that year, fifty-seven of the ninety were categorized as "Master Hairdressers." "British Hairdressers' Benevolent and Provident Institution," *THC* 1, no. 3 (January 1, 1867): 2, 6; and "British Hairdressers' Provident and Benevolent Institution," *The Perruquier: A Monthly Trade Journal for Hairdressers, Perfumers, Brush & Comb Manufacturers* 1 (December 1877–December 1878): 4–5. On Queen Adelaide and the "Buy British" campaign of 1830, see Alison Adburgham, *Shops and Shopping, 1800–1914: Where and in What Manner the Well-Dressed Englishwoman Bought Her Clothes* (London: Allen & Unwin, [1964] 1981), chapter 4.

51　On the establishment of French authorities as "taste masters" in the early beauty business, see Morag Martin, *Selling Beauty: Cosmetics, Commerce, and French Society 1750–1830* (Baltimore, MD: Johns Hopkins Press, 2009).

52　Andrew Halliday, "Court, Ball, Powder and Evening," *All the Year Round* 15 (February 10, 1866): 109–12.

53　The Société moved to 11 Denman Street, Soho, in the 1870s and Maddox Street in May 1882.

54　La Société du Progrès de la Coiffure, *Rules of the School* (London: No publisher, 1893), 38–9. Booth Archive, F 2/4/7.

55　"Société du Progrès de la Coiffure," *THC* 1, no. 7 (May 1, 1867): 4.

56　"Société du Progrès de la Coiffure," *HWJ* (September 29, 1883): 636.

57　"Société du Progrès de la Coiffure," *THC* 1, no. 7 (May 1, 1867): 4.

58　Booth Archive, B160, p. 57; and La Société du Progrès de la Coiffure, 38–9. Booth Archive, F 2/4/7.

59　Jerry White notes that, according to the census, Germans were the largest foreign-born population in London before the 1890s. In 1861, there were 16,082 German nationals in London. See White, *London in the Nineteenth Century: 'A Human Awful Wonder of God'* (London: Jonathan Cape, 2007), 106–13; and Panikos Panayi, "Germans in 19th-Century Britain," *History Today* 43, no. 1 (January 1993): 50.

60　This group, later renamed the International Union of Journeymen Hairdressers, was one of the primary nineteenth-century labor organizations serving German tradesmen in London. See Panikos Panayi, "German Immigrants in Britain, 1815–1914," in *Germans in Britain since 1500*, ed. Panikos Panayi (London: Hambledon Press, 1996), 87.

61　Harmony Club, *Rules of the School* (London: No publisher, 1893), 38–9. Booth Archive, F 2/4/7.

62　Booth Archive, B160, p. 66. According to Ellen Ross, the 1901 Census counted 135,000 Jewish Londoners. Up until 1910, London's Jewish population was concentrated in St. Giles and Whitechapel. See Appendix 1 in Ellen Ross, *Slum Travelers: Ladies and London Poverty, 1860–1920* (Berkeley: University of California Press, 2007), 281.

63　Quick to criticize skilled and well-trained French and German workers "taking" situations in the West End, *THC* ignored the case of recently immigrated Eastern European workers, subsequently leaving no record of the demanding conditions they most probably experienced. See Panikos Panayi, *Immigration, Ethnicity, and Racism in Britain, 1815–1945* (New York: Manchester University Press, 1994); and Laura Tabili, "'Having Lived Close Beside Them All the Time': Negotiating National Identities through Personal Networks," *Journal of Social History* 39, no. 2 (2005): 369–87.

64 Booth, *Life and Labour of the People in London, Volume VIII*, 278; and Booth Archive, B160.

65 Booth Archive, B160, p. 91.

66 "Correspondence: 'Foreigners,'" *HWJ* 2, no. 67 (August 11, 1883): 516.

67 Booth, *Life and Labour of the People in London, Volume VIII*, 277.

68 Christopher P. Hosgood, "'Mercantile Monasteries': Shops, Shop Assistants, and Shop Life in Late-Victorian and Edwardian Britain," *Journal of British Studies* 38, no. 3 (1999): 352.

69 "Hairdressers," *THC* 1, no. 3 (January 1, 1867): 5.

70 "British Hairdressers' Benevolent and Provident Institution," *THC* 1, no. 3 (January 1, 1867): 2.

71 Zdatny, *Fashion*, 26.

72 See, for example, Lynda Nead, *Victorian Babylon: People, Streets and Images in Nineteenth-Century London* (New Haven, CT: Yale University Press, 2000); and Judith R. Walkowitz, *City of Dreadful Delight: Narratives of Sexual Danger in late-Victorian London* (Chicago, IL: University of Chicago Press, 1992).

73 Geographic divides also shaped perfumers' and wholesalers' stock lists for West End versus City and East End shops. While Hovenden's West End locations stocked high-end perfumery and "laboratory" items, locations on Berners Street and City Road depended on "Manufacturing Hair" or wigs, and also carried masculine items like walking sticks, cricket bats, and umbrellas. Jones, "R. Hovenden," 33.

74 Booth Archive, B160, p. 58. See also "The Education of the Shop," *The Pall Mall Gazette* 635 (February 21, 1867): 3.

75 "'Call a Spade a Spade': A History of the Now Defunct Master Hairdressers' Co-Operative Society," *HWJ* (October 14, 1882): 379.

76 Booth, *Life and Labour of the People in London, Volume VIII*, 275.

77 "Such Luxuries Are Costly," *Cassell's Saturday Magazine* (April 6, 1898): 628. For more on the history of upper-middle-class male grooming, see Paul Deslandes's forthcoming study of male beauty from the University of Chicago Press. See also Christopher Oldstone-Moore, "The Beard Movement in Victorian Britain," *Victorian Studies* 48, no. 1 (2005): 7–34; Brent Shannon, *The Cut of His Coat: Men, Dress, and Consumer Culture in Britain, 1860–1914* (Athens: Ohio University Press, 2006), 85–9; and Susan Walton, "Squalid Impropriety to Manly Respectability: The Revival of Beards, Moustaches and Martial Values in the 1850s in England," *Nineteenth-Century Contexts* 30, no. 3 (2008): 229–45. For a discussion of the methodological possibilities engendered by the study of male grooming and aesthetics, see Deslandes, "The Male Body, Beauty and Aesthetics in Modern British Culture," *History Compass* 8, no. 10 (October 2010): 1191–208.

78 Vincent, *Hair*, 67; and Catherine Maxwell, *Scents and Sensibility: Perfume in Victorian Literary Culture* (Oxford: Oxford University Press, 2017), 41–6.

79   Booth Archive, B160, p. 78.

80   "A West-End Hairdressers' Establishment Described," *THC* 14, no. 351 (July 17, 1880): 109–10.

81   On hairdressers' hours in this period, see "Hairdressers," *THC* 1, no. 3 (January 1, 1867): 5.

82   "The Hairdressers' Saturday Early Closing Movement," *THC* (November 1, 1866): 5; and "Hairdressers' Sunday Closing Association," *THC* (December 1, 1866): 5.

83   "The Hairdressers' Saturday Early Closing Movement," *THC* (November 1, 1866): 5; and "Ourselves and the British Hairdressers' Institute," *THC* 1, no. 4 (February 1, 1867): 4–5.

84   "Employers," *THC* 1, no. 2 (December 1, 1866): 7.

85   "Ourselves and the British Hairdressers' Institute," *THC* 1, no. 4 (February 1, 1867): 4–5.

86   "The Fashions," *THC* 1, no. 3 (January 1, 1867): 3.

87   "Hairdressers' Conversazione," *THC* 83, no. 5 (June 3, 1871): 49.

88   *Census Returns of England and Wales, 1861*, class RG 9, piece 44, folio 8, p. 14, www.ancestry.co.uk.

89   Specifically, Douglas, Truefitt, John Marsh of 175 Piccadilly, William Wilcox of 36 Glasshouse Street, and William Hewson of 104 Cromer Street became vice presidents of the Hairdressers' Sunday Closing Movement Association, a group primarily consisting of assistants. *The Queen: The Lady's Newspaper* (January 3, 1880): 19.

    The few histories that address the Early Closing Movement privilege a small group as key political agitators, typically "Linen Drapers, Silk Mercers, Hosiers, and Lacemen of the British Metropolis." Entire groups of London workers (including hairdressers and barbers) do not feature in the literature. See Gregory Anderson, *Victorian Clerks* (Manchester: Manchester University Press, 1976); John Benson and Laura Ugolini, eds. *A Nation of Shopkeepers: Five Centuries of British Retailing* (London: I. B. Tauris, 2003); Geoffrey Crossick and Heinz-Gerhard Haupt, *Shopkeepers and Master Artisans in Nineteenth-Century Europe* (New York: Methuen, 1984); Crossick and Haupt, *The Petite Bourgeoisie in Europe, 1780–1914: Enterprise, Family, and Independence* (New York: Routledge, 1995); Christopher P. Hosgood, "A 'Brave and Daring Folk'? Shopkeepers and Trade Associational Life in Victorian and Edwardian England," *Journal of Social History* 26, no. 2 (Winter 1992): 285–308; William Lancaster, *The Department Store: A Social History* (London: Leicester University Press, 1995), 132–4; and Wilfred B. Whitaker, *Victorian and Edwardian Shopworkers: The Struggle to Obtain Better Conditions and a Half-Holiday* (Newton Abbot: David and Charles, 1973). Exceptions include Lee Holcombe, *Victorian Ladies at Work; Middle-Class Working Women in England and Wales, 1850–1914* (Hamden, CT: Archon Books,

1973); Hosgood, "Mercantile Monasteries," 352; and Michael J. Winstanley, *The Shopkeeper's World, 1830–1914* (Manchester: Manchester University Press, 1983).

90   Through the nineteenth century, "Hairdressers and Perfumers" was a distinct category from "Perfumers" in *Kelly's Directory,* the latter denoting retail and manufacturing perfumers.

91   For more on factors limiting women's appearances in trade directories, see Kay, "Retailing," 153.

92   "Female Hairdressers" from *The British Quarterly Review.* Quoted in *THC* 4, no. 47 (September 1, 1870): 76. See also Vincent, *Hair,* 64–6. However, the German trade publication *Der Friseur* maintained that "English ladies seldom call in a hairdresser," save for "foreign ladies and … certain ladies who make a moonlight study of Virtue in and about Regent-street." Quoted in "The Hairdressing Trade in London," *THC* 12 (March 2, 1878): 37.

93   On the employment of urban middle-class and upper working-class women in the late nineteenth century, see Lancaster *The Department Store,* 125–58; Erika D. Rappaport, *Shopping for Pleasure: Women in the Making of London's West End* (Princeton, NJ: Princeton University Press, 2000), chapter 3; and Lise Sanders, *Consuming Fantasies: Labor, Leisure, and the London Shopgirl, 1880–1920* (Columbus: Ohio State University Press, 2006), chapter 2.

94   "Correspondence," *Pall Mall Gazette* (September 13, 1867): 3.

95   "The Present Fashions in Hair," *The Graphic* (May 28, 1870): 603.

96   "Another Lady Hairdresser," *Women's Penny Paper* 10 (December 29, 1888): 3; and "Female Hairdressers," *THC* 10, no. 256 (August 5, 1876): 118.

97   Quoted in "Valets and Ladies' Maids," *THC* 3, no. 29 (March 1, 1868): 32.

98   Advertisement in Leonard de Vries and Ilonka van Amstel, *Victorian Advertisements* (London: John Murray, 1968).

99   "Trade Enterprise," *HWJ* 1, no. 5 (June 3, 1882): 48. These developments echo the amenities offered by the department store in the late nineteenth century. Scholars argue their emergence facilitated the expansion of West End consumption and pleasure to increasingly mobile upper-middle-class women. See Rappaport, *Shopping for Pleasure,* especially chapters 3 and 5. See also Lancaster, *The Department Store,* 171–94; William R. Leach, "Transformations in a Culture of Consumption: Women and Department Stores, 1890–1925," *Journal of American History* 71, no. 2 (September 1984): 319–42; and Mica Nava, "Modernity's Disavowal: Women, the City, and the Department Store," in *Modern Times: Reflections on a Century of Modernity,* ed. Mica Nava and Alan O'Shea (London: Routledge, 1996), 38–76.

100 "A West-End Hairdressers' Establishment Described," 109. The construction of gendered boundaries also extended to employee space, and the discrepancies between women's and men's workrooms speak to contrasting labor conditions for the two groups. Lady hairdressers spent their "leisure" time in "nice, comfortable

rooms" on the second floor at No. 23, rooms which apparently "showed Mr. Douglas's paternal care for his 'retainers.'" By contrast, the men's workroom was located in the basement of No. 21, from which they were "called upstairs by telegraph" as required. "A West-End Hairdressers' Establishment Described, Cont." *THC* 14, no. 352 (August 7, 1880): 115.

101 "Lease for 21 years, counterpart," Henry White Hitchins and Jean Nestor Marie Tirard for 39 Curzon Street, Mayfair, Middlesex (June 26, 1865) LMA O/108/014/001.

102 "A West-End Hairdressers' Establishment Described," 109.

103 "A West-End Hairdressers' Establishment Described," 109.

104 The men's rooms also featured private boxes, although the columnist found "'gentlemen' scorn even to be shaved in 'camera,' and the snug green curtains in each and every box remain undrawn, while each and every operation is performed on manly heads." This illusion of privacy, created by the careful construction of public space, mirrored other popular mixed-gender venues like churches, reading rooms, and the theater. The construction of these spaces—including pews, cabinets, and personal boxes—facilitated what Erika Rappaport terms a "public privacy" by engendering within visitors a false sense of seclusion. See Rappaport, *Shopping*, 124; and Ruth Hoberman, "Women in the British Museum Reading Room during the Late-Nineteenth and Early-Twentieth Centuries: From Quasi- to Counterpublic," *Feminist Studies* 28 no. 3 (Autumn 2002): 489–512.

105 "A West-End Hairdressers' Establishment Described," 109–10.

106 "A West-End Hairdressers' Establishment Described," 110.

107 Vincent, *Hair*, 64–6.

108 "Women at Work, No. 5. By Our Special Commissioner. Hairdressers," *Women and Work* 12 (August 22, 1874): 2.

109 Mercy Grogan, *How Women May Earn a Living* (London: Cassell, Petter, Galpin, 1880), 109.

110 "Women at Work, No. 5. By Our Special Commissioner. Hairdressers," 2. Employment at a hairdressing shop in any capacity was contingent on personal appearance. One advertisement for a "first-class shopwoman" requested the applicant's references, terms, and a photograph. "Classifieds," *THC* 8, no. 194 (January 3, 1874): 8.

111 "Women at Work, No. 5. By Our Special Commissioner. Hairdressers," 2.

112 "Another Lady Hairdresser," 3.

113 Birmingham and Liverpool registered 392 and 581 hairdressers, respectively. "The Census and Hairdressers," *THC* 18, no. 443 (May 17, 1884): 101.

114 *Census Returns of England and Wales, 1871*, class RG10, piece 3195, folio 58, p. 12, www.ancestry.co.uk; *Census Returns of England and Wales, 1881*, class

RG11, piece 133, folio 49, p. 28, www.ancestry.co.uk; *Census Returns of England and Wales, 1891*, class RG12, piece 67, folio 39, p. 28, www.ancestry.co.uk; and *Census Returns of England and Wales, 1901*, class RG13, piece 81, folio 6, p. 3, www.ancestry.co.uk.

115 "Record of Events," *Englishwoman's Review* (November 15, 1881): 506.

116 "Shows in the London Shops," *Pall Mall Gazette* 7634 (September 5, 1889): n.p.

117 "Another Lady Hairdresser," 3. Latter did not advertise in trade directories.

118 "Shows in the London Shops," n.p. On advances in hair dyeing in the French context, see Geoffrey Jones, *Beauty Imagined: A History of the Global Beauty Industry* (New York: Oxford University Press, 2010), 49–51; and Zdatny, *Fashion*, 19–21.

119 "Shows in the London Shops," n.p. Mrs. H. Coleman Davidson wrote, "A young Frenchwoman whom we once knew in England attended ladies and even gentlemen in their own homes, and did extremely well; indeed, she had as much work as she could possibly manage. Certainly her care achieved the most wonderful restoration of thin or dull hair, and a few months of treatment was sufficient to make scanty locks luxuriant. She had, of course, a specific which she used in conjunction with a system of massage, her idea being to stimulate the hair into growth." Davidson, *What Our Daughters Can Do for Themselves* (London: Smith, Elder, 1894), 110.

120 "Shows in the London Shops," n.p.

121 "Women at Work, No. 5. By Our Special Commissioner. Hairdressers," 2.

122 Booth, *Life and Labour of the People in London, Volume VIII*, 284.

123 "Meeting of Master Hairdressers on the Customs of the Trade" *THC* 3, no. 38 (December 1, 1869): 1.

4 Professionalizing Perfumery: Eugène Rimmel

1 "Celebrities Connected with the Trade. No. 1–Rimmel," *Hairdressers' Weekly Journal* (February 24, 1883): 121 (hereafter *HWJ*).

2 The series ran through 1885 and also featured Alfred Colin, Alfred Low, John Carter, Olivier Rolland (Isidore Ville), and Gustav Boehm.

3 On Victorian biography as a form, see David Amigoni, ed., *Life Writing and Victorian Culture* (New York: Ashgate, 2006); and Juliette Atkinson, *Victorian Biography Reconsidered: A Study of Nineteenth-Century 'Hidden' Lives* (New York: Oxford University Press, 2010).

4 "Eugène Rimmel," *The Chemist and Druggist* (February 14, 1874): 38. This profile was part of another celebratory series, that of the *C&D* "Portrait Gallery." Rimmel was one of the only manufacturing perfumers featured in this series.

5 Mary B. Rose, "The Family Firm in British Business, 1780–1914," in *Business Enterprise in Modern Britain: From the Eighteenth to the Twentieth Century*, ed. Maurice W. Kirby (New York: Routledge, 1994), 62.

6 Geoffrey Jones, *Beauty Imagined: The History of the Global Beauty Business* (New York: Oxford University Press, 2010), 18. On Rimmel, see also Jonathan Reinarz, *Past Scents: Historical Perspectives on Smell* (Urbana: University of Illinois Press, 2014), 71; and Catherine Maxwell, *Scents and Sensibility: Perfume in Victorian Literary Culture* (Oxford: Oxford University Press, 2017), 21–2.

7 On the establishment of French authorities as "taste masters" in the early beauty business, see Morag Martin, *Selling Beauty: Cosmetics, Commerce, and French Society 1750–1830* (Baltimore, MD: Johns Hopkins Press, 2009); and Eugénie Briot, "From Industry to Luxury: French Perfume in the Nineteenth Century," *Business History Review* 85 (Summer 2011): 273–94.

8 Critics have challenged the romanticization of "authentic" ethnic communities and subjects as existing outside capitalist venture and liberal agendas. See Sarah Joseph, *Interrogating Culture: Critical Perspectives on Contemporary Social Theory* (London: Sage, 1998).

9 On "entrepreneurial manliness," see John Benson and Laura Ugolini, "Introduction," in *A Nation of Shopkeepers: Five Centuries of British Retailing* (London: I. B. Tauris, 2003), 3.

10 Jerry White, *London in the 19th Century: 'A Human Awful Wonder of God'* (London: Jonathan Cape, 2007), 141–2. See also Panikos Panayi, *Immigration, Ethnicity, and Racism in Britain, 1815–1945* (Manchester: Manchester University Press, 1994), 56–7; and Panikos Panayi, *An Immigration History of Britain: Multicultural Racism since 1800* (London: Pearson Longman, 2010).

11 Hyacinthe studied in Paris under Lubin, who was a key player in perfumery from the 1830s through the 1860s. He was engaged at Delcroix's for four years. "Eugène Rimmel," *Chemist and Druggist,* 38.

12 On bankruptcy in English consumer culture, see Tammy Whitlock, *Crime, Gender, and Consumer Culture in Nineteenth-Century England* (Burlington, VT: Ashgate, 2005), 97–9.

13 *Census Returns of England and Wales, 1851*, class HO107, piece 1510, folio 532, p. 20, www.ancestry.co.uk.

14 H. R., "A Tour of Little France," *Cassell's Family Magazine* 8 (London: Cassell, 1886), 734. Historian Panikos Panayi writes that "a significant number of French shops had previously existed in Bond Street in London." See Panayi, *Immigration*, 69.

15 Paul Villars, "French London," in *Living London: Its Work and Its Play, Its Humour and Its Pathos, Its Sights and Its Scenes, Volume II*, ed. George R. Sims (London: Cassell, 1902), 33.

16 "Eugène Rimmel," *Chemist and Druggist,* 38.

17 "Dissolution of Partnerships," *London Gazette* 20560 (January 13, 1846): 18.

18 "From Gay to Grave," *All the Year Round* (March 21, 1874): 488–92.

19 H. R., "A Tour of Little France," 734.

20 On the longstanding relationship between Soho and cosmopolitanism, see Judith R. Walkowitz, *Nights Out: Life in Cosmopolitan London* (New Haven, CT: Yale University Press, 2012), especially chapter 1.

21 Lynda Nead, *Victorian Babylon: People, Streets, and Images in Nineteenth-Century London* (New Haven, CT: Yale University Press, 2000), 161.

22 *Census Returns of England and Wales, 1861,* class RG 9, piece 179, folio 41, p. 14, www.ancestry.co.uk; and *Census Returns of England and Wales, 1851,* class HO107, piece 1510, folio 532, p. 20, www.ancestry.co.uk.

23 On the importance of commercial geography to Parisian perfumers, see Briot, "From Industry to Luxury," 290–1. See also Susan M. Yohn, "The Primacy of Place, Collaborations, and Alliances: Mapping Women's Businesses in Nineteenth-Century Brooklyn," *Journal of Urban History* 36 no. 4 (2010): 411. Christopher Breward emphasizes the Strand's more questionable associations with the cheap theaters and music halls spilling over from neighboring Covent Garden. A move from Gerrard Street, Soho to the Strand nonetheless represented upward spatial mobility for Rimmel. See Christopher Breward, *Fashioning London: Clothing and the Modern Metropolis* (Oxford: Berg, 2004), chapter 3 and especially 71–2.

24 "Celebrities Connected with the Trade.—Alfred Low," *HWJ* (May 26, 1883): 334.

25 "Celebrities Connected with the Trade.—Eugène Rimmel," 121. 96 the Strand is near the current site of the Savoy Theatre.

26 It had also accommodated celebrated perfumer Charles Lillie through the 1820s. See Lillie, *The British Perfumer: Being a Collection of Choice Receipts and Observations Made During an Extensive Practice of Thirty Years, By Which Any Lady or Gentleman may Prepare their own Articles of the Best Quality, Whether of Perfumery, Snuffs, or Colours* (London: J. Souter, 1822).

27 "Making Valentines," *Illustrated London News* 1799 (February 14, 1874): 151; and Reinarz, *Past Scents,* 136.

28 "Literature," *The Ladies' Treasury* (February 1, 1871): 30.

29 On display windows and shop displays, see Rachel Bowlby, *Carried Away: The Invention of Modern Shopping* (New York: Columbia University Press, 2001), chapter 4; Claire Walsh, "Shop Design and the Display of Goods in Eighteenth-Century London," *Journal of Design History* 8, no. 3 (1995): 157–76; and Whitlock, *Crime,* 85–8.

30 "Literature and Art," *Illustrated London News* 1056 (October 27, 1860): 401. In 1875, the Embankment stores burnt down. "Fire in Beaufort Buildings," *Illustrated London News* 1859 (March 27, 1875): 305.

31 One of the first almanacs produced after Rimmel's death featured "Scientific Celebrity" (1889). It included images of great English and French scientific minds of the period: Faraday, Watt, and Montgolfier.

32 The most popular ether at the Exhibition was pineapple oil, made from butyrate of ethyloxide. A. W. Hofmann, "On the Application of Organic Chemistry to Perfumery," *Annalen der Chemie.* Reprinted in G. W. Septimus Piesse, *The Art of Perfumery* (Philadelphia, PA: Lindsay and Blakiston, [1855] 1857), 293–4.

33 Piesse, *Art*, 34. There would be an "explosion in the range of scents that a perfumer could utilize" in the late 1890s with the availability of new chemicals. Jones, *Beauty Imagined*, 23.

34 Traditional processes of extracting materials from botanical sources were expression, distillation, maceration, or "*enfleurage* (absorption) for flowers; tincturation for roots; and distillation for seeds." When dissolved in alcohol, these simple odors were known as "essences." Piesse, *Art*, 112, 132; and Jones, *Beauty Imagined*, 15.

35 "Concrete essence extraction," a new process developed in the 1870s, produced concentrated substances soluble in alcohol. Jones, *Beauty Imagined*, 21–2. For more traditional modes of extracting essential oils, see "The Perfumer" in James Wylde, *The Book of Trades* (Edinburgh: Gall & Inglis, 1866); and Andrew Wynter, "Britannia's Smelling Bottle," *Our Social Bees; or, Pictures of Town & Country Life, and Other Papers* (London: Robert Hardwicke, 1861), 96–105.

36 "Reports and Analyses and Descriptions of New Inventions in Medicine, Surgery, Dietetics, and the Allied Sciences," *British Medical Journal* 1, no. 1156 (February 24, 1883): 365; and "Useful Hints for the Season by Septimus Piesse," *Scientific American* 19, no. 8 (August 19, 1868): 118.

37 "From Gay to Grave," 489.

38 Ess Bouquet was reportedly Queen Victoria's favorite scent. Maxwell, *Scents and Sensibility*, 31.

39 Piesse, *Art*, 234.

40 Piesse, *Art*, 301.

41 Perfumers also manufactured soap, typically refashioning it according to their preferences. Piesse, *Art*, 176. On soap, marketing, and the British consumer, see Bowlby, *Carried Away*, 95–100; Brian Lewis, *So Clean: Lord Leverhulme, Soap and Civilization* (Manchester: Manchester University Press, 2008); and Anne McClintock, *Imperial Leather: Race, Gender and Sexuality in the Colonial Contest* (New York: Routledge, 1995), 207–31.

42 "From Gay to Grave," 489.

43 Laura Ugolini, *Men and Menswear: Sartorial Consumption in Britain 1880–1939* (Burlington, VT: Ashgate, 2007), 13–14.

44 Bernard Porter, *The Refugee Question in Mid-Victorian Politics* (New York: Cambridge University Press, [1979] 2008), 4–5.

45 "Naturalisation Papers: Rimmel, Eugène, from France. Certificate 2524" (September 10, 1857) The National Archives (hereafter TNA), HO 1/81/2524.

46 Piesse, *Art*, 29.

47 McClintock, *Imperial Leather*, 45.

48 McClintock, *Imperial Leather*, 57. On cultures of exhibition, see Jeffrey A. Auerbach and Peter H. Hoffenberg, eds. *Britain, the Empire, and the World at the Great Exhibition of 1851* (Aldershot: Ashgate, 2008); and Lara Kriegel, *Grand Designs: Labor, Empire and the Museum in Victorian Culture* (Durham, NC: Duke University Press, 2007).

49 "Eugène Rimmel," *Chemist and Druggist*, 41.

50 McClintock, *Imperial Leather*, 60.

51 Jones, *Beauty Imagined*, 18.

52 *Official Catalogue of the Great Exhibition of the Works of Industry of All Nations* (London: Commissioners for the Exhibition of 1851, 1851), 142.

53 Piesse, *Art*, 33.

54 According to Lawrence Wright, the soap and perfumery section had a total of 727 exhibitors. Almost half of them represented Britain. Wright, *Clean and Decent: The Fascinating History of the Bathroom & the Water Closet and of Sundry Habits, Fashions & Accessories of the Toilet Principally in Great Britain, France, & America* (London: Routledge & Kegan Paul, 1960), 242.

55 Piesse, *Art*, 155.

56 Jones, *Beauty Imagined*, 22.

57 Piesse, *Art*, 118.

58 Piesse, *Art*, 119–23.

59 Civet remains "a fundamental French perfume material, a historic girder of the industry and the quintessential scent of France," although Chanel reportedly switched to a synthetic form in 1998. See Chandler Burr, "The Talk: Meow Mix," *The New York Times* (October 21, 2007); and Maxwell, *Scents and Sensibility*, 29.

60 "109 exhibited perfumery materials, and 123 manufactured perfumery and toilet soaps." Eugène Rimmel, "On the Perfumery Trade," in *The Technologist, Volume 3* (London: Kent, 1863): 176.

61 His resultant publication *Recollections* contained no less than 313 illustrations and plates and helped establish Rimmel as a translator of international commodities for Britain's consuming classes. Rimmel, *Recollections of the Paris Exposition of 1867* (London: Chapman and Hall, 1868); and "Literature," *The Ladies' Treasury* (May 1, 1868): 1.

62 *Exhibition of the Works of Industry of all Nations, 1851. Reports by the Juries on the Subjects in the Thirty Classes into Which the Exhibition Was Divided* (London: William Clowes, 1852), 612; and Maxwell, *Scents and Sensibility*, 22.

63 Rimmel, *Recollections*, 298. For more on Pears, see Francis Pears, *The Skin, Baths, Bathing, and Soap* (London: The Author, 1859).

64 His success at the Great Exhibition was confirmed in the Crystal Palace's move to Sydenham, when he was asked to reconstruct three fountains "in exchange [for] the monopoly of the sale of perfumery on the ground floor." "Eugène Rimmel," *The Chemist and Druggist,* 41.

65 In advertisements for his Patent Vaporizer appearing in *The Lady's Newspaper,* the Vaporizer appeared not in the operating theater (as it had in *The Lancet*), but in Princess Alexandra's Bridal Boudoir at Windsor Castle. "Advertisements," *The Lady's Newspaper* 849 (April 4, 1863): 440.

66 Eugène Rimmel, *The Book of Perfumes* (London: Chapman and Hall, 1865), vi, emphasis his. See also Reinarz, *Past Scents,* 123; and Maxwell, *Scents and Sensibility,* 2.

67 Rimmel, *Book of Perfumes,* vii–viii.

68 McClintock, *Imperial Leather,* 32. Andrew Wynter suggested the opposite, arguing that women should take up their own perfumery production, as "the lady who takes the trouble to perform the operation may be sure that she possesses a perfume which money cannot buy from the best perfumer's in the metropolis." Wynter, "Britannia's Smelling Bottle," 101.

69 "Celebrities Connected with the Trade. No. 1—Eugène Rimmel," 121.

70 "Eugène Rimmel," *The Chemist and Druggist,* 38.

71 "Eugène Rimmel," *The Chemist and Druggist,* 39.

72 "Dr. G. W. Septimus Piesse, PhD," *Scientific American Supplement* No. 366 (January 6, 1883): 5844. This was followed soon after by "Stolen Kisses" and "Box His Ears." Wynter, "Britannia's Smelling Bottle," 102. On "Kiss-Me-Quick," see Laura Wright, "*Kiss Me Quick*: On the Naming of Commodities, 1650 to the First World War," in *Merchants of Innovation: The Language of Traders,* ed. Esther-Miriam Wagner, Bettina Beinhoff, and Ben Outhwaite (Boston: Walter de Gruyter, 2017), 120–9.

73 Lori Loeb, *Consuming Angels: Advertising and Victorian Women* (New York: Oxford University Press, 1994), 152–3; McClintock, *Imperial Leather,* chapter 5; Robert Opie, *Rule Britannia: Trading on the British Image* (New York: Viking Penguin, 1985); and Thomas Richards, *The Commodity Culture of Victorian England: Advertising and Spectacle, 1851–1914* (Stanford, CA: Stanford University Press, 1990), 135–6.

74 McClintock, *Imperial Leather,* 352.

75 McClintock, *Imperial Leather,* 50. On the relationship between cosmetics and the creation of "national essence" in the eighteenth century, see Lynn Festa, "Cosmetic Differences: The Changing Faces of England and France," *Studies in Eighteenth-Century Culture* 34 (2005): 27.

76 John M. Mackenzie, *Orientalism: History, Theory, and the Arts* (Manchester: Manchester University Press, 1995), 89.

77 Rimmel, *Rimmel's Perfumed Almanack* (London: The Author, 1852–71). On the fusion of "aesthetic values with emerging categories of nation and race" in the eighteenth century, see Festa, "Cosmetic Differences," 41.

78 These criticisms worked both ways. English women were renowned on the
    continent for their outlandish sartorial choices, enhanced by aniline dyes.
    Wrote "Chroniqueuse" in her 1859 text, "Purple bonnets, green dresses,
    and pink parasols form a combination far from elegant. These varieties of
    colours seem to charm the rosy-cheeked English girls who abound in the
    streets of Paris. Why! I actually saw, the other day, walking on the Boulevard,
    an English lady, wearing a fine mauve velvet shawl, or rather mantle, with a
    yellow cotton fringe!" Chroniqueuse, *Photographs of Paris Life: A Record of the
    Politics, Art, Fashion and Anecdote of Paris during the Past Eighteen Months*
    (London: William Tinsley, 1861), 157. Quoted in Amy Montz, "Dressing for
    England: Fashion and Nationalism in Victorian Novels" (PhD dissertation,
    Texas A&M, 2008), 21.

79 Montz, "Dressing for England," 80. For eighteenth-century precedents, see Festa,
    "Cosmetic Differences," 29–30.

80 For more on the relationship between domesticity and the nineteenth-century
    colonial project, see McClintock, *Imperial Leather*, 36.

81 On "artificial naturalness," see Montz, "Dressing for England," 116.

82 "From Gay to Grave," 489.

83 Margaret Schabas, "Victorian Economics and the Science of the Mind," in
    Victorian Science in Context, ed. Bernard V. Lightman (Chicago, IL: University of
    Chicago Press, 1997), 86.

84 Seth Koven, *Slumming: Sexual and Social Politics in Victorian London* (Princeton,
    NJ: Princeton University Press, 2004), 49.

85 "Celebrities Connected with the Trade. No. 1—Eugène Rimmel," 122.

86 The Commune brought over one thousand new French to Britain. Many stayed
    until 1879–80, when they were granted amnesty. Colin Holmes, *John Bull's Island;
    Immigration and British Society, 1871–1971* (London: Macmillan Education,
    1988), 35.

87 "Latest Telegrams: The Floods in France," *Daily News* 9105 (June 30, 1875): n.p.

88 "Obituary," *The Chemist and Druggist* 30 (March 5, 1887): 292.

89 "From Gay to Grave," 490. See also "Eugène Rimmel," *Chemist and Druggist,* 38.

90 "Metropolitan News," *The Illustrated London News* 1524 (February 6, 1869): 127;
    and "French Hospital and Dispensary," *The Lancet* (February 6, 1869): 216.

91 "From Gay to Grave," 490–1.

92 Carl Deite, *A Practical Treatise on the Manufacture of Perfumery* (Philadelphia, PA: H.
    C. Baird, 1892), 29; Jones, *Beauty Imagined*, 16; and Reinarz, *Past Scents*, 67–8.

93 Despite political instability, the French trade made a rapid recovery. Their exports
    between 1827 and 1836 totaled some 6 million francs. By 1858, it was 12 million
    francs, followed by a substantial leap in 1860 to 31 million francs. Rimmel, "On
    the Perfumery Trade," 183.

94 Jones, *Beauty Imagined*, 18.

95 Piesse, *Art*, 114; and George William Septimus Piesse, *The Art of Perfumery*, 3rd edition (London: Longman, Green, Longman, and Roberts, 1862), xi.

96 *Catalogue of the British Section, Paris Universal Exhibition of 1867* (London: Spottiswoode, 1867), 68; and Jones, *Beauty Imagined*, 20.

97 Wynter, "Britannia's Smelling Bottle," 105.

98 "The Old English Lavender Water," *The London and Paris Ladies' Magazine of Fashion, Polite Literature, Etc.* 55, no. 619 (July 1882): 10.

99 J. L. Grossmith of Newgate and Smyth & Nephew of New Bond Street. Rimmel, *Book of Perfumes*, 253.

100 Piesse, *Art*, 303.

101 Geoffrey Jones notes how French "sales increased dramatically; production of perfume and other beauty products soared from 45 million francs in 1878 to 100 million francs ($19 million) in 1912." Jones, *Beauty Imagined*, 20–1, 23, 26–7. The exception to this remained soap, which Britain continued to dominate. See Briot, "From Industry to Luxury," 275.

102 Piesse, *Art*, 31. See also Maxwell, *Scents and Sensibility*, 19–20; and Reinarz, *Past Scents*, 73.

103 Rimmel, *Book of Perfumes*, 232–3.

104 Rimmel, *Book of Perfumes*, 224.

105 French materials were transported to perfume manufactories across continental Europe and North America. According to Rimmel, however, manufactories in Germany, Russia, Spain, and the United States could not be "considered a legitimate business," as "their chief trade consist[ed] in counterfeiting the articles of London and Parisian manufacturers." In the period leading up to the American Civil War, London perfumers did considerable trade with the United States. However, "this branch of the export trade was seriously interfered with by the action of the United States Government after the Civil War, in imposing most enormous duties upon all foreign goods." Some savvy entrepreneurs like Alfred Low (son of Robert) established a branch factory in the United States and circumvented the duties. "Celebrities Connected with the Trade. Alfred Low," 335; and Rimmel, *Book of Perfumes*, 233.

106 Piesse, *Art*, 142–5.

107 Jones, *Beauty Imagined*, 34. English lavender was held in high estimation, and in continental Europe, cold cream was known as "Cold Crême Anglaise." Piesse, *Art*, 206.

108 Jones, *Beauty Imagined*, 34; and Rimmel, *Book of Perfumes*, 235. Rimmel was a vocal advocate for a permanent "Colonial Museum" in London. He called for the museum to blend scientific and commercial elements of imperialism to form "a permanent connecting link between the manufacturer and the colonist." Eugène

Rimmel, "Notes on the Permanent Exhibition of Algerian and Other French Colonial Products in Paris," in *The Technologist, Volume* 1 (London: Kent & Co., 1861), 26.

109   Rimmel, *Book of Perfumes*, 234. These were modest estimates according to Rimmel. Official returns purportedly recorded only one-fourth of the total exports. Exports to Australia, for example, "appear[ed] ridiculously small," and Rimmel knew of "several manufacturers in London" who individually conducted that much trade with the colony each year.

110   "From Gay to Grave," 489.

111   Jones, *Beauty Imagined*, 22.

112   Kim F. Hall, *Things of Darkness: Economies of Race and Gender in Early Modern England* (Ithaca, NY: Cornell University Press, 1995); Jennifer L. Morgan, *Laboring Women: Reproduction and Gender in New World Slavery* (Philadelphia: University of Pennsylvania Press, 2004), 14–16; and Kimberly Poitevin, "Inventing Whiteness: Cosmetics, Race, and Women in Early Modern England," *Journal for Early Modern Cultural Studies* 11, no. 1 (Spring/Summer 2011): 59–89. See also Sharon Block, "Early American Bodies: Creating Race, Sex, and Beauty," in *Connexions: Histories of Race and Sex in North America*, ed. Jennifer Brier, Jim Downs, and Jennifer L. Morgan (Urbana: University of Illinois Press, 2016), 85–112; Stephanie M. H. Camp, "Black Is Beautiful: An American History," *Journal of Southern History* 81, no. 3 (August 2015): 675–90; Stephanie M. H. Camp, "Making Racial Beauty in the United States: Toward a History of Black Beauty," in *Connexions: Histories of Race and Sex in North America*, ed. Jennifer Brier, Jim Downs, and Jennifer L. Morgan (Urbana: University of Illinois Press, 2016), 113–26; and Roxann Wheeler, *The Complexion of Race: Categories of Difference in Eighteenth-Century British Culture* (Philadelphia: University of Pennsylvania Press, 2000), 99–101.

113   For the American context, see Camp, "Black Is Beautiful," 690; and Camp, "Making Racial Beauty in the United States," 113–26.

114   Sadiah Qureshi, *Peoples on Parade: Exhibitions, Empire, and Anthropology in Nineteenth-Century Britain* (Chicago, IL: University of Chicago Press, 2011), 10–11, 211–8, and 275–6.

115   See, for example, Douglas A. Lorimer, *Science, Race Relations and Resistance: Britain, 1870–1914* (Manchester: Manchester University Press, 2013). On mid-century shifts in ethnology and anthropology, see Qureshi, *Peoples on Parade*, chapter 6 and 278–80. See also Timothy Burke, *Lifebuoy Men, Lux Women: Commodification, Consumption, and Cleanliness in Modern Zimbabwe* (Durham, NC: Duke University Press, 1996), 18–19, 31–2; Rebecca Herzig, *Plucked: A History of Hair Removal* (New York: New York University Press, 2015),

22; and Sharrona Pearl, *About Faces: Physiognomy in Nineteenth-Century Britain* (Cambridge, MA: Harvard University Press, 2010).

116   McClintock, *Imperial Leather*, 32; and Anandi Ramamurthy, *Imperial Persuaders: Images of Africa and Asia in British Advertising* (Manchester: Manchester University Press, 2003), chapter 2.

117   This contrasts an 1865 claim by Rimmel that there was "very limited use" of "perfumes, properly speaking" among those who he characterized as "know[ing] little or nothing of civilisation." See "Chapter IX: Uncivilized Nations" in Rimmel, *The Book of Perfumes*, 168.

118   "From Gay to Grave," 489.

119   "From Gay to Grave," 489.

120   "From Gay to Grave," 490.

121   Burke, *Lifebuoy Men, Lux Women*, 18.

122   Burke, *Lifebuoy Men, Lux Women*, especially 202–7.

123   Jones, *Beauty Imagined*, especially 287, 289, and chapter 9; and Timothy Burke, "The Modern Girl and Commodity Culture," in *The Modern Girl around the World: Consumption, Modernity, and Globalization*, ed. Alys Weinbaum et al. (Durham, NC: Duke University Press, 2008), 362–9.

124   This was especially evident in the growing popularity of skin-whitening products across global markets of colonial and postcolonial consumers. Burke, *Lifebuoy Men, Lux Women*, 158–61; Lynn M. Thomas, "Skin Lighteners, Black Consumers, and Jewish Entrepreneurs in South Africa," *History Workshop Journal* 73, no. 1 (2012): 263; and Alys Eve Weinbaum et al., "The Modern Girl around the World: Cosmetics Advertising and the Politics of Race and Style," in *The Modern Girl around the World: Consumption, Modernity, and Globalization*, ed. Alys Weinbaum et al. (Durham, NC: Duke University Press, 2008), 50.

125   Weinbaum et al., "Modern Girl," 51.

126   On commercial exploitation of colonial sites in the soap industry, see Ramamurthy, *Imperial Persuaders*, 25.

127   See, for example, Anandi Ramamurthy on representations of race in early-twentieth-century advertisements for Grossmith perfumes. Ramamurthy, *Imperial Persuaders*, 20. See also ads for New York firm Murray & Lanman in *Belgravia Holiday Number Advertiser, Midsummer 1881* (London: 214 Picadilly W., 1881), 11.

128   The pursuit of whiteness often led to the consumption of deleterious goods, including Laird's Bloom of Youth, as detailed by Alison Matthews David in *Fashion Victims: The Dangers of Dress Past and Present* (London: Bloomsbury,

2015), 22–4. For considerations of modern skin lightening, see Thomas, "Skin Lighteners" and her forthcoming work.

129	Steven R. B. Smith, "The Centenary of the London Chamber of Commerce: Its Origins and Early Policy," *London Journal* 8, no. 2 (1982): 156–70.

130	This included the gradual entry of Russian perfumery. Jones, *Beauty Imagined*, 27–8. For other nations, see Sydney Whiting, "Report on Perfumery. –(Class 25.)—," *Reports on the Paris Universal Exhibition, 1867, Volume II* (London: George E. Eyre and William Spottiswoode, 1868), 569–79.

131	Chemical Trades Section Minute Books (July 10, 1883), CLC/B/150/MS16583, 1883–1907, London Metropolitan Archives (LMA); and "The Manufacture of Perfumery," *Illustrated Weekly News* (September 20, 1862): 797.

132	"Export Trade and the Spirit Duties," *The Chemist and Druggist: The Newsweekly for Pharmacy* 29 (November 6, 1886): 615–16.

133	"Export Trade and the Spirit Duties," 616.

134	Specifically, in 1883, members of the LCC elected to remain under Customs regulations (or the bonded warehouse system) rather than come under the control of the Excise in the exporting of spirituous compounds. "[E]ven if extended facilities were given," LCC members concluded, "it was not to the interest of the Perfumery Trade that the facilities already enjoyed should be taken away." This failed to resolve the situation for firms that did not manufacture in bond. LCC members subsequently received complaints from a firm, in 1892, "that the Chamber had shown partiality in having hitherto only consulted the interests of a few of the firms in the trade," accusations that members "entirely repudiated." Chemical Trades Section Minute Books (July 10, 1883); Chemical Trades Section Minute Books (December 22, 1891); and Chemical Trades Section Minute Books (January 22, 1892), CLC/B/150/MS16583, 1883–1907, LMA.

135	Following Rimmel's death in 1887, the brand lost market share when his sons assumed its management. Jones, *Beauty Imagined*, 27. See also "Obituary," *The Chemist and Druggist* 30 (March 5, 1887): 292; "Obituary," *Aberdeen Weekly Journal* 9990 (February 28, 1887): n.p.; and "Obituary," *Pall Mall Gazette* 6849 (February 28, 1887): n.p.

136	"Between Ourselves," *Hairdressers' Chronicle and Trade Journal* 28 (London: R. Hovenden & Sons, Ltd., 1904): 2.

137	See, for example, Jones, *Beauty Imagined*, 20–1, 26–7.

138	Briot, "From Industry to Luxury"; and Jones, *Beauty Imagined*, 19–20.

139	On small-scale traders' resistance to universal providers and department stores more generally, see Erika D. Rappaport, *Shopping for Pleasure: Women in the Making of London's West End* (Princeton, NJ: Princeton University Press, 2000), 17–19.

5 Female Enterprise at the *Fin-de-Siècle:* Jeannette Pomeroy

1   In later years, Mrs. Pomeroy featured alongside complexion specialists like
    Madame Kadijah, Mrs. Spencer Ward, and H. P. Truefitt. By 1905, the number of
    complexion specialists listed in the *Post Office Directory* swelled to nine; by 1906,
    it featured twelve traders, of which nine were women. See *Post Office London
    Directory, 1897* (London: W. Kelly, 1897), 1805; *Post Office London Directory, 1903*
    (London: W. Kelly, 1903), 2692; *Post Office London Directory, 1904* (London: W.
    Kelly, 1904), 2024; *Post Office London Directory, 1905* (London: W. Kelly, 1905),
    2027; and *Post Office London Directory, 1906* (London: W. Kelly, 1906), 2033.

2   H. Ellen Browning, *Beauty Culture* (London: Hutchinson, 1898), 171; and "At Mrs.
    Pomeroy's," *Hearth and Home: An Illustrated Weekly Journal for Gentlewomen* 292
    (December 17, 1896): 239.

3   "Health and Personal Appearance," *Woman at Home* (n.d.): 185; "Advertisement,"
    Hearth and Home (April 6, 1899): 412; and *Post Office London Directory, 1903*
    (London: Kelly's & Co., 1903), 2692.

4   "Special Law Reports: Complexion Specialists at Law," *Daily Telegraph* (December
    13, 1906): 4. According to the National Archives, £21,000 in 1900 would have the
    same spending worth of £1,641,616 in 2017. See http://www.nationalarchives.gov.
    uk/currency, accessed September 19, 2011.

5   Great Britain Patent Office, *Reports of Patent, Design, and Trademark Cases* 24
    (London: Patent Office, 1907), 178.

6   "Miscellaneous," *The London Times* (October 6, 1906): 3.

7   The plaintiffs challenged Scalé's choice of locale, not to mention her use of a
    facsimiled signature, "which … appeared on the outside of all the preparations
    sold both by the old and new companies." The plaintiffs alleged that Scalé hired
    sandwich-board men who deliberately "promenaded in front of the [old company's]
    premises"; on their signs, "the word 'Jeannette' [appeared] very small, while 'Mrs.'
    and 'Pomeroy' were very large." "Miscellaneous," 3.

8   Pamela Sharpe, *Adapting to Capitalism: Working Women in the English Economy,
    1700–1850* (New York: St. Martin's Press, 1996), 149, adapted from W. A. Lewis,
    "Economic Development with Unlimited Supplies of Labour," *The Manchester
    School of Economic and Social Studies* 12 (1954): 139–91.

9   Ongoing work by Jennifer Aston and others challenge traditional narratives
    of the decline of female enterprise in this moment. See Jennifer Aston and Paolo
    Di Martino, "Risk, Success, and Failure: Female Entrepreneurship in Late Victorian
    and Edwardian England," *The Economic History Review* 70, no. 3 (2017):
    837–58; and Jennifer Aston, *Female Entrepreneurship in Nineteenth-Century
    England: Engagement in the Urban Economy* (London: Palgrave, 2016). For
    overviews, see Pat Hudson, "Women and Industrialization," in *Women's*

History: Britain, 1850–1945: An Introduction, ed. Jane Purvis (London: Routledge, 2000), 23–50; Nicola Phillips, *Women in Business, 1700–1850* (Woodbridge: Boydell Press, 2006), 3–14; Sharpe, *Adapting to Capitalism*, 6–8; and Sharpe, "Continuity and Change: Women's History and Economic History in Britain," *Economic History Review* 48, no. 2 (1995): 353–69.

10 New systems of advertising, growing anonymity in the expanding urban market, and novel forms of self-representation opened up possibilities for a certain kind of celebrated female entrepreneur that did not necessarily impinge upon businesswomen's respectability. For an earlier moment, see Alison C. Kay *The Foundations of Female Entrepreneurship: Enterprise, Home and Household, London c. 1800–1870* (London: Routledge, 2009), chapters 1 and 2.

11 On self-fashioning, see Jennifer Craik, *The Face of Fashion: Cultural Studies in Fashion* (London: Routledge, 1993), 4–5.

12 Great Britain Patent Office, *Reports of Patent*, 184.

13 I refer to Jeannette Scalé's "performance" in the Butlerian sense. Judith Butler, "Performative Acts and Gender Constitution: An Essay in Phenomenology and Feminist Theory," in *Performing Feminisms: Feminist Critical Theory and Theatre*, ed. Sue-Ellen Case (Baltimore, MD: The Johns Hopkins University Press, 1990), 279.

14 "At Mrs. Pomeroy's," 239.

15 On West End commercial development and constructions of bourgeois femininity, see Erika D. Rappaport, *Shopping for Pleasure: Women in the Making of London's West End* (Princeton, NJ: Princeton University Press, 2001), 5 and chapter 1. See also Lynne Walker, "Vistas of Pleasure: Women Consumers of Urban Space in the West End of London, 1850–1900," in *Women in the Victorian Art World*, ed. Clarissa Campbell Orr (Manchester: Manchester University Press, 1995), 70–85; and Judith R. Walkowitz, *City of Dreadful Delight: Narratives of Sexual Danger in Late-Victorian London* (Chicago, IL: University of Chicago Press, 1992), 46-52.

16 On the influx of lower-middle-class consumers, see Christopher P. Hosgood, "Mrs. Pooter's Purchase: Lower-Middle-Class Consumerism and the Sales, 1870–1914," in *Gender, Civic Culture and Consumerism: Middle-Class Identity in Britain, 1800-1940*, ed. Alan J. Kidd and David Nicholls (Manchester: Manchester University Press, 1999), 146. On Bond Street as an ongoing site of luxury retail, see Ivor Halstead, *Bond Street* (London: Barcliff Advertising, 1952), chapter 1.

17 *Olivia's Shopping and How She Does It: A Prejudiced Guide to the London Shops* (London: Gay and Bird, 1906), 24. On this text and other West End shopping guides, see Rappaport, *Shopping for Pleasure*, chapter 4.

18 Ina Zweiniger-Bargielowska, *Managing the Body: Beauty, Health, and Fitness in Britain 1880–1939* (New York: Oxford University Press, 2010).

19   Zweiniger-Bargielowska, *Managing the Body*, 4–5.

20   For example, John Gosnell & Co. registered as a limited liability corporation in 1898 and relocated to a large manufactory on Blackfriars Road in 1900.

21   This figure is from a 1911 survey. Halstead, *Bond Street*, 97.

22   In 1905, fifteen out of thirty-three beauty vendors on Bond Street were female. *Post Office London Directory, 1905* (London: W. Kelly, 1905), 615–16 and 638–9; and H. B. Wheatley, *A Short History of Bond Street, Old & New* (London: The Fine Art Society, 1911), 32–6. See Kathy Peiss, *Hope in a Jar: The Making of America's Beauty Culture* (New York: Metropolitan, 1998), chapter 3 for corresponding developments in the American beauty industry.

23   Jessica P. Clark, "Clever Ministrations: Regenerative Beauty at the *Fin de Siècle*," *Palgrave Communications* 3, no. 47 (2017): n.p. For historical takes, see, for example, "Curious Characters of Modern Life: The Beauty Doctor," *The Morpeth Herald* (November 5, 1904): 6.

24   *Post Office London Directory, 1911* (London: W. Kelly, 1911), 1555; "The Woman about Town," *The Sketch* (September 16, 1908): 332; and "The Highway of Fashion," *The Tatler* (January 28, 1920): 34.

25   James Bennett, "Cyclax," *Cosmetics and Skin*, January 23, 2019, http://www.cosmeticsandskin.com/companies/cyclax.php.

26   "Mrs. Adair, Patronised by Royalty," *The Tatler* 271 (September 5, 1906): iv. On Adair, see the exhaustive research of James Bennett, http://www.cosmeticsandskin.com/companies/adair.php.

27   For more on conceptions of glamour and its effects on twentieth-century beauty culture, see Carol Dyhouse, *Glamour: Women, History, Feminism* (London: Zed Books, 2010). For more on Rubinstein, see chapter 6. See also Ruth Brandon, *Ugly Beauty: Helena Rubinstein, L'Oreal, and the Blemished History of Looking Good* (New York: HarperCollins, 2011); Geoffrey Jones, *Beauty Imagined: A History of the Global Beauty Industry* (New York: Oxford University Press, 2010), 59–60; and Lindy Woodhead, *War Paint: Madame Helena Rubinstein and Miss Elizabeth Arden: Their Lives, Their Times, Their Rivalry* (London: Virago, 2003).

28   Woodhead, *War Paint*, 92; and *Post Office London Directory, 1905* (London: W. Kelly, 1905).

29   "La Toilette des Mains," *Le Follet, Journal du Grand Monde, Fashion, Polite Literature, Beaux Arts &c. &c.* 5201 (December 1, 1889): 58.

30   "Your Finger Nails," *Pall Mall Gazette* 7491 (March 21, 1899): 7.

31   Carmichael offered manicure services alongside neighbors Sarah Dean, who ran a parlor at 26 Old Bond Street, and Grace Maud Stanley, who worked out of a private residence at 41 New Bond Street. Madame Gwen Curzon of 118 New Bond Street was the thoroughfare's earliest female manicurist, but seems to have moved on by the mid-1890s. *Post Office London Directory, 1895* (London: W. Kelly, 1895); *Post*

Office London Directory, 1900 (London: W. Kelly, 1900); and *Census Returns of England and Wales, 1901*, class RG13, piece 81, folio 57, p. 55, www.ancestry.co.uk.

32 *Post Office London Directory, 1915* (London: W. Kelly, 1915), 1713. The six non-female listings were large (familiar) firms that most likely employed female manicurists to serve customers: Melville Carmichael, Robert Douglas, Arthur Kosmeo, Shipwright's & The Universities' Toilet Club & Hat Co. Ltd., H. P. Truefitt, and Willshear & Boome.

33 Anna Ruppert published a number of tracts. See, for example, *Dermatology. A Book of Beauty: Containing a Choice Collection of Receipts for Beautifying the Face and Form* (London: Anna Ruppert, 1892); and *Natural Beauty: Or, the Secrets of the Toilet. A Lecture, etc.* (London: Anna Ruppert, 1892).

34 "Advertisement," *Hearth and Home* (December 3, 1891): 61; "Mrs. Anna Ruppert's Lecture," *Hearth and Home* (December 24, 1891): 181; and Miscellaneous, *Hearth and Home* (May 26, 1892): 53.

35 Carolyn Rance, "Madame Ruppert's Beauty Secrets," *Wellcome Library Blog*, February 3, 2016, http://blog.wellcomelibrary.org/2016/02/madame-rupperts-beauty-secrets/. For Ruppert's *Hearth and Home* columns see, for example, Ruppert, "A Few Wrinkles Upon Wrinkles," *Hearth and Home* (February 9, 1893): 384; "Health and Beauty," *Hearth and Home* (May 4, 1893): 794; and "Natural Beauty," *Hearth and Home* (January 19, 1893): 284.

36 Three excellent blog posts explore Ruppert's legacy as an individual provider and alleged fraud. See Rance, "Madame Ruppert's Beauty Secrets," 2016; Michelle Smith, "Friday Essay: Toxic Beauty, Then and Now," *The Conversation*, October 19, 2017, http://theconversation.com/friday-essay-toxic-beauty-then-and-now-84267; and Lee Jackson, "Who Was Anna Ruppert?" *The Cat Meat's Shop*, September 24, 2010, http://catsmeatshopblogspot.ca/2010/09/who-was-anna-ruppert.html.

37 Anne M. Sebba, "Ballin, Ada Sarah (1862–1906)," in *Oxford Dictionary of National Biography*, September 23, 2004, http://www.oxforddnb.com/view/article/55732. Ballin's fall from a window at her Portland Square home was ruled accidental.

38 "A Good Complexion," *Woman's Signal* (December 17, 1896): 155.

39 Ruppert, *Dermatology*, preface.

40 Arthur Marwick, *Beauty in History: Society, Politics and Personal Appearance c. 1500 to the Present* (London: Thames and Hudson, 1988), 220–6.

41 See also "Mrs. Anna Ruppert's Lecture," *Myra's Journal* (January 1, 1892): 30.

42 I have yet to locate a surviving copy of Pomeroy's *Beauty Rules*, although advertisements and personal correspondence describe the "little booklet" as providing advice on health, exercise, and appearance. See also E. Sanders, *Practical Face Treatment and Natural Beauty* (London: Truslove, Hanson & Comba, 1903); M. Elise, *Secrets of Fascination* (Birmingham: W. Lake, 1906); OH Hara, *Complexion Beautiful; or New Skins for Old* (London: L. N. Fowler, 1907);

and Helen Gent, *Health and Beauty for Women and Girls* (London: Health & Strength, 1909).

43   Sanders, *Practical*, 7.

44   Marwick cites the lack of advertisements in some texts to argue that "[i]f one were to comb through the literature constantly seeking overt commercial motivation one would be disappointed." However, this fails to take into account the commercial standing of many of these authors, who encouraged custom merely through their textual presence as experts and arbiters of taste. Marwick, *Beauty in History*, 230.

45   "Making New Faces," *Daily Mail* (November 16, 1898): 7.

46   On women's shifting public role at the *fin de siècle*, see, for example, Kay Heath, *Aging by the Book: The Emergence of Midlife in Victorian Britain* (Albany: State University of New York Press, 2009), 15; Sandra Holton, "The Women's Movement, Politics and Citizenship from the Late Nineteenth Century until 1918," in *Women in Twentieth-Century Britain*, ed. Ina Zweiniger-Bargielowska (Harlow: Longman, 2001), 247–61; Kathryn Gleadle, *British Women in the Nineteenth Century* (New York: Palgrave Macmillan, 2001), chapter 11; Ellen Jordan, *The Women's Movement and Women's Employment in Nineteenth Century Britain* (New York: Routledge, 1999); and Judith R. Walkowitz, "Going Public: Shopping, Street Harassment, and Streetwalking in Late Victorian London," *Representations* 62 (1998): 1–30.

47   "The Hunt after Beauty," *Daily Mirror* (January 12, 1904): 11

48   Peiss observes corresponding rhetorics in the American case. Peiss, *Hope in a Jar*, 86.

49   "The Hunt after Beauty," *Daily Mirror* (December 9, 1903): 6.

50   There was also the process of facial skinning or early chemical peels, perhaps the least publicized of beauty treatments. Quoting Joan Kron, Teresa Riordan notes that the 1880s saw the proliferation of "skinning" in the United States as a "thriving, unregulated business." Kron, *Lift: Wanting, Fearing, and Having a Facelift* (New York: Penguin Books, 2000), 145 in Teresa Riordan, *Inventing Beauty: A History of the Innovations That Have Made Us Beautiful* (New York: Broadway, 2004), 164.

51   Peiss, *Hope in a Jar*, 31–5; and Lynn M. Thomas, "Skin Lighteners, Black Consumers, and Jewish Entrepreneurs in South Africa," *History Workshop Journal* 73, no. 1 (2012): 263.

52   On mid-century developments leading up to this shift, see Sadiah Qureshi, *Peoples on Parade: Exhibitions, Empire, and Anthropology in Nineteenth-Century Britain* (Chicago, IL: University of Chicago Press, 2011), 211–18.

53   Timothy Burke, *Lifebuoy Men, Lux Women: Commodification, Consumption, and Cleanliness in Modern Zimbabwe* (Durham, NC: Duke University Press, 1996); Anne McClintock, *Imperial Leather: Race, Gender, and Sexuality in the*

Colonial Contest (New York: Routledge, 1995), chapter 5; and John M. MacKenzie, *Propaganda and Empire: The Manipulation of British Public Opinion, 1880–1960* (Manchester: Manchester University Press, 1984), 7 and chapter 1.

54 Peiss, *Hope in a Jar*, 42. On cosmetics, ethnic identity, and physical appearance in *fin de siècle* literature, see Elizabeth Carolyn Miller, "'Shrewd Women of Business': Madame Rachel, Victorian Consumerism, and L.T. Meade's *The Sorceress of the Strand*," *Victorian Literature and Culture* 34, no. 1 (2006): 324–6.

55 Kim F. Hall, *Things of Darkness: Economies of Race and Gender in Early Modern England* (Ithaca, NY: Cornell University Press, 1995).

56 Smith, "Friday Essay." On skin lighteners in the American context and Ruppert's bleach, see Peiss, *Hope in a Jar*, 40–3 and 85.

57 Alison Matthews David, *Fashion Victims: The Dangers of Dress Past and Present* (London: Bloomsbury, 2015), 22–4. See also Gwen Kay, *Dying to Be Beautiful: The Fight for Safe Cosmetics* (Columbus: Ohio State University, 2005); and Peiss, *Hope in a Jar*, 21–2 and 41–3.

58 See, for example, Thomas, "Skin Lighteners," 264; Tania Woloshyn, *Soaking Up the Rays: Light Therapy and Visual Culture in Britain, c. 1890–1940* (Manchester: Manchester University Press, 2017); and Zweiniger-Bargielowska, *Managing the Body*, 167–8 and 293–309.

59 Thomas Richards, *The Commodity Culture of Victorian England: Advertising and Spectacle, 1851–1914* (Stanford, CA: Stanford University Press, 1990), 5. See also Heath, *Aging by the Book*, 16; Lori Loeb, *Consuming Angels: Advertising and Victorian Women* (New York: Oxford University Press, 1994), 5; and T. R. Nevett, *Advertising in Britain: A History* (London: Heinemann, 1982), chapter 5.

60 On advertorials, see Margaret Beetham and Kay Boardman, eds. *Victorian Women's Magazines: An Anthology* (Manchester: Manchester University Press, 2001), 5; and Michelle J. Smith, "Beauty Advertising and Advice in the *Queen* and *Woman*," in *Women, Periodicals and Print Culture in Britain, 1830s-1900s: The Victorian Period*, ed. Alexis Easley, Clare Gill, and Beth Rodgers (Edinburgh: University of Edinburgh Press, 2019), 225–9.

61 One strategy to combat criticism was to emphasize the "natural" qualities of beauty goods and services. This was especially evident in another textual form of the *fin de siècle*, the woman's magazine. In periodicals like *The Queen* and *Woman*, Smith shows that magazine copy advanced messages about natural beauty, often on the very same page as promotions for artificial beauty goods and regimens. Smith, "Beauty Advertising."

62 Church notes that, in general, "products linked to personal hygiene and appearance were … the subjects of persuasive advertising from the mid-century." Roy Church, "Advertising Consumer Goods in Nineteenth-Century Britain: Reinterpretations," *Economic History Review* 53, no. 4 (2000): 642–3.

63 For example, the London Metropolitan Police investigated female-run massage and manicure parlors at the turn of the century. On the "Massage Scandal," see Takahiro Ueyama, *Health in the Marketplace: Professionalism, Therapeutic Desires, and Medical Commodification in Late-Victorian London* (Palo Alto, CA: The Society for the Promotion of Science and Scholarship, 2010); Julia Laite, *Common Prostitutes and Ordinary Citizens: Commercial Sex in London, 1885–1960* (London: Palgrave Macmillan, 2012), chapter 3; and "Bylaws: London County Council, Registration of Massage Establishments," The National Archives PRO HO 45/10912/A56.145/25.

64 Zweiniger-Bargielowska, *Managing the Body*, 4–5.

65 "Special Law Reports: Complexion Specialists at Law," 4.

66 "Up and Down Bond Street," *The Graphic* (May 12, 1883): 702. There was also the matter of national competition from across the Channel. See, for example, Rose Barton, *Familiar London* (London: Adam and Charles Black, 1904), 189–90.

67 Mrs. Aria, "My Lady's Afternoon in London," in *Living London: Its Work and Its Play, Its Humour and Its Pathos, Its Sights and Its Scenes, Volume I...* , ed. George Robert Sims (London: Cassell, 1902), 42.

68 Another notable characteristic of Mrs. Pomeroy, Ltd. shareholders was their gender and marital status; the majority of stakeholders were widows. Stana Nenadic finds similar trends among businesses run by women in Edinburgh. See Nenadic, "Gender and the Rhetoric of Business Success: The Impact on Women Entrepreneurs and the 'New Woman' in Late Nineteenth Century Edinburgh," in *Women's Work in Industrial England: Regional and Local Perspectives*, ed. Nigel Goose (Hatfield: Location Population Studies, 2007), 272–3.

69 "Special Law Reports: Complexion Specialists at Law," 4.

70 Jones, *Beauty Imagined*, chapter 1.

71 "A Chat with Mrs. Pomeroy," *Hearth and Home* 16, no. 405 (February 16, 1899): 589.

72 Mrs. Aria, *Living London*, 44.

73 "Beauty's Penetralia," *Daily Mail* (January 1, 1904): 10.

74 "A Good Complexion," *Woman's Signal* (December 17, 1896): 155.

75 "The Experiences of a Pilgrim of Seventeen in Search of Prettiness: The Hunt after Beauty," *Daily Mirror* (December 10, 1903): 11.

76 The Pomeroy case represents an early mode of marketing. See Roy Church and Andrew Godley, "The Emergence of Modern Marketing: International Dimensions," *Business History* 45, no. 1 (2003): i–v.

77 Jeannette Shepherd Hauser to Jeannette Hauser Jobbins, February 24, 1901, Rosser-Hauser Family Papers, Archives of Ohio United Methodism, Delaware Ohio (hereafter AOUM).

78 "Result of Mrs. Pomeroy's Design Competition," *Hearth and Home* 425 (July 6, 1899): 355.

79 Jeannette Shepherd Hauser to Jeannette Hauser Jobbins, February 24, 1901, AOUM.

80 Smith, "Beauty Advertising," 225. On actresses, self-fashioning, and artificiality, see also Christopher Breward, *Fashioning London: Clothing and the Modern Metropolis* (Oxford: Berg, 2004), chapter 3.

81 Joseph Roach, "Celebrity Erotics: Pepys, Performance, and Painted Ladies," *Yale Journal of Criticism* 16, no. 1 (2003): 215. See also Lenard R. Berlanstein, "Historicizing and Gendering Celebrity Culture: Famous Women in Nineteenth-Century France," *Journal of Women's History* 16, no. 4 (2004): 67; and Catherine Hindson, *Female Performance Practice on the Fin-de-Siècle Popular Stages of London and Paris: Experiment and Advertisement* (Manchester: Manchester University Press, 2007).

82 By contrast, Roach argues for the erotic dimensions of these public intimacies, but this was not the apparent motivation behind Mrs. Pomeroy's revelations.

83 "A Chat with Mrs. Pomeroy," 589.

84 John Duguid Milne, *Industrial Employment of Women in the Middle and Lower Ranks* (London: Longmans, Green, 1870), 129. Cited in Kay, *Foundations*, 11.

85 "She Comes to Beautify Women," *Olympia Recorder* 4, no. 181 (December 8, 1905): 11.

86 On nineteenth-century developments in middle-class domestic ideology and models of femininity, see Elizabeth Langland, *Nobody's Angels: Middle-Class Women and Domestic Ideology in Victorian Culture* (Ithaca, NY: Cornell University Press, 1995).

87 "She Comes to Beautify Women," 11.

88 Iveta Jusová, *The New Woman and the Empire* (Columbus: Ohio State University Press, 2005), 34.

89 "A Chat with Mrs. Pomeroy," 589.

90 "A Chat with Mrs. Pomeroy," 589.

91 Jeannette Hauser Jobbins to Miriam Hauser Rosser, February 19, 1903, AOUM.

92 Jeannette Shepherd Hauser to Miriam Hauser Rosser, November 24, 1902, AOUM.

93 By fixing the focus on Mrs. Pomeroy, "the single human being," Scalé ensured her "constantly replicated image [began] to create in the beholder an entirely specious sense of knowing the person depicted." Alison Hennegan, "Personalities and Principles: Aspects of Literature and Life in *Fin-De-Siècle* England," in *Fin de Siècle and Its Legacy*, ed. Mikuláš Teich and Roy Porter (London: Cambridge University Press, 1990), 186.

94 Scalé's mother, Jeannette Shepherd Hauser (1840–1923), led the first Woman's Christian Temperance Union in India and authored *The Orient and Its People* (Milwaukee: I. L. Hauser, 1876). See Ian R. Tyrell, *Woman's World/Woman's Empire: The Woman's Christian Temperance Union in International Perspective, 1800–1930* (Chapel Hill: University of North Carolina Press, 1991), 164.

95 Jeannette Hauser Jobbins to Jeannette Shepherd Hauser, October 2, 1895, AOUM.

96 Jeannette Hauser Jobbins to Jeannette Shepherd Hauser, October 22, 1895, AOUM.

97 Great Britain Patent Office, *Reports of Patent*, 180. Inspiration for the name "Pomeroy" originated during Jeannette and Bernard's honeymoon at Berry Pomeroy Castle in Devon, with Jeannette also claiming matrilineal connections to the Pomeroy line. National Society, Daughters of the American Revolution, *Lineage Books of the Charter Members of the National Society of the Daughters of the American Revolution*. Vol. I-CLII (152 vols.) (Washington, DC, 1899–1938).

98 Jeannette Shepherd Hauser to Miriam Hauser Rosser, November 11, 1902, AOUM.

99 Bernard Scalé to Miriam Hauser Rosser, April 16, 1905, AOUM.

100 Great Britain Patent Office, *Reports of Patent*, 184.

101 Jeannette Shepherd Hauser to Miriam Hauser Rosser, November 11, 1902, AOUM.

102 Jeannette Shepherd Hauser to Miriam Hauser Rosser, October 20, 1903, AOUM.

103 Jeannette Shepherd Hauser to Miriam Hauser Rosser, November 24, 1902, AOUM.

104 Jeannette Shepherd Hauser to Miriam Hauser Rosser, June 8, 1903, AOUM; and G. S. Street, "Bayswater and St. John's Wood," in *A Book of Essays* (London: A. Constable, 1902), 41.

105 Jeannette Hauser Jobbins to Miriam Hauser Rosser, November 8, 1905, AOUM; and Bernard Scalé to Miriam Hauser Rosser, February 28, 1905, AOUM.

106 Jeannette Shepherd Hauser to Miriam Hauser Rosser, October 20, 1903, AOUM.

107 "Lady's Name Riddle," *Daily Mirror* (December 12, 1906): 4.

108 Jeannette Hauser Jobbins to Miriam Hauser Rosser, November 5, 1905, AOUM.

109 Jeannette Shepherd Hauser to Miriam Hauser Rosser, November 24, 1902, AOUM.

110 Jeannette Shepherd Hauser to Miriam Hauser Rosser, June 8, 1903, AOUM.

111 Jeannette Shepherd Hauser to Miriam Hauser Rosser, April 19, 1903, AOUM.

112 Rappaport, *Shopping*, 144–51.

113 Jeannette Shepherd Hauser to Jeannette Hauser Jobbins, January 13, 1901, AOUM.

114 Jeannette Hauser Jobbins to I. L. Hauser, September 22, 1908, AOUM.

115 Rappaport, *Shopping*, especially chapter 1.

116 Rappaport, *Shopping*, especially chapter 5. For criticisms of these shifts in an earlier moment aimed specifically at William Whiteley's Bayswater operations, see Rappaport, *Shopping*, 37–9.

117 Margot C. Finn, *The Character of Credit: Personal Debt in English Culture, 1740-1914* (New York: Cambridge University Press, 2003), 89. Finn contests this narrative, arguing for the perpetuation of traditional vendor–patron relations in modern shopping experiences.

118 See Craig Muldrew, *The Economy of Obligation: The Culture of Credit and Social Relations in Early Modern England* (Basingstoke: Palgrave Macmillan, 1998), 148; Finn, *The Character of Credit*, 279; Wendy Gamber, "A Gendered Enterprise: Placing Nineteenth-Century Businesswomen in History," *Business History Review* 72, no. 2, Gender and Business (Summer 1998): 188–217; and Michael Winstanley, *The Shopkeeper's World 1830–1914* (Manchester: Manchester University Press, 1983), 217.

119 See Finn, *The Character of Credit*, 279. On conceptions of modernity in the Victorian metropolis, see Simon Gunn, "The Public Sphere, Modernity, and Consumption: New Perspectives on the History of the Middle Class," in *Gender, Civic Culture and Consumerism: Middle-Class Identity in Britain, 1800-1940*, ed. Alan J. Kidd and David Nicholls (London: Manchester University Press, 1999), 12; and Martin Daunton and Bernhard Rieger, eds. *Meanings of Modernity: Britain from the Late-Victorian Era to World War II* (Oxford: Berg, 2001), particularly the contribution by Erika Rappaport.

120 Great Britain Patent Office, *Reports of Patent*, 183.

121 "Special Law Reports: Complexion Specialists at Law," 4.

122 "Lady's Name Riddle," 4.

123 "'Beauty' In the Courts," *Daily Mirror* (December 11, 1906): 4.

124 "Special Law Reports: Complexion Specialists at Law," 4.

125 "Special Law Reports: Complexion Specialists at Law," 4.

126 "Special Law Reports: Complexion Specialists at Law," 4.

127 "Special Law Reports: Complexion Specialists at Law," 4.

128 "How Mrs. Pomeroy Got Her Name," *Daily Mirror* (December 13, 1906): 4.

129 "Special Law Reports: Complexion Specialists at Law," 4.

130 Great Britain Patent Office, *Reports of Patent*, 186. Emphasis theirs.

131 Great Britain Patent Office, *Reports of Patent*, 187.

132 John Millar, *An Historical View of English Government, Volume IV* (London: Mawman, 1803), 279, quoted in Phillips, *Women in Business*, 69.

133 Great Britain Patent Office, *Reports of Patent*, 192.

134 London Chamber of Commerce, "Use of Name on Sale of Business," *The Chamber of Commerce Journal* 26 (1907): 70.

135 Great Britain Patent Office, *Reports of Patent*, 191. Emphasis in original.

136 "Lady's Name Riddle," 4.

137 "How Mrs. Pomeroy Got Her Name," 4.

138 The second short-lived business was registered as "Altona."

139 Jeannette Shepherd Hauser to Miriam Hauser Rosser, April 15, 1910, AOUM. Jeannette Hauser attempted to aid Scalé. She invested substantial funds in all three of Scalé's companies and registered the latter two in her own name. Following Scalé's final failure, creditors contacted Hauser, who was "liable for a claim which

[Scalé's] partner could make if she was ugly or unprincipled." Scalé used the money Hauser forwarded "to start the business [Altona] instead of coming [home] to America," as her mother had requested. Jeannette Shepherd Hauser to Miriam Hauser Rosser, August 21, 1910, AOUM.

140   Jeannette Hauser Jobbins to Miriam Hauser Rosser, March 3, 1909, AOUM; Jeannette Hauser Jobbins to Miriam Hauser Rosser, October 16, 1909, AOUM; and Jeannette Hauser Jobbins to Miriam Hauser Rosser, July 20, 1909, AOUM. Departing Southampton at age 48, Scalé listed her mother's Chicago address as her American destination. Ellis Island Foundation, "The American Family Immigration History Center's Ellis Island Archive," *Ellis Island* (The Statue of Liberty-Ellis Island Foundation Inc., 2009) Web (February 24, 2009), http://www. ellisislandrecords.org/.

141   "Classified Advertisements," *London Times* 51175 (September 13, 1948): 7.

142   On the importance of "business personas," see Kay, *Foundations*, 26–7.

143   On Ruppert's demise, see Clark, "Clever Ministrations"; Jackson, "Who Was Anna Ruppert?"; Rance, "Madame Ruppert's Beauty Secrets"; and Smith, "Beauty Advertising," 227.

144   See Clark, "Clever Ministrations," for further examples of beauty "doctor" scandals.

6 From Beauty Culturists to Beauty Magnates: Helena Rubinstein

1   Ann-Carol Grossman et al., "Film Description," *The Powder & the Glory Promotional Website*, December 21, 2011, www.powderandglory.com/ filmdescription.php.

2   See, for example, Lindy Woodhead, *War Paint: Madame Helena Rubinstein and Miss Elizabeth Arden: Their Lives, Their Times, Their Rivalry* (London: Virago, 2003); and Grossman et al., *The Powder & the Glory* (Alexandria: PBS Home Video, 2007).

3   According to Woodhead, "Australia was her testing ground, Europe her finishing school, but America was her goldmine." Woodhead, *War Paint*, 105. See also the 2007 documentary film *The Powder & the Glory*. Transforming herself into an international brand through the 1920s, Rubinstein's expansion into wholesaling was reportedly one source of her considerable financial success. In 1928, the sale of her American firm to major chemist wholesalers made her one of the richest women in America; her repurchase of the firm some three years later garnered a $6 million profit. With a passion for modernist art and architecture, Rubinstein

also became a generous benefactor of New York's art community and a fixture on the urban art scene.

4   A focus on individual enterprise engendered by the modern American market is a common trend in business and entrepreneurial history and a result of both historical and historiographic trends. See, for example, Virginia Drachman, *Enterprising Women: 250 Years of American Business* (Chapel Hill: University of North Carolina Press, 2002); Alfred Allan Lewis and Constance Woodworth, *Miss Elizabeth Arden* (New York: Coward, McCann & Geoghegan, 1972); Patrick O'Higgins, *Madame: An Intimate Biography of Helena Rubinstein* (New York: Viking Press, 1971); and Suzanne Slesin, *Over the Top: Helena Rubinstein: Extraordinary Style, Beauty, Art, Fashion, and Design* (New York: Pointed Leaf Press, 2003).

5   This suggests the transnational implications of Rubinstein's story. On global beauty markets and their consumers, see Geoffrey Jones, *Beauty Imagined: A History of the Global Beauty Industry* (New York: Oxford University Press, 2010); Timothy Burke, *Lifebuoy Men, Lux Women: Commodification, Consumption, and Cleanliness in Modern Zimbabwe* (Durham, NC: Duke University Press, 1996); and Alys Weinbaum et al., *The Modern Girl around the World: Consumption, Modernity, and Globalization* (Chapel Hill, NC: Duke University Press, 2010).

6   Ruth Brandon, *Ugly Beauty: Helena Rubinstein, L'Oreal, and the Blemished History of Looking Good* (New York: HarperCollins, 2011), 7.

7   The Valaze line included a Cream, Herbal Complexion Soap, Skin Lotion, Face Powder, Skin Tonic, and Hair Tonic. See, for example, "Classified Advertisements," *The Argus [Melbourne]* (March 5, 1903): 10; "Classified Advertisements," *Australian Town and Country Journal* (December 14, 1904): 15; and "Classified Advertisements," *The [Adelaide] Register* (November 1904): 3. On Australian women and colonial whiteness, see Angela Woollacott, "'All This Is the Empire, I Told Myself': Australian Women's Voyages 'Home' and the Articulation of Colonial Whiteness," *American Historical Review* 102, no. 4 (October 1997): 1003–29.

8   "At the Maison de Beauté Valaze," *Strand Magazine* 36 (May–December 1908): 152. On her naturalization in 1907, see Woodhead, *War Paint*, 48.

9   Angela Woollacott, *To Try Her Fortune in London: Australian Women, Colonialism, and Modernity* (London: Oxford University Press, 2001), 6–7.

10 Helena Rubinstein, *My Life for Beauty* (New York: Simon and Schuster, 1966), 34.

11 The Charles Booth Archive at the London School of Economics and Political Science, Notebook B358 (January 30, 1899): 176–7.

12 Quoted in Woodhead, *War Paint*, 71. See also Erika D. Rappaport, *Shopping for Pleasure: Women in the Making of London's West End* (Princeton, NJ: Princeton University Press, 2001), 151.

13 Rubinstein, *My Life*, 35.

14 During her search, Rubinstein shared rooms in Arlington Street with a young Australian woman who had arrived in London around the same time. Rubinstein, *My Life*, 36–7. On Australian women's emigration to London in this period, see Woollacott, *To Try Her Fortune*.

15 Rubinstein, *My Life*, 37. She reportedly came to London with £12,000 from her Australian venture.

16 *Census Returns of England and Wales, 1911*, class RG14, piece 417, enumeration district 3, www.ancestry.co.uk; and Rubinstein, *My Life*, 45. This seemingly did not induce the opprobrium of the previous century, however, and Rubinstein describes hosting elaborate dinner parties for leading Mayfair personalities and "creative people."

17 In 1908, the West End also hosted ten electrolysis operators, all women; twenty nine manicurists, of which twenty two were obviously female; and thirty one masseuses, of which sixteen were obviously female. *Post Office London Directory, 1908* (London: W. Kelly, 1908), 2120, 2309, 2314.

18 See chapter 5, note 46.

19 Jessica P. Clark, "Clever Ministrations: Regenerative Beauty at the *Fin de Siècle*," *Palgrave Communications* 3, no. 47 (2017): n.p.; and Michelle Smith, "Beauty Advertising and Advice in the *Queen* and *Woman*," in *Women, Periodicals and Print Culture in Britain, 1830s-1900s: The Victorian Period*, ed. Alexis Easley, Clare Gill, and Beth Rodgers (Edinburgh: University of Edinburgh Press, 2019), 218–31.

20 "Special Law Reports," *Daily Mail* 4752 (July 1, 1911): 6.

21 Brandon, *Ugly Beauty*, 21.

22 [Rebecca Insley Casper], *Intimacies of Court and Society; an Unconventional Narrative of Unofficial Days by the Widow of a Diplomat* (London: Hurst and Blackett, 1912), 216.

23 Rubinstein took careful steps to prevent the public revelation of her client list. As Leverson and Scalé had done before her, Rubinstein refused to submit her books—and subsequently disclose her list of clientele—in the course of the 1911 trial. "King's Bench Division," *The London Times* 39626 (July 1, 1911): 3.

24 Rubinstein, *My Life*, 33. Also quoted in Brandon, *Ugly Beauty*, 22.

25 Despite losing money in her first two years of business, she reportedly spent £20,000 on advertising in 1911. "King's Bench Division," 3. She was not the only London-based firm offering "free trials" of beautifying goods and services. Through 1911, Oatine Company of Southwark distributed sample kits to potential new clients. "Free Toilet Soap," *Penny Illustrated Paper* 2599 (March 18, 1911): 350.

26 Helena Rubinstein, *Beauty in the Making* (New York: Mme. Helena Rubinstein, 1915), 39–40. Available at *Cosmetics and Skin*, http://www.cosmeticsandskin.com/booklets/rubinstein-making.php.

27 "Maison de Beauté Valaze. II.—The New Cult of Beauty," *London Times* (July 13, 1909): 12; and James Bennett, "Helena Rubinstein," *Cosmetics and Skin*, http://www. cosmeticsandskin.com/companies/helena-rubinstein.php, accessed April 25, 2019.

28 Bennett, "Helena Rubinstein." Rubinstein tells of one famous patron who had "suffered for years with acute acne." She describes using daring new peeling treatments, which transformed her from a "hurt, tragic woman" to one who was free of selfconsciousness. Rubinstein, *My Life*, 43.

29 Rubinstein, *My Life*, 43.

30 "Maison de Beauté Valaze. II.—The New Cult of Beauty," 12.

31 Woodhead, *War Paint*, 35.

32 "'Beauty' Specialist's Action," *Birmingham Mail* (July 1, 1911): 6.

33 Woodhead, *War Paint*, 87. This characterization of Putney comes from Charles Booth's analysis of local church attendance. See Booth, *Life and Labour of the People in London: South-East and South-West London. Third Series: Religious Influences* (London: Macmillan, 1902), 210. On Rubinstein's New York salons, see Marie J. Clifford, "Helena Rubinstein's Beauty Salons, Fashion, and Modernist Display," *Winterthur Portfolio* 38, nos. 2/3 (Summer-Autumn 2003): 83–108. Rubinstein's two sons were born during her time in London. When they relocated to Paris, she left her sister Manka in charge of the London shop, another move reminiscent of an earlier generation of London's beauty entrepreneurs.

34 Kristin Hoganson, "The Fashionable World: Imagined Communities of Dress," in *After the Imperial Turn: Thinking with and Through the Nation*, ed. Antoinette Burton (Durham, NC: Duke University Press, 2003), 260–78.

35 For their wedding dinner menu, see Rare Book Division, New York Public Library, "Dinner [held by] H. Winterfeldt [at] 'Waldorf-Astoria, New York' (Hotel)," New York Public Library Digital Collections, http://digitalcollections.nypl.org/ items/510d47db-7566-a3d9-e040-e00a18064a99. I am indebted to the work of family researchers at Ancestry.co.uk, who charted and made public Louise Winterfeldt's early—and complicated—life story. This includes Diane Hitchcox (DianeHitchcox64) and Mrs. L. Blake-Mizen (LBlakeMizen).

36 See, for example, "A Pot-Pourri of Fashions—Millinery and Spring Gowns," *New York Times* (March 24, 1907): S7; "Social Notes," *New York Times* (December 19, 1909): 11; and "Social Notes," *New York Times* (March 4, 1910): 9. On American aristocrats, identity, and fashion writing, see Hoganson, "The Fashionable World," 265–6.

37 Woollacott, *To Try Her Fortune*, 5.

38 On London as a financial and imperial hub in this period, see Jonathan Schneer, *London 1900: The Imperial Metropolis* (New Haven, CT: Yale University Press, 1999), 7; and Joseph De Sapio, *Modernity and Meaning in Victorian London: Tourist Views of the Imperial Capital* (Basingstoke: Palgrave Macmillan, 2014).

39 The London season was "roughly the period from late March until early August, which coincided with the sitting of Parliament, when the wealthy and influential came to the capital for a hectic round of social engagements." On the social season, see Alison C. Kay, "Retailing, Respectability and the Independent Woman in Nineteenth-Century London," in *Women, Business and Finance in Nineteenth-Century Europe: Rethinking Separate Spheres*, ed. Robert Beachy, Béatrice Craig, and Alastair Owens (Oxford: Berg, 2006), 161; and Leonore Davidoff, *The Best Circles: Society Etiquette and the Season* (London: Croom Helm, 1973).

40 See, for example, Antoinette Burton, *At the Heart of the Empire: Indians and the Colonial Encounter in Late-Victorian Britain* (Berkeley: University of California Press, 1998); Cecilia Morgan, *A Happy Holiday: English Canadians and Transatlantic Tourism, 1870–1930* (Toronto: University of Toronto Press, 2007); Schneer, *London 1900*; and Woollacott, *To Try Her Fortune*.

41 Insley Casper, *Intimacies of Court and Society*, 216–17 and 277. For an earlier moment, see William W. Stowe, *Going Abroad: European Travel in Nineteenth-Century American Culture* (Princeton, NJ: Princeton University Press, 1994).

42 Insley Casper, *Intimacies of Court and Society*, 231.

43 Insley Casper, *Intimacies of Court and Society*, 220. Insley Casper describes an incident at the opening of Parliament in February 1911 when two peers stumbled upon "a lady's powder puff in a little blue silk bag" that induced fits of laughter. "If the gallant Edward had been there to come upon the scene, wearing his Order of the Garter, *Honi soit qui mal y pense*, he might have again turned feminine embarrassment into lasting glory, and instituted 'The Royal Order of the Powder Puff.'" Insley Casper, *Intimacies of Court and Society*, 236–7.

44 Insley Casper, *Intimacies of Court and Society*, 271.

45 Insley Casper, *Intimacies of Court and Society*, 272.

46 On Americans in the West End, see Rappaport, *Shopping for Pleasure*, 138–9 and 149–53.

47 For example, following her loss of the Mrs. Pomeroy name, Jeannette Scalé's final business suffered in the wake of Edward VII's death in 1910. "The brilliant social season, which she depended on so much to tide her over the beginning of her new business venture, is all turned to mourning," wrote her mother, "And we can't help her. What luck!!" Jeannette Shepherd Hauser to Miriam Hauser Rosser, May 20, 1910, Archives of Ohio United Methodism.

48 Rubinstein, *My Life*, 34.

49 Hoganson, "The Fashionable World," 266. On London's "American Phase" in relation to commercial providers, see Rappaport, *Shopping for Pleasure*, 144–51. On early twentieth-century transnational cosmopolitanism, see also Judith R. Walkowitz, "The 'Vision of Salome': Cosmopolitanism and Erotic Dancing

in Central London, 1908–1918," *American Historical Review* 108, no. 2 (April 2003): 338.

50 Hoganson, "The Fashionable World," 262. The clothing trade was London's largest industry in the early twentieth century. Beauty and grooming services acted as ancillary arms to the trade, rounding out the acquirement of fashionable toilettes. Schneer, *London 1900*, 6.

51 Insley Casper, *Intimacies of Court and Society*, 276. On the centrality of fashion to elite feminine power, see also Hoganson, "The Fashionable World," 266–7. It was not only via money that American women "conquered" Britain; it was also through trans-Atlantic marriages. Dana Cooper has found that 588 American heiresses married British elites between the US Civil War and the Great War in what she terms "poli-social marriages." *Informal Ambassadors: American Women, Transatlantic Marriages, and Anglo-American Relations, 1865–1945* (Kent: Kent State University Press, 2014), 4.

52 On the American context, see Kathy Peiss, *Hope in a Jar: The Making of America's Beauty Culture* (New York: Metropolitan, 1998).

53 Walkowitz, "Salome," 340.

54 By 1900, Breidenbach had relocated their head office from 157b New Bond Street to Greek Street, Soho. Travellers Order Book for the London area, and Guard Book of Invoices, 1885–1896, Reference 2242, City of Westminster Archives Centre.

55 Unlabeled images from John Gosnell & Co., *c.*1900, private collection, Lewes, East Sussex.

56 See, for example, an 1874 account that reported Rimmel's employment of 150 "contented and well-to do young women, nicely dressed and nicely mannered." "From Gay to Grave," *All the Year Round* (March 21, 1874): 488–92.

57 *Census Returns of England and Wales, 1911*, class RG14, piece 3374; schedule number 289, www.ancestry.co.uk; and "American Lady Sued," *The Globe* (June 30, 1911): 9.

58 "Special Law Reports," 6.

59 "'Beauty' Specialist's Action," 6.

60 "Special Law Reports," 6.

61 "'Beauty' Specialist's Action," 6.

62 Steven Zdatny, *Fashion, Work, and Politics in Modern France* (New York: Palgrave, 2006), 113. The Savoy opened in August 1889, some two years after Rimmel's death.

63 Madeleine Henrey, *Madeleine Grown Up* (London: Dent, 1952), 51.

64 Henrey, *Madeleine Grown Up*, 18. Working as a West End manicurist in the late 1950s, Carolyn Steedman's mother described "how she 'flung' a sixpenny piece back at a titled woman who'd given it her as a tip: 'If you can't afford any more than that, Madame, I suggest you keep it.' Wonderful!—like tearing up the ration books."

Steedman, *Landscape for a Good Woman: A Story of Two Lives* (New Brunswick, NJ: Rutgers University Press, 1987), 37–8.

65 The Statue of Liberty-Ellis Island Foundation, Inc. "Ellis Island Port of New York Passenger Records Search," https://www.libertyellisfoundation.org, Stock, Dora Isabel, January 14, 1909, Passenger ID 104355010017, Frame 829, Lines 17.

66 "Special Law Reports," 6.

67 United States Census, 1910, Manhattan Ward 21, ED 1170, Image 9 of 18, NARA microfilm publication T624, Washington, DC: National Archives and Records Administration, www.FamilySearch.org.

68 UK Incoming Passenger Lists, 1878–1960, Board of Trade: Commercial and Statistical Department and Successors: Inwards Passenger Lists, class BT26, piece 424, www.ancestry.co.uk.

69 "King's Bench Division. Complexion Specialist's Action," 3.

70 Clark, "Clever Ministrations."

71 "King's Bench Division. Complexion Specialist's Action," 3.

72 "American Lady Sued," 9.

73 See, for example, "From the Social World: A Group of Portraits of New York Women," *The Sun* (August 14, 1910): n.p.

74 "Won Beauty Case," *New York Times* (July 11, 1911): 12.

75 Winterfeldt's elite standing, with its attendant lifestyle, continued in the years following the trial, until she retired to the Hotel Victoria in Grasse, France where she died in 1914. *London Gazette* 29012 (March 16, 1915): 2668; and Principal Probate Registry, *Calendar of the Grants of Probate and Letters of Administration Made in the Probate Registries of the High Court of Justice in England*, London, England ©Crown copyright.

76 "King's Bench Division. Complexion Specialist's Action," 3.

77 At the time of the trial, a news article noted that Stock travelled to France to await Winterfeldt's return to Europe in the Fall of 1911. "Won Beauty Case," 12.

78 The salon was at 15 East 49th Street.

79 The Statue of Liberty-Ellis Island Foundation, Inc. "Ellis Island Port of New York Passenger Records Search," https://www.libertyellisfoundation.org, Stock, Dora Isabel, December 16, 1915, Passenger ID 610120110189, Frame 746, Line 5; and England & Wales, National Probate Calendar (Index of Wills and Administrations), 1858–1966, 1973–95; England & Wales, Civil Registration Death Index, 1916–2007.

80 As we have seen, generations of British beauty providers employed strategies remarkably similar to those celebrated by historians as unique to Rubinstein: the developing of boutique businesses that catered to elite women, the centrality of trade secrets to developing personal lines of wares, and the amplification of circulating narratives about women's roles in society.

81 That is not to say that beauty consumption was relegated to women. See Matt
    Houlbrook, "'The Man with the Powder Puff' in Interwar London," *Historical
    Journal* 50, no. 1 (March 2007): 145–71.

82 Katrina Honeyman, "Doing Business with Gender: Service Industries and British
    Business History," *Business History Review* 81, no. 3 (Autumn 2007): 492. For
    the British case, see also Robert Beachy, Béatrice Craig, and Alaister Owens, eds.,
    *Women, Business, and Finance in Nineteenth-Century Europe: Rethinking Separate
    Spheres* (Oxford: Berg, 2006), 7–8, 10. In the American case, see Wendy Gamber,
    "A Gendered Enterprise: Placing Nineteenth-Century Businesswomen in History,"
    Business History Review 72, no. 2 (1998): 191.

83 This is also a condition of the historical archive and the economic actors who
    feature therein.

Epilogue

1   See Paul Deslandes's forthcoming study of male beauty from the University of
    Chicago Press; Paul Deslandes, "The Male Body, Beauty and Aesthetics in Modern
    British Culture," *History Compass* 8, no. 10 (2010): 1191–208; Paul Deslandes,
    "Selling, Consuming and Becoming the Beautiful Man in Britain: The 1930s
    and 1940s," *Consuming Behaviours: Identity, Politics and Pleasure in Twentieth-
    Century Britain*, ed. Erika Rappaport, Sandra T. Dawson, and Mark Crowley
    (London: Bloomsbury, 2015), 53–70; Alys Eve Weinbaum et al., eds., *The Modern
    Girl around the World: Consumption, Modernity, and Globalization* (Durham,
    NC: Duke University Press, 2008); Ina Zweiniger-Bargielowska, *Managing the
    Body: Beauty, Health, and Fitness in Britain 1880–1939* (New York: Oxford
    University Press, 2010); and Zweiniger-Bargielowska, "The Making of a Modern
    Female Body: Beauty, Health and Fitness in Interwar Britain," *Women's History
    Review* 20, no. 2 (2011): 299–317.

2   See Geoffrey Jones, *Beauty Imagined: A History of the Global Beauty Industry*
    (New York: Oxford University Press, 2010), 98, 107–8, 121–2, and 125–7.

3   *The London Gazette* 33930 (April 14, 1933): 2581.

4   *The London Gazette* 40298 (October 12, 1954): 5793.

5   "R. Hovenden and Sons," *Grace's Guide to British Industrial History*, https://www.
    gracesguide.co.uk/R._Hovenden_and_Sons, accessed September 10, 2013; *The
    London Gazette* 40679 (January 6, 1956): 164; *The London Gazette* 44650 (August
    8, 1968): 8723; *The London Gazette* 44788 (February 11, 1969); and *The London
    Gazette* 44848 (May 15, 1969): 5089–90.

6   "J. Grossmith and Sons," *Grace's Guide to British Industrial History*, https://www.
    gracesguide.co.uk/J._Grossmith_and_Sons, accessed January 5, 2017; and *The
    London Gazette* 45888 (January 23, 1973): 1069.

7　Jones, *Beauty Imagined*, 2–3. This extends to the present, and Jones notes that we can attribute over half of all current global beauty sales to just ten companies. On issues in defining the beauty industry, see Jones, "Blonde and Blue-Eyed? Globalizing Beauty, c.1945-c.1980," *Economic History Review* 61, no. 1 (2008): 131.

8　Jones, *Beauty Imagined*, 183.

9　Jones, *Beauty Imagined*, 132–3, n182.

10　Jones, *Beauty Imagined*, 133–4. On Yardley, see Jones, *Beauty Imagined*, 253–4.

11　Jones, *Beauty Imagined*, 253–4; and Jones, "Blonde and Blue-Eyed?," 149.

12　"A. and F. Pears," *Grace's Guide to British Industrial History*, https://www.gracesguide.co.uk/A._and_F._Pears.

13　See "James and Edward Atkinson," *Grace's Guide to British Industrial History*, https://www.gracesguide.co.uk/James_and_Edward_Atkinson; *The Times* (November 30, 1957); and Jones, *Beauty Imagined*, 209.

14　In 1971 it was acquired by ITT; in 1978, it was acquired by Schering-Plough. Jones, *Beauty Imagined*, 183 and 252; and "Rimmel," *Grace's Guide to British Industrial History*, https://www.gracesguide.co.uk/Rimmel.

15　For more, see Jessica P. Clark, "Buying Beauty: Female Beauty Consumption in the Modern British World," *History Compass* 14, no. 5 (May 2016): 206–17.

16　Jones, *Beauty Imagined*, 108–9 and 125–34.

17　Alys Eve Weinbaum et al., "The Modern Girl around the World: Cosmetics Advertising and the Politics of Race and Style," in *The Modern Girl around the World: Consumption, Modernity, and Globalization,* ed. Alys Weinbaum et al. (Durham, NC: Duke University Press, 2008), 31.

18　Weinbaum et al., "Modern Girl," 38, 50.

19　Jones argues that "[b]y 1980, globalization had not resulted in a pervading Americanization of global beauty." "Blonde and Blue-Eyed?," 150.

20　Timothy Burke, *Lifebuoy Men, Lux Women: Commodification, Consumption, and Cleanliness in Modern Zimbabwe* (Durham, NC: Duke University Press, 1996), 202.

21　Timothy Burke, "The Modern Girl and Commodity Culture," in *The Modern Girl around the World: Consumption, Modernity, and Globalization*, ed. Alys Weinbaum et al. (Durham, NC: Duke University Press, 2008), 365–6; and Burke, *Lifebuoy Men, Lux Women*, 193–202.

22　Burke, "Modern Girl," 367.

23　For early and important work that considers the relationship between colonial rule, grooming practices, and symbols of cleanliness, see Anne McClintock, *Imperial Leather: Race, Gender, and Sexuality in the Colonial Contest* (New York: Routledge, 1995), chapter 5.

24　Priti Ramamurthy, "All-Consuming Nationalism: The Indian Modern Girl in the 1920s and 1930s," in *The Modern Girl around the World: Consumption, Modernity, and Globalization*, ed. Alys Weinbaum et al. (Durham, NC: Duke University Press, 2008), 150. See also Weinbaum et al., "Modern Girl," 51.

25   Rochelle Rowe, *Imagining Caribbean Womanhood: Race, Nation, and Beauty Contests, 1929-70* (Manchester: Manchester University Press, 2013), 10.

26   Rowe, *Imagining Caribbean Womanhood*, 8. See also Rowe, "'Glorifying the Jamaican Girl': The 'Ten Types–One People' Beauty Contest, Racialized Femininities and Jamaican Nationalism," *Radical History Review* 103 (2009): 36–58.

27   Rowe, *Imagining Caribbean Womanhood*, 182.

28   Rowe, *Imagining Caribbean Womanhood*, 152.

29   Rowe, *Imagining Caribbean Womanhood*, 3.

30   Susan Vincent, *Hair: An Illustrated History* (London: Bloomsbury, 2018), 220.

31   Kim Smith, "Strands of the Sixties. A Cultural Analysis of the Design and Consumption of the New London West End Hair Salons, c.1954–1975" (PhD dissertation, University of East London, 2014), 126.

32   On the importance of beauty politics in Britain's Afro-Caribbean youth culture, see Tanisha C. Ford, *Liberated Threads: Black Women, Style, and the Global Politics of Soul* (Chapel Hill: University of North Carolina Press, 2015), 128–32.

33   Smith, "Strands of the Sixties," 218; Rowe, *Imagining Caribbean Womanhood*, 168 and 172; and Peter Fraser, "Carmen England," in *The Oxford Companion to Black British History*, ed. David Dabydeen, John Gilmore, and Cecily Jones (Oxford: Oxford University Press, 2007). England was one of the cofounders of the Caribbean Carnival. As Smith notes, England appeared in a 1948 British Pathé production on hairdressing: https://www.britishpathe.com/video/hairdressing.

34   Smith, "Strands of the Sixties," 218; and Philip Herbert, "Winifred Atwell," in *The Oxford Companion to Black British History*, ed. David Dabydeen, John Gilmore, and Cecily Jones (Oxford: Oxford University Press, 2007).

35   Smith notes that the business continued on Bond Street until 1967. Smith, "Strands of the Sixties," 220.

36   Fraser, "Carmen England"; and Ford, *Liberated Threads*, 132.

37   Rowe, *Imagining Caribbean Womanhood*, 167–8; and Smith, "Strands of the Sixties," 221–2. On Ghanaian students in British beauty schools, see Doris S. Essah, "Fashioning the Nation: Hairdressing, Professionalism, and the Performance of Gender in Ghana, 1900–2006" (PhD dissertation, University of Michigan, 2008), 138–9, cited in Smith.

38   Smith, "Strands of the Sixties," 224.

39   Ford, *Liberated Threads*, 132. In the American context, Tiffany Gill has shown how African-American women's activism was bolstered by the creation of spaces specifically devoted to black female consumers, including beauty salons and schools. Gill, *Beauty Shop Politics: African American Women's Activism in the Beauty Industry* (Chicago: University of Illinois Press, 2010), 1 and 99. See also Blain Roberts, *Pageants, Parlors, and Pretty Women: Race and Beauty in the Twentieth-Century South* (Chapel Hill: University of North Carolina Press,

2014); Noliwe M. Rooks, *Hair Raising: Beauty, Culture and African American Women* (New Brunswick: Rutgers University Press, 1996); Susannah Walker, *Style and Status: Selling Beauty to African American Women, 1920–1975* (Lexington: University Press of Kentucky, 2007); and Julie Willett, *Permanent Waves: The Making of the American Beauty Shop* (New York: New York University Press, 2000).

40 Ford, *Liberated Threads*, 132.

41 Jones, *Beauty Imagined*, 283–5. Another example is Lush Cosmetics, launched by Brit Mark Constantine in 1995. See Jones, *Beauty Imagined*, 284.

42 Anita Roddick, *Body and Soul. Profits with Principles: The Amazing Success Story of Anita Roddick and the Body Shop* (New York: Crown, 1991), 14. Quoted in Jones, *Beauty Imagined*, 291.

43 Roddick, *Body and Soul*, 16.

44 Roddick, *Body and Soul*, 17. Also quoted in Jones, *Beauty Imagined*, 284–5.

45 Roddick, *Body and Soul*, 26; and Jones, *Beauty Imagined*, 285.

46 British Society of Perfumers, *British Perfumery: A Fragrant History* (Frome: Butler, Tanner, & Dennis, 2013), 131. The company was acquired by Brazilian firm Natura in 2017.

47 For the complicated relationship between masculinity and grooming in twentieth-century Britain, see Matt Houlbrook, "'The Man with the Powder Puff' in Interwar London," *Historical Journal* 50, no. 1 (2007): 145–71.

48 British Society of Perfumers, *British Perfumery*, 169. My thanks to the Brookes family for meeting me in 2015.

49 British Society of Perfumers, *British Perfumery*, 21.

Select Bibliography

Archival Sources

Archives of Ohio United Methodism, Delaware Ohio
    Rosser-Hauser Family Papers
Bodleian Libraries, Oxford
    John Johnson Collection of Printed Ephemera
City of Westminster Archives Centre, London
    Blake, Sandford, and Blake, Pharmaceutical Chemists
    Breidenbach & Co., Perfumers
Croydon Museum and Archives Service, Croydon
    Breidenbach's Perfumery, Croydon: records c, 1869–90, Acc 478
Floris of London
    Private Collections
John Gosnell & Co., Lewes, East Sussex
    Private Collections
London Metropolitan Archives
    Apprenticeship Indentures
    H.P. Truefitt Limited
    London Chamber of Commerce
        Chemical Trades Section minute books, 1883–1938
        Perfumery and Toilet Preparations Section minute books, 1893–1946
    Noble Collection
    Sun Fire Insurance Records
    Trade Card Collection
London Probate Registry
London School of Economics, Archives and Special Collections
    Charles Booth Collection
National Archives at Kew
    Board of Trade Papers (BT)
    Court of Chancery (C)
    Home Office: Census of Population 1851–1911
    Records created or inherited by the Registry of Friendly Societies (FS)
    Records of the Prerogative Court of Canterbury (PROB)
National Art Library, London
    F. Gillham Collection

Prospectuses of Exhibitors, Great Exhibition 1851
V&A Theatre and Performance Collections
   Willy Clarkson Scrapbooks
Worshipful Company of Barbers, London
   Papers of R. Hovenden

Primary Sources

Andrews, William. *At the Sign of the Barber's Pole*. Cottingham: J. R. Tutin, 1904.

Aria, Mrs. "My Lady's Afternoon in London." In *Living London: Its Work and Its Play, Its Humour and Its Pathos, Its Sights and Its Scenes, Volume 1*, edited by George R. Sims, 42–8. London: Cassell, 1902.

Arlidge, J. T. *The Hygiene, Diseases, and Mortality of Occupations*. London: Percival, 1892.

The Art of Being Beautiful: A Series of Interviews with a Society Beauty. London: Henry J. Drane, 1902.

Ballantine, William. *Some Experiences of a Barrister's Life*. London: R. Bentley, 1882.

Barton, Rose. *Familiar London*. London: Adam and Charles Black, 1904.

Beauty and How to Keep It. London: Brentano's, 1889.

Beauty: Its Attainment and Preservation. New York: Butterick Publishing, 1890.

Beerbohm, Max. "A Defence of Cosmetics." In *The Yellow Book: An Illustrated Quarterly* 1, 65–82. London: E. Matthews & J. Lane, 1894.

Booth, Charles, ed. "Inner South London." *Life and Labour of the People in London. Volume IV*. New York: Macmillan, 1902.

Booth, Charles, ed. *Life and Labour of the People in London. Final Volume: Notes on Social Influences and Conclusion*. London: Macmillan, 1903.

Booth, Charles, ed. *Life and Labour of the People in London: Population Classified by Trades. Volume VIII*. London: Macmillan, 1896.

Booth, Charles, ed. *Life and Labour of the People in London: South-East and South-West London. Third Series: Religious Influences*. London: Macmillan, 1902.

Braddon, Mary Elizabeth. *Lady Audley's Secret*. London: Tinsley Bros., 1862.

Browning, H. Ellen. *Beauty Culture*. London: Hutchinson, 1898.

[Casper, Rebecca Insley]. *Intimacies of Court and Society: An Unconventional Narrative of Unofficial Days by the Widow of a Diplomat*. London: Hurst and Blackett, 1912.

Catalogue of the British Section. Paris Universal Exhibition of 1867. London: Spottiswoode, 1867.

Chroniqueuse. *Photographs of Paris Life: A Record of the Politics, Art, Fashion and Anecdote of Paris during the Past Eighteen Months*. London: William Tinsley, 1861.

Collins, Wilkie. *Armadale*. London: Harper, 1866.

Collins' Illustrated Guides to London and Neighborhood. London: William Collins, 1871.

Cook, Emily Constance Baird. *Highways and Byways in London*. London: Macmillan, 1902.

Cooley, Arnold James. *The Toilet in Ancient and Modern Times; with a Review of the Different Theories of Beauty and Copious Allied Information, Social, Hygienic, and Medical*. London: Robert Hardwicke, 1866.

Corisande. "Aids to Beauty." *Illustrated Household Journal and Englishwoman's Domestic Magazine* (May 1, 1882): 115.

Cross, Francis. *Hints to All about to Rent, Buy, or Build House Property*. London: J. K. Starling, 1851.

Davidson, Mrs. H. Coleman. *What Our Daughters Can Do for Themselves*. London: Smith, Elder, 1894.

Deite, Carl. *A Practical Treatise on the Manufacture of Perfumery*. Philadelphia, PA: H. C. Baird, 1892.

Dickens, Charles Jr. *Dickens' Dictionary of London*. London: The Author, 1879.

Elise, M. *Secrets of Fascination*. Birmingham: W. Lake, 1906.

Exhibition of the Works of Industry of all Nations, 1851. Reports by the Juries on the Subjects in the Thirty Classes into Which the Exhibition Was Divided. London: William Clowes, 1852.

The Extraordinary Life & Trial of Madame Rachel at the Central Criminal Court, Old Bailey, London, On the 22, 23, 24, & 25, September, 1868, Before Mr. Commissioner Kerr, in the New Court. London: Diprose and Bateman, 1868.

Faithfull, Emily. *Three Visits to America*. Edinburgh: David Douglas, 1884.

General Register Office. *England and Wales Civil Registration Indexes*. London: General Register Office, July-August-September 1905.

General Register Office. *Fourteenth Annual Report of the Registrar-General of Births, Deaths, and Marriages in England*. London: Eyre and Spottiswoode, 1855.

General Register Office. *Supplement to the Fifty-Fifth Annual Report of the Registrar-General for England and Wales, Volume 55*. London: Eyre and Spottiswoode, 1897.

Gent, Helen. *Health and Beauty for Women and Girls*. London: Health & Strength, 1909.

Great Britain Patent Office. *Reports of Patent, Design, and Trademark Cases* 24. London: Patent Office, 1907.

Greenwood, James. *In Strange Company: Being the Experiences of a Roving Correspondent*. London: Vizetelly, [1873] 1883.

Grogan, Mercy. *How Women May Earn a Living*. London: Cassell, Petter, Galpin, 1880.

The Habits of Good Society: A Handbook for Ladies and Gentlemen. New York: Carleton, 1863.

Haight, Gordon S., ed. *The George Eliot Letters, Volume 9: 1871–1881*. New Haven, CT: Yale University Press, 1978.

The Handbook of the Toilette. By the Author of "Familiar Hints on Sea-Bathing," The Handbook of Cookery, &c. London: W. S. Orr, 1839.

Hara, O.H. *Complexion Beautiful; or New Skins for Old*. London: L. N. Fowler, 1907.

Hauser, Jeannette L. *The Orient and Its People*. Milwaukee, WI: I. L. Hauser, 1876.

Henrey, Madeleine. *Madeleine Grown Up*. London: Dent, 1952.

History and Trial of Madame Rachel or Beautiful for Ever. London: William Swift, 1868.

Hollingshead, John. *Ragged London in 1861*. London: Smith, Elder, 1861.

Leverson, Madame Rachel. *Beautiful for Ever!* London: Madame Rachel, 47a New Bond Street, 1863.

Life in London by a Town Traveller. London: 4, Ludgate Circus Buildings, 1879.

Lillie, Charles. *The British Perfumer: Being a Collection of Choice Receipts and Observations Made During an Extensive Practice of Thirty Years, By Which Any Lady or Gentleman May Prepare Their Own Articles of the Best Quality, Whether of Perfumery, Snuffs, or Colours*. London: J. Souter, 1822.

Linton, Eliza Lynn. *Modern Women and What Is Said of Them*. New York: J. S. Redfield, 1868.

Loftie, William John. *Kensington Picturesque & Historical*. London: The Leadenhall Press, 1888.

Mayhew, Henry. *London Labour and the London Poor, Volume I: London Street Folk*. London: Charles Griffin, 1851.

Meade, L. T. *The Sorceress of the Strand*. London: Ward, Lock, 1903.

Milne, John Duguid. *Industrial Employment of Women in the Middle and Lower Ranks*. London: Longmans, Green, 1870.

Montez, Lola. *The Arts of Beauty*. London: James Blackwood, Paternoster Row, 1858.

Official Catalogue of the Great Exhibition of the Works of Industry of All Nations. London: Commissioners for the Exhibition of 1851, 1851.

Olivia's Shopping and How She Does It: A Prejudiced Guide to the London Shops. London: Gay and Bird, 1906.

Osborne's Stranger's Guide and Directory to Hastings and St. Leonards. Hastings: Osborne, 1854.

Pears, Francis. *The Skin, Baths, Bathing, and Soap*. London: The Author, 1859.

Philp, Robert Kemp. *The Shopkeeper's Guide*. London: Houlston and Stoneman, 1853.

Piesse, George William Septimus. *Chymical, Natural, and Physical Magic*. London: Longman, Brown, Green, Longmans & Roberts, 1858.

Piesse, George William Septimus. *The Laboratory of Chemical Wonders, a Scientific Melange*. London: Longman, Brown, Green, Longmans & Roberts, 1860.

Piesse, George William Septimus. *Lecture on Perfumes, Flower Farming, and the Methods of Obtaining the Odours of Plants, Delivered before the Royal Horticultural Society, etc.* London: Robert Hardwicke, 1865.

Piesse, George William Septimus. *[Piesse's] Art of Perfumery*. Philadelphia, PA: Lindsay and Blakiston, [1855] 1857.

Rimmel, Eugène. *A History of Perfumery and the Toilet*. London: S. O. Beeton, 1864.

Rimmel, Eugène. *A Lecture on the Commercial Use of Flowers and Plants: Delivered on the 27th July, 1865, at the Royal Horticultural Society*. London: The Author, 1865.

Rimmel, Eugène. *Recollections of the Paris Exposition of 1867*. London: Chapman and Hall, 1868.

Rimmel, Eugène. *Rimmel's Perfume Vaporizer for Diffusing the Fragrance of Flowers in Apartments, Ball Rooms, etc.* London: The Author, 1865.

Rimmel, Eugène. *Rimmel's Perfumed Almanack.* London: The Author, 1852–71.

Rimmel, Eugène. *Souvenirs de l'Exposition Universelle.* Paris: The Author, 1868.

Rimmel, Eugène. *The Book of Perfumes, etc. [With Plates and Illustrations].* London: Chapman & Hall, 1865.

Roddick, Anita. *Body and Soul. Profits with Principles: The Amazing Success Story of Anita Roddick and the Body Shop.* New York: Crown, 1991.

Ross, Miriam. *Against Tide: A Story of a Poor Street Arab.* London: John Dicks, 1871.

Rubinstein, Helena. *My Life for Beauty.* New York: Simon and Schuster, 1966.

Ruppert, Anna. *Dermatology. A Book of Beauty: Containing a Choice Collection of Receipts for Beautifying the Face and Form.* London: Anna Ruppert, 1892.

Ruppert, Anna. *Natural Beauty: Or, the Secrets of the Toilet. A Lecture, etc.* London: The Author, 1892.

Sampson, Henry. *History of Advertising: From the Earliest Times.* London: Chatto and Windus, 1874.

Sanders, E. *Practical Face Treatment and Natural Beauty.* London: Truslove, Hanson & Comba, 1903.

[Shaw, Donald]. *London in the Sixties. With a Few Digressions. By One of the Old Brigade.* London: Everett, 1908.

Smith, Charles Manby. *The Little World of London: Or, Pictures in Little of London Life.* London: Arthur Hall, Virtue, 1857.

Staffe, Baronness Blanche. *My Lady's Dressing Room.* Translated by Harriet Hubbard Ayer. New York: Cassell, 1892.

Street, G. S. "Bayswater and St. John's Wood." In *A Book of Essays.* London: A. Constable, 1902.

Thornbury, Walter. *Old and New London: A Narrative of Its History, Its People, and Its Places,* Volume 3. London: Cassell, Petter, & Galpin, 1878.

Villars, Paul. "French London." In *Living London: Its Work and Its Play, Its Humour and Its Pathos, Its Sights and Its Scenes, Volume 2,* edited by George R. Sims, 133–8. London: Cassell, 1902.

Walker, Mrs. Alexander. *Female Beauty: As Preserved and Improved by Regimen, Cleanliness and Dress.* London: Thomas Hurst, 1837.

Wheatley, H. B. *A Short History of Bond Street, Old & New.* London: The Fine Art Society, 1911.

Whitehead, Henry. *The Cholera in Berwick Street.* London: Hope, 1854.

Whiting, Sydney. "Report on Perfumery. –(Class 25.)—." In *Reports on the Paris Universal Exhibition, 1867, Volume II,* 563–79. London: George E. Eyre and William Spottiswoode, 1868.

Williams, Montagu. *Leaves of a Life Being the Reminiscences of Montagu Williams, Q.C.* London: Macmillan, 1890.

Wylde, James. *The Book of Trades.* Edinburgh: Gall & Inglis, 1866.

Wynter, Andrew. *Our Social Bees; or, Pictures of Town & Country Life, and Other Papers.* London: Robert Hardwicke, 1861.

Yonge, Charlotte M. *Love and Life: An Old Story in Eighteenth Century Costume.* London: Macmillan, 1880.

Young, Austin T. *The Annals of the Barber-Surgeons of London. Compiled from Their Records and Other Sources by Sidney Young, One of the Court of Assistants of the Worshipful Company of Barbers of London.* London: Blades, East & Blades, 1890.

Secondary Sources

Adburgham, Alison. *Shops and Shopping, 1800–1914: Where and in What Manner the Well-Dressed Englishwoman Bought her Clothes.* London: Allen & Unwin, [1964] 1981.

Alexander, Andrew, Gareth Shaw, and Deborah Hodson. "Regional Variations in the Development of Multiple Retailing in England, 1890–1939." In *A Nation of Shopkeepers: Five Centuries of British Retailing*, edited by John Benson and Laura Ugolini, 127–54. London: I. B. Tauris, 2003.

Alexander, David. *Retailing in England during the Industrial Revolution.* London: Athlone Press, 1970.

Altick, Richard Daniel. *The Presence of the Present: Topics of the Day in the Victorian Novel.* Columbus: Ohio State University Press, 1991.

Amigoni, David, ed. *Life Writing and Victorian Culture.* New York: Ashgate, 2006.

Anderson, Gregory. *Victorian Clerks.* Manchester: Manchester University Press, 1976.

Anderson, Patricia. *The Printed Image and the Transformation of Popular Culture, 1790–1860.* Oxford: Clarendon Press, 1991.

Angeloglou, Maggie. *A History of Make-Up.* New York: Macmillan, 1970.

Ashikari, Mikiko. "The Memory of the Women's White Faces: Japaneseness and the Ideal Image of Women." *Japan Forum* 15, no. 1 (2003): 55–79.

Aston, Jennifer. "Female Business Ownership in Birmingham 1849–1901." *Midland History* 37, no. 2 (September 2012): 187–206.

Aston, Jennifer. *Female Entrepreneurship in Nineteenth-Century England: Engagement in the Urban Economy.* London: Palgrave, 2016.

Aston, Jennifer, and Paolo Di Martino. "Risk, Success, and Failure: Female Entrepreneurship in Late Victorian and Edwardian England." *The Economic History Review* 70, no. 3 (2017): 837–58.

Atkins, P. J. "The Spatial Configuration of Class Solidarity in London's West End, 1792–1939." *Urban History Yearbook* 17 (1990): 36–65.

Atkinson, Juliette. *Victorian Biography Reconsidered: A Study of Nineteenth-Century "Hidden" Lives.* New York: Oxford University Press, 2010.

Auerbach, Jeffrey A., and Peter H. Hoffenberg, eds. *Britain, the Empire, and the World at the Great Exhibition of 1851*. Aldershot: Ashgate, 2008.

Ballaster, Ros, Margaret Beetham, and Sandra Hebron. *Women's Worlds: Ideology, Femininity, and the Woman's Magazine*. London: Macmillan, 1991.

Barker, Hannah, and Karen Harvey. "Women Entrepreneurs and Urban Expansion: Manchester 1760–1820." In *Women and Urban Life in Eighteenth-Century England: "On the Town,"* edited by Rosemary Sweet and Penelope Lane, 111–30. Burlington, VT: Ashgate, 2003.

Barker, Hannah. *The Business of Women: Female Enterprise and Urban Development in Northern England, 1760–1830*. Oxford: Oxford University Press, 2006.

Barnes, Natasha B. "Face of the Nation: Race, Nationalisms, and Identities in Jamaican Beauty Pageants." In *Daughters of Caliban: Caribbean Women in the Twentieth Century*, edited by Consuelo López-Springfield, 471–97. Bloomington: Indiana University Press, 1997.

Bartrip, Peter W. J. "How Green Was My Valance?: Environmental Arsenic Poisoning and the Victorian Domestic Ideal." *English Historical Review* 109, no. 433 (September 1994): 891–913.

Beachy, Robert, Béatrice Craig, and Alaister Owens, eds. *Women, Business, and Finance in Nineteenth-Century Europe: Rethinking Separate Spheres*. Oxford: Berg, 2006.

Beaujot, Ariel. *Victorian Fashion Accessories*. London: Berg, 2013.

Becattini, Giacomo. "The Industrial District as a Creative Milieu." In *Industrial Change and Regional Development: The Transformation of New Industrial Spaces*, edited by Georges Benko and Mick Dunford, 102–14. London: Belhaven Press, 1991.

Beetham, Margaret, and Kay Boardman, eds. *Victorian Women's Magazines: An Anthology*. Manchester: Manchester University Press, 2001.

Beetham, Margaret. *A Magazine of Her Own?: Domesticity and Desire in the Woman's Magazine, 1800–1914*. London: Routledge, 1996.

Belussi, Fiorenza, and Katia Caldari. "At the Origin of the Industrial District: Alfred Marshall and the Cambridge School." *Cambridge Journal of Economics* 33 (2009): 335–55.

Bengry, Justin. "Courting the Pink Pound: *Men Only* and the Queer Consumer, 1935–39." *History Workshop Journal* 68, no. 1 (Autumn 2009): 122–48.

Bennett, James. *Cosmetics and Skin*. http://www.cosmeticsandskin.com/index.php.

Benson, John, and Gareth Shaw, eds. *The Evolution of Retail Systems, c. 1800–1914*. Leicester: Leicester University Press, 1992.

Benson, John, and Laura Ugolini, eds. *A Nation of Shopkeepers: Five Centuries of British Retailing*. London: I. B. Tauris, 2003.

Benson, John, and Laura Ugolini, eds. *Cultures of Selling: Perspectives on Consumption and Society Since 1700*. Aldershot: Ashgate, 2006.

Berg, Maxine. *Luxury and Pleasure in Eighteenth-Century Britain*. Oxford: Oxford University Press, 2005.

Berlanstein, Lenard R. "Historicizing and Gendering Celebrity Culture: Famous Women in Nineteenth-Century France." *Journal of Women's History* 16, no. 4 (2004): 65–91.

Bindman, David. *Ape to Apollo: Aesthetics and the Idea of Race in the Eighteenth Century*. London: Reaktion Books, 2002.

Block, Sharon. "Early American Bodies: Creating Race, Sex, and Beauty." In *Connexions: Histories of Race and Sex in North America*, edited by Jennifer Brier, Jim Downs, and Jennifer L. Morgan, 85–112. Urbana: University of Illinois Press, 2016.

Bowlby, Rachel. *Carried Away: The Invention of Modern Shopping*. New York: Columbia University Press, 2001.

Boyd, Robert L. "Black Retail Enterprise and Racial Segregation in Northern Cities Before the 'Ghetto.'" *Sociological Perspectives* 53, no. 3 (Fall 2010): 397–417.

Boyd, Robert L. "Race, Labor Market Disadvantage, and Survivalist Entrepreneurship: Black Women in the Urban North during the Great Depression." *Sociological Forum* 15, no. 4 (December 2000): 647–70.

Brandon, Ruth. *Ugly Beauty: Helena Rubinstein, L'Oreal, and the Blemished History of Looking Good*. New York: HarperCollins, 2011.

Bratton, Jacky Susan. *The Making of the West End Stage: Marriage, Management and the Mapping of Gender in London, 1830–1870*. New York: Cambridge University Press, 2011.

Bressey, Caroline. "The Black Presence in England and Wales after the Abolition Act, 1807–1930." *Parliamentary History* 26 (2007): 224–37.

Breward, Christopher. *Fashioning London: Clothing and the Modern Metropolis*. Oxford: Berg, 2004.

Breward, Christopher. *The Hidden Consumer: Masculinities, Fashion, and City Life, 1860–1914*. Manchester: Manchester University Press, 1999.

Breward, Christopher. "Sartorial Spectacle: Clothing and Masculine Identities in the Imperial City, 1860–1914." In *Imperial Cities: Landscape, Display and Identity*, edited by Felix Driver and David Gilbert, 244–51. Manchester: Manchester University Press, 1999.

Breward, Christopher, and Caroline Evans, eds. *Fashion and Modernity*. Oxford: Berg, 2005.

Breward, Christopher, and David Gilbert, eds. *Fashion's World Cities*. Oxford: Berg, 2006.

Breward, Christopher, Becky Conekin, and Caroline Cox, eds. *The Englishness of English Dress*. Oxford: Berg, 2002.

Breward, Christopher, Edwina Ehrman, and Caroline Evans. *London Look: Fashion from Street to Catwalk*. New Haven, CT: Yale University Press, 2004.

Brewer, John, and Roy Porter, eds. *Consumption and the World of Goods*. London: Routledge 1993.

Briefel, Aviva. "Cosmetic Tragedies: Failed Masquerade in Wilkie Collins's *The Lady and the Law*." *Victorian Literature and Culture* 37, no. 2 (2009): 463–81.

Briot, Eugénie. "From Industry to Luxury: French Perfume in the Nineteenth Century." *Business History Review* 85 (Summer 2011): 273–94.

British Society of Perfumers. *British Perfumery: A Fragrant History*. Frome: Butler, Tanner, & Dennis, 2013.

Burke, Timothy. *Lifebuoy Men, Lux Women: Commodification, Consumption, and Cleanliness in Modern Zimbabwe*. Durham, NC: Duke University Press, 1996.

Burke, Timothy. "The Modern Girl and Commodity Culture." In *The Modern Girl around the World: Consumption, Modernity, and Globalization*, edited by Alys Weinbaum et al., 362–9. Durham, NC: Duke University Press, 2008.

Burnby, J. G. L. "Women in Pharmacy." *Pharmaceutical Historian* 20, no. 2 (1990): 6–8.

Burney, Ian. *Poison, Detection, and the Victorian Imagination*. Manchester: Manchester University Press, 2006.

Burton, Antoinette. *At the Heart of the Empire: Indians and the Colonial Encounter in Late-Victorian Britain*. Berkeley: University of California Press, 1998.

Butler, Judith. "Performative Acts and Gender Constitution: An Essay in Phenomenology and Feminist Theory." In *Performing Feminisms: Feminist Critical Theory and Theatre*, edited by Sue-Ellen Case, 270–82. Baltimore, MD: Johns Hopkins University Press, 1990.

Camp, Stephanie M. H. "Black Is Beautiful: An American History." *Journal of Southern History* 81, no. 3 (August 2015): 675–90.

Camp, Stephanie M. H. "Making Racial Beauty in the United States: Toward a History of Black Beauty." In *Connexions: Histories of Race and Sex in North America*, edited by Jennifer Brier, Jim Downs, and Jennifer L. Morgan, 113–26. Urbana: University of Illinois Press, 2016.

Canning, Kathleen. *Gender History in Practice: Historical Perspectives on Bodies, Class, and Citizenship*. Ithaca, NY: Cornell University Press, 2006.

Chancellor, E. Beresford. *Liberty and Regent Street*. London: Liberty, 1926.

Church, Roy. "Advertising Consumer Goods in Nineteenth-Century Britain: Reinterpretations." *Economic History Review* 53, no. 4 (2000): 621–45.

Church, Roy, and Andrew Godley. "The Emergence of Modern Marketing: International Dimensions." *Business History* 45, no. 1 (2003): 1–5.

Clark, Jessica P. "Buying Beauty: Female Beauty Consumption in the Modern British World." *History Compass* 14, no. 5 (2016): 206–17.

Clark, Jessica P. "Clever Ministrations: Regenerative Beauty at the *Fin de Siècle*." *Palgrave Communications* 3, no. 47 (2017): n.p.

Clark, Jessica P. "Grooming Men: The Material World of the Nineteenth-Century Barbershop." In *Gender and Material Culture in Britain since 1600*, edited by Hannah Greig, Jane Hamlett, and Leonie Hannan, 104–19. London: Palgrave Macmillan, 2015.

Clark, Jessica P. "*Pomeroy v. Pomeroy*: Beauty, Modernity, and the Female Entrepreneur in *Fin-De-Siècle* London." *Women's History Review* 22, no. 6 (2013): 877–903.

Clark, Jessica P. "'Will You Give Me Your Opinion?': Mundane Beauty in the *Englishwoman's Domestic Magazine*, 1860–1875." *Victorian Periodicals Review* 52, no. 3 (Fall 2019): 540–65.

Clifford, Marie J. "Helena Rubinstein's Beauty Salons, Fashion, and Modernist Display." *Winterthur Portfolio* 38, nos. 2/3 (Summer-Autumn 2003): 83–108.

Cohen, Deborah. *Family Secrets: Living with Shame from the Victorians to the Present Day*. London: Viking, 2013.

Corson, Richard. *Fashions in Makeup: From Ancient to Modern Times*. London: Owen, 1972.

Craik, Jennifer. *The Face of Fashion: Cultural Studies in Fashion*. London: Routledge, 1993.

Crossick, Geoffrey, and Heinz-Gerhard Haupt. *The Petite Bourgeoisie in Europe, 1780–1914: Enterprise, Family, and Independence*. New York: Routledge, 1995.

Crossick, Geoffrey, and Heinz-Gerhard Haupt. *Shopkeepers and Master Artisans in Nineteenth-Century Europe*. New York: Methuen, 1984.

Crossick, Geoffrey, and Serge Jaumain, eds. *Cathedrals of Consumption: The European Department Store, 1850-1939*. Aldershot: Aldergate, 1999.

Cunnington, Cecil Willett. *Handbook of English Costume in the Nineteenth Century*. London: Faber and Faber, 1959.

Dabydeen, David, John Gilmore, and Cecily Jones, eds. *The Oxford Companion to Black British History*. Oxford: Oxford University Press, 2007.

Daunton, Martin, and Bernhard Rieger, eds. *Meanings of Modernity: Britain from the Late-Victorian Era to World War II*. Oxford: Berg, 2001.

David, Alison Matthews. *Fashion Victims: The Dangers of Dress Past and Present*. London: Bloomsbury, 2015.

Davidoff, Leonore. *The Best Circles: Society Etiquette and the Season*. London: Croom Helm, 1973.

Day, Carolyn. *Consumptive Chic: A History of Beauty, Fashion, and Disease*. London: Bloomsbury, 2017.

de Lauretis, Teresa. *Technologies of Gender: Essays on Theory, Film, and Fiction*. Bloomington, IN: Indiana University Press, 1987.

de Vries, Leonard, and Ilonka van Amstel. *Victorian Advertisements*. London: John Murray, 1968.

Deslandes, Paul. "The Male Body, Beauty and Aesthetics in Modern British Culture." *History Compass* 8, no. 10 (2010): 1191–208.

Deslandes, Paul. "Selling, Consuming, and Becoming the Beautiful Man in Britain: The 1930s and 1940s." In *Consuming Behaviors: Identity, Politics and Pleasure in Twentieth-Century Britain*, edited by Erika Rappaport, Sandra Trudgen Dawson, and Mark J. Crowley, 53–70. London: Bloomsbury, 2015.

Dolan, Frances E. "Taking the Pencil Out of God's Hand: Art, Nature, and the Face–Painting Debate in Early Modern England." *PMLA* 108, no. 2 (1993): 224–39.

Drachman, Virginia. *Enterprising Women: 250 Years of American Business.* Chapel Hill: University of North Carolina Press, 2002.

Drew–Bear, Annette. "Cosmetics and Attitudes towards Women in the Seventeenth Century." *Journal of Popular Culture* 9, no. 1 (1975): 31–7.

Drew–Bear, Annette. "Face Painting in Renaissance Tragedy." *Renaissance Drama* 12 (1981): 71–93.

Drew–Bear, Annette. "Face Painting Scenes in Ben Jonson's Plays." *Studies in Philology* 77. no. 4 (1980): 388–401.

Dugan, Holly. *The Ephemeral History of Perfume: Scent and Sense in Early Modern England.* Baltimore, MD: Johns Hopkins University Press, 2011.

Dyhouse, Carol. *Glamour: Women, History, Feminism.* London: Zed Books, 2010.

Elliot, Blanche B. *A History of English Advertising.* London: B. T. Batsford, 1962.

Emsley, Clive. *Crime and Society in England, 1750–1900.* New York: Longman, [1987] 1996.

Essah, Doris S. "Fashioning the Nation: Hairdressing, Professionalism, and the Performance of Gender in Ghana, 1900–2006." PhD dissertation, University of Michigan, 2008.

Festa, Lynn. "Cosmetic Differences: The Changing Faces of England and France." *Studies in Eighteenth-Century Culture* 34 (2005): 25–54.

Finke, Laurie. "Painting Women: Images of Femininity in Jacobean Tragedy." *Theatre Journal* 36, no. 3 (1984): 357–70.

Finn, Margot C. *The Character of Credit: Personal Debt in English Culture, 1740–1914.* New York: Cambridge University Press, 2003.

Finn, Margot C. "Women, Consumption, and Coverture in England, c. 1760–1860." *Historical Journal* 39, no. 3 (1996): 703–22.

Finn, Margot C. "Working-Class Women and the Contest for Consumer Control in Victorian County Courts." *Past & Present* 161 (1998): 116–54.

Flinn, Laurel. "Social and Spatial Politics in the Construction of Regent Street." *Journal of Social History* 46, no. 2 (Winter 2012): 364–90.

Ford, Tanisha C. *Liberated Threads: Black Women, Style, and the Global Politics of Soul.* Chapel Hill: University of North Carolina Press, 2015.

Foster, David. "Albion's Sisters: A Study of Trade Directories and Female Economic Participation in the Mid-Nineteenth Century." MPhil dissertation, University of Exeter, 2002.

Foucault, Michel. *The History of Sexuality, Volume I.* Translated by Robert Hurley. New York: Vintage Books, 1978.

Gamber, Wendy. *The Female Economy: The Millinery and Dressmaking Trades, 1860–1930.* Urbana: University of Illinois Press, 1997.

Gamber, Wendy. "A Gendered Enterprise: Placing Nineteenth-Century Businesswomen in History." *The Business History Review* 72, no. 2, Gender and Business (Summer 1998): 188–217.

Garner, Shirley Nelson. "'Let Her Paint an Inch Thick': Painted Ladies in Renaissance Drama and Society." *Renaissance Drama* 20 (1989): 123–39.

Gill, Tiffany. *Beauty Shop Politics: African American Women's Activism in the Beauty Industry*. Urbana: University of Illinois Press, 2010.

Gleadle, Kathryn. *British Women in the Nineteenth Century*. New York: Palgrave Macmillan, 2001.

Greenblatt, Stephen. *Renaissance Self-Fashioning, from More to Shakespeare*. Chicago, IL: University of Chicago Press, [1980] 2005.

Grossman, Ann-Carol, and Arnie Reisman, dir. *The Powder & the Glory*. Alexandria, VA: PBS Home Video, 2007.

Grout, Holly Lynn. *The Force of Beauty: Transforming French Ideas of Femininity in the Third Republic*. Baton Rouge: Louisiana State University Press, 2015.

Gunn, Simon. "The Public Sphere, Modernity, and Consumption: New Perspectives on the History of the Middle Class." In *Gender, Civic Culture and Consumerism: Middle-Class Identity in Britain, 1800-1940*, edited by Alan J. Kidd and David Nicholls, 12–29. Manchester: Manchester University Press, 1999.

Hall, Kim F. *Things of Darkness: Economies of Race and Gender in Early Modern England*. Ithaca, NY: Cornell University Press, 1995.

Halstead, Ivor. *Bond Street*. London: Barcliff Advertising & Publishing, 1952.

Halttunen, Karen. *Confidence Men and Painted Women: A Study of Middle-Class Culture in America, 1830–1870*. New Haven, CT: Yale University Press, 1982.

Hammerton, A. James. *Cruelty and Companionship: Conflict in Nineteenth-Century Married Life*. New York: Routledge, 1992.

Haupt, Heinz-Gerhard. "Small Shops and Department Stores." In *The Oxford Handbook of the History of Consumption*, edited by Frank Trentmann, 267–88. New York: Oxford University Press, 2012.

Heath, Kay. *Aging by the Book: The Emergence of Midlife in Victorian Britain*. Albany: State University of New York Press, 2009.

Hennegan, Alison. "Personalities and Principles: Aspects of Literature and Life in Fin-De-Siècle England." In *Fin de Siècle and Its Legacy*, edited by Mikuláš Teich and Roy Porter, 190–215. Cambridge: Cambridge University Press, 1990.

Herzig, Rebecca. "Subjected to the Current: Batteries, Bodies, and the Early History of Electrification in the United States." *Journal of Social History* 41, no. 4 (Summer 2008): 867–85.

Herzig, Rebecca. *Plucked: A History of Hair Removal*. New York: New York University Press, 2015.

Herzog, Don. "The Trouble with Hairdressers." *Representations* 53 (Winter 1996): 21–43.

Herzog, Don. *Poisoning the Minds of the Lower Orders*. Princeton, NJ: Princeton University Press, 1998.

Higgs, Edward, and Amanda Wilkinson. "Women, Occupations and Work in the Victorian Censuses Revisited." *History Workshop Journal* 81, no. 1 (Spring 2016): 17–38.

Hill, Bridget. "Women, Work, and the Census: a Problem for Historians of Women." *History Workshop Journal* 35 (Spring 1993): 78–94.

Hindson, Catherine. *Female Performance Practice on the Fin-de-Siècle Popular Stages of London and Paris: Experiment and Advertisement.* Manchester: Manchester University Press, 2007.

Hoberman, Ruth. "Women in the British Museum Reading Room during the Late-Nineteenth and Early-Twentieth Centuries: From Quasi- to Counterpublic." *Feminist Studies* 28, no. 3 (Autumn 2002): 489–512.

Hobhouse, Hermione. *A History of Regent Street: A Mile of Style.* Chichester: Phillimore, 2008.

Hoganson, Kristin. "The Fashionable World: Imagined Communities of Dress." In *After the Imperial Turn: Thinking with and Through the Nation*, edited by Antoinette Burton, 260–78. Durham, NC: Duke University Press, 2003.

Holcombe, Lee. *Victorian Ladies at Work; Middle-Class Working Women in England and Wales, 1850–1914.* Hamden, CT: Archon Books, 1973.

Holmes, Colin. *John Bull's Island: Immigration and British Society, 1871–1971.* London: Macmillan, 1988.

Holt, Robin, and Andrew Popp. "Emotion, Succession, and the Family Firm: Josiah Wedgwood & Sons." *Business History* 55, no. 6 (2013): 892–909.

Holton, Sandra. "The Women's Movement, Politics and Citizenship from the late Nineteenth Century until 1918." In *Women in Twentieth-Century Britain*, edited by Ina Zweiniger-Bargielowska, 247–61. Harlow: Longman, 2001.

Honeyman, Katrina. "Doing Business with Gender: Service Industries and British Business History." *Business History Review* 81, no. 3 (Autumn 2007): 471–93.

Honeyman, Katrina. *Women. Gender and Industrialisation in England, 1700–1870.* New York: St. Martin's Press, 2000.

Hosgood, Christopher P. "A 'Brave and Daring Folk'? Shopkeepers and Trade Associational Life in Victorian and Edwardian England." *Journal of Social History* 26, no. 2 (Winter 1992): 285–308.

Hosgood, Christopher P. "'Mercantile Monasteries': Shops, Shop Assistants, and Shop Life in Late-Victorian and Edwardian Britain." *Journal of British Studies* 38, no. 3 (1999): 322–52.

Hosgood, Christopher P. "Mrs. Pooter's Purchase: Lower-Middle-Class Consumerism and the Sales, 1870–1914." In *Gender, Civic Culture and Consumerism: Middle-Class Identity in Britain, 1800-1940*, edited by Alan J. Kidd and David Nicholls, 143–63. Manchester: Manchester University Press, 1999.

Houlbrook, Matt. "'The Man with the Powder Puff' in Interwar London." *Historical Journal* 50, no. 1 (March 2007): 145–71.

Houlbrook, Matt. *Prince of Tricksters: The Incredible True Story of Netley Lucas, Gentleman Crook*. Chicago, IL: University of Chicago Press, 2016.

Hudson, Pat. "Women and Industrialization." In *Women's History: Britain, 1850–1945: An Introduction*, edited by Jane Purvis, 23–50. London: Routledge, 2000.

Hunt, Lynn. *The Middling Sort: Commerce, Gender, and the Family in England, 1680–1780*. Berkeley: University of California Press, 1996.

Jackson, Lee. "Who Was Anna Ruppert?" *The Cat Meat's Shop*, September 24, 2010 http://catsmeatshop.blogspot.ca/2010/09/who-was-anna-ruppert.html.

Jackson, W. A. *The Victorian Chemist and Druggist*. Princes Risborough: Shire, 1981.

Jefferys, James B. *Retail Trading in Britain, 1850–1950*. Cambridge: Cambridge University Press, 1954.

Jones, Geoffrey. *Beauty Imagined: A History of the Global Beauty Industry*. New York: Oxford University Press, 2010.

Jones, Geoffrey. "Blonde and Blue-Eyed? Globalizing Beauty, c.1945–c.1980." *Economic History Review* 61, no. 1 (2008): 125–54.

Jones, Stephanie. "R. Hovenden & Sons, Ltd." *Business Archives* 56 (1988): 29–38.

Jordan, Ellen. "'The Great Principle of English Fair-Play': Male Champions, the English Women's Movement and the Admission of Women to the Pharmaceutical Society in 1879." *Women's History Review* 7, no. 3 (1998): 381–410.

Jordan, Ellen. *The Women's Movement and Women's Employment in Nineteenth Century Britain*. New York: Routledge, 1999.

Jusová, Iveta. *The New Woman and the Empire*. Columbus: Ohio State University Press, 2005.

Kaplan, Morris B. *Sodom on the Thames: Sex, Love, and Scandal in Wilde Times*. Ithaca, NY: Cornell University Press, 2005.

Kay, Alison C. "A Little Enterprise of Her Own: Lodging-House Keeping and the Accommodation Business in Nineteenth-Century London." *The London Journal* 28, no. 2 (2003): 41–53.

Kay, Alison C. *The Foundations of Female Entrepreneurship: Enterprise, Home and Household in London c. 1800–1870*. London: Routledge, 2009.

Kay, Alison C. "Reconstructing the Role of the Household in Businesswomen's Networks of Support, London 1851–1861." Presented to XIV International Economic History Congress, Helsinki, Finland (August 21–5, 2006).

Kay, Alison C. "Retailing, Respectability and the Independent Woman in Nineteenth-Century London." In *Women, Business and Finance in Nineteenth-Century Europe: Rethinking Separate Spheres*, edited by Robert Beachy, Béatrice Craig, and Alastair Owens, 152–66. Oxford: Berg, 2006.

Kay, Alison C. "Revealing Her Assets: Liberating the Victorian Businesswoman from the Sources." *Business Archives: Sources and History* 92 (2006): 1–16.

Kay, Alison C. "Small Business, Self-Employment and Women's Work-Life Choices in Nineteenth Century London." In *Origins of the Modern Career*, edited by J. Brown, D. Mitch and M. Van Leeuwen, 191–206. Aldershot: Ashgate, 2004.

Kay, Gwen. *Dying to Be Beautiful: The Fight for Safe Cosmetics*. Columbus: Ohio State University Press, 2005.

Kling, Rebecca. "'It Is Only Colour That You Want': *Lady Audley's Secret* and Cosmetics as Discursive Fantasy." *Victorian Periodicals Review* 50, no. 3 (Fall 2017): 560–84.

Kortsch, Christine Bayles. *Dress Culture in Late Victorian Women's Fiction: Literacy, Textiles, and Activism*. Farnham: Ashgate, 2009.

Koven, Seth. *Slumming: Sexual and Social Politics in Victorian London*. Princeton, NJ: Princeton University Press, 2004.

Kowaleski-Wallace, Elizabeth. *Consuming Subjects: Women, Shopping, and Business in the Eighteenth Century*. New York: Columbia University Press, 1997.

Kriegel, Lara. *Grand Designs: Labor, Empire and the Museum in Victorian Culture*. Durham, NC: Duke University Press, 2007.

Kron, Joan. *Lift: Wanting, Fearing, and Having a Facelift*. New York: Penguin Books, 2000.

Kuchta, David. *The Three-Piece Suit and Modern Masculinity. England, 1550–1850*. Berkeley: University of California Press, 2002.

Kwass, Michael. "Big Hair: A Wig History of Consumption in Eighteenth-Century France." *American Historical Review* 111, no. 3 (2006): 631–59.

Laite, Julia. *Common Prostitutes and Ordinary Citizens: Commercial Sex in London, 1885–1960*. New York: Palgrave Macmillan, 2012.

Lancaster, William. *The Department Store: A Social History*. London: Leicester University Press, 1995.

Langland, Elizabeth. *Nobody's Angels: Middle-Class Women and Domestic Ideology in Victorian Culture*. Ithaca, NY: Cornell University Press, 1995.

Leach, William R. "Transformations in a Culture of Consumption: Women and Department Stores, 1890–1925." *Journal of American History* 71, no. 2 (September 1984): 319–42.

Ledbetter, Kathryn. *British Victorian Women's Periodicals: Beauty, Civilization, and Poetry*. New York: Palgrave Macmillan, 2009.

Lewis, Alfred Allan and Constance Woodworth. *Miss Elizabeth Arden*. New York: Coward, McCann & Geoghegan, 1972.

Lewis, Brian. *So Clean: Lord Leverhulme, Soap and Civilization*. Manchester: Manchester University Press, 2008.

Light, Ivan, and Carolyn Rosenstein. *Race, Ethnicity, and Entrepreneurship in Urban America*. Hawthorne: Aldine de Gruyter, 1995.

Linnane, Fergus. *London: The Wicked City: A Thousand Years of Prostitution and Vice*. London: Robson Books, 2003.

Linnane, Fergus. *London's Underworld: Three Centuries of Vice and Crime*. London: Robson Books, 2003.

Loeb, Lori. *Consuming Angels: Advertising and Victorian Women*. New York: Oxford University Press, 1994.

Lorimer, Douglas A. *Science, Race Relations and Resistance: Britain, 1870–1914.* Manchester: Manchester University Press, 2013.

MacKenzie, John M. *Orientalism: History, Theory, and the Arts.* Manchester: Manchester University Press, 1995.

Marcus, Sharon. *Between Women: Friendship, Desire, and Marriage in Victorian England.* Princeton, NJ: Princeton University Press, 2007.

Marshall, Alfred. *Industry and Trade.* London: Macmillan, 1919.

Marshall, Alfred. *Principles of Economics, Volume I.* London: Macmillan, 1890.

Martin, Morag. *Selling Beauty: Cosmetics, Commerce, and French Society, 1750–1830.* Baltimore, MD: Johns Hopkins University Press, 2009.

Marwick, Arthur. *Beauty in History: Society, Politics and Personal Appearance c. 1500 to the Present.* London: Thames and Hudson, 1988.

Maxwell, Catherine. *Scents and Sensibility: Perfume in Victorian Literary Culture.* Oxford: Oxford University Press, 2017.

McClintock, Anne. *Imperial Leather: Race, Gender, and Sexuality in the Colonial Contest.* New York: Routledge, 1995.

McKendrick, Neil, John Brewer, and J. H. Plumb. *The Birth of a Consumer Society: The Commercialization of Eighteenth-Century England.* Bloomington: Indiana University Press, 1982.

McLaren, Angus. *Sexual Blackmail: A Modern History.* Cambridge, MA: Harvard University Press, 2002.

McLaren, Angus. "Smoke and Mirrors: Willy Clarkson and the Role of Disguises in Inter-War England." *Journal of Social History* 40, no. 3 (2007): 597–618.

Miller, Elizabeth Carolyn. *Framed: The New Woman Criminal in British Culture at the Fin de Siècle.* Ann Arbor: University of Michigan Press, 2008.

Miller, Elizabeth Carolyn. "'Shrewd Women of Business': Madame Rachel, Victorian Consumerism, and L.T. Meade's *The Sorceress of the Strand.*" *Victorian Literature and Culture* 34, no. 1 (2006): 311–32.

Milne-Smith, Amy. *London Clubland: A Cultural History of Gender and Class in Late Victorian Britain.* New York: Palgrave Macmillan, 2011.

Montwieler, Katherine. "Marketing Sensation: *Lady Audley's Secret* and Consumer Culture." In *Beyond Sensation: Mary Elizabeth Braddon in Context,* edited by Marlene Tromp, Pamela K. Gilbert, and Aeron Haynie, 43–61. Albany: State University of New York Press, 2000.

Montz, Amy. "Dressing for England: Fashion and Nationalism in Victorian Novels," PhD dissertation, Texas A&M University, 2008.

Morgan, Cecilia. *A Happy Holiday: English Canadians and Transatlantic Tourism, 1870–1930.* Toronto: University of Toronto Press, 2007.

Morgan, Jennifer L. *Laboring Women: Reproduction and Gender in New World Slavery.* Philadelphia: University of Pennsylvania Press, 2004.

Muldrew, Craig. *The Economy of Obligation: The Culture of Credit and Social Relations in Early Modern England.* Basingstoke: Palgrave Macmillan, 1998.

Nava, Mica. "Modernity's Disavowal: Women, the City, and the Department Store." In *Modern Times: Reflections on a Century of Modernity*, edited by Mica Nava and Alan O'Shea, 38–76. London: Routledge, 1996.

Nead, Lynda. *Victorian Babylon: People, Streets, and Images in Nineteenth-Century London*. New Haven, CT: Yale University Press, 2000.

Nelson, Charmaine. *Representing the Black Female Subject in Western Art*. New York: Routledge, 2010.

Nenadic, Stana. "Gender and the Rhetoric of Business Success: The Impact on Women Entrepreneurs and the 'New Woman' in Late Nineteenth-Century Edinburgh." In *Women's Work in Industrial England: Regional and Local Perspectives*, edited by Nigel Goose, 269–88. Hatfield: Local Population Studies, 2007.

Nevett, T. R. *Advertising in Britain: A History*. London: Heinemann, 1982.

Niles, Lisa. "Owning 'the Dreadful Truth'; or, Is Thirty-Five Too Old? Age and the Marriageable Body in Wilkie Collins's *Armadale*." *Nineteenth-Century Literature* 65, no. 1 (June 2010): 65–92.

O'Higgins, Patrick. *Madame: An Intimate Biography of Helena Rubinstein*. New York: Viking Press, 1971.

Ofek, Galia. *Representations of Hair in Victorian Literature and Culture*. Burlington, VT: Ashgate 2009.

Oldstone-Moore, Christopher. "The Beard Movement in Victorian Britain." *Victorian Studies* 48, no. 1 (2005): 7–34.

Opie, Robert. *Rule Britannia: Trading on the British Image*. New York: Viking Penguin, 1985.

Panayi, Panikos, ed. *Germans in Britain since 1500*. London: Hambledon Press, 1996.

Panayi, Panikos. "Germans in 19th-Century Britain." *History Today* 43, no. 1 (January 1993): 48–53.

Panayi, Panikos. *Immigration, Ethnicity, and Racism in Britain, 1815–1945*. Manchester: Manchester University Press, 1994.

Panayi, Panikos. *An Immigration History of Britain: Multicultural Racism since 1800*. London: Pearson Longman, 2010.

Pearl, Sharrona. *About Faces: Physiognomy in Nineteenth-Century Britain*. Cambridge, MA: Harvard University Press, 2010.

Peiss, Kathy. "Educating the Eye of the Beholder: American Cosmetics Abroad." *Daedalus: Proceedings of the American Academy of Arts and Sciences*, 131, no. 4 (2002): 101–9.

Peiss, Kathy. *Hope in a Jar: The Making of America's Beauty Culture*. New York: Metropolitan, 1998.

Peiss, Kathy. "Making Faces: The Cosmetics Industry and the Cultural Construction of Gender, 1890–1930." *Genders* (Spring 1990): 143–69.

Peiss, Kathy. "Making Up, Making Over: Cosmetics, Consumer Culture, and Women's Identity." In *The Sex of Things: Gender and Consumption in Historical Perspective*, edited by Victoria de Grazia and Ellen Furlough, 311–36. Berkeley: University of California Press, 1996.

Peiss, Kathy. "On Beauty ... and the History of Business." In *Beauty and Business: Commerce, Gender, and Culture in Modern America*, edited by Philip Scranton, 7–22. New York: Routledge, 2001.

Peiss, Kathy. "'Vital Industry' and Women's Ventures: Conceptualizing Gender in Twentieth Century Business History." *Business History Review* 72, no. 2, Gender and Business (Summer 1998): 219–41.

Pelling, Margaret. "Appearance and Reality: Barber-Surgeons, the Body and Disease." In *London 1500–1700: The Making of the Metropolis*, edited by A. L. Beier and Roger Finlay, 82–112. London: Longman Group, 1985.

Phillippy, Patricia. *Painting Women: Cosmetics, Canvases and Early Modern Culture.* Baltimore, MD: Johns Hopkins University Press, 2006.

Phillips, Nicola. *Women in Business, 1700–1850.* Woodbridge: Boydell Press, 2006.

Poitevin, Kimberly. "Inventing Whiteness: Cosmetics, Race, and Women in Early Modern England." *Journal for Early Modern Cultural Studies* 11, no. 1 (Spring/Summer 2011): 59–89.

Pollard, Tanya. "Beauty's Poisonous Properties." *Shakespeare Studies* 27 (1999): 187–210.

Poovey, Mary, ed. *The Financial System in Nineteenth Century Britain.* Oxford: Oxford University Press, 2003.

Poovey, Mary. *Uneven Developments: The Ideological Work of Gender in Mid-Victorian England.* Chicago, IL: University of Chicago Press, 1988.

Popp, Andrew. *Entrepreneurial Families: Business, Marriage and Life in the Early Nineteenth Century.* London: Pickering & Chatto, 2012.

Porter, Bernard. *The Refugee Question in Mid-Victorian Politics.* New York: Cambridge University Press, [1979] 2008.

Porter, Roy, and Lesley A. Hall. *The Facts of Life: The Creation of Sexual Knowledge in Britain, 1650–1950.* New Haven, CT: Yale University Press, 1995.

Prior, Mary. "Women and the Urban Economy." In *Women in English Society*, edited by Mary Prior, 93–117. London: Methuen, 1985.

Pritchard, Will. "Masks and Faces: Female Legibility in the Restoration Era." *Eighteenth-Century Life* 24, no. 3 (2000): 31–52.

Qureshi, Sadiah. *Peoples on Parade: Exhibitions, Empire, and Anthropology in Nineteenth-Century Britain.* Chicago, IL: University of Chicago Press, 2011.

Ramamurthy, Anandi. *Imperial Persuaders: Images of Africa and Asia in British Advertising.* Manchester: Manchester University Press, 2003.

Rance, Carolyn. "Madame Ruppert's Beauty Secrets." *Wellcome Library Blog*, February 3 2016. http://blog.wellcomelibrary.org/2016/02/madame-rupperts-beauty-secrets/.

Rappaport, Erika D. "'A Husband and His Wife's Dresses': Consumer Credit and the Debtor Family in England, 1864–1914." In *The Sex of Things: Gender and Consumption in Historical Perspective*, edited by Victoria de Grazia and Ellen Furlough, 163–87. Berkeley: University of California Press, 1996.

Rappaport, Erika D. *Shopping for Pleasure: Women in the Making of London's West End.* Princeton, NJ: Princeton University Press, 2000.

Rappaport, Helen. *Beautiful for Ever: Madame Rachel of Bond Street –Cosmetician, Con-Artist, and Blackmailer.* Ebrington: Long Barn Books, 2010.

Reichardt, Dosia. "'Their Faces Are Not Their Own': Powders, Patches and Paint in Seventeenth–Century Poetry." *Dalhousie Review* 84, no. 2 (2004): 195–214.

Reinarz, Jonathan. *Past Scents: Historical Perspectives on Smell.* Urbana: University of Illinois Press, 2014.

Richards, Thomas. *The Commodity Culture of Victorian England: Advertising and Spectacle, 1851–1914.* Stanford, CA: Stanford University Press, 1990.

Riordan, Teresa. *Inventing Beauty: A History of the Innovations That Have Made Us Beautiful.* New York: Broadway, 2004.

Roach, Joseph. "Celebrity Erotics: Pepys, Performance, and Painted Ladies." *Yale Journal of Criticism* 16, no. 1 (2003): 211–30.

Robb, George. "Circe in Crinoline: Domestic Poisonings in Victorian England." *Journal of Family History* 22, no. 2 (1997): 176–90.

Robb, George. *White-Collar Crime in Modern England: Financial Fraud and Business Morality, 1845–1929.* Cambridge: Cambridge University Press, 1992.

Roberts, Blain. *Pageants, Parlors, and Pretty Women: Race and Beauty in the Twentieth-Century South.* Chapel Hill: University of North Carolina Press, 2014.

Rooks, Noliwe M. *Hair Raising: Beauty, Culture, and African American Women.* New Brunswick, NJ: Rutgers University Press, 1996.

Rose, Mary B. "The Family Firm in British Business, 1780–1914." In *Business Enterprise in Modern Britain: From the Eighteenth to the Twentieth Century*, edited by Maurice W. Kirby, 61–87. New York: Routledge, 1994.

Ross, Ellen. *Love and Toil: Motherhood in Outcast London, 1870–1918.* New York: Oxford University Press, 1993.

Ross, Ellen, ed. *Slum Travelers: Ladies and London Poverty, 1860–1920.* Berkeley: University of California Press, 2007.

Rowe, Rochelle. "'Glorifying the Jamaican Girl': The 'Ten Types–One People' Beauty Contest, Racialized Femininities, and Jamaican Nationalism." *Radical History Review* 103 (2009): 36–58.

Rowe, Rochelle. *Imagining Caribbean Womanhood: Race, Nation, and Beauty Contests, 1929-70.* Manchester: Manchester University Press, 2013.

Sanders, Lise. *Consuming Fantasies: Labor, Leisure, and the London Shopgirl, 1880–1920.* Columbus: Ohio State University Press, 2006.

Savage, Gail. "'The Wilful Communication of a Loathsome Disease': Marital Conflict and Venereal Disease in Victorian England." *Victorian Studies* 34, no. 1 (Autumn 1990): 35–54.

Schabas, Margaret. "Victorian Economics and the Science of the Mind." In *Victorian Science in Context*, edited by Bernard V. Lightman, 72–93. Chicago, IL: University of Chicago Press, 1997.

Scheer, Monique. "Are Emotions a Kind of Practice (And Is That What Makes Them Have a History)? A Bourdieuian Approach to Understanding Emotion." *History and Theory* 51 (May 2012): 193–220.

Schneer, Jonathan. *London 1900: The Imperial Metropolis*. New Haven, CT: Yale University Press, 1999.

Scranton, Philip, ed. *Beauty and Business: Commerce, Gender, and Culture in Modern America*. New York: Routledge, 2001.

Scranton, Philip. "Introduction: Gender and Business History." *The Business History Review* 72, no. 2, Gender and Business (Summer 1998): 185–7.

Sebba, Anne M. "Ballin, Ada Sarah (1862–1906)." *Oxford Dictionary of National Biography*, September 23, 2004. http://www.oxforddnb.com/view/article/55732.

Shannon, Brent. *The Cut of His Coat: Men, Dress, and Consumer Culture in Britain, 1860–1914*. Athens: Ohio University Press, 2006.

Sharpe, Pamela. *Adapting to Capitalism: Working Women in the English Economy, 1700–1850*. New York: St. Martin's Press, 1996.

Sharpe, Pamela. "Continuity and Change: Women's History and Economic History in Britain." *Economic History Review* 48, no. 2 (1995): 353–69.

Sharpe, Pamela. "Lace and Place: Women's Business in Occupational Communities in England, 1550–1950." *Women's History Review* 19, no. 2 (2010): 283–306.

Shaw, Gareth, and Allison Tipper. *British Directories: A Bibliography and Guide to Directories Published in England and Wales 1850–1950 and Scotland 1773–1950*. London: Mansell, 1996.

Slesin, Suzanne. *Over the Top: Helena Rubinstein: Extraordinary Style, Beauty, Art, Fashion, and Design*. New York: Pointed Leaf Press, 2003.

Smith, Kim. "Strands of the Sixties. A Cultural Analysis of the Design and Consumption of the New London West End Hair Salons. c.1954–1975." PhD dissertation, University of East London, 2014.

Smith, Michelle J. "Beauty Advertising and Advice in the *Queen* and *Woman*." In *Women, Periodicals and Print Culture in Britain, 1830s-1900s: The Victorian Period*, edited by Alexis Easley, Clare Gill, and Beth Rodgers, 218–31. Edinburgh: Edinburgh University Press, 2019.

Smith, Michelle J. "Friday Essay: Toxic Beauty, Then and Now." *The Conversation* (blog), October 19, 2017, http://theconversation.com/friday-essay-toxic-beauty-then-and-now-84267.

Smith, Steven R. B. "The Centenary of the London Chamber of Commerce: Its Origins and Early Policy." *London Journal* 8, no. 2 (1982): 156–70.

Snook, Edith. "Beautiful Hair, Health, and Privilege in Early Modern England." *Journal for Early Modern Cultural Studies* 15, no. 4 (Fall 2015): 22–51.

Snook, Edith. "'The Beautifying Part of Physic': Women's Cosmetic Practices in Early Modern England." *Journal of Women's History* 20, no. 3 (Fall 2008): 10–33.

Snook, Edith. *Women, Beauty, and Power in Early Modern England: A Feminist Literary History*. London: Palgrave Macmillan, 2011.

Steedman, Carolyn. *Landscape for a Good Woman: A Story of Two Lives*. New Brunswick, NJ: Rutgers University Press, [1986] 1987.

Steele, Valerie. *Fashion and Eroticism: Ideals of Feminine Beauty from the Victorian Era to the Jazz Age*. New York: Oxford University Press, 1985.

Stoler, Ann Laura. *Race and the Education of Desire: Foucault's* History of Sexuality *and the Colonial Order of Things*. Durham, NC: Duke University Press, 1995.

Tabili, Laura. "'Having Lived Close Beside Them All the Time': Negotiating National Identities Through Personal Networks." *Journal of Social History* 39, no. 2 (2005): 369–87.

Talairach-Vielmas, Laurence. *Moulding the Female Body in Victorian Fairy Tales and Sensation Novels*. Burlington, VT: Ashgate, 2007.

Tebbutt, Melanie. *Making Ends Meet: Pawnbroking and Working-Class Credit*. Leicester: Leicester University Press, 1983.

Thomas, Lynn M. "Skin Lighteners, Black Consumers, and Jewish Entrepreneurs in South Africa." *History Workshop Journal* 73, no. 1 (2012): 259–83.

Tosh, John. *A Man's Place: Masculinity and the Middle-Class Home in Victorian England*. New Haven, CT: Yale University Press, 1999.

Turner, E. S. *The Shocking History of Advertising!* London: Michael Joseph, 1952.

Ueyama, Takahiro. *Health in the Marketplace: Professionalism, Therapeutic Desires, and Medical Commodification in Late-Victorian London*. Palo Alto, CA: Society for the Promotion of Science and Scholarship, 2010.

Ugolini, Laura. *Men and Menswear: Sartorial Consumption in Britain, 1880–1939*. Burlington, VT: Ashgate, 2007.

Vernon, James. *Distant Strangers: How Britain Became Modern*. Berkeley: University of California Press, 2014.

Vincent, Susan. *Hair: An Illustrated History*. London: Bloomsbury, 2018.

Walker, Lynne. "Vistas of Pleasure: Women Consumers of Urban Space in the West End of London, 1850–1900." In *Women in the Victorian Art World*, edited by Clarissa Campbell Orr, 70–85. Manchester: Manchester University Press, 1995.

Walker, Susannah. *Style and Status: Selling Beauty to African American Women, 1920–1975*. Lexington: University Press of Kentucky, 2007.

Walkowitz, Judith R. *City of Dreadful Delight: Narratives of Sexual Danger in Late-Victorian London*. Chicago, IL: University of Chicago Press, 1992.

Walkowitz, Judith R. "Going Public: Shopping, Street Harassment, and Streetwalking in Late Victorian London." *Representations* 62 (Spring 1998): 1–30.

Walkowitz, Judith R. *Nights Out: Life in Cosmopolitan London*. New Haven, CT: Yale University Press, 2012.

Walsh, Claire. "Shop Design and the Display of Goods in Eighteenth-Century London." *Journal of Design History* 8, no. 3 (1995): 157–76.

Walton, Susan. "Squalid Impropriety to Manly Respectability: The Revival of Beards, Moustaches and Martial Values in the 1850s in England." *Nineteenth-Century Contexts* 30, no. 3 (2008): 229–45.

Weinbaum, Alys Eve et al., eds. *The Modern Girl around the World: Consumption, Modernity, and Globalization*. Durham, NC: Duke University Press, 2008.

Westall, Oliver M. "The Competitive Environment of British Business, 1850–1914." In *Business Enterprise in Modern Britain, from the Eighteenth to the Twentieth Century*, edited by Maurice W. Kirby and Mary B. Rose, 223–30. London: Routledge, 2004.

Wheeler, Roxann. *The Complexion of Race: Categories of Difference in Eighteenth-Century British Culture*. Philadelphia: University of Pennsylvania Press, 2000.

Whitaker, Wilfred B. *Victorian and Edwardian Shopworkers: The Struggle to Obtain Better Conditions and a Half-Holiday*. Newton Abbot: David and Charles, 1973.

White, Jerry. *London in the Nineteenth Century: 'A Human Awful Wonder of God.'* London: Jonathan Cape, 2007.

Whitlock, Tammy. "A 'Taint Upon Them': The Madame Rachel Case, Fraud, and Retail Trade in Nineteenth-Century England." *Victorian Review* 24, no. 1 (Summer 1998): 29–52.

Whitlock, Tammy. *Crime, Gender, and Consumer Culture in Nineteenth-Century England*. Burlington, VT: Ashgate, 2005.

Whorton, James C. *The Arsenic Century: How Victorian Britain was Poisoned at Home, Work, and Play*. New York: Oxford University Press, 2010.

Willett, Julie. *Permanent Waves: The Making of the American Beauty Shop*. New York: New York University Press, 2000.

Williams, Neville. *Powder and Paint: A History of the Englishwoman's Toilet, Elizabeth I – Elizabeth II*. London: Longmans Green, 1957.

Winstanley, Michael. *The Shopkeeper's World, 1830–1914*. Manchester: Manchester University Press, 1983.

Winter, James. *London's Teeming Streets, 1830–1914*. London: Routledge, 1993.

Withey, Alun. "Shaving and Masculinity in Eighteenth-Century Britain." *Journal for Eighteenth-Century Studies* 36, no. 2 (June 2013): 225–43.

Withey, Alun. *Technology, Self-Fashioning and Politeness in Eighteenth-Century Britain: Refined Bodies*. London: Palgrave Macmillan, 2016.

Woodhead, Lindy. *War Paint: Madame Helena Rubinstein and Miss Elizabeth Arden: Their Lives, Their Times, Their Rivalry*. London: Virago, 2003.

Woods, Kathryn. "'Facing' Identity in a 'Faceless' Society: Physiognomy, Facial Appearance and Identity Perception in Eighteenth-Century London." *Cultural & Social History* 14, no. 2 (2017): 137–53.

Woollacott, Angela. *To Try Her Fortune in London: Australian Women, Colonialism, and Modernity*. London: Oxford University Press, 2001.

Wright, Laura. "*Kiss Me Quick*: On the Naming of Commodities, 1650 to the First World War." In *Merchants of Innovation: The Languages of Traders*, edited by Esther-Miriam Wagner, Bettina Beinhoff, and Ben Outhwaite, 120–9. Boston, MA: Walter de Gruyter, 2017.

Wright, Lawrence. *Clean and Decent: The Fascinating History of the Bathroom & the Water Closet and of Sundry Habits, Fashions & Accessories of the Toilet Principally in Great Britain, France, & America*. London: Routledge & Kegan Paul, 1960.

Yohn, Susan M. "The Primacy of Place, Collaborations, and Alliances: Mapping Women's Businesses in Nineteenth-Century Brooklyn." *Journal of Urban History* 36 no. 4 (2010): 411–28.

Zdatny, Steven. *Fashion, Work, and Politics in Modern France*. New York: Palgrave, 2006.

Zweiniger-Bargielowska, Ina. "The Body and Consumer Culture." In *Women in Twentieth-Century Britain*, edited by Ina Zweiniger-Bargielowska, 183–97. Harlow: Longman, 2001.

Zweiniger-Bargielowska, Ina. "The Making of a Modern Female Body: Beauty, Health and Fitness in Interwar Britain." *Women's History Review* 20, no. 2 (2011): 299–317.

Zweiniger-Bargielowska, Ina. *Managing the Body: Beauty, Health, and Fitness in Britain 1880–1939*. New York: Oxford University Press, 2010.

Index